# Terrorism

# Terrorism
## A Critical Introduction

**Richard Jackson**
**Lee Jarvis**
**Jeroen Gunning**
and
**Marie Breen Smyth**

palgrave
macmillan

First published 2011 by
PALGRAVE MACMILLAN

Palgrave Macmillan in the UK is an imprint of Macmillan Publishers Limited, registered in England, company number 785998, of Houndmills, Basingstoke, Hampshire RG21 6XS.

Palgrave Macmillan in the US is a division of St Martin's Press LLC, 175 Fifth Avenue, New York, NY 10010.

Palgrave Macmillan is the global academic imprint of the above companies and has companies and representatives throughout the world.

Palgrave® and Macmillan® are registered trademarks in the United States, the United Kingdom, Europe and other countries

ISBN 978–0–230–22117–8    hardback
ISBN 978–0–230–22118–5    paperback

This book is printed on paper suitable for recycling and made from fully managed and sustained forest sources. Logging, pulping and manufacturing processes are expected to conform to the environmental regulations of the country of origin.

A catalogue record for this book is available from the British Library.

A catalog record for this book is available from the Library of Congress.

10  9  8  7  6  5  4  3  2  1
20  19  18  17  16  15  14  13  12  11

Printed and bound in Great Britain
by the MPG Books Group, Bodmin and King's Lynn

# Summary of Contents

# Contents

# List of Illustrations

## Figures

## Images

## Tables

# Boxes

# Preface and Acknowledgements

Attempting to write a new type of textbook on terrorism was never going to be easy. Not only is there a voluminous literature on the subject, but it is expanding and changing day by day. Terrorism is also a subject of endless debate, including among this book's authors, and one which evokes strong emotions and polarized opinions; it generates a great deal of heat and only a small amount of light. In undertaking this challenging task, we are therefore very grateful to the staff at Palgrave Macmillan for their professional and timely assistance in the production of this book. Steven Kennedy in particular gave his unstinting support to this project, and as an editor should he kept up the pressure to make it the best book it could possibly be. The helpful and very encouraging feedback we received from Steven and two anonymous reviewers was also of great assistance to us in the final preparation of our manuscript. Gareth Hall and Ruth Blakeley also went far beyond the obligations of friendship and provided invaluable comments and suggestions for improving the manuscript. Naturally, all remaining errors and omissions are ours alone.

We are also grateful for valuable research assistance provided by Daniel McCarthy, previously of Aberystwyth University, and Nathan Roger at Swansea University. Michelle Jackson, as she has faithfully done in the past, not only provided essential familial support to Richard but also turned her considerable editing skills to greatly improving the manuscript. We are deeply grateful for this generous assistance which went well beyond the bounds of spousal obligation.

A great many other colleagues, friends and family members contributed to this book with comments, suggestions, rebukes, challenges, encouragement and favours, both large and small. Among many others, we are deeply grateful to: Helen Dexter, Elaine Martin, Emmanuel-Pierre Guittet, David Miller, Eric Herring, Jonathan Joseph, Claes Belfrage, Daniela Tepe, Michael Lister, Matt McDonald, Doug Stokes, Ken Booth, Michael Boyle, Andreas Gofas, Joseba Zulaika, Michael Stohl, Ayla Gol, Sam Raphael, Richard English, George Kassimeris, Piers Robinson and Susan Patania.

As usual, we would like to thank our families and friends who provided emotional support, encouragement, friendship and respite, and who tolerated our absences from family life and social occasions with patience, good humour and graciousness. In particular, we thank Ken Sparks, Michelle Jackson, David and Kathryn Wells, I-Chant Chiang,

Daniel Logan, Aya Oyama, Geoff and Eleanor Jarvis, Greg and Kerri Jarvis, Toru and Mitsuko Oyama, Takako Oyama, Christopher O'Rourke and Shirley Gunn.

Finally, we want to thank all of our past and present students at the University of Manchester; Aberystwyth University; Oxford Brookes University; Swansea University; Castellon University, Spain; and Smith College, Northampton, Massachusetts, USA, who engaged intelligently with our ideas and continually challenged and encouraged us in writing this book. Ultimately, we wrote this book for them and all future students of terrorism seeking to navigate their own way through this field of study. To assist them in this challenging task, we have included a glossary of key terms at the end of the book. This glossary contains short summaries of every concept that first appears in **bold** type in the text.

RICHARD JACKSON, LEE JARVIS, JEROEN GUNNING AND MARIE BREEN SMYTH

The authors and publishers are grateful to the Metropolitan Police Authority in London for permission to reproduce the public warning poster on page 52 (© Adam Hinton), and also to Steve Wells for permission to reproduce the photograph on the front cover of the book.

# List of Abbreviations

| | |
|---|---|
| 9/11 | 11 September 2001 terrorist attacks |
| ACTA | American Council of Trustees and Alumni |
| ANC | African National Congress |
| ASEAN | Association of Southeast Asian Nations |
| ATF | Bureau of Alcohol, Tobacco, Firearms and Explosives |
| AU | African Union |
| BBC | British Broadcasting Corporation |
| BISA | British International Studies Association |
| CCTV | closed-circuit television |
| CDA | Critical Discourse Analysis |
| CIA | Central Intelligence Agency |
| CPA | Coalition Provision Authority |
| CRTPV | Consortium for Research on Terrorology and Political Violence |
| CSS | Critical Security Studies |
| CSTPV | Centre for the Study of Terrorism and Political Violence (University of St Andrews) |
| CSTWG | Critical Studies on Terrorism Working Group |
| CTF | Counterterrorism Foundation |
| CTS | Critical Terrorism Studies |
| DHS | Department of Homeland Security |
| DOD | Department of Defense |
| DOJ | Department of Justice |
| DOS | Department of State |
| DRC | Democratic Republic of Congo |
| ETA | Euskadie ta Askatasuna (Basque Homeland and Freedom) |
| EU | European Union |
| FARC | Fuerzas Armadas Revolucionarias de Colombia (Armed Revolutionary Forces of Colombia). |
| FBI | Federal Bureau of Investigation |
| FEMA | Federal Emergency Management Agency |
| FLN | Front de Libération Nationale (National Liberation Front) |
| GIA | al-Jama'ah al-Islamiyah al-Musallaha, from French Groupe Islamique Armé (Armed Islamic Group of Algeria) |
| GNP | gross national product |
| GTD | Global Terrorism Database |
| GWOT | Global War on Terrorism |
| ICC | International Criminal Court |
| ICTR | International Criminal Tribunals for Rwanda |

| | |
|---|---|
| ICTY | International Criminal Tribunals for the Former Yugoslavia |
| INLA | Irish National Liberation Army |
| INS | (United States) Immigration and Naturalization Service |
| IR | International Relations |
| IRA | Irish Republican Army |
| IRSP | Irish Republican Socialist Party |
| JI | Jemaah Islamiyah (Islamic Congregation) |
| LRA | Lord's Resistance Army (also known as Lord's Resistance Movement or Lakwena Part Two) |
| LTTE | Liberation Tigers of Tamil Eelam |
| NASPIR | Network of Activist Scholars of Politics and International Relations |
| NATO | North Atlantic Treaty Organization |
| NCTC | National Counterterrorism Center |
| NGO | non-governmental organization |
| OAS | Organization of American States |
| OSCE | The Organization for Security and Co-operation in Europe |
| PA | Palestinian Authority |
| PFLP | Popular Front for the Liberation of Palestine |
| PIRA | Provisional Irish Republican Army |
| PIRN | Public Interest Research Network |
| PKK | Patiya Karkeren Kurdistan (Kurdish Workers Party) |
| PLO | Palestine Liberation Organization |
| PMC | private military company |
| PNAC | Project for the New American Century |
| PSC | private security company |
| RAF | Red Army Faction |
| RAND | The Research and Development Corporation |
| RDWTI | RAND Database of Worldwide Terrorism Incidents |
| RUF | Revolutionary United Front (Sierra Leone) |
| SAS | Special Air Service |
| START | Study of Terrorism and Responses to Terrorism |
| SWAPO | South West African People's Organization |
| TIPS | Terrorism Information and Prevention System |
| TTSRL | Transnational Terrorism, Security and the Rule of Law |
| UK | United Kingdom of Great Britain and Northern Ireland |
| UN | United Nations |
| UNDP | United Nations Development Project |
| UNITA | Uniao Nacional para a Independencia Total de Angola (National Union of Total Independence of Angola) |
| UNSC | United Nations Security Council |
| USA | United States of America |
| USIP | United States Institute of Peace |
| USSR | Union of Soviet Socialist Republics |
| WITS | Worldwide Incidents Tracking System |
| WMD | Weapons of Mass Destruction |

# Introduction

In the twenty-first century, terrorism, it seems, is everywhere. It is in the headlines and stories of our newspapers, websites and nightly television news, and in the plotlines and characters of films, TV programmes and plays we watch, and the thriller novels and comics we read. Themes related to terrorism also feature in the popular music we listen to, in the jokes that circulate through society, in the tattoos and T-shirts we wear, and in the sermons and *khutbahs* we hear in church or in the mosque. Terrorism is also a part of many of the courses we study at school and university, and it features regularly in parliamentary and political debates, community meetings and legal rulings by the courts. Terrorism is often in the mind of police officers who stop and question people at train stations and on the street, and it is part of the rules governing where tourists can take photos, the security measures at airports and football matches, the installation of new CCTV cameras, the routine risk assessments for shopping malls and theatres, and the regulations governing our bank accounts. Terrorism is often stated as one of the reasons for foreign wars and military interventions, and organizations like the UN, the EU and NATO try to coordinate action to counter it. If we look carefully, we can see the traces of terrorism or, more accurately, efforts to protect society against it in numerous aspects of modern life. Yet, most of the time, unless a spectacular terrorist attack is splashed across the media, we hardly even notice its pervasive influence on all of these aspects of our everyday lives.

What is particularly interesting is that, although the term goes back several hundred years to the French Revolution and while it appears to be a permanent part of modern life, from another perspective, terrorism is a very recent addition to modern society. Until the early 1970s, it was hardly visible at all. Before then there was little mention of terrorism in the media, very few states had laws specifically designed to deal with the threat, there were few organizations specifically devoted to responding to it, and there were virtually no films, television programmes, novels or other cultural portrayals of what we understand as terrorism today. Similarly, there were very few scholars researching the topic, and virtually no university courses where students could study it as a stand-alone subject. In contrast, terrorism is today a major focus of scholarly research and teaching, with thousands of new publications every year and courses on terrorism-related sub-

1

jects taught in every major university in the world. Terrorism, or more accurately, the responses of governments around the world to acts of terrorism – whether we live in Chicago or Canberra, Mumbai or Manchester – has left very few aspects of our lives untouched.

Taking this historical context into consideration, there are at least two compelling reasons for writing a book such as this. First, despite the rapidity with which the field of terrorism research has grown, especially in the years following the attacks of 11 September 2001, there is still something of a dearth of variety in terrorism-related texts available today. Certainly, in comparison to other fields like International Relations (IR), Security Studies or Criminology, there is not the same rich array of literature available to interested students, particularly in terms of texts offering approaches and perspectives which fall outside of the mainstream.

Second, the fact that terrorism is not simply an abstract academic field of study, but now infuses and impacts upon virtually every aspect of modern life, means there is a real imperative to try and explain how terrorism came to occupy such an important part of modern life in such a relatively short period of time, and to explain the political, social and ideological consequences of this remarkable development. In particular, there is a need to try and understand how this comparatively minor form of violence responsible for the deaths of a few thousand people every year globally – a figure dwarfed by those killed through war, insurgency, repression, poverty, disease and global warming, among others – generates such a vast amount of intellectual, cultural, political, legal and security activity accompanied by the investment of vast expenditures. It is not that as a real (though relatively minor and historically ever-present) threat terrorism is not worth any attention at all; rather, the question is why it has come to garner so much attention relative to other pressing threats, and why this has occurred at this particular historical juncture. Related to this, there is a need to understand how terrorism came to be understood as a special or exceptional type of violence totally unrelated to war, insurgency, repression, torture and other forms of political violence. To try and understand these developments requires going some way beyond traditional IR-based approaches which focus on the security threat posed by terrorism, its history and causes, and its management by states. Instead, we need to treat terrorism as a phenomenon embedded within broader political, cultural and academic processes. Only in this way can we seek to understand how terrorism has come to dominate society in the early twenty-first century and what impacts these developments have had.

In short, *Terrorism: A Critical Introduction* is a textbook with a difference. Its most important point of difference is that it does not simply assume that terrorism exists independently of the way in which we seek to study and understand it. Nor does it assume that terrorism exists as an objective, freestanding phenomenon, or that terrorism is a unique kind of political violence. Terrorism is not a self-evident, exceptional category of political violence. Rather, it is a social construction – a linguistic term or label that is applied to certain acts through a range of specific political, legal and academic processes. This is not the same thing as saying that terrorism is not real; there are real people causing real harm and death to other real people. Instead, it is to say that the *meaning* of (and subsequent responses to) those real acts of violence is determined by a complex series of social and political practices which contribute to the labelling and categorization of events. In a similar process to that by which a boxing ring, an official referee, a set of rules and the expectations of an audience transforms a fist-fight into a socially accepted sporting match, the actions and pronouncements of politicians, academics, lawyers and others transform a particular act of violence – such as a bombing or murder – into an act of 'terrorism'. When and how these processes work to construct certain acts as 'terrorism' – and others as 'war' or 'insurgency', for example – depends on history, context and the actors involved.

Understanding terrorism as a social construction has obvious implications for the way we approach it as an object of knowledge and a subject for scholarly research. In the first instance, this decision means we need to examine the political violence which is today understood as 'terrorism' in order to appreciate better its real-world manifestations and causes, for example. In the second, it means we also need to explore the social processes which construct some acts as 'terrorism' (and not others) in particular times and places. More importantly, it means that we need to study and interrogate the relationship between the real violence and the 'terrorism' label used to describe it, because this relationship is neither necessary nor obvious, and it is historically changeable. In other words, the relationship between the category used and the real-world violence the category describes must be a critical focus of attention. And, of course, it also implies that the usual responses taken to terrorism by governments cannot simply be assumed to be necessary or effective.

Related to this, a social constructivist stance towards terrorism means that widely accepted knowledge about this phenomenon should not be taken for granted but approached with caution and seen as open to question. In other words, while other books may treat terrorism as an unproblematic, stable and unique type of political violence that can be objectively defined, categorized, explained and solved, we suggest that the way in which terrorism is defined, represented and studied is an intrinsic part of how the thing itself – 'terrorism' – came to exist as a social phenomenon in the late twentieth century. How we study terrorism, in other words, is as important as the subject itself, and has a range of important real-world consequences. We have therefore tried to incorporate a focus on the study of terrorism – and the philosophy of social science more broadly – throughout the book. In short, understanding how the central issues and debates of terrorism have been constructed must come before any discussion of the substantive issues themselves.

Conceiving of the subject in this way, we believe, offers a new, substantive approach to the study of terrorism, not least because it opens up the possibility of asking different kinds of questions to those asked in much of the established literature on this topic. It also offers new perspectives on traditional subjects and adds some new issues for research and study. In particular, unlike many existing texts, this book does not provide a chronological history of terrorism because it recognizes that those groups and acts of violence which are called 'terrorism' in one society or era may be called something else in another context. Similarly, it does not focus only on those groups and tactics widely seen to pose the greatest threat today, because these concerns are actually a reflection of the politics, values, and self-image of Western societies and their governmental, cultural and other elites.

Instead, the aim of this book is to ask important and pressing questions about the role of scholars and experts themselves in constructing terrorism as an object of knowledge and practice, and in determining which groups and forms of terrorism should have priority. Sustained attention is also given to exploring how the subject of terrorism is shaped and moulded by broader practices of popular culture and socially embedded attitudes towards gender, for example. These topics are a long way from the study of terrorism as it has been traditionally approached, particularly within IR and political science. We also take the neglected topic of state terrorism seriously. Not just the terror carried out by so-called 'rogue states', but any terror perpetrated by or on behalf of a state, including liberal democries. This is because we believe that state terrorism is an important part of the terrorism phenomenon, and that its study can tell us a great deal about the way in which non-state terrorism has been constructed and treated as a major threat. More importantly, going beyond a critique of the existing field, we try to show how our approach provides an alternative lens through which to study many of the traditional questions and puzzles about terrorism, such as: How do we define terrorism? What kind of threat does terrorism pose? Are there different types of terrorism? What are the causes of terrorism? How should societies respond to acts of terrorism?

So our aims in this text are twofold. First, we want to interrogate, question and destabilize dominant understandings of, and approaches to, terrorism, exploring the relationship between knowledge, power and practice in the process. Second, we want to approach the subject of terrorism – or 'terrorism' – from a fresh perspective and find new ways of understanding key issues and topics associated with its study. A few of the important questions we address in the textbook include:

- How has terrorism been socially constructed within modern societies?
- How, why and with what consequences has terrorism been constructed specifically as a form of non-state political violence, and what are the consequences of the silence on state terrorism?
- What social, political and ideological impacts have dominant constructions of terrorism, and its causes and effects, had for individuals and communities across the world?
- How can we think differently about terrorism, its causes and its effects, and how will this affect counter-terrorism policies?
- What role has the academic study of terrorism played in the social construction of terrorism, and how is the study of terrorism shaped by the cultural and political context in which it occurs?
- How does the power–knowledge relationship shape our understanding of terrorism and counter-terrorism?
- Which groups benefit from dominant understandings of terrorism, and for whom does knowledge of terrorism work in society?
- How do dominant understandings of terrorism affect or determine the responses to terrorism?
- What is the role of critical scholars in the study of terrorism and counter-terrorism?
- What ethical principles should we apply to the study of terrorism and the evaluation of counter-terrorism?

At a minimum, our intention in writing this textbook is to show that *how* we think about terrorism, whether as students, citizens, consumers, politicians or counter-terrorism officials, matters a great deal. Demonstrating that it is possible to study and understand terrorism in very different ways is an important end in itself, one too often neglected within traditional approaches to the topic. More optimistically, we hope that many of our readers will be as persuaded as we are by the value of the critical approaches we chart in this book, taking these questions and viewpoints with them to the cinema, church, shopping mall or library on their next visit, and applying them when they read a newspaper or watch television. It is precisely *because of* terrorism's – and counter-terrorism's – increasing influence over our lives that we have a responsibility to try and understand it, to ask difficult questions and to challenge dominant and embedded forms of knowledge about the subject.

## Organization of the book

In order to address the aims and questions we have set out above, the text is divided into two parts. Part I examines core conceptual issues relating to the way terrorism is studied and understood; it describes the theoretical lenses or prisms we use in approaching the subject. It begins with an outline of the way terrorism has typically been approached in the past, or what has been called orthodox terrorism studies, and the consequences of this approach for our understanding of the subject. It then outlines our own alternative approach, what has been termed Critical Terrorism Studies (CTS). This is followed by an examination of how a culturally informed perspective can help us to understand terrorism as a particular kind of cultural–political construct, and how a focus on gender can open up new kinds of questions and issues that have until now been largely missing from orthodox approaches. The chapters in Part I are crucial because they provide the theoretical and analytical framework through which we approach the central issues of terrorism research. As we hope to demonstrate, the ways in which terrorism is framed as an object of research greatly influence the formulation and study of political, strategic, ethical and other questions associated with this particular form of violence.

Part II examines some of the key issues and concerns of terrorism research through the prism of the critical lens outlined in Part I. It starts by revisiting the definitional debate – how we distinguish terrorism from other forms of political violence, its primary characteristics and how we might retain the term without falling into some of the mistakes and misconceptions that have characterized earlier approaches to terrorism. The next chapter takes a critical perspective to the nature and extent of the terrorist threat. We then turn our attention to understanding the different types of terrorism, including the problematic notions of 'new terrorism' and 'religious terrorism', and the frequently neglected category of state terrorism. This is followed by an examination of different approaches to the causes or origins of terrorism. The final two chapters focus on responses to terrorism, including an in-depth critical analysis of the 'war on terrorism'.

# Part I
# The Study of Terrorism

# Part I

## The Study of Terrorism

Chapter 1

# The Orthodox Study of Terrorism

## Chapter Contents

- Introduction
- Terrorology and the terrorism industry
- The limitations of orthodox approaches to terrorism
- Knowledge, power and problem-solving theory
- The myths of political terrorism
- Conclusion

## Reader's Guide

In this chapter we examine the nature and origins of the orthodox terrorism studies field, the way its evolution and practices have shaped our understanding of terrorism, and some of its main weaknesses and failings. We start by describing how terrorism research emerged as a branch of counter-insurgency studies and soon established itself as an influential epistemic community centred on the work and activities of a key set of scholars and research institutions. We then go on to examine in detail some of the main problems and limitations of the orthodox study of terrorism in relation to definition and theory, methodology and research practice, the politics of researching terrorism, and the impact of the war on terror. In the following section we examine how orthodox accounts of terrorism are rooted in a classic problem-solving approach that is insufficiently sensitive to the ways in which knowledge and power are connected. The final section explores some of the popular myths of terrorism, the ways in which they have been propagated by the terrorism industry, and how and why they have dominated policy and public debate for so long. In the conclusion, we reflect on the implications of this analysis of the orthodox field. We describe how its origins in counter-insurgency studies shaped its evolution and character, and suggest that the time is ripe for an explicitly critical approach to terrorism.

## Introduction

The study of terrorism as a separate and distinct subject began in the late 1960s and early 1970s. Before this time, political violence by state or non-state actors was studied as part of war, insurgency, repression, revolution and the like, and acts of terrorism were most often described simply as bombings, kidnappings, hijackings, assassinations and so on (Zulaika and Douglass 1996). During the 1960s at the height of the cold war, Western states and their allies were battling anti-colonial movements, left-wing guerrilla groups and revolutionary insurgencies in Indochina, Africa, Latin America and many other parts of the world. As part of the broader struggle against communism and decolonization, they began to refer to such groups as 'terrorists' (see Winkler 2006). In the Malayan insurgency for example, the British forces called their opponents 'communist terrorists' or 'CTs' as a way of delegitimizing them and undermining the community support they enjoyed. At the same time, some of these revolutionary groups started to adapt their strategies towards urban guerrilla warfare, with bombings, assassinations and military assaults in towns and cities. The Front de Libération Nationale (FLN) in Algeria, for example, planted bombs at cafes and other public places where French settlers gathered and assassinated soldiers and officials, while the Palestine Liberation Organization (PLO) began to hijack international airliners to publicize the Palestinian cause.

In this situation, a number of scholars and analysts who had previously been studying counter-insurgency in order to help Western militaries fight communist insurgencies better began to turn their attention specifically to acts of terrorism and the non-state groups who committed them. A key purpose of this initial research was to bolster Western counter-insurgency efforts more broadly and to help design counter-terrorism measures specifically. As a consequence, much of the terrorism field's early output has been described as 'counterinsurgency masquerading as political science' (Schmid and Jongman 1988: 182; see also Raphael 2010). From the 1970s onwards, the field quickly began to grow and establish itself. A group of recognized scholars soon emerged as '**terrorism experts**', conferences were held, new research centres were established, specialized academic journals on terrorism were founded, and a body of literature was published. The field received another important boost in a second wave of research following the terrorist attacks on 11 September 2001, when many hundreds of scholars turned their attention to the study of terrorism as a way of aiding efforts to try and prevent further such attacks (see Ranstorp 2006), including hundreds of new doctoral research students (see Price 2010).

That the orthodox study of terrorism emerged in the context of state-based attempts to defeat challengers, and has since worked primarily in the service of Western states, is not at all surprising. This is because the production of knowledge, particularly knowledge *for* policy, is never a neutral process but is intimately connected to structures of power in society (Foucault 1991). In this case, the study of non-state terrorism and ways to defeat it was part of a broader strategy by powerful Western states to maintain their dominance of the international system and defeat groups which sought to challenge Western **hegemony** (see Raphael 2009; Blakeley 2009). Moreover, the context in which the field of terrorism studies emerged – as part of the West's counter-insurgency efforts during the cold war and later as a response to 9/11 – is crucial to understanding its evolution and its fundamental characteristics today.

## Terrorology and the terrorism industry

The orthodox study of terrorism – sometimes termed the discipline of **'terrorology'** by critics (George 1991b) – began to coalesce into a recognizable field from the early 1970s. From this time, a core group of academics and terrorism experts could be identified as the leading scholars in the field (Herman and O'Sullivan 1991; Reid 1997; Raphael 2009; Miller and Mills 2009). Key figures in this group (see for example Box 1.1) were influential in establishing the field's two main scholarly journals, *Studies in Conflict and Terrorism* and *Terrorism and Political Violence*, and in organizing important conferences and seminars on terrorism. They also published the most widely cited and authoritative books and articles on the subject, established the parameters for its study and set the terms for key debates (Ranstorp 2009; Jackson 2009a; Raphael 2010). Important terrorism research centres were also established at this time, such as the St Andrews Centre for Studies in Terrorism and Political Violence (CSTPV). The Research and Development Corporation (RAND), a non-profit research foundation established by the United States Air Force with ties to the American military and political establishments, as well as private security and military companies, was also highly influential in consolidating the terrorism field (Burnett and Whyte 2005). By the 1980s, therefore, terrorism studies possessed all the characteristics of a stand-alone academic field: a core group of leading experts, a corpus of published work on the subject, a body of accepted knowledge, scholarly journals, research institutions and a set of regular scholarly activities such as conferences and seminars.

However, terrorism studies has always been more than just an academic field of research. In its make-up and knowledge production practices, it shows all the characteristics of an **'invisible college'**, which is a group of scholars who exchange ideas, share each other's work,

**Box 1.1  Influential terrorism experts**

Yonah Alexander
J. B. Bell
Ray Cline
Richard Clutterbuck
Martha Crenshaw
Michael Crozier
Rohan Gunaratna
Ted Robert Gurr
Bruce Hoffman
I. L. Horowitz
Brian Jenkins
Walter Laqueur
Neil Livingstone
Robert Kupperman
Ariel Merari
Alexander Schmid
Stephen Sloan
Claire Sterling
Graham Wardlaw
Paul Wilkinson

*Sources*: Compiled from Herman and O'Sullivan 1991; Reid 1997; Miller and Mills 2009; Raphael 2010.

present at the same conferences, use the same information channels and maintain informal links (Reid 1997: 92, 97). From another perspective, it can also be described as an **'epistemic community'** or a network of 'specialists with a common world view about cause and effect relationships which relate to their domain of expertise, and common political values about the type of policies to which they should be applied' (Stone 1996: 86). Crucially, a great many of the leading experts in the field and several of the central research institutions have demonstrable links to the state through funding sources, institutional positions, interlocking personnel and policy advice channels. Some of the leading scholars at the RAND Corporation for example, have previously served as senior officials in several US administrations. Their positions within state-linked institutions and their role in providing counter-terrorism advice to the government has led some observers to describe them as **'embedded experts'** (Burnett and Whyte 2005), similar in function to the embedded journalists in the US military. From a Gramscian perspective, some scholars of terrorism studies could be described as **'organic intellectuals'** because they are institutionally, financially, politically and ideologically tied to the state and function as an integral part of the state's apparatus of power – even if they do not always necessarily agree on what causes terrorism or how it should be dealt with and sometimes criticize state actions and policies.

Although the terrorism field was relatively small until 2001, it has arguably wielded a significant level of political and social–cultural influence in Western societies. This is partly because the leading terrorism scholars have frequently had access to state power through their institutional positions and links to officials. As a consequence of their positional influence and recognized expertise, they have also been regularly called on to provide policy advice to counter-terrorism officials (Reid 1997). In addition, they frequently appear in the media to provide commentary and explanation of terrorism-related stories to the wider public (Miller and Mills 2009). As we have shown, they also lead and dominate the scholarly study and teaching of terrorism. In effect, through these processes the leading terrorism scholars ensure that their perspectives and approaches – their 'knowledge' of terrorism – remain influential among politicians, scholars, the media and the wider public.

As a consequence of these processes, it can be argued that the orthodox terrorism field has developed a long-term material interest in the maintenance of terrorism as a major public policy concern: the funding, prestige, careers and ongoing influence of scholars within the field depends on it (see also the analysis of the broader **terrorism industry** in Chapter 6). As a number of studies have documented (Ilardi 2004: 222; Reid 1997), in order to protect its privileged position, the field has developed a number of subtle gate-keeping procedures which function to ensure that scholars or critics who do not share dominant views and beliefs are marginalized and denied access to policymakers and the main forums for discussion. In these myriad ways, as well as through their links to centres of power in the state, media and society, it has been argued that the orthodox terrorism studies field has become something of a 'terrorism industry' which generates a great deal of intellectual, cultural and political activity and wields genuine influence (Herman and O'Sullivan 1989; Mueller 2006). As we will demonstrate later, the broader terrorism industry helps to construct terrorism as a popularly understood subject (see Chapter 3) and, through counter-terrorism theory and practice, it functions to help maintain the dominance of powerful Western states in the international system (see Chapters 6 and 11).

It is important to recognize that the terrorism industry and the scholarly field of terrorism studies are neither monolithic nor completely hegemonic; they have their share of critical voices, rebels, factions and internal disputes. Nor do their deep ties to the state preclude them from criticizing the government on aspects of counter-terrorism policy. Moreover, this understanding of the terrorism industry does not imply

---

**Key Points**

- By the 1980s, terrorism research had emerged as a stand-alone field with its own recognized experts, an authoritative body of work, academic journals, research centres and scholarly activities.
- The terrorism field showed all the characteristics of being an invisible college, an epistemic community and an influential terrorism industry.
- The terrorism industry has maintained its power and influence through gate-keeping and links to the media and the state.
- The concept of the terrorism industry is not a bad faith model relating to individual terrorism scholars, but rather an attempt to understand the wider processes of knowledge production and the ways in which knowledge intersects with the wielding of power in society.

---

a 'bad faith' model in which individual scholars deliberately try to work on behalf of state power or pursue their own interests. All scholarly fields develop their own material interests that they must maintain, and all scholars are embedded within historical–political structures which shape their values. Neither does it necessarily mean that more orthodox scholars cannot produce accurate explanations or even predictions of particular types of political violence. Instead, it is simply, but importantly, an attempt to understand how the production of terrorism knowledge – and forms of academic and scientific knowledge more broadly – functions at a broader societal level, intersecting with the ways power is wielded in modern society. It is about recognizing that the study of terrorism does not proceed in a vacuum or in an objective, wholly scientific manner. Rather, knowledge is produced within particular contexts and power relationships which then shape it in important ways.

## The limitations of orthodox approaches to terrorism

The orthodox field of terrorism research – the terrorism industry – has faced serious criticisms over the years from three different groups. First, a number of left-wing scholars have argued that the terrorism industry has often acted as an arm of Western state policy and an apologist for state terrorism carried out by Western states and its allies (see for example Chomsky and Herman 1979; Herman 1982; Herman and O'Sullivan 1989; George 1991a; Burnett and Whyte 2005). Second, anthropologists and area studies specialists have criticized the orthodox field for taking a restrictive view on what constitutes terrorism, for not engaging directly with their subject, for lacking in-depth contextual knowledge and for failing to study the more serious issue of state terrorism (see, for example, Zulaika 1984; Zulaika and Douglass 1996; Sluka 2009). Third, as we discuss in Chapter 2, a number of openly 'critical' scholars have in recent years started to question and challenge a number of the most fundamental assumptions underpinning this orthodox research, such as its **ontology**, its **epistemology** and its **normative** orientation (see Gold-Biss 1994; Gunning 2007a; Hulsse and Spencer 2008; Jackson *et al.* 2009a; Jarvis 2009a).

In addition to these external criticisms, a number of orthodox terrorism scholars, as well as some sociologists, have sought to review the state of the field in mapping and assessment exercises to determine where gaps and weaknesses are and to suggest ways forward (see Schmid and Jongman 1988; Reid 1993, 1997; Silke 2004b; Ranstorp 2006). Together, these critiques and mapping exercises suggest that orthodox terrorism studies has a number of serious problems and weaknesses related to the broad areas of: (1) definition and theory; (2) methods and research; (3) the politics of researching terrorism; and (4) the impact of the war on terrorism.

## Definition and theory

The orthodox field has tended on the whole to treat terrorism as a free-standing, ontologically stable phenomenon which can be objectively identified and studied using traditional social scientific methods. As Chapter 5 shows, this is a highly simplistic and problematic assumption on which to base the field. The failure to recognize that 'terrorism' is a label given to acts of political violence by outside observers, and that the designation of what constitutes terrorism has historically changed according to political context, is a serious problem for the field. A related problem is that a great many leading terrorism scholars have employed an *actor-based* definition of terrorism, describing it as illegitimate violence by non-state actors, rather than as a *strategy* of political violence which any type of actor can employ.

A consequence of these weaknesses is that the field has largely failed to develop sophisticated theories of terrorism to help us understand the ways in which this strategy has been employed by different political groups and actors. In part, this is also because the field has until recently been dominated by IR and political science scholars, and has lacked input from other disciplines and approaches such as anthropology, criminology, sociology and the like.

## Methods and research

The field has been greatly criticized by both orthodox and critical scholars for its generally poor research practices and methods. Terrorism scholars have, with few notable exceptions and particularly before the second wave of terrorism studies after 9/11, relied primarily on secondary sources like the media for information about terrorism; and most have never met or spoken to any 'terrorists' – the people they are studying (Gunning 2007a). In part, it has been argued that this could be related to the **taboo** of 'talking to terrorists' (Zulaika and Douglass 1996), in which experts fear that doing so would risk contaminating their work with sympathy for their actions or causes. A related research failure has been a tendency to accept information from state sources such as the security services without question (Raphael 2010), leading in some notorious cases to the inadvertent publishing of disinformation and propaganda (see for example Zulaika and Douglass's 1996 discussion of Claire Sterling). These broader failings have led to research that is often descriptive, narrative-based and propagandistic, rather than analytical in nature (Schmid and Jongman 1988; Silke 2004a; Ranstorp 2006; Gunning 2007a). It has also resulted in a restricted research focus on groups and events that receive major media coverage, rather than systematic analyses of all relevant cases. Finally, terrorism scholars have often fallen into the temptation of thinking that the current wave of terrorism is entirely new and unprecedented (see Lesser *et al.* 1999; Simon and Benjamin 2000; Neumann 2009). The tendency to ignore history has been particularly noticeable following the 9/11 attacks when a new generation of scholars emerged who tended to treat terrorism as an entirely novel phenomenon and who appeared to believe that the attacks on America were entirely without precedent.

## The politics of terrorism research

As a number of studies have shown, orthodox terrorism research has in a number of important ways revealed a distinct political and ideological bias (see Herman and O'Sullivan 1989; George 1991b; Gold-Biss 1994; Miller and Mills 2009; Raphael 2010). In terms of its focus, for example, the orthodox field has tended to concentrate primarily on those groups and states that are in direct conflict with Western states and their allies (Herman and O'Sullivan 1989; Raphael 2010). Thus, during the cold war, the vast majority of terrorism research focused on left-wing groups such as the Italian **Red Brigades** and German **Red Army Faction** that could be identified – however tangentially – with the spectre of a threatening Soviet Union. After 9/11, on the other hand, the vast majority of research has focused on so-called 'Islamist terrorism' (Silke 2009). This failure to study – or what can be described as a 'silence' on – right-wing terrorism, state terrorism (including that committed by Western states) or the terrorism of Western-supported groups like the Nicaraguan Contras expresses an underlying ideological bias: a bias that risks replicating official, state-based accounts of danger and threat (see Raphael 2009, 2010).

More broadly, the adoption of research agendas based on state counter-terrorism priorities, or the **securitization** of academic research, reveals that the field is oriented towards helping Western governments in their short-term and immediate struggles against perceived enemies. At the same time, the claim to academic objectivity and the failure to acknowledge the politics involved in determining which groups are considered 'terrorist' functions as a deeper kind of ideological bias because it obscures the political values which determine who to study and how to study them. Finally, it has long been acknowledged that there is a real danger of bias creeping in when terrorism scholars receive most of their funding from state sources (Ranstorp 2006). As occurred with tobacco-industry-funded research on the effects of smoking, scholars researching terrorism face both overt and subtle forms of pressure to produce results and advice which will satisfy their (government) donors. As before, this is not a bad faith argument which questions the integrity of individual scholars; rather, it is simply to highlight the kinds of relationships and practices which impact upon the way the broader field conceives of, and studies, its primary subject.

## The impact of the war on terrorism

The war on terrorism launched after 2001 has had a noticeably chilling effect on terrorism research. This is due in large part to the disciplinary nature of the 'either for us or against us' rhetoric of political elites such as President George W. Bush, the political demands for displaying national unity in the fight against terrorism, and the co-option of researchers into government research programmes on radicalization, for example. In some cases, censorship and self-censorship appear to have led some scholars to alter the focus of their research and downplay findings which are critical of state policies or which challenge widely accepted knowledge. Importantly, the war on terrorism has also created a legal environment which means that scholars who withhold information about informants, or who possess certain kinds of widely available materials, or who speak directly with terrorist groups, can be charged under anti-terrorism laws. There has also been pressure from security services on academics in the UK and elsewhere to inform on their students and report suspicious behaviour or the expression of extremist views (see Breen Smyth 2009). An effect of these types of pressure has been to further focus and channel terrorism research in particular directions, such as towards state priorities, and close down other areas of research.

To conclude, as we noted above, it is important to recognize that not all orthodox terrorism research is necessarily poor or politically biased

---

### Key Points

- Orthodox terrorism research has come in for criticism over the years by left-wing scholars, anthropologists and area study specialists, orthodox scholars themselves and, more recently, critical scholars.
- A key problem for orthodox terrorism research has been its tendency to treat terrorism as an objective phenomenon which is defined by the actor rather than the act.
- Orthodox terrorism research has often relied on poor and secondary research methods, and has limited itself to a narrow set of research questions.
- Orthodox terrorism research has frequently been politically and ideologically biased towards Western governments and their security agendas.
- The war on terrorism has had politicizing and chilling effects on terrorism research in recent years.
- While not all orthodox terrorism research is necessarily poor, a great deal of the voluminous literature in the field is overly descriptive, condemnatory and biased.

---

in the ways we have described here, nor do all orthodox terrorism scholars act solely in the state's interests. Some important and rigorous analyses based on primary research by orthodox scholars have challenged existing understandings of terrorism and made a real contribution to knowledge (see, for example, Gurr 1970; Crenshaw 1981, 1995, 2008; Porta 1992, 1995b; Pape 2005). However, such rigorous non-traditional work has been relatively rare and unrepresentative of the field as a whole, much of whose research can be described as overly descriptive, theoretically unsophisticated, condemnatory and ideologically biased. The situation has improved somewhat in the years since 9/11 (Silke 2004a; Ranstorp 2006), but many of the major problems we have described remain.

## Knowledge, power and problem-solving theory

Another important means of assessing the field of terrorism studies lies in understanding the difference between **traditional** or **problem-solving theory** and **critical theory** (Cox 1981). This distinction is an important one because it encourages us to think rather more carefully about the purposes or functions of knowledge claims, as well as their accuracy. It encourages us to question, in other words, *why* particular understandings of our social and political existence become popular when others do not – how specific models and frameworks of our world come to dominate certain historical moments.

For a very long time, social scientists across the disciplines have laboured under the belief that an objective and value-free understanding of the social world is achievable. This approach – often referred to as **positivism** – views the study of social problems and issues as a practice that is essentially identical to the study of scientific questions. Knowledge here is seen as something that is neutral and independent from its creator, something unaffected by the researcher's own interests, status or background. The Truth (with a capital T), in other words, is out there simply waiting to be discovered by the scientific observer.

This traditional approach to theory suffers from a number of problems. In the first instance, it fails to recognize the ways in which all theorists and analysts are submerged within particular social worlds, histories and practices (Glynos and Howarth 2007: 9). Yet, as we have already seen in this chapter, many of the most influential experts on terrorism are thoroughly embedded in a range of state institutions and interests – as well as in their Western cultural and historical contexts. Second, because traditional theory takes the world 'out there' as its point of departure, it tends to focus on attempting to resolve problems as they arise in this world without questioning how and why this status quo came into being. In the words of Robert Cox (1981: 128–9), this problem-solving approach to theoretical knowledge 'takes the world as it finds it, with the prevailing social and power relationships and the institutions into which they are organised, as the given framework for action', and then tries to 'make these relationships and institutions work smoothly by dealing effectively with particular sources of trouble'. This rather conservative stance means that problem-solving approaches do not seek to challenge the status quo with all of its hierarchies, inequalities and injustices. Instead, they tend to serve it by assuming that existing power structures are natural and immutable and then attempt to ally or control challenges to that existing order. Finally, by adopting what appear to be scientific language and methods, with their impression of accuracy, traditional theory also transforms the management of social conflict into a series of technical problems, thereby obscuring the deeper political and ethical questions at the heart of managing social conflict.

Although this traditional approach to knowledge has historically dominated all areas of the social sciences, there has been a number of prominent efforts at challenging its assumptions. Some of these challenges are based on the recognition that **knowledge and power** are intimately connected – that 'theory is always *for* someone and *for* some purpose' (ibid.: 128; see also Gunning 2007a; Toros and Gunning 2009). From this standpoint, all efforts to explain the social world are

---

### Box 1.2  Problem-solving and critical theory: some key quotations

The critical theory of society ... has for its object men as producers of their own historical way of life in its totality. The real situations which are the starting-point of science are not regarded simply as data to be verified and to be predicted according to the laws of probability. Every datum depends not on nature alone but also on the power man has over it. Objects, the kind of perception, the questions asked, and the meaning of the answers all bear witness to human activity and the degree of man's power.

(Horkheimer 1972: 244)

Theory is always *for* someone and *for* some purpose.

(Cox 1981: 128)

A critique is not a matter of saying that things are not right as they are. It is a matter of pointing out on what kinds of assumptions, what kinds of familiar, unchallenged, unconsidered modes of thought the practices that we accept rest.

(Foucault 1988: 155)

Adopting a Critical Theory approach to the study of terrorism first of all means uncovering the ideological, conceptual and institutional underpinnings of terrorism studies.

(Toros and Gunning 2009: 90)

---

tied up with the interests and perspectives of their creators (Held 1990: 192), and, just as importantly, they all have consequences for the worlds that are being explained. For example, the IR theory of political realism, which argues that states are the main legitimate unit within global politics and that national interests are more important than transnational moral concerns, clearly works *for* the interests of states and their ruling elites. The knowledge of realist-based IR, therefore, is part of the structures and processes that consolidate state power. More than this, however, critical approaches also acknowledge that theory and knowledge always comes *from* somewhere; that is, it is located in, and reflects, the values and assumptions of the particular historical and social context in which it emerges. Critical theorists thus not only question whether completely objective knowledge and theory is possible; they also question who benefits by claiming that it is (see Box 1.2).

Applying this framework to the field of terrorism studies, it appears obvious that orthodox terrorism research is an example of traditional

> **Key Points**
>
> - Traditional or problem-solving theory takes existing power structures for granted and attempts to solve the 'problems' which threaten the status quo.
> - Critical theory acknowledges the power–knowledge connection and argues that theory always works for someone and for some purpose.
> - The orthodox terrorism studies field is an example of problem-solving theory which treats terrorism primarily as a problem to be solved.
> - Studying terrorism from a problem-solving perspective has lead to a number of serious weaknesses and problems, such as lack of context, equating state security with human security, ignoring state violence and working to maintain Western hegemony.

or problem-solving theory (Gunning 2007a). From its origins in counterinsurgency studies, it has always proceeded on the basis that the status quo needs protection from the 'problem' of terrorism, and it has sought to help the state deal more effectively with that problem. It has also largely ignored historical and political contexts, particularly in terms of examining whether the state itself and its repressive apparatus might have played a role in creating an environment in which terrorism may seem desirable (and even legitimate) to some actors. This **state-centric** and status quo-oriented nature of orthodox terrorism research has resulted in a series of important weaknesses and problems. For example, the field has tended to equate human security with state security, ignored numerous instances of state terrorism, marginalized and excluded alternative perspectives and explanations, and, as we have already described, worked to uphold Western hegemony and dominance (Toros and Gunning 2009).

## The myths of political terrorism

A common criticism of the orthodox terrorism studies field is that it has long maintained and propagated a number of dubious knowledge claims or myths of terrorism (Gold-Biss 1994; Stohl 1979, 2008; Jackson 2009a). That is, over time, a number of key assumptions and arguments about the nature, causes and responses to terrorism have become accepted as common knowledge. While there is no hard and fast agreement on which knowledge claims are myths – Stohl's myths of terrorism (see Box 1.3) include the statement that one person's terrorist may be someone else's freedom fighter, which we argue is a useful expression of the subjectivity involved in defining terrorism – it

---

**Box 1.3   Michael Stohl's ten myths of political terrorism**

According to Michael Stohl (1979, 2008), ten common myths of terrorism are:

1. Political terrorism is exclusively the activity of non-governmental actors.
2. All terrorists are madmen.
3. All terrorists are criminals.
4. One persons' terrorist is another's freedom fighter.
5. All insurgent violence is political terrorism.
6. The purpose of terrorism is the production of chaos.
7. Governments always oppose non-governmental terrorism.
8. Political terrorism is exclusively a problem relating to internal political conditions.
9. The source of contemporary political terrorism may be found in the evil of one or two major actors.
10. Political terrorism is a strategy of futility.

---

is possible to identify a number of frequently expressed claims which make up the accepted myths of terrorism.

First, as we have already argued (see also Chapter 5), much orthodox terrorism research assumes that terrorism exists as an ontologically stable, identifiable phenomenon which can be understood and studied objectively and scientifically, and without any obvious political bias. Related to this, it is commonly believed that terrorism refers solely to forms of illegitimate violence committed by non-state actors like rebel groups and insurgents, although **rogue states** might sometimes sponsor the terrorism of non-state groups. In other words, while states do commit violence, it is commonly believed that this particular type of violence is essentially different to the terrorism committed by non-state actors. Another widely accepted myth about terrorism is that liberal democratic (mainly Western) states never engage in terrorism as a matter of policy, only in error or misjudgement. Instead, they are always implacably opposed to the use of terrorism.

However, as Chapter 6 demonstrates, the core sustaining myth of the field is that non-state terrorism poses such an urgent and existential threat to modern societies that, without significant investment in counter-terrorism, could be catastrophic to Western states and the international system. A related myth is the belief that the world now faces a 'new terrorism' which is religiously motivated, willing to employ weapons of mass destruction (WMD) and aimed primarily at causing mass casualties (see Chapter 7). Other popular myths of terrorism include: terrorism aims primarily to cause destruction and chaos; terrorism is futile and irrational because it is rarely if ever successful; the roots of terrorism lie in poverty, religious extremism and individual psychology, and not necessarily in state policies, occupation or legitimate grievances (see Chapter 9); individuals become involved in terrorism through personality defects, deviance, criminal tendencies, religious radicalization or psychological abnormalities; democratic states are more vulnerable to terrorism because of their inherent rights and freedoms; the media often aids terrorism by providing it with the oxygen of publicity; force-based counter-terrorism is legitimate and effective as a response to terrorist campaigns; because terrorism represents an extraordinary threat, sometimes extraordinary measures are required to deal with it, such as employing torture or restricting civil liberties (see Chapter 10).

While not every one of these myths is necessarily accepted or repeated by all orthodox terrorism scholars (there is a growing consensus that terrorists are not psychologically abnormal, for example, and a great many orthodox scholars oppose torture), collectively they make up the common knowledge of terrorism which is generally accepted by politicians, the media, a great many scholars and the wider society. They are continuously reproduced in articles in the main terrorism studies and IR journals, at conferences and seminars, in the media, in official government reports and statements, and in hundreds of publications every year by academics, terrorism experts and think-tanks. They are also reproduced culturally and socially through teaching in schools and universities, and through popular entertainment and the arts (see Chapter 3). There are literally hundreds of films and television shows such as *Die Hard*, *The Kingdom* and *24* which show deranged or fanatical religious terrorists threatening to attack Western cities with WMD, for example. In these processes of knowledge diffusion, the terrorism industry has played an important role by providing academic and scientific authority to the main claims. More directly, a number of the core terrorism experts regularly appear in the media and provide advice to politicians (see Miller and Mills 2009).

As will become obvious over the course of this book, virtually all of these assumptions and arguments about terrorism are contestable and open to question. For example, in Chapter 5 we show that terrorism is a social fact which cannot be defined or studied objectively, while Chapter 6 demonstrates that terrorism is by any measure actually a fairly minor threat to society. In Chapter 7, we debunk the idea of a 'new terrorism' and 'religious terrorism', while Chapter 8 clearly shows that states can be terrorists too, *including* Western states. Chapter 9 demonstrates that the causes of terrorism do not necessarily lie in poverty, psychopathy or religion, while Chapter 10 questions whether countering terrorism ever requires extraordinary methods like suspending civil liberties. A key question, therefore, is: How are these myths maintained as widely accepted knowledge in society if they are so easily refuted and open to challenge? How does dubious and biased knowledge such as this maintain its influence in society? Who gains power and benefits from this knowledge?

There are different perspectives we can use to try and answer these types of question. First, at the level of the terrorism industry itself, it can be argued that its poor theories and research methods – and in particular its lack of primary research – mean that it rarely questions its primary findings or asks the kinds of challenging questions which might raise doubts about its knowledge. A detailed study of prominent scholars of terrorism studies found that the research process among these intellectuals was a closed, circular and static system of information which tended to accept dominant myths about terrorism without strong empirical investigation for long periods of time before research later disproved them (Reid 1993: 28). In Thomas Kuhn's (1996) language, these researchers were working within a particular form of intellectual **paradigm** based on a shared understanding of terrorism itself, and of the ways in which knowledge about terrorism could be acquired. Under such circumstances, it is very difficult indeed for an individual scholar to challenge commonly held assumptions and beliefs.

It is also important to ask for whom this knowledge works and who benefits from its wide acceptance. There are a range of powerful actors in society who directly benefit from the maintenance of these myths and who therefore have a vested interest in their continuation – not least, the terrorism industry itself which depends on them for its funding, influence, prestige and careers (Chapter 6). The state for example, benefits from the extra powers it can claim in the fight against terrorism, while the media benefits from the never-ending supply of dramatic stories and sensational scenarios (Chapter 3). Materially, a whole range of government departments and private companies benefit from the myths of terrorism, such as the police and security services who receive increased funding and extra powers to fight the 'new terrorism', and the private security firms contracted to provide screening services at airports and other protection services (Chapter 11).

Importantly, those that seek to question these established understandings can often be targeted not only with criticism but also hostility for their views (see, for example, Der Derian 2009: xx–xxi). A well known public report in the USA from the immediate post-9/11 period, for example, picked out a number of American academics by name in order to decry their lack of patriotism, arguing: 'rarely did professors publicly mention heroism, rarely did they discuss the difference between good and evil, the nature of Western political order or the virtue of a free society. Indeed, the message of many in academe was clear: BLAME AMERICA FIRST' (ACTA 2001). As this suggests, there are a range of powerful social actors who would not want the myths of terrorism to be disproved or questioned because they are tied to important material, political and ideological interests. In other words, the terrorism industry itself has an incentive to maintain these myths.

A final perspective on the question of how the myths of terrorism are maintained is the notion that these myths have become, and now function as, a dominant **discourse** or a **regime of truth** in Western societies. In other words, the myths and **narratives** about terrorism have been repeated so many times by so many authoritative actors in society, and have then been acted upon as if they were indeed true (through counter-terrorism practices, for example), that they have taken on a sense of external reality which in turn seems to confirm the myths. For example, through the daily counter-terrorism actions of the police, security services, airline officials and others, the 'truth' of the great threat posed by terrorism has become a concrete, living reality which seems intuitively commonsensical to most people. In part, this is because people are inclined to assume that the government would not expend so much money, effort and intellectual capital trying to counter something that was not demonstrably threatening and not in any way exaggerated.

At the same time, the terrorism discourse is functional to the state because it can be employed as a way of directly exercising power: the state can use the terrorist threat as an excuse to crack down on dissent and protest, for example. More prosaically, the state needs to be seen to be protecting its citizens from threats in order to legitimize its continued authority. The discourse can also be directly employed to reinforce and bolster a sense of national identity (see Campbell 1998): the

---

## Key Points

- There is a series of myths that collectively make up commonly accepted knowledge about terrorism, such as the notion that terrorism is a major threat, that it is caused by radicalization and that countering it with force is effective and legitimate.
- These myths have spread across society, with the terrorism industry playing a key role in their dissemination.
- Virtually all the myths of terrorism are questionable and open to challenge.
- The myths of terrorism are maintained as accepted knowledge in society because of the closed knowledge system of the terrorism industry, the vested interests in maintaining such knowledge and the operation of the terrorism truth regime.

state can claim that terrorists are attacking us because of our values and who we are, for example. One of the consequences of the established truth regime about terrorism is that it is extremely difficult to oppose or counter, because alternative arguments both contradict accepted commonsense and seem disloyal to the nation, even when they are based on concrete evidence and arguments. This is why the publicly available evidence and arguments which we have marshalled in the following chapters is often not widely known or publicly discussed.

## Conclusion

It is important to reiterate that not all orthodox terrorism research is beset by the problems and weaknesses we have described in this chapter; nor are all orthodox scholars implicated in the political relationships we have outlined. A number of terrorism scholars working within the problem-solving framework have produced outstanding research which to this day informs our understanding of terrorism (see for example Gurr 1970; Crenshaw 1995; Pape 2005). Moreover, terrorism research has greatly improved in recent years following the 9/11 attacks. Nonetheless, the broader field continues to be characterized by some serious weaknesses and problems which continue to taint its output and hamper its progress (see Burnett and Whyte 2005; Gunning 2007a; Jackson 2008, 2009a; Jackson *et al.* 2009b).

The origins of the field in counter-insurgency studies and its subsequent evolution into a powerful terrorism industry has profoundly shaped the nature and characteristics of terrorism studies to this day. Among others, there are four important legacies of these early developments. First, the field has focused almost entirely on the issue of non-state terrorism, with the much greater and more endemic terrorism perpetuated by states (Chapter 8), and the more costly and damaging results of state counter-terrorism (Chapters 10 and 11), having remained largely unstudied within its confines. Second, the field has concentrated largely on anti-Western revolutionary groups, whether communist or Islamist, and largely ignored pro-state terrorism and the experience of terrorism in the developing world. Third, the field has adopted a problem-solving orientation and allowed the imperatives of state counter-terrorism largely to determine the research agenda. As a consequence, the vast majority of studies on terrorism aim to provide specific advice for state counter-terrorism policy, rather than, say, improving the lives of ordinary people (although the two are not mutually exclusive). Lastly, the field has largely studied terrorism as a separate, stand-alone phenomenon, rather than in the context of broader conflicts, forms of structural violence, social movements and history.

In summary, the field's origins in cold war counter-insurgency efforts, as well as the impact of 9/11, have left a lasting legacy of state-centrism and **Eurocentrism** in which the study of terrorism functions largely as an effort to find effective means for countering perceived anti-Western terrorism. This is not at all surprising. In fact, it is indicative of the way in which power and knowledge functions in the maintenance of hegemony in modern states.

Despite, and perhaps because of, this situation, a number of openly critical scholars of terrorism have put forward the argument that the time is now ripe for a new, openly critical approach to the study of terrorism – one which is theoretically and methodologically rigorous, sensitive to the politics of labelling, self-reflective about issues of knowledge and power, and committed to conflict resolution and human security (Gunning 2007a; Jackson *et al.* 2009a; Jarvis 2009b). Moreover, these scholars suggest that the failures in counter-terrorism strategy shown up in Iraq and Afghanistan, the revelations of torture and abuse in the war on terrorism and the election of President Barack Obama in 2008 have created an openness by officials and scholars towards alternative approaches and ideas. The present historical juncture, in other words, seems ripe for CTS.

## Discussion Questions

1. What are the origins of terrorism studies and how did these roots affect its evolution as a field?
2. In what ways does the orthodox terrorism studies field constitute an epistemic community or terrorism industry?
3. How does the terrorism industry wield influence?
4. What main problems of definition and theory does the orthodox field face?
5. What main problems of methodology and approach does the orthodox field face?
6. In what ways is the orthodox field politically biased?
7. What have been some of the effects of the war on terrorism on terrorism research?
8. What are some of the main terrorism myths maintained by the terrorism industry?
9. Who benefits from the commonly accepted knowledge about terrorism?
10. How is the terrorism truth regime maintained in society?
11. What makes the current historical juncture a ripe moment for the adoption of a more critical approach to the study of terrorism?

## Recommended Reading

George, A., ed., 1991. *Western State Terrorism*, Cambridge: Polity Press. An edited collection of articles examining the terrorism industry and its role in concealing Western state terrorism across the world.

Herman, E., 1982. *The Real Terror Network: Terrorism in Fact and Propaganda*, Cambridge, MA: South End Press. A critical analysis of the terrorism industry and its assistance to Western-supported anti-communist state terror in many developing nations allied to the West.

Herman, E. and O'Sullivan, G., 1989. *The 'Terrorism' Industry: The Experts and Institutions that Shape our View of Terror*, New York: Pantheon Books. The classic critical analysis of the terrorism industry, its central scholars and its political bias towards Western geostrategic interests.

Ranstorp, M., ed., 2006. *Mapping Terrorism Research: State of the Art, Gaps and Future Direction*, London: Routledge. An edited collection of articles analysing the state of the art in contemporary terrorism research, particularly as it relates to the post-9/11 period.

Silke, A., ed., 2004. *Research on Terrorism: Trends, Achievements and Failures*, London: Frank Cass. An edited collection which examines some of the most important trends in the study of terrorism over the past few decades.

## Web Resources

The Terrorism Expertise Portal: *www.powerbase.info/index.php?title=Terrorism_Expertise_Portal*
   A portal with a wide range of links and articles about the role of terrorism experts in shaping the views of the public, policy-makers and the academy.

The Consortium for Research on Terrorology and Political Violence (CRTPV): *www.publicinterest.ac.uk/working-groups/40-consortium-for-research-on-terrorology-and-political-violence-crtpv*
   CRTPV is a consortium of academics operating under the auspices of the Network of Activist Scholars of Politics and International Relations (NASPIR) and the Public Interest Research Network (PIRN) on issues surrounding terrorism experts and counter-terrorism. The website has links to numerous articles analysing the personnel and practices of terrorology.

The RAND Corporation: *www.rand.org/research_areas/terrorism/*
   The RAND Corporation is one of the most important security think-tanks in the USA. This webpage provides information about its counter-terrorism research.

The Centre for the Study of Terrorism and Political Violence: *www.st-andrews.ac.uk/~wwwir/research/cstpv/*
   The CSTPV at the University of St Andrews is one of the oldest and most important research centres on the study of terrorism.

## Chapter 2

# Critical Approaches to Terrorism Studies

## Chapter Contents

- Introduction
- Critical approaches to terrorism
- The critical turn and CTS
- A critical research agenda
- Conclusion

## Reader's Guide

This chapter introduces the reader to some of the main critical approaches to terrorism research, outlining their unique character-istics and primary commitments, and drawing out their points of difference from the orthodox terrorism studies field. It begins with a brief discussion of what is meant by the term 'critical', the broad characteristics of critical approaches to terrorism and a few key differences between critical and orthodox approaches. This is fol-lowed by a description and explanation of two long-standing crit-ical approaches to terrorism, namely political-economy approaches and anthropology, sociology and area studies approaches. Scholars from these perspectives have long contested the orthodox approach to terrorism research, but have always done so from outside the main confines and activities of the field. Next, we describe the 'critical turn' which has taken place within terrorism studies in recent years, before briefly outlining some of the core characteris-tics and commitments of the CTS approach. The final section out-lines a critical research agenda, arguing for a widening and deepening of research on terrorism, as well as the inclusion of some long-ignored subjects. In the conclusion, we reflect on the current successes of critical approaches, the obstacles that will need to be overcome for their wider acceptance, and how a broadly crit-ical approach helps to frame the rest of this textbook.

## Introduction

As Chapter 1 showed, there have been a great many long-standing criticisms of the orthodox terrorism field from left-wing scholars, anthropologists, sociologists, area studies specialists, historians and others. However, any critical approach must do more than simply criticize the existing state of the field; it must also suggest an alternative way of studying terrorism and a concrete research agenda for the future. Having outlined the main problems of the orthodox field in the previous chapter, the purpose of this chapter is to explore what a critical approach to the study of terrorism might consist of – in terms of its underlying assumptions, aims, methods, orientation and future research agenda. This will provide us with a set of concepts and tools – a broad framework and set of key questions – for considering the topics examined in the remainder of the book.

However, before we begin, we must be clear on what we mean by the term 'critical', because the term itself, like the term 'terrorism', has also been the subject of intense debate. In this book, we conceive of the term 'critical' in two primary senses. First, in a very broad sense, we take it simply to mean trying to stand apart from the existing order, questioning what passes for commonsense or accepted knowledge and asking deeper questions about how the existing order came to be and how it is sustained. This process involves, at the same time, acknowledging our own situatedness and biases. In other words, it is not a 'critique from nowhere' or from some illusory vantage point. Second, in a much narrower sense, 'critical' refers to approaches which draw upon the tools and insights of Critical Theory, a social theory oriented towards critiquing and changing society as a whole, which is most commonly associated with the so-called Frankfurt School. Some of the approaches we examine in this chapter are critical in the first, broader sense, whereas CTS is arguably more firmly rooted in Critical Theory.

Despite the differences between these broad and narrow senses, all critical approaches share a number of key concerns and commitments. First, they are characterized by scepticism towards accepted knowledge claims and dominant ideas and seek continuously to question and interrogate that which is taken for granted. Second, they value and prioritize the gathering and analysis of primary data, even when it is difficult and dangerous, rather than relying on second-hand information. Third, critical approaches display sensitivity towards issues of knowledge and power. They understand that knowledge always works for some purpose and is never neutral, and that, as well, researchers always bring with them a set of attitudes and preconceptions that are rooted in their own particular context. They therefore accept the need for careful self-reflection about their work and its outputs. Finally, critical approaches are characterized by an ethical commitment to human rights, progressive politics and improving the lives of individuals and communities. They follow the dictum that the point of knowledge is not just to understand the world, but to change it for the better.

Although many orthodox scholars share some or all of these concerns, at the broadest level, there are a number of key differences between orthodox and critical approaches. These differences relate to questions of ontology, epistemology and normative values (see definitions of these terms below). In terms of ontology, for example, critical approaches tend to view terrorism as a label or a social construct which evolves and changes over time and place, whereas orthodox approaches often treat it as an ontologically stable, objective and scientifically identifiable phenomenon. Such fundamentally different assumptions about the nature of what is being studied – 'terrorism' – can lead to very different methods, questions, priorities and outputs in the subsequent research. Similarly, on issues of epistemology, critical approaches are usually far more sensitive to issues of knowledge and power, the politics of labelling, the consequences of academic research on individuals and communities, and the generally unstable nature of knowledge claims. Lastly, in terms of normative or ethical values, orthodox approaches tend to prioritize national security and the maintenance of the status quo – what is sometimes called a problem-solving attitude (Gunning 2007a). Critical approaches are very different in that they tend to prioritize individual or **human security** and **societal security** instead, and they continuously question the ways in which violence and injustice are the consequence of the status quo. In other words, they tend to be **counter-hegemonic** and politically progressive.

## Critical approaches to terrorism

Critical approaches to terrorism have existed as long as the field itself, and from this perspective they are not in any way new. The aim of this section is to explore briefly two important critical approaches from the last few decades.

As Chapter 1 indicated, the first set of challenges to the orthodox conception and study of terrorism came from what might broadly be termed political-economy approaches. Scholars in this tradition produced a number of important critical works on the terrorism industry and state terrorism during the cold war (Chomsky and Herman 1979; Herman 1982; Herman and O'Sullivan 1989; George 1991a; Gold-Biss 1994). Another wave of this type of critical research followed the initiation of the war on terrorism in 2001 (see, for example, Stokes 2005; Blakeley 2007, 2009; Raphael 2009, 2010; Miller and Mills 2009). Research in this tradition has tended to focus on: the links between orthodox terrorism studies, counter-insurgency and the political establishment; the political biases and propagandistic elements of the orthodox field; the role of the terrorism discourse in legitimizing Western imperialism and hegemony, particularly in the global South; and the ways in which the state terrorism of Western states and their allies have been ignored and excused.

On the basis of these criticisms, political-economy approaches have sought to demonstrate, and argue for, an alternative approach to terrorism research. Among other commitments, these approaches seek to adhere to a definition of terrorism which recognizes it as a tactic or strategy that any actor can employ – including states. They argue that this has two main consequences: first, it makes for a more objective (in the traditional social scientific sense) rather than propagandistic study of terrorism; and second, it reprioritizes research towards the much greater problem of state terrorism (sometimes called 'wholesale terrorism') rather than non-state terrorism (or 'retail terrorism'; see Chomsky 1991). Political-economy approaches also argue that terrorism research needs to examine the role that the language of terrorism and counter-terrorism plays in advancing Western state interests; the ways in which forms of Western state violence, such as counter-terrorism programmes, can sometimes constitute state terrorism; and the underlying motives and interests for the willingness of dominant Western states to use violent strategies across the world.

A second broad critical approach comes from anthropology, sociology, history and area studies. Over the past few decades, scholars from these disciplines have produced a great many important works on aspects of terrorism which implicitly or explicitly adopt a critical approach to the dominant ideas of the orthodox field, even if they don't always use the term 'terrorism' in their work (Townshend 1983, 2002; Zulaika 1984; Sluka 1989; Feldman 1994; Mahmood 1996; Zulaika and Douglass 1996; Oliveiro 1998; English 2003, 2006, 2009; Gunning 2007c). These studies suggest that much commonly accepted knowledge about terrorism amounts to stereotypes and misconceptions, which is often a direct consequence of the failure to engage in primary research, especially in terms of 'talking to terrorists', or to appreciate fully the historical, cultural and social context in which terrorism always takes place. Often, scholars from these perspectives start from the premise that the term 'terrorism' is an unhelpful and distorting frame through which to study political violence and that terrorism should not be treated as exceptional and unrelated to the other forms of violence which typify intense social conflicts.

By virtue of the methods and types of question they adopt, these studies demonstrate an alternative 'critical' approach to terrorism research. First, they show that primary research among the groups under scrutiny is both possible and necessary for gaining an in-depth, richly textured and nuanced understanding of the subject. Second, they prove that terrorism cannot be fully understood outside of the historical, political, social and cultural context in which it occurs, or outside of the wider forms of political violence which take place during periods of social conflict. In fact, they suggest that generalizing about terrorism – comparing the Irish Republican Army (IRA) or Euskadie ta Askatasuna (ETA) with **al-Qaeda** or Hamas, for example – has to be undertaken with extreme care, as terrorism and the groups that employ it can only be fully understood within their local context. Finally, these approaches show how a range of different methodologies, from archival research to ethnographic observation, symbolic analysis and cultural studies, can produce different layers and types of understanding which produce a 'thick' account of political violence.

Although these two broad sets of critical approaches have been present for several decades, they have not been brought together into a recognized body of research or a new field. Instead, they have tended to remain isolated and idiosyncratic. They have also largely taken place outside of the orthodox field: such critical research has only rarely been published in the main Terrorism Studies journals or included in its conferences. In part, this is because scholars from these perspectives have generally shunned the orthodox field and simply got on with researching terrorism, often without using the term (see Gunning 2007b). For these reasons and because of the gate-keeping measures of the terrorism industry discussed in Chapter 1, these critical approaches have had little cross-fertilization with the orthodox field and have largely failed to alter its practices, priorities, approaches, outputs and myths.

## Key Points

- Critical approaches to the study of terrorism are not new, but have existed for many decades within political-economy, anthropology, sociology, history and area studies.
- Political-economy approaches argue for an objective definition of terrorism, a greater focus on state terrorism and the analysis of the role of violence in Western foreign policy.
- Anthropology, sociology, history and area studies approaches argue for the necessity of conducting primary research, taking full account of context, and methodological pluralism as a means of gaining a deeper understanding of terrorism.
- Critical approaches to the study of terrorism have thus far taken place outside of the activities of the orthodox field and have failed to make a significant impact on its practices, priorities and outputs.

## The critical turn and CTS

In the past few years, a growing number of publications and related scholarly activities indicate that a 'critical turn' has been taking place within the broader terrorism studies field (see Gunning 2007a; Jackson 2007b; Burke 2008; Horgan and Boyle 2008; Hulsse and Spencer 2008; Weinberg and Eubank 2008; Jarvis 2009a; Jones and Smith 2009; Joseph 2009; Stokes 2009; Egerton 2009). The emergence of what has become known as CTS is rooted in the earlier critical approaches to terrorism research we described above. Unlike these earlier efforts however, CTS has made a genuine effort to engage directly with the orthodox terrorism studies field and its scholars. As a consequence, CTS has had a real impact on the broader study and teaching of terrorism and is now a regular part of debates in the field and teaching programmes. The purpose of this section is to explain the broad contours of the CTS approach. Before we begin, however, it is important to note that, as with most academic approaches, CTS is a broad and evolving church made up of diverse perspectives and a series of ongoing disagreements over key issues. In this sense, the version of CTS we present here is only one perspective on this dynamic new field, and even in this case there are points of divergence between us on some of the issues covered in this book.

CTS can be understood first and foremost as a critical orientation, a sceptical attitude and a willingness to challenge received wisdom and knowledge about terrorism. In this sense, CTS can be conceived of as a broad scholarly movement that allows multiple perspectives, some of which have been considered outside of the mainstream, to be brought into the same forum. In other words, CTS seeks to engage with, and learn from, a range of perspectives and approaches, including excellent research within the orthodox field which may originate within a problem-solving approach. Most importantly, CTS entails an ongoing process of intellectual engagement and debate with a wide range of perspectives and approaches, rather than a fixed position or endpoint. In this sense, it is a dynamic and continuously evolving field.

However, beyond the adoption of a broadly 'critical' attitude, we suggest that CTS can be characterized by an identifiable set of key ontological, epistemological, methodological and ethical-normative commitments related to the study of terrorism. These commitments distinguish CTS from other approaches to terrorism research.

### Ontological commitments

As discussed above, ontology refers to the nature, essence or 'being' of the object under scrutiny, in this case, terrorism. That is, is terrorism a physical phenomenon, an ideology, a behavioural characteristic or some other thing? What is its essence? CTS adopts the ontological position that terrorism is fundamentally a **social fact** rather than a brute fact, because deciding whether a particular act of violence constitutes an 'act of terrorism' relies on judgements about the context, circumstances and intent of the violence, rather than any objective characteristic inherent to it (Schmid and Jongman 1988: 101). As such, 'terrorism' has no pure essence. For example, if a group of civilians are killed in a bomb blast or a policeman is shot, it is not obvious whether either of these events necessarily constitutes an act of terrorism; there is nothing inherent or objective to the violence itself which makes it 'terrorism' per se. Instead, it requires an outsider's analysis of the circumstances and context of the events and the intentions of the perpetrators to determine whether it fits current understandings of 'terrorism'. In other words, while acts of violence are a brute physical fact for the victims and onlookers, the meaning or labelling of the acts – as a 'crime', an act of 'war' or an act of 'terrorism', for example – is a social process that depends upon different actors making judgements about its nature. In contemporary society, deciding which events come to be viewed as terrorism depends upon a series of social, cultural, legal and political processes of interpretation, categorization and labelling (Zulaika and Douglass 1996; see also Gold-Biss 1994).

In addition, terrorism is not an ideology like socialism or liberalism; it is not a set of ideas or perspectives for making sense of the world; nor is it a set of aims for constructing a just society. Rather, it is a violent *strategy* or tactic of political struggle which actors can employ to try and achieve their goals; it is a *means* to some kind of political end. Groups specializing in terror and no other forms of political action do sometimes form, but they are extremely rare and typically highly unstable and relatively short-lived. In reality, most terrorism occurs in the context of wider political struggles in which terror is used as one strategy among other more routine forms of contentious action (Tilly 2004: 6). In other words, ontologically we could say that while there is the strategy of terror which actors can adopt or discard, there is no terror*ism* as such – although this is the common term used to describe the strategy.

Importantly, CTS adopts the same ontological position in relation to the 'terror*ist*' label. CTS argues that calling a group or individual a 'terrorist' is not an ontological statement about the nature or status of a particular individual: 'terrorist' is not an identity like 'Amish' or 'Canadian', nor is it the case that 'once a terrorist, always a terrorist' (Schmid 2004: 205; Toros 2008). As we will show in Chapter 5, a number of people formerly labelled 'terrorist' have later become respected heads of state, with some like Nelson Mandela and Yasser Arafat even having won the Nobel Peace Prize. Most so-called terror-

ists eventually stop using the terrorism strategy and go on to live relatively ordinary lives or pursue their goals using non-violent political
strategies. In other words, CTS would argue that there is little intellectual value to be gained by reducing a person or group to what is
usually a subset of their overall behaviour and not a reflection of their
ideological beliefs. More than this, CTS believes that essentialist reduc-
tions of this sort can pose very harmful effects for those individuals
and for society more broadly.

CTS scholars argue that there are some important implications and
advantages to the ontological position they adopt towards terrorism.
First, they suggest that recognizing terrorism as a social fact with no
objective essence means scholars should be extremely careful in their
use of the term and should always be aware of the politics involved in
naming individuals or groups as 'terrorists'. A second implication is the
rejection of the frequent tendency to universalize or generalize about
terrorism from one context to another, to assume that terrorism has a
single essential and recognizable nature, and to treat acts of terrorism
as wholly exceptional kinds of events that have nothing in common
with other forms of social and political activity. More specifically, this
means refusing to treat terrorism as an exceptional form of political
violence, wholly unrelated to other kinds of violence like war, insurgency, repression, sexual violence and the like. Finally, an advantage of
this ontological position is that it permits us to study the legal, academic and cultural processes by which certain acts come to be accepted
as 'terrorism', as well as the actual political violence being named.

## Epistemological commitments

Epistemology deals with questions relating to the nature of knowledge,
including the forms it takes and how it is gathered and put to use by
different actors. In relation to the ways in which knowledge about terrorism is collected and used, CTS adopts a number of important positions. First, it argues that creating knowledge is ultimately a social
process which depends on a range of contextual factors, including the
social positions of the researchers (whether they are recognized academics, for example), the institutional context within which they operate
(whether they are working primarily within an academic context), the
kinds of methods they employ (whether they use accepted social scientific methods), and the intended consumers of the knowledge produced
(whether it is for other academics or students). These kinds of factors
will greatly impact on the kinds of knowledge produced, as well as the
kinds of purposes to which it will be put. In this example, academically
produced knowledge will often have greater social acceptance and
political influence than a blog written by a layperson working from
home.

In other words, CTS scholars argue that we must remain sensitive to, and be continuously aware of, the different ways in which context and process impact on knowledge about terrorism. In addition, the recognition that knowledge is a social process and that societies change, means that what we 'know' about terrorism today differs from previous societies and will likely differ from future ones. Crucially, this means there are few if any knowledge claims about terrorism today that cannot be challenged or questioned.

Second, CTS recognizes that no individual, including academic researchers, can completely put aside their personal identity, values, perceptions and world view to engage in objective, dispassionate, value-free research. Rather, all researchers bring with them a particular culture and set of values and understandings which shape their research in a variety of important ways. CTS scholars argue that recognizing and acknowledging the personal **subjectivity** of the researcher during the research process is an important step, not least because such continuous **reflexivity** acts as an antidote to the dangerous claim that some kinds of knowledge are objective and wholly unbiased – and therefore superior to others.

Third, as shown in Chapter 1, CTS is deeply aware of the linkages between power and knowledge, particularly in terms of the different ways in which knowledge can be employed by actors as a political tool of influence and domination. CTS scholars are critical of the way in which certain kinds of knowledge claims about terrorism – the widely accepted knowledge that terrorism poses a serious ongoing or even existential threat to Western societies, for example – have been used by governments to increase their own power, suppress opposition and restrict civil liberties. As a consequence, CTS scholars are concerned with questions like: Who is terrorism research for? How does terrorism research support particular interests? What are the effects of terrorism research on society?

In summary, a CTS approach to terrorism research begins with the acceptance that wholly objective or neutral knowledge – any kind of absolute or real 'truth' – about terrorism is impossible and that there is always an ideological, ethical and political dimension to the research process (Toros and Gunning 2009). Crucially, for CTS scholars this does not mean that all knowledge of the social world is hopelessly insecure or that what might be called 'anchorages' – relatively secure knowledge claims – cannot be found and built upon (Booth 2008; Herring 2008; Toros and Gunning 2009). It also does not mean that we should reject the rigorous application of scholarly standards and procedures in research on terrorism. Rather, it suggests that, in addition to a commitment to the highest standards of scholarship, research on terrorism should remain continuously aware of the ways in which its unique context and the values of the individual researcher impact upon its nature and outcomes, and how it is always an inherently political or ideological process.

An important consequence of this epistemological perspective (and its related ontological position) is an opening of the broader intellectual project of studying terrorism to new questions and topics, as well as new methods and approaches (see following sections). The acceptance of the socially constructed nature of terrorism and terrorism knowledge, for example, raises new kinds of questions about how the phenomenon we now know as 'terrorism' came to be viewed primarily as a kind of non-state violence and how the academic study of terrorism contributed to this process. Similarly, questioning the terrorism knowledge produced by the dominant social scientific approaches which stress objectivity and quantifiable data suggests that other kinds of knowledge produced by ethnography, discourse analysis, constructivism, sociology, history, philosophy, law and beyond could also be extremely helpful to our understanding of terrorism and its social construction.

## Methodological commitments

As we have already alluded to, the particular ontological and epistemological commitments at the heart of CTS have a number of important consequences for method and approach in researching terrorism. First, CTS scholars are committed to transparency about their own values and standpoints, particularly as they relate to the interests and values of the societies in which they live and work. For Western-based scholars, this translates into an abiding commitment to being aware of, and trying to overcome, the Eurocentric, **orientalist** and **patriarchal** forms of knowledge which currently dominate the terrorism studies and security studies fields, and to an extent social science more generally (see Toros and Gunning 2009; Gunning 2009; Sylvester and Parashar 2009).

Second, as we have noted above, CTS scholars are committed to taking subjectivity seriously, in terms of both the researcher and the research subject (see Breen Smyth 2009). This means being aware of, and transparent about, the values and impact of the researcher on the conduct and outcomes of research and being willing to engage seriously with the viewpoint and perceptions of the 'terrorist'. This latter point implies an additional commitment to engaging in primary research when relevant, as opposed to the too frequent habit of relying principally on secondary sources, as identified in Chapter 1. Specifically, this means that CTS scholars value 'talking to terrorists' as one way of obtaining primary data (Gunning 2007a).

Third, CTS scholars are committed to methodological and disciplinary pluralism in terrorism research – a willingness to embrace the insights and perspectives of different academic disciplines, intellectual approaches and schools of thought. In particular, CTS sees value in **post-positivist** and non-IR-based methods and approaches, including **discourse analysis, post-structuralism, constructivism,** Critical Theory, **historical materialism,** history, **ethnography** and others.

Finally, and importantly, CTS refuses to privilege the dominant social scientific methods of terrorism research which stress **rationalism, empiricism** and positivism. Instead, it argues that interpretive and **reflectivist approaches** can be equally valuable in expanding the study and understanding of terrorism. In one respect, this means refusing to be limited by the narrow logic of traditional social scientific explanation based on linear notions of cause and effect – in which terrorism is caused by 'Islamic extremism' or 'anti-Americanism', for example. Instead, CTS argues that adopting an interpretive 'logic of understanding' rooted in 'how possible' rather than 'what causes' questions can open space for inquiries and perspectives often foreclosed by traditional social science (see Doty 1993). Asking 'How does terrorism become possible in a particular social and political context?', for example, can open up new possibilities of understanding which are potentially foreclosed by the question 'What causes terrorism?'. Importantly, this can also be seen as a political commitment because it refuses to treat (i) one model of social science as the sole legitimate method of research and (ii) the researchers who employ this model as the only legitimate producers of knowledge (Smith 2004: 514).

## Ethical-normative commitments

There are a number of ethical-normative commitments which flow directly from the ontological, epistemological and methodological commitments we have described above. First, CTS is committed to a permanent set of responsible research ethics which take account of, and try to avoid harming, the various end-users of terrorism research. These may include informants or interviewees (who may be considered 'terrorists' by the state), the **'suspect communities'** from which terrorists often emerge and the populations or groups who bear the brunt of terrorist campaigns and counter-terrorism policies – as well as the wider public, other academics and policymakers (Breen Smyth 2009). In practical terms, these research ethics mean: the adoption of a 'do no harm' approach to research; operating transparently as a researcher in terms of aims and values; 'recognising the human behind the [terrorist] label' (Booth 2008: 73) and consequently the vulnerability of those being researched; honouring undertakings of confidentiality and protecting interviewees; utilizing principles of informed consent; and taking responsibility for the anticipated impact of the research and the ways in which it may be utilized. For example, in the current legal and political environment, research on certain Islamist groups could lead to the arrest or persecution of individual Muslims or the demonization of Muslims more broadly if extreme care in the conduct and presentation of such research is not taken.

Second, the broader CTS approach involves a shift from state-centrism and the privileging of state security to a focus on the security, freedom and well-being of human individuals (Toros and Gunning 2009; Sluka 2009). Just as **Critical Security Studies** (CSS) has argued that the primary actor to be secured should be the human individual and not the state, CTS scholars also tend to be concerned with ending the avoidable suffering of human beings than with bolstering the state. In other words, CTS scholars tend to prioritize human security over **national security**, and they work towards minimizing all forms of physical, **structural** and **cultural violence** (Toros and Gunning 2009). Related to this, they take seriously the scholarly and practical exploration of non-violence, conflict transformation and reconciliation as practical alternatives to terrorist and counter-terrorist violence. Importantly, this does not mean that CTS scholars are necessarily anti-state or that the state should never be the focus of research. What it means is that one of the key measures by which we can judge legitimacy is by asking whether an act or an organization (including both states and oppositional groups) improves human well-being.

Third, CTS scholars are committed to trying to influence public policy, because not being concerned with policy is not an option for scholars committed to improving human security and well-being (Gunning 2007b; Toros and Gunning 2009). Importantly, this does not mean that CTS scholars conduct their research around the needs of state elites. Instead, CTS argues that critical scholars need to engage equally with both policy*makers* – the state elites who have to make policies to deal with non-state terrorism – and policy*takers* – the groups and wider societies who bear the brunt of counter-terrorism policies. Engaging with policytakers lessens the risk of co-option by the status quo, particularly if those thus engaged include members of communities labelled 'suspect' by the state, those designated 'terrorists', and so on. However, to be effective in realizing the potential for positive change within the status quo, critical scholars must simultaneously strive to engage with those who are embedded in the state, members of the 'counter-terrorist' forces, the political elite, and so on. This is an area where some critical scholars have arguably been weak in the past.

Fourth, CTS involves a continuous process of **'immanent critique'** of society's power structures and oppressive practices and a simultaneous commitment to action and struggle aimed at bringing about the positive transformation of existing structures (Herring 2008; Toros and Gunning 2009). More specifically, CTS scholars see an important task in questioning both morally and intellectually the dominant paradigm of political violence which promotes the idea of violence as a rational instrument for positive change, whether by governments or non-state groups (Burke 2008). From this perspective, CTS can be understood as a kind of 'outsider theorising' which seeks to go 'beyond problem-solving within the status quo and instead ... to help engage through critical theory with the problem of the status quo' (Booth 2007).

Collectively, these commitments – to human security over state security, to ending avoidable suffering, to minimizing and questioning all forms of violence, to continuous immanent critique and to transforming positively existing structures – can be described as a broad commitment to the concept of **emancipation** (see Box 2.1). Despite objections to the term and its past implication in hegemonic projects, and its being rooted in a philosophical commitment to **praxis**, CTS scholars for the most part see emancipation as a process of trying to construct 'concrete utopias' by realizing the unfulfilled potential of existing structures, freeing individuals from unnecessary structural constraints and the democratization of the public sphere (Ashley 1981: 227; Wyn Jones 2005: 229–32; McDonald 2009; Toros and Gunning 2009). In other words, as with all 'critical' research, CTS involves an underlying conception of a different social and political order (Alker 2004: 192; Wyn Jones 2005: 217–20). Importantly, as CTS understands it, emancipation is a continuous *process* of struggle and critique, rather than any particular endpoint or universal grand narrative.

---

## Box 2.1  Conceptualizing emancipation

[Emancipation is concerned with] securing freedom from unacknowledged constraints, relations of domination, and conditions of distorted communication and understanding that deny humans the capacity to make their future through full will and consciousness.

(Ashley 1981)

Emancipation is the freeing of people (as individuals and groups) from those physical and human constraints which stop them carrying out what they would freely choose to do. War and the threat of war is one of those constraints, together with poverty, poor education, political oppression and so on.

(Booth 1991)

Emancipation is the theory and practice of inventing humanity, with a view to freeing people, as individuals and collectivities, from contingent and structural oppressions. It is a discourse of human self-creation and the politics of trying to bring it about.

(Booth 2005)

---

Emancipation, then, can never be fully and finally achieved: it is something for us as scholars, students and practitioners of global politics to continuously aim *towards*.

Within the context of critical research on terrorism, emancipation expresses itself in a variety of ways, including, among others: efforts to end the use of terrorist violence whether by state or non-state actors; the promotion of human rights and well-being in situations of terrorist and counter-terrorist violence; the refusal to sanction illegal and immoral practices such as targeted killings and torture; explorations in non-violent and conflict-resolution-based responses to terrorism; and addressing the conditions that might impel actors to resort to terrorist tactics. In short, CTS imbues many of the values, concerns and orientations of peace research, conflict resolution and CSS. It is a vigorous anti-terror project based on: fundamental human rights and values; a concern for social justice and equality; and an end to structural and physical violence and discrimination.

Finally, the adoption of a 'critical' standpoint which seeks to critique and transform the status quo requires a certain amount of intellectual and moral courage because it invariably leads to vigorous opposition from interests vested in the status quo (Herring 2008; Breen Smyth 2009). CTS scholars therefore try to adopt a prior commitment to refusing to give in to intimidation, to abandoning research that is controversial or to self-censorship. In the current political and legal environment, CTS scholars are prepared to say the unsayable, whether it is to governments, the wider society, particular communities or terrorists. In a very real sense, they take the view that 'blasphemy is our business' (Booth 2008: 68).

## Key Points

- CTS is a set of approaches and commitments shared by a growing number of scholars around the world and expressed through a number of activities, publications and networks.
- The central ontological commitment of CTS is the notion that terrorism is a social construction.
- The central epistemological commitment of CTS is that knowledge of terrorism can never be neutral or divorced from power and context.
- CTS is committed to disciplinary pluralism and opening up to new, often reflectivist, approaches to research and study.
- CTS is committed to responsible research ethics, continuous immanent critique and the broader project of emancipation.
- More specifically, CTS is committed to human security over state security, to ending avoidable human suffering, to minimizing and questioning all forms of violence, and to positively transforming existing structures.

## A critical research agenda

The value of any critical approach lies not only in the insights it can provide through a critique and deconstruction of the existing field, but also in the extent to which it can provide an alternative and credible future research agenda for the subject (Jackson *et al.* 2009b). In relation to terrorism research, critical approaches like CTS aim to encourage three broad developments. First, they argue for *broadening* the study of terrorism to include subjects that have often been neglected by the leading scholars of the field, including the wider social context of political violence, the nature and causes of state violence, non-violent practices, gendered aspects of terrorism and the nature and impact of terrorism and counter-terrorism in the developing world. Second, they argue for *deepening* terrorism research by uncovering the field's underlying ideological, institutional and material interests (as we have attempted to do briefly in Chapter 1), exploring the forms of knowledge and practice which socially construct terrorism (see Chapter 3), and making the values, perspectives and normative commitments of both researchers and the researched more open and explicit. Third, they argue for making a commitment to *emancipatory praxis* central to the terrorism research enterprise (see above).

More specifically, we suggest that an initial critically oriented research agenda should include some of the following subjects, among others. While there is a growing literature on some of these subjects already, much of this research occurs largely outside of the wider Terrorism Studies field. Indeed, one of the tasks of a critical approach is to gather in these fragmented voices and serve as a tent under which research from other disciplines and approaches can coalesce and cross-pollinate (Gunning 2007a).

First, as suggested, there is a need to examine more thoroughly and systematically the linguistic, conceptual, ideological and institutional underpinnings of the Terrorism Studies field and its related practices of counter-terrorism. As mentioned, the language and widely accepted knowledge of terrorism and the institutionalized practices of counter-terrorism are actually a very recent invention; even one hundred years ago, the term 'terrorism' was rarely spoken in public discourse and there were few laws or counter-terrorism institutions in existence. Systematic research is needed to uncover how and why the term entered public consciousness and how it became such a powerful discourse able to generate vast amounts of research and political activity. The linguistic and conceptual processes by which this came about can be understood as the field's 'conditions of possibility'.

Directly related to this, there is a further need to explore in much more detail the political-economic contexts of both the Terrorism Studies field as a politically embedded domain of knowledge and the theory and practice of counter-terrorism. In other words, applying historical materialist approaches and taking material reality seriously, there is a need for further exploration of how counter-terrorism functions as a form of ideology; that is, how it works to promote certain kinds of material and class interests, maintain hegemony and sustain dominant economic relationships. As we demonstrate in Chapter 6, there are a great many actors who benefit directly from efforts to counter the terrorist threat as it is commonly understood. This means that critical analyses of the theory and practice of counter-terrorism need to be rooted within theories of class, capitalism, hegemony and imperialism (Herring 2008).

Third, as we show in Chapter 8, there is a real need for more systematic research on the nature, causes and consequences of state terrorism and state repression more broadly. In particular, there is a need for wider research into those forms of state terrorism that have remained virtually invisible in terrorism research so far, including that of Western states and that practised by many Western allies, such as Israel, Egypt, Saudi Arabia, Pakistan, Sri Lanka and Colombia, to name but a few. We also need more research into how state terrorism ends and how it might more effectively be dealt with.

Fourth, it is imperative to broaden the research agenda to include the wider social and historical context within which terrorism occurs, instead of artificially singling it out as a unique phenomenon. Terrorism is always part of a wider context in which other forms of violent and non-violent behaviour takes place, and militants are almost always part of a broader social movement struggling for political goals. At present, too little is understood about the interaction between militants and non-militants within social movements, and between militant and non-militant forms of behaviour. We also do not fully understand the role played by bystander publics, political elites, state forces and wider ideological debates in the evolution of violent militancy (Gunning 2009). Similarly, more research is needed into the effect of movement participation on individual motivation and behaviour, the effects of the internet and wider international networks on militancy, the relationship between political and domestic violence, and the interactions between structural and political violence – among others.

Fifth, there is a need to take gender much more seriously in terrorism research (see Chapter 4). A number of important topics suggest themselves here, including: examining the gendered nature of the terrorism studies field itself, the kinds of masculinized forms of knowledge it produces and the silences it contains about women, gender and gendered identities; uncovering the role of masculinity in terrorist and counter-terrorist violence; exploring the various perspectives, motivations, ambitions, goals and political agency of female participants in terrorism, counter-terrorism and political violence more broadly;

applying a gender-sensitive perspective towards militant groups and movements, and exploring how women join, mediate, subvert and resist such movements; comparative research on women in different societies who join terrorist and counter-terrorist groups; and the impact of counter-terrorist measures on women and children.

Sixth, there is a real need to address the Eurocentric and Western state-orientation of much terrorism research. This means expanding the study of terrorism to include the voices and perspectives of those in the global South who have in fact been the most frequent victims of both terrorism and counter-terrorism. It can be argued that the war on terror has had its greatest impact on the South, but this impact has yet to be the subject of systematic research (see the special issue of *Critical Studies on Terrorism*, 3(1), 2010). This concern is related to the emancipatory agenda of critical approaches, as it involves seeking to include and empower marginalized groups and individuals (McDonald 2009). Of particular importance is the need to move beyond explanations which suggest that violence in the developing regions is due to inherent cultural characteristics or pathological inclinations, or which assume that actors in the South are passive victims lacking their own agency.

Finally, there is a need to analyse further the ethics, impacts and effectiveness of different approaches to counter-terrorism. In the first instance, there is a real need to find transparent and meaningful ways of evaluating the success of counter-terrorism policies and to examine critically the accepted wisdom, such as the popular argument that 'we do not negotiate with terrorists'. Other questions which need to be explored in greater detail include: the impact of counter-terrorism policies on specific communities and individuals, the legal order, domestic society and the international system; the effects of counter-terrorism policy on issues like human rights, social trust, community cohesion, democratic culture, academic research, the media and policing prac-

---

### Key Points

- Critical approaches must go beyond critique and suggest alternative and credible future research agendas.
- CTS argues for widening, deepening and including an emancipatory element to the existing terrorism research agenda.
- Among others, a future critical research agenda calls for more systematic research on the underlying conditions and material interests of the terrorism studies field, state terrorism, the social and historical context of terrorism, gender and terrorism, the experience and perspectives of the developing world, and the impacts and ethics of counter-terrorism, particularly the war on terrorism.

tices; the role of civil society and socio-economic change in ending campaigns of political violence; the effectiveness or otherwise of dialogue with groups practising terrorism; the precise role and dynamics of demilitarization strategies, police reform, truth and reconciliation mechanisms, and the like; and the successes and failures of the current war on terrorism and other previous experiences of terrorism. In particular, the impact of the war on terrorism is in need of much more systematic research, given its global reach and size, and the vast areas of social and political life on which it has thus far impacted.

## Conclusion

It could be tempting to think that critical approaches to terrorism research amount to little more than criticism of existing studies, combined with a call for better research. We argue that they are much more than this because not only do they provide a convincing critique of the existing state of the field, they also suggest an alternative framework for looking at, understanding and studying terrorism, as well as a concrete research agenda for the future. In terms of this textbook, the critical approach we have outlined in this chapter provides an important new framework and a set of conceptual tools and key questions for considering the topics covered in Part II of the book. At the very least, it provides a framework for questioning and interrogating commonly accepted 'knowledge' and ideas about terrorism. Thus, in Chapter 6 for example, we question whether terrorism really does constitute a major threat to security; in Chapter 7 we question whether there really is a *new* type of terrorism; in Chapter 8 we ask why the state terrorism of Western states has been ignored; in Chapter 9 we question whether religion is a significant cause of terrorism; in Chapter 10 we question whether the use of force is the best way to deal with terrorism; and so on. More specifically, approaching many of these subjects from the perspective that terrorism is a social construction rather than an objective, stable phenomenon, we argue that it is not an exceptional form of violence unrelated to other kinds of political violence and struggle, and that knowledge about terrorism is never neutral but always serves someone's interests, allowing us to ask new kinds of questions and to see the topic of terrorism from new angles.

It is clear that critical approaches are now having a major impact on the terrorism studies field as whole. Not only is there a growing body of literature which adopts an explicitly critical orientation, but there are new teaching programmes, conferences, journals, book series and networks which all take an openly 'critical' perspective. As a consequence, it can be argued that anyone seriously interested in the subject of terrorism is now bound to consider the critical perspective we have outlined in this book. The success of critical approaches, CTS in particular, is in part due to the historical juncture at which they have emerged. The failures and difficulties of counter-terrorism efforts in the war on terrorism in Iraq, Afghanistan and elsewhere, combined with growing dissatisfaction with the over-reaction and damaging consequences of domestic counter-terrorism efforts and the optimism engendered by the election of Barack Obama in the USA, means that policymakers, scholars and the wider public are increasingly open to new, fresh approaches. In other words, past and continuing failures, and a widespread sense of pessimism about the state of counter-terrorism, have opened the door to new approaches like CTS.

However, notwithstanding the impact that critical approaches have had thus far, there are some dangers and obstacles which must be carefully negotiated (see Gunning 2007a; Jackson *et al.* 2009b). For example, there is a danger that the growth of critical approaches will have the effect of splitting the broader terrorism field into critical and orthodox intellectual ghettos which then refuse to speak to each other. There is a related danger that the critical side of the field will remain isolated and marginalized, and as a consequence remain locked out of being able to influence policymakers or compete for research funding. There are also continuing debates and arguments between critical scholars and others over what it really means to be 'critical' and what 'emancipation' means in practice (see 'Forum' in *International Relations*, 23(1), 2009). None of these challenges are insurmountable, but they will require careful attention and effort by critical scholars and students over the next few years.

## Discussion Questions

1.  What broadly distinguishes critical approaches to terrorism research from orthodox terrorism studies?
2.  What is meant by the term 'critical'?
3.  What are the main arguments of political-economy-based approaches to terrorism?
4.  What distinguishes anthropology, sociology, history and area studies approaches from orthodox approaches to terrorism?
5.  What are the broad characteristics of the CTS approach?
6.  How does the CTS approach to the ontology of terrorism differ from the orthodox approach?
7.  What is the CTS approach to epistemological issues in terrorism research and how does this differ from orthodox approaches?
8.  What are the core methodological commitments of the CTS approach?
9.  What does it mean to adopt an emancipatory agenda in terrorism research?
10. What does it mean to widen the study of terrorism?
11. What does it mean to deepen the study of terrorism?
12. What key issues and subjects take priority in a critical research agenda?
13. Are critical approaches just a call for better research on terrorism?
14. What tools does the critical approach outlined in this chapter provide for considering the other terrorism-related topics which follow in the book?

## Recommended Reading

Gunning, J., 2007a. 'A Case for Critical Terrorism Studies?', *Government and Opposition*, 42(3): 363–93. The first published article exploring the main weaknesses of problem-solving approaches to terrorism research and outlining the case for CTS.

Jackson, R., Breen Smyth, M., and Gunning, J., eds, 2009. *Critical Terrorism Studies: A New Research Agenda*, Abingdon: Routledge. The first book-length explanation of the CTS approach.

'Symposium: The Case for Critical Terrorism Studies', *European Political Science*, 6(3): 225–59. A symposium of papers which explores some of the main ideas and perspectives of an explicitly critical approach to the study of terrorism.

'Symposium: Critical Terrorism Studies: Foundations, Issues, Challenges', *Critical Studies on Terrorism*, 1(1–2). A symposium of papers debating the new field of critical terrorism studies from a number of leading scholars. Arguments both for and against CTS are included in the symposium.

Zulaika, J., and Douglass, W., 1996. *Terror and Taboo: The Follies, Fables, and Faces of Terrorism*, London: Routledge. The first comprehensive critical dissection of the field of terrorism studies and the broader terrorism discourse utilizing the tools and perspectives of anthropology.

## Web Resources

The journal *Critical Studies on Terrorism*: *www.tandf.co.uk/journals/titles/17539153.asp*
   The journal is a key outlet for critical terrorism-related research.

The British International Studies Association (BISA) Critical Studies on Terrorism Working Group CSTWG): *www.bisa.ac.uk/index.php?option=com_content&view=article&id=93-cst&catid=37-working-groups&Itemid=68*
   An international network of scholars working on terrorism-related research from broadly critical perspectives.

The Stanford Encyclopedia of Philosophy: *http://plato.stanford.edu/entries/critical-theory/*
   A detailed explanation of Critical Theory.

## Chapter 3

# The Cultural Construction of Terrorism

## Chapter Contents

- Introduction
- The role of the media in terrorism
- Terrorism in popular culture
- 9/11 and the construction of a social narrative
- Terrorism and national identity
- Conclusion

## Reader's Guide

This chapter explores some of the main ways in which terrorism has been socially and culturally constructed. In many Western societies, terrorism has come to saturate virtually every area of life and it is now a central element of contemporary culture. Across newspaper headlines, television programmes, films, literature, computer games, internet websites and many other cultural sites, terrorism attracts, excites and frightens us as consumers and citizens. In this chapter, we identify some of the ways in which critical approaches can contribute to an understanding of these social forms and the power/knowledge relations in which they are located. We begin by introducing the concept of media frames to help us explore the importance of the mainstream news media in mediating and reproducing dominant perspectives on terrorism. The next section then investigates some of the ways in which films and other forms of popular culture depict terrorism as a modern taboo. A third section introduces a detailed case study of these processes, exploring the construction and consolidation of a powerful 9/11 narrative in the years since 2001. This remarkably consistent presentation of those events as an *exceptional* act of terrorism was central, we suggest, to justifying the war on terrorism that followed. In the final section, we investigate the link between representations of terrorism and constructions of national identity by drawing on rhetorical theory to approach terrorism as a negative ideograph.

## Introduction

In contemporary Western societies, the threat of terrorism permeates almost every aspect of our daily lives. The newspapers we read inundate us with headlines about imminent or recent terrorist plots. On television and in film, terrorist attacks – past and future, real and imagined – are depicted with increasing frequency, as the popularity of Jack Bauer's exploits in *24* (Yin 2008) or the box office success of the film, *Baader–Meinhof Complex*, demonstrates. The video games we play transport us to the hidden worlds of the terrorists, injecting our own responsibility into 'their' death and 'our' safety. Even the landscapes in which we live, shop and relax serve as a constant reminder of the threat's omnipresence, with daily terrorist threat level reports (see Image 3.1), warning posters (see Image 3.2), CCTV cameras, concrete crash barriers and armed police all increasingly visible on the streets of our cities. Terrorism, it seems, is everywhere. This is interesting and important, because as we have demonstrated terrorism is actually a very recent addition to our store of wider cultural narratives, even though the term was first used as far back as the French Revolution. Before the 1960s, there were few counter-terrorism laws or public safety measures designed to deal with the threat, virtually no films or television programmes on the subject, and few mentions of it in the news media (Zulaika and Douglass 1996).

In this chapter, we explore how these and other forms of cultural activity draw upon and reproduce a shared social discourse about ter-

**Image 3.1**   *The US Daily Threat advisory Scale*

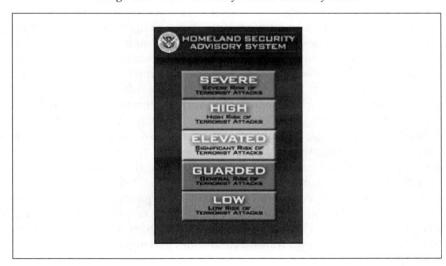

**Image 3.2**    *A popular UK counter-terrorism public warning poster*

These chemicals won't be used in a bomb because a neighbour reported the dumped containers to the Anti-Terrorist Hotline.

Don't rely on others.
If you suspect it, report it.
Confidential Anti-Terrorist Hotline
Call 0800 789 321

rorism as an ever-present **existential threat** to Western societies. Perpetuating a particular commonsense 'knowledge' about terrorism – what it is, what causes it and how we should combat it – these activities function as an important process in the social production of terrorism. In other words, they help to co-construct the terrorism phenomenon, rather than simply describe or reflect it. They also provide the context within which the study of terrorism takes place, a context that scholars never completely escape. For these reasons, critical scholars argue that engaging with these cultural processes is crucial for analysing where and how 'terrorism' is constructed, and for investigating who benefits from the dominant discourses about terrorism. As we will demonstrate, many of these social objects and practices are now so embedded in our cultural and political landscape that we are frequently oblivious to their significance or even their presence. Because of this, the dominant discourses and narratives on terrorism and their effects often go unnoticed and unchallenged, with potentially serious consequences.

## The role of the media in terrorism

Since the 1970s, a growing body of academic research has emerged to help us understand the link between terrorism and the media (Ross 2007). Because terrorism now constitutes such a major part of the daily news coverage that is consumed by citizens on their television screens, newspapers, personal computers and elsewhere, this realm is integral to its social construction as a cultural object. As Chermak (2003: 6) argues, 'the mass media is the primary vehicle [through which] the public has come to know and thus fear terrorism'. This section explores some of the ways in which the media helps to produce both knowledge and fear in this context and the political and ideological importance of these constructions.

For many analysts, terrorism and the media exist in a relationship that is best described as symbiotic; that is, a mutually beneficial coexistence from which each profits (Biernatzki 2002: 6). Thus, on the one hand, media coverage of terrorism offers political actors access to particular audiences with whom they wish to communicate, as the reporting of a violent event helps to extend its impact beyond those directly affected. As Zulaika and Douglass (1996: 7) express it, 'without television, terrorism becomes rather like the philosopher's hypothetical tree falling in the forest: no one hears it fall and therefore it has no reason for being'. On the other hand, media outlets themselves benefit from larger audiences, increased sales, associated revenues and so forth from their coverage of 'terrorist' threats and attacks. On 11 September 2001, for example, the intense public interest in unfolding events led the average American to view an incredible eight hours of television news coverage (Heller 2005: 7; see also Mogensen 2008). On the same day, online news sites experienced unprecedented numbers of hits. CNN.com, for example, recorded 162 million views of its pages compared to a daily average of only 14 million (Allan 2002: 123; see also Denton 2004). While the magnitude of these figures is considerable, they are by no means unique. Earlier events such as **Black September**'s kidnapping of Israeli athletes at the 1972 Munich Olympics, for example, which drew a worldwide audience of half a billion or 13 per cent of the world's population at the time, had already highlighted the importance of the terrorism–media relationship (see Box 3.1).

This understanding of the media–terrorism nexus as a symbiotic relationship is intuitively appealing. Not only does it correspond to a sophisticated understanding of terrorism as a form of instrumental violence (Nacos 2002: 38), it also approaches media elites and their employees as similarly rational utility-maximizers. However, even if we accept the basic premise that this relationship operates as a 'positive-sum game' from which everyone benefits, it is far more difficult to know

---

**Box 3.1  Case study: Black September and the 1972 Munich Olympics**

In September 1972, eight individuals belonging to the Palestinian organization Black September catapulted their cause to the world's attention during the Olympic Games in Munich, Germany. Having burst into the bedrooms of the Israeli athletes staying in the Olympic Village, Black September took nine athletes hostage and began negotiating for their release with the German authorities. With the world's media already concentrated on Munich, much of the subsequent crisis unfolded live on television with half a billion people tuning in to coverage of the incident and its aftermath (Harmon 2008: 8). The events culminated in a dramatic shoot-out at the airport in which all the hostages were killed, along with a number of the terrorists. The more recent conversion of these events into successful, critically acclaimed, feature-length films, including *One Day in September* and *Munich*, demonstrates their continuing ability to attract viewing audiences.

---

whether this constitutes a *causal* connection. Here, debate continues between those scholars for whom the sensationalist coverage of attacks encourages further incidents from those, on the one hand, who would use violence to pursue political programmes and those, on the other hand, who approach the media as victims rather than perpetrators of terrorism – as manipulated by, rather than beneficiaries of, those engaging in spectacular acts of violence (Picard 1991; Schlesinger 1991).

Whether or not media coverage directly causes terrorist violence, it certainly helps to *constitute* terrorism as a social construction. To understand how this takes place, critical scholars take an interest in the news frames used by the media in the stories on terrorism they produce and disseminate. News media frames refer to the interpretive structures that journalists employ to help their audiences locate an event within a broader context of historical, political, social and normative dynamics. They are collections of concepts, phrases, narratives and images that are instantly familiar to their viewers and readers. Crucially, because of this familiarity, they encourage very particular understandings of the events being depicted, giving them broader meaning (Norris *et al.* 2003: 10–11). They do this, in large part, by magnifying or shrinking certain elements of an event to make those elements appear more or less relevant than others (Entman 1991: 9). Examples of common frames used in the coverage of political violence include: terrorists as monsters, villains and evildoers; terrorist attacks as national traumas; terrorism as evidence of broader cultural clashes; the need for resilience in the face of adversity; and the heroism of post-attack efforts to rescue innocent victims, which are often heavily gendered due to their focus on courageous men (frequently in uniform) saving helpless women and children (Kellner 2002; Rai 2004; Anker 2005; Devetak 2005; Mogensen 2008; Masters 2009; Steuter and Wills 2010).

This notion of news frames is a useful one for critical scholars because it encourages us to understand media presentations of terrorism as choices rather than neutral or objective representations of external events. How an attack is depicted by journalists and their editors always involves a process of selection. Certain causes, backgrounds, consequences and evaluations will be prioritized at the expense of others, and the foregrounding and camouflaging of particular parts of a story will have cognitive and evaluative effects on its audiences. Cognitively, a news frame works to produce a coherent narrative or story by shaping its empirical 'facts' into a reasonable explanation of what has occurred, and why. By joining actors and events around specific backdrops, frames encourage particular readings of violence, such as by asking their audiences to focus on the biography of a 'terrorist' leader or on religious tensions as the ongoing context of an attack. The evaluative dimension of a frame, in contrast, encourages audiences to assess and condemn a violent action by 'naming perpetrators, identifying victims, and attributing blame' (Norris *et al.* 2003: 15). Simply by referring to an act of violence as 'terrorism', the media is already condemning that which has occurred.

When a particular narrative of terrorism is regularly repeated by influential figures, such as media elites, it can become embedded within social and political life and gain widespread currency as the truth. A number of important political and ideological consequences then follow. In the first instance, the narrative will appear as an obvious, even commonsense, explanation of what has occurred. As a consequence, certain policy options begin to seem not only possible, but also necessary in response to the violence in question. A terrorist attack that is widely understood to be the consequence of religious extremism, for example, is likely to bring very different reactions in a secularized, nation-centric context to one viewed as a consequence of nationalist aspirations.

Second, dominant narratives help to shape social and national identities by encouraging audiences to identify with certain characters in a story whilst rejecting others. This can have very real material consequences, ranging from encouraging the public to donate their money, time or blood to the victims of terrorism, to fuelling vigilante attacks on those seen as 'others' and somehow responsible for the violence.

Third, a dominant narrative may also help to constitute a framework of understanding or 'grid of intelligibility' through which subsequent political events are interpreted or 'read'. Here, the 'lessons' learned from an attack will be used to legitimate particular types of political practice, helping to 'crowd out' the emergence of critical voices and exclude alternatives.

## Key Points

- Terrorism now represents a major part of the news coverage received by citizens within Western states.
- Media coverage of political violence as terrorism is a comparatively recent phenomenon that only began in earnest from the early 1970s.
- The framing of terrorism has different dimensions because these 'frames' help shape how we understand and judge an event.
- Frames may therefore be said to co-construct acts of political violence as terrorism.
- When a particular framing is regularly repeated it can become embedded in social life with political consequences.

Finally, a dominant narrative may be used instrumentally by political and other elites to serve their own interests. Media elites, for example, may recycle a successful terrorism-related narrative to further their readership. Political elites, on the other hand, may do so to discredit their opponents or strengthen their position (see the examples on pp. 261–2). Many of these processes occurred during the construction of the dominant 9/11 narrative.

## Terrorism in popular culture

As we have noted, terrorism is now a major part of the news coverage consumed by Western and global publics. However, terrorism has also permeated many other sectors of the entertainment industry and these representations are equally important for its social construction. For example, terrorism has become an increasingly prominent topic for feature-length movies and television serials (Prince 2009). While cultural producers have long been attracted to the intrigue, drama and excitement of terrorist plots (Jackson 2005: 111; Morgan 2009), the post-9/11 era in particular has witnessed a surge in screened depictions of terrorism (Riegler 2010). Box 3.2 lists some of the most popular and profitable screen productions of this phenomenon.

The depictions of terrorism and counter-terrorism we encounter on our cinema and television screens have different social effects, depending upon how the work is interpreted by its audiences. Some like *Team America: World Police* work, at least in part, by critiquing contemporary counter-terrorism efforts. The film lampoons an inept, over-zealous US government which tries to restore global order, irrespective of the consequences of its actions – including the destruction of Paris in a counter-terrorist operation in the film's opening scene (Gow 2006).

## Box 3.2  Terrorism in television and film: selected examples

| Terrorism-themed movies pre-9/11 | Terrorism-themed movies post-9/11 | Television programmes with terrorism-themed episodes |
|---|---|---|
| *Arlington Road* (1999) | *Four Lions* (2010) | *Sleeper Cell* (2005) |
| *American History X* (1999) | *The Kingdom* (2007) | *Numb3rs* (2005) |
| *The Siege* (1998) | *Die Hard 4* (2007) | *Criminal Minds* (2005) |
| *The Devil's Own* (1997) | *Rendition* (2007) | *NCIS: Naval Crime Investigative Service* (2003) |
| *Speed* (1994) | *The Wind that Shakes the Barley* (2006) | *Ultimate Force* (2002) |
| *True Lies* (1994) | *United 93* (2006) | *Spooks* (2002) |
| *In the Name of the Father* (1993) | *Munich* (2005) | *24* (2001) |
| *Die Hard* (1988) | *Syriana* (2005) | *The Agency* (2001) |
| *Little Drummer Girl* (1984) | *Team America: World Police* (2004) | *Alias* (2001) |
| *Who Dares Wins* (1982) | *Collateral Damage* (2002) | *Cover Me: Based on the True Life of an FBI Family* (2000) |
| *The Battle of Algiers* (1966) | *The Quiet American* (2002) | *The West Wing* (1999) |
| *Sabotage* (1936) | *The Sum of All Fears* (2002) | *JAG* (1995) |

*Source*: The Internet Movie Database.

Others, such as *24* and *The Agency*, seem to simulate the work of counter-terrorist institutions doing a difficult job in a world of uncertainty. Some productions have even become directly involved in recruiting for Western intelligence agencies (Erickson 2007: 207–8). For example, the lead actress of the television serial *Alias*, Jennifer Garner, recorded a series of CIA recruitment videos that included the following remarks: 'I'm Jennifer Garner. I play a CIA officer on the ABC TV series *Alias* … Since the tragic events of 9/11, the CIA has an even stronger need for creative, innovative, flexible men and women from diverse backgrounds and a broad range of perspectives' (cited in ibid.: 208).

Television shows and Hollywood movies are thus capable of presenting different types of knowledge claims about terrorism. They can reproduce or subvert official discourses of threat and danger. How they do this is of great significance to critical scholars, as these screenings contribute to the broader social construction of terrorism occurring in the news media and terrorism industry. Films such as the *Die Hard* franchise and *Rules of Engagement*, for example, encourage viewers to inhabit particular identities or **subject positions** in relation to terrorism, by soliciting our sympathy or empathy for particular characters and what they stand for. Even allegorical references to contemporary events, such as those depicted in *The Incredibles*, help to reinforce particular perspectives on what it means to be a 'terrorist' or an 'American' (Croft 2006).

Related to this, by narrating their plot from particular perspectives these cinematic depictions shape public understandings of the causes of non-state terrorism against Western societies. The historical and political reasons for violence are rarely afforded much attention, and because of the nature of the medium, cinematic depictions tend to simplify terrorism, often presenting it as the outcome of flawed or psychotic individuals (Riegler 2010). This is most pronounced in films or TV shows offering crudely moralistic interpretations of terrorism as the product of evil fanatics (such as the film *True Lies*). Yet, even in more ambiguous depictions like *The Siege*, scant attention is afforded to the backdrop of the Muslim Arab attacks on New York City that dominate the film's storyline. As Wilkins and Downing (2002: 428) note, the film contains very little reference to 'the political economy of oil supplies, of long-running US, British, and French military interventions in the "Middle East", of Israeli settlement and ongoing annexation' and other potentially relevant factors. Finally, because Islam, in particular, has long been associated in Western narratives with violence in general (Said 1978; Wolff 1998) and terrorism specifically (Jackson 2007d), these television and film productions may also be complicit in helping to reproduce crude stereotypes of social and cultural difference (Shaheen 2001; see also Simon 1989; Hafez 2000; Said 2003; Richardson 2004; Poole and Richardson 2006).

An increased willingness to use terrorism as a subject of entertainment can also be observed within popular video games. Through this newer medium, younger audiences in particular are encountering terrorism and terrorists in increasingly graphic, seemingly realistic, scenarios (see Box 3.3). What differentiates this format from the television and film industries is the sense of direct involvement that gaming offers. Participation in games such as *Pandora Tomorrow* (from the successful series of *Tom Clancy's Splinter Cell* games) allows a gamer to be projected into a futuristic world of conflict with Indonesian cyber-terrorists as the character 'Sam Fisher, a deadly stealth operative waging a one-man war'. In others, such as *Terrorist Takedown: Mogadishu* (2009), the player is transported back to 1993 Somalia to revisit (or perhaps rewrite) past confrontations with terrorists, as a 'member of Army Rangers, the elite special operations force, [from which] you'll engage the fanatical followers of terrorist warlords in a furious battle for control of the city'. (The descriptions of these video games are taken from the manufacturers' information found on the Amazon website.)

The capacity for consumers to be transported by video games into these fictitious scenarios, again, means that very particular understandings of terrorism and counter-terrorism are reinforced. First, often with few opportunities to participate as the (typically non-Western) 'terrorist', these games invariably encourage their users to identify with particular actors in global politics, namely the soldier, the special agent and so forth (Sisler 2008: 208). At the same time, they solicit hostility and suspicion towards particular others, who are often heavily racialized and portrayed as though they exist in the 'real' world (Power 2007: 273).

Second, because these games tend to focus on character biography rather than social and political contexts they reinforce simple, one-dimensional understandings of the causes of terrorism as a phenomenon reducible to personality defects or choices (Sisler 2008). Third, the tendency to locate many terrorism-themed games in an imaginary Middle Eastern context reaffirms a pervasive and widespread understanding of terrorism as something that is geographically or culturally specific. The frequent use of stereotypical icons associated with the Middle East, such as the camel, the sheik or the belly dancer, draws on long-established orientalist tropes that exoticize a diverse region and present the Middle East as a singular world of danger and excitement (ibid.: 206–8; see also Said 1978; Wolff 1998).

Fourth, many of the most successful video games in this genre emulate television and film depictions in reproducing the dominant discourse on terrorism as an exceptional threat from which we are all constantly at risk. The *War on Terror* PC game, for example, asked of its users: 'In a world where terror is just around the corner, can you be the one to stop it … Can you rid the world of terror once and for all?'.

---

**Box 3.3  Terrorism-themed video games**

| Title | Manufacturer's description |
| --- | --- |
| *Tom Clancy's Splinter Cell: Double Agent* | 'Play as a double agent spy for the first time ever. Take on dual roles of covert operative and ruthless terrorist, where your choices of whom to betray and whom to protect actually affect the outcome of your game. Experience the relentless tension and gut-wrenching dilemmas of life as a double agent. Lie. Kill. Sabotage. Betray. All to protect the innocent.' |
| *Just Cause* | 'Take on the role of the flamboyant Rico Rodriguez – an undercover CIA operative specializing in regime change – as he tries to overthrow the corrupt government of San Esperito. This rogue South American island is suspected of stockpiling WMDs and it's your job to negate the threat to world peace. It could be to your advantage that this tropical paradise is about to implode as various factions vie for power – it just needs a gentle nudge in the right direction.' |
| *Tom Clancy's Rainbow Six: Vegas* | 'Rainbow operatives take to the chaotic streets of Las Vegas as an escalating terrorist siege in Sin City threatens to take world terrorism to new, uncontrollable heights. The future of global security hangs in the balance as you battle to defend classic Vegas locations and environments like Fremont Street, the Strip, and casinos.' |
| *Metal Gear Solid 2: Sons of Liberty* | 'Assume the role of Solid Snake, a one-man army determined to stop a deadly high-tech weapon from falling into the hands of the wrong people. Snake must utilize his skills in stealth, weaponry and counter-terrorism to fight off the competing powers and destroy the gigantic killing machine Metal Gear Ray.' |
| *Black Hawk Down* | 'Delta Force Black Hawk Down lets you experience 10 extraordinary months in 1993, fighting in Somalia as a member of the US Special Operations Forces.' |

Finally, just as Hollywood producers and television actors have become increasingly linked to military and political elites (Der Derian 2009), so too have video games (Power 2007). The game, *America's Army*, is officially funded and developed by Western state militaries and promises to provide players 'with the most authentic military experience available'.

## Box 3.4 The Danish cartoon controversy

On 30 September 2005, the Danish newspaper *Jyllands-Posten* published twelve cartoons caricaturing the Prophet Muhammad. These pictures provoked considerable controversy, initially in Denmark, and later further afield, after they were republished across a number of other countries. More than simply depicting Muhammad – an action seen by many as prohibited under Islamic law – the more controversial of these cartoons drew a link between the Prophet and terrorism, and therefore between Islam and terrorism. In one cartoon, Muhammad's turban appeared to contain a bomb with a lit fuse in it; another depicted the Prophet baring an unsheathed sword. The publication of these cartoons led to much public discussion over the right to, and limits of, freedom of expression in European societies and elsewhere, not least in a context where Islam has been repeatedly constructed as a social and cultural threat. It also resulted in violent protests and deaths of protestors, the burning of Danish embassies and the organization of consumer boycotts of Danish products. Controversy has continued to surround the affair with revelations of additional cartoons being added by protestors for their own interests and more recently with the shooting of a would-be attacker in the home of the original cartoonist in Denmark.

*For a useful introduction to the different positions taken on the cartoon controversy and the issues it raised, see Modood, 2006.*

Television shows, films and computer games are only three of the most important cultural sites in which the social construction of terrorism takes place. Popular novels, popular music, comic books, plays, websites, blogs, jokes, cartoons, public art, poetry, children's books, postage stamps, tattoos and many other areas of contemporary culture have also increasingly begun to engage with issues surrounding terrorist violence (see Zulaika and Douglass 1996; Foster 2005; Hart 2005; Jackson 2005; Croft 2006; Dodds 2007; Holloway 2008; Versluys 2009). Although these cultural objects and processes may seem inconsequential, collectively they all contribute to a shared understanding of terrorism, the threat that it poses and how we should respond to this threat as consumers and citizens. At times, as with the Danish Cartoon controversy (Box 3.4), this can lead to social division and hostility, and even to further violence. More often though, by replicating a dominant understanding of terrorism, these products assist in reproducing a shared worldview or 'grid of intelligibility' on which political elites can subsequently draw in their attempts to justify or 'sell' new anti-terrorism policies and programmes (Jackson 2009c: 30).

> ## Key Points
>
> - Terrorism has become increasingly prominent within the entertainment industries.
> - Films, computer games, novels and other media which explore terrorism and counter-terrorism all contribute to the social construction of this phenomenon.
> - By encouraging audiences to identify with particular characters, these products also help in the shaping of national, cultural and other identities.
> - In so doing, they contribute to the creation of a 'grid of intelligibility' through which 'real' events and people are interpreted or 'read'.

## 9/11 and the construction of a social narrative

In this chapter we have thus far explored the roles of the news and entertainment media in the social construction of terrorism. In this section, we look at perhaps the most important contemporary case study of these processes, namely the consolidation of a social-political narrative surrounding the events of 11 September 2001. The following discussion shows that violent events never simply 'speak for themselves', even if their meaning may seem self-evident. Instead, they acquire their meaning through processes of interpretation that are usually organized and driven by powerful social actors with their own interests.

The 9/11 attacks acquired their meaning through an evolving, yet remarkably coherent, narrative that was picked up and reproduced across numerous social sites within the USA and beyond (Silberstein 2002; Jackson 2005; Croft 2006; Jarvis 2008, 2009b). Importantly, in the immediacy of the attacks no commentator seemed able to pinpoint what they signified or represented, with politicians and others regularly referring to them as indescribable or incomprehensible. Gradually, however, this 'void of meaning' (Campbell 2002; Jackson 2005) began to be filled, initially through the identification of the events as an exceptional moment of national trauma. Politicians in the US and beyond were quick to point to the uniqueness of the attacks, presenting 11 September 2001 as a 'day like no other' (Jackson 2009c: 27). Memorial practices that sprang forth in America and elsewhere seemed to confirm the significance and innocence of the 9/11 victims (Jarvis 2009b: 54–6, 2010). Newspapers reinforced this sense of exceptionality by seeking to remember those that had died in dedicated sections such as the *New York Times*'s 'Portraits of Grief' series (Simpson 2006: 21–53). Later, body art, poems, children's essays and many other forms of cultural practice all emerged to further testify to 9/11's destabilizing impact on the American public (Croft 2006: 86–95). The overtly nationalistic flavour of many of these practices both reproduced and extended the wave of patriotism that swept the USA (Silberstein 2002: 107–25).

The gradual emergence of this dominant 9/11 narrative not only confirmed the importance of the attacks for America and Americans, it also helped to establish – or co-construct – the attacks' meaning: how audiences should interpret the events (see Box 3.5). Although the 9/11 events were initially framed as 'acts of murder' – and therefore criminal – they were swiftly rhetorically recast by the Bush administration and others as 'terrorist attacks' and 'acts of war'. Analogies drawn with earlier military conflicts, such as the Pearl Harbor attack, and the recycling of earlier war imagery such as the Iwo Jima iconography of the 9/11 memorial stamp and the *New York Times*'s adaptation of Rockwell's 1943 painting *Freedom From Fear* (Frascina 2005), helped to confirm this militarized understanding of the events. Televized news also added to this nationalistic, war-based narrative of the attacks, with stars and stripes imagery and 'AMERICA UNDER ATTACK' banners ubiquitous in coverage of the events and their aftermath (Silberstein 2002: 71).

Another part of the narrative suggested that the attacks' unique and unexpected character provided irrefutable evidence for the emergence of a new type of terrorist threat confronting the USA and its allies. In this construction, the new threat was so severe that 'our' values, as well as 'our' lives, were at stake: civilization, freedom, democracy and justice were under attack. Those responsible for 9/11 were branded evil, cowardly, savage and inhuman, and their actions were the result of a psychological deviance that was unrelated to politics or history. And, because language tends to function in a binary manner, the victims and those associated with them were implicitly scripted as good, heroic, civilized and innocent. Importantly, this new enemy was seen to be both within and outside of the USA, so that 'according to the administration, there were so-called terrorist "sleeper cells" who were "living in our communities", like "ticking time-bombs" just waiting to go off' (Jackson 2009c: 27).

Finally, because the 9/11 attacks were depicted as 'acts of war' as well as 'acts of terrorism', this narrative also underpinned America's response to the attacks. The Bush administration (and others) quickly (and frequently) asserted that the only appropriate response to 9/11 would be a 'war on terrorism', one that would differ from earlier conflicts because of the new type of enemy being confronted. Because America had been already attacked and remained under threat, this conflict was constructed as both necessary and legitimate. The new 'war on terrorism' would be successful and just – proportionate to the threat, but reflecting US global superiority. However, as we shall see in Chapter 11, critical scholars argue that this conflict was neither successful nor just in its global prosecution.

## Box 3.5  Key features of the 9/11 narrative

### Narrating 9/11

- An exceptional and unprecedented strike on US soil.
- A historical dividing point, separating past security from present insecurity.
- An 'act of war'.
- A new Pearl Harbor. A surprise attack and a 'wake-up call' to the USA.
- A part of America's enduring struggle against evil, savagery and totalitarianism.
- An attack on the USA by terrorists because of their hatred of its values and success.

### Narrating the terrorist threat

- Terrorism as the most serious contemporary security threat to individuals, states and global values.
- Terrorism as a growing security threat: the next attack could be even worse if it involved WMD.
- Terrorist groups like al-Qaeda seen as ruthless and sophisticated.
- Terrorism as an internal and external security challenge.
- Terrorism as the instigator of a permanent state of emergency.

### Narrating the terrorist other

- Terrorists as evil, cruel and inhuman, yet also sophisticated and ruthless.
- Contemporary terrorists as different from earlier terrorists because they are religiously motivated, incorrigible and unconstrained in their methods.
- Terrorists as primarily aimed at causing maximum casualties and chaos.

### Narrating response

- 9/11 as the start of a new war on terrorism.
- The war on terrorism as necessary, legitimate, proportionate and just.
- The war on terrorism as a new, different type of war requiring new methods and ways of thinking.
- The war on terrorism as successful if it receives long-term commitment and sustained national and international effort.
- America as a nation called by history to lead the war on terrorism because of its universal values and global position.

*Sources*: Jackson 2005; Jarvis 2009b; Silberstein 2002.

The consolidation of this understanding as the accepted common-sense view of the 9/11 events was successful for a number of reasons, not least because American society (and by extension, the wider world) was saturated with the key narratives of senior Bush administration officials and world leaders. In the months and years following the attacks, for example, the administration made on average ten speeches, statements to the press, interviews and the like, *per day*, about 9/11 and the war on terrorism (Nacos 2002: 148–9; Jackson 2005), and during his term President Bush discussed terrorism in over 3,000 public speeches (Bartolucci 2010: 134). The mainstream media gave extensive coverage to many of these statements. In other words, given that the core narratives were in every newspaper, on every radio and television station, as well as in novels, films, sermons and on the internet, continuously for several years, it is perhaps unsurprising that it became the dominant interpretation.

Second, and equally important, the Bush administration's narrative succeeded because it built on long-standing political myths relating to 'American exceptionalism', 'manifest destiny' and the 'chosen nation' (Hughes 2003). With these myths already well-established and accepted within American society, this narrative was always likely to resonate with the broader American public. Many in the USA believed it was attacked because of its unique role as a global beacon of liberty and democracy, and that it was acting appropriately in its forceful, wide-ranging reaction to 9/11 because of its historic duty to spread these values to the world. Also, although pre-emptive military responses (such as the attack against Iraq) may be unpopular, the USA was uniquely positioned to engage in such actions because of its pre-eminent global position. Similarly, by comparing 9/11 and its aftermath to earlier American triumphs – such as the World War II confrontation with fascism and the cold war defeat of communism – the narrative helped to convince audiences of both the righteousness and ultimate success of the present confrontation.

Potential challenges to the dominant narrative were also effectively countered by the Bush administration and their allies through vigorous public diplomacy campaigns, protracted appeals to patriotism, the discrediting of political opponents and the use of pressure groups such as Campus Watch and the American Council of Trustees and Alumni (ACTA) (see Peterson 2002; Kennedy 2003; Kennedy and Lucas 2005; Aysha 2005). Its reproduction and consolidation, moreover, was further aided by a generally docile media which either directly repeated the understanding of official sources or simply relied on those sources for cues on how to interpret best the attacks (Al-Sumait *et al.* 2009; Altheide 2009).

Beyond discrediting alternative understandings of 9/11 and the USA-led response, this socially constructed narrative also had a number of other key ideological and political effects. First, because 9/11 was systematically constructed as both an 'act of war' and evidence of a new type of terrorist threat, this narrative helped to make a number of subsequent policy choices possible by presenting them as conceivable, respectable and plausible responses to the attacks (Doty 1993). In other words, the subsequent military conflicts in Afghanistan and Iraq were in part able to proceed because 9/11 had first been constructed as the start of a new war on terrorism. Similarly, the foundations for the widespread incursions on civil liberties that followed the attacks were laid by the interpretation of 9/11 as the start of a new age of terror, and through the construction of terrorism as an existential threat requiring exceptional measures.

A second consequence was that this narrative helped to 'sell' all of these policy responses to the domestic American and international publics. Because it built on well-established political myths and was repeated continuously throughout the war on terrorism's early years, the narrative came to be viewed as an accurate representation of what had happened – a form of accepted commonsense or regime of truth. Against this background, it then became easier to argue that the war on terrorism was both necessary and right.

Third, and perhaps most significantly, the dominant 9/11 narrative directly served a range of material and political interests within the USA and beyond. A large array of actors directly benefited from this particular understanding of the events and their responses: state security institutions received increased resources and authority; military-industrial corporations benefited in their roles as suppliers to the military and intelligence agencies; private security corporations were contracted to provide security at airports elsewhere; and academics and think-tanks saw considerable increases in research funding because of the perceived terrorist threat (see further examples on pp. 141–2, 270). These actors then had a direct material interest in the continuation of the dominant narrative.

In summary, the 9/11 narrative helped to co-construct our contemporary social world by giving meaning to a set of events and a sense of legitimacy to the response. The narrative was successful in part because it reinforced the notion that the events 'speak for themselves'. From a critical perspective, public narratives like the 9/11 one are important, because they help to structure political decisions and choices and to make some policy options appear obvious (such as invading two states and declaring war on armed groups regardless of whether they have directly attacked US interests), whilst camouflaging others (such as pursuing terrorists through legal and community policing means). They are also important because they may be used instrumentally by political and other elites to achieve specific political goals.

> ### Key Points
>
> * The aftermath of 9/11 was marked by the emergence of a remarkably powerful social narrative about the meaning of the attacks.
> * The Bush administration-led narrative constructed 9/11 as an evil act of terrorism against innocent Americans and the start of a new USA-led war on terrorism.
> * The narrative's consolidation across cultural and media sites helped to discredit alternative understandings of the attacks and the response that followed.
> * The narrative also had a number of political and ideological effects, including justifying the war on terrorism and helping to serve existing material and political interests.

## Terrorism and national identity

Terrorism, as we have seen, represents something far more than one of the main security threats facing Western states; it is a socially constructed cultural object with wide-ranging effects across society. The seemingly insatiable appetite for terrorism within our news media, films and so on illustrates how terrorism now operates as a common and popular source of entertainment. Yet, as we have seen, social productions of terrorism do far more than keep us entertained. By marking out whom and what 'we' should fear, these depictions also tell us who and what 'we' are. In this sense, terrorism represents an ideological, symbolic marker of British, American and perhaps even Western culture. It has become a negative ideograph of Western society (Winkler 2006).

The term 'ideograph' was originally developed by the rhetorical scholar Michael McGee (1999: 428) to help understand how dominant discourses about society are internalized by individuals. According to McGee, this happens because the privileged cultural values we inherit, such as freedom, democracy and justice, in many Western contexts function as 'ideographs' or as ordinary language terms used by elites and wider populations alike. Ideographs function as 'collective terms of political allegiance that embody a society's ideals' (Winkler 2006: 12), marking out a shared identity's primary values. Terms that fulfil this role are typically abstract with a flexible, imprecise and shifting quality. They are bound by their cultural context, characterized by a highly charged process of labelling and are dependent on broader cultural and political narratives that give coherence to the scenes, characters and themes that guide the moral conduct of a society and provide meaning to the lives of its members.

This notion of ideographs is a useful one for understanding how members of a society perceive their cultural identity through acceptance of idealized values. Yet, the practice of identity formation also involves identifying differences or oppositions between oneself and others: in other words, 'to know what a culture is requires an understanding of what it is not' (ibid.). In order to establish a particular cultural identity it is therefore necessary to label those behaviours that represent a negation of 'our' societies: we are good/they are evil; we are strong/they are weak; we are normal/they are deviant; and so forth. In this respect, American and British societies, for example, define themselves as much by their opposition to tyranny as they do by their commitment to liberty. This process has expanded to include terrorism, in part because of the way events like 9/11 have been narrated. That is, Western societies have over the past few decades come to define themselves in opposition to terrorism, to the point that 'terrorism' now functions as a negative marker – a negative ideograph – of Western identity (Winkler 2006). Whatever the terrorists are, we are the opposite: the terrorists hate freedom, we love freedom; they are anti-democratic, we are pro-democratic; they destroy life, we value life. Labelling something or someone as 'terrorist', in other words, not only condemns the actions of the 'other', it also, importantly, helps to construct the identity of the 'self'.

In this chapter we have examined a considerable amount of evidence suggesting that terrorism now represents a negative ideograph of Western societies. The saturation of popular culture and mass media broadcasting with terrorism-related themes means that the term certainly qualifies as a common term in political and everyday discourse (ibid.). Yet, the ambiguous and highly charged threat of terrorism has also become institutionalized and normalized in many other areas of Western societies. In recent years, for example, terrorism has increasingly dominated the realms of government and high politics. Western states have established new departments, offices and legislation for combating terrorism, such as the US Department of Homeland Security and the 2005 Australian Anti-Terrorism Act. Public spending on terrorism has increased considerably; the UK, for example, has recently committed itself to increased spending on counter-terrorism, intelligence and resilience from £2.5 billion in 2007–08 to £3.5 billion in 2010–11 (BBC News Online 2007). Also, a host of new action plans, resolutions, operating procedures and resources devoted to countering terrorism have emerged domestically and internationally through the auspices of the EU, the UN, the Organization for Security and Co-operation in Europe (OSCE), NATO and many other international organizations.

Second, anti-terrorism measures have also become normalized in the everyday lives of Western citizens. Security checks and mechanisms are now ubiquitous on public transport, at public gatherings, in government buildings, and so on. The streets of our cities have been transformed with warning posters, bollards, barriers, armed guards and collapsible street furniture, all of which are now increasingly prominent (Coaffee *et al.* 2009). A pervasive and extensive restructuring of immigration powers, policies and programmes throughout Western states has occurred, and there has been an embedding of anti-terrorism programmes in everyday life (Jarvis and Lister 2010), such as the US Terrorism Information and Protection System (TIPS) programme, the trucker's Eyes of the Road programme and emergency preparedness and response pamphlets such as the Federal Emergency Management Agency's (FEMA) 2002 booklet *Are You Ready: A Guide to Citizen Preparedness*.

Third, we have also recently seen an embedding of a terrorism focus within Western universities and the wider education sector. Following 9/11, in particular, Western universities introduced numerous new study and research centres, degree schemes and academic appointments dedicated to the study of terrorism. Virtually all areas of the academy have now benefited from significant sums of research funding relating to terrorism, despite the concerns of critical academics (Breen Smyth 2009: 206). In the UK, universities and lecturers have been asked to help the government fight terrorism and extremism by challenging radical views in the classroom and reporting suspicious students to the authorities. We have also seen the publication of a staggeringly high output of books and scholarly articles on terrorism every year since 9/11, such that, 'by June 2008, 2,281 non-fiction books with "terrorism" in the title had been published since September 2001. In comparison, prior to September 2001 only 1,310 such books had been published in entirety' (Silke 2009: 34). There is even the emergence of a substantial body of children's educational literature on the threat of terrorism and the war on terrorism.

Fourth, in the USA in particular, terrorism has become a significant dimension of religious life encountered in numerous religious books, magazines, television and radio broadcasts, home study materials, websites and sermons (see, for example, Croft 2006: 31–2). Finally, terrorism has also increasingly featured as a major part of the retail sector's output, with the design, manufacture and sale of a range of products promoted to help protect consumers from terrorism. These include home kits for WMD protection, parachutes for high-rise office workers and vast quantities of 9/11 and war on terrorism memorabilia. There have also emerged a range of new services designed to connect the public directly to counter-terrorism, including the recent trialling of mobile telephone kits directly linking the consumer to the security services.

Taken together, these developments indicate the pervasiveness and embedding of terrorism within the cultures of Western states. Because of terrorism's ubiquity, the national identities of countries such as the USA and UK have been gradually reshaped around a shared opposition to this constructed threat. As a result, measures have been introduced to combat terrorism which previously would have been viewed as excessive, but are now accepted as commonplace by the very people potentially victim to their scrutiny. The threat and our expected responses to it have become normalized in many aspects of our everyday lives.

The existence of terrorism as an extremely powerful negative symbol of Western identity also means that it may be thought of as a contemporary cultural taboo or myth (in the anthropological sense). Associated with evil, monstrosity and barbarism (see Steuter and Wills 2010), and presented as a ubiquitous threat to our values and our very existence, terrorism has become the epitome of everything we are not – the ultimate transgression of everything we stand for (see Asad 2007). This construction is simplistic. As we have seen, it is always possible to interpret acts of political violence differently: some of the violence carried out in response to terrorism, such as the invasion of Iraq for example, is perceived as terror by its many victims. It is also counterproductive: when something exists as a taboo it will often be segregated and removed from the rest of society (Zulaika and Douglass 1996: 153). Here, the war on terrorism's programmes of rendition and indefinite detention represent only the most visible example of recent efforts to remove tabooed individuals from society. At the same time, those seeking to understand why terrorism happens, or, indeed, to offer alternative perspectives on the threat that it poses, will often be viewed with suspicion and derision. Therefore, practices such as these not only reproduce an existing grid of intelligibility – making it harder still to critique the dominant discourse on terrorism – they also, potentially, increase the risk of future violence from opponents or victims of political oppression conducted in the guise of counter-terrorism.

## Key Points

- Ideographs are privileged symbols of cultural identity found in the everyday language of political elites and the wider society.
- Negative ideographs identify a society's key values by negation, defining what a society is not.
- Terrorism increasingly functions as a negative ideograph within Western states, the threat of which encroaches more and more on our everyday lives.
- The power of terrorism as a negative ideograph means that it now functions as a cultural taboo.

## Conclusion

In this chapter we have explored some of the insights derived from cultural studies for those seeking to study terrorism critically. As we have seen, critical scholars view representations of terrorism in the news media, films, video games and elsewhere as central to the social construction of this phenomenon. Understood in this way, these cultural objects and processes do not simply represent or reflect an external reality. They actively help to shape the ways in which terrorism is understood and assessed by consumers. In so doing, they also contribute to the formation of shared national and cultural identities, marking out who 'we' are by telling 'us' who and what to fear. As such, the practices explored in this chapter help to reproduce a dominant regime of truth about terrorism, maintaining the myth that a ubiquitous existential threat to 'our' security and shared values confronts us from both within and without.

The social-political narratives and practices related to terrorism, however, do even more than contribute to the construction of identities and threats. As outlined above, they also have a direct impact on political decisions and responses to attacks or perceived threats. How an event is viewed or narrated works to make counter-terrorism programmes seem necessary, legitimate and commonsensical. At the same time, this process militates against considering alternative options and approaches. When particular narratives become embedded within social life they help to constitute a grid of intelligibility through which other events, risks and threats are interpreted. When this happens, a range of different actors can capitalize on these narratives to further their own material and political interests.

## Discussion Questions

1. How is the relationship between terrorism and the news media best understood?
2. What does it mean to suggest that media representations 'frame' terrorist violence? How useful is the concept of media frames?
3. How, and in what ways, are video games, cartoons and other forms of popular culture important in the social construction of terrorism?
4. How were the 9/11 attacks socially constructed in the USA and beyond? Who was responsible for this construction?
5. Why were the dominant narratives relating to 9/11 so widely accepted?
6. Why does this particular social construction of 9/11 matter?
7. In what ways has the threat of terrorism become integrated into the everyday life of Western societies?
8. How are cultural constructions of terrorism and national identity related to one another?
9. What does it mean to say that terrorism is a modern cultural taboo?
10. To what extent does terrorism today function as a negative ideograph of Western states?

## Recommended Reading

Croft, S., 2006. *Culture, Crisis and America's War on Terror*, Cambridge: Cambridge University Press. A critical investigation of the ways in which the war on terrorism was co-constituted within the sites of popular culture.

Hill, A., 2009. *Re-Imagining the War on Terror: Seeing, Waiting, Travelling*, Basingstoke: Palgrave Macmillan. A slightly more advanced exploration of the role of images in the recent war on terrorism.

Jackson, R., 2005. *Writing the War on Terrorism: Language, Politics and Counter-Terrorism*, Manchester: Manchester University Press. A critical discourse analysis of the ways in which the war on terrorism was simultaneously constructed and justified within the language employed by the Bush administration and others.

Morgan, M., ed., 2009. *The Impact of 9/11 on the Media, Arts and Entertainment: The Day that Changed Everything?*, New York: Palgrave Macmillan. A collection of essays on the far-reaching and complex impacts of 9/11 on the media, arts and entertainment.

Norris, P., Kern, M., and Just, M., eds, 2003. *Framing Terrorism: The News Media, the Government, and the Public*, London: Routledge. An edited collection of chapters exploring the ways in which terrorist attacks are framed in the news media.

Shaheen, J., 2001. *Reel Bad Arabs: How Hollywood Vilifies a People*, New York: Olive Branch Press. A study of the widespread stereotyping of Arabs within films and television programmes made by Hollywood.

Winkler, C., 2006. *In the Name of Terrorism: Presidents on Political Violence in the Post-World War II Era*, New York: SUNY. A study of the evolution of terrorism as an ideological marker – a negative ideograph – of American culture that focuses primarily on the language of US presidents.

## Web Resources

The National Commission on Terrorist Attacks upon the United States, also known as the 9/11 Commission: *www.9-11commission.gov/report/index.htm*
> The website includes the final report on the 9/11 events, as well as a wealth of other information related to the Commission's work.

The September 11 Digital Archive: *http://911digitalarchive.org/*
> A website dedicated to the collection and preservation of electronic media related to the history of 11 September 2001 and its aftermath. The Archive contains more than 150,000 digital items, including more than 40,000 emails and other electronic communications, more than 40,000 first-hand stories and more than 15,000 digital images.

US public service advertising campaign: *www.ready.gov*
> A US-based 'national public service advertising campaign designed to educate and empower Americans to prepare for and respond to emergencies including natural and man-made disasters', such as terrorist attacks.

Metropolitan Police warning posters: *www.met.police.uk/campaigns/counter_terrorism/index.htm*
> A sample of counter-terrorism public warning posters used in the UK.

America's Army video game: *www.americasarmy.com/*
> US military website, home to the United States Army's online video game. The website also includes features such as a free graphic novel, access to social networking sites and testimonials of the 'Real Heroes' from the US army.

Terrorism Warfare video game: *www.terrorismwarfare.com/login.php*
> An online video game where it is possible to play either as a terrorist or as a counter-terrorist.

# Chapter 4

# Bringing Gender into the Study of Terrorism

## Reader's Guide

In this chapter we examine how the issue of gender applies to, and shapes, understandings of terrorism and political violence. We start by introducing key terms such as gender, sex, masculinity, stereotypes and heteronormativity, before explaining the notion of gender hierarchies. This is followed by a critical examination of the reliability of essentialist ideas about men, women and political violence, and the role of hypermasculinity in the causation of violence. To do this, we explore a range of examples of women who have been involved in political violence and terror, both as combatants and victims. Next, we examine gender-based political violence through the example of rape as a war crime, tracing how women's victimhood is also frequently used to justify the use of force and glorify terror. We then look at how the gendering of terrorism and political violence replicates stereotypical notions of gender roles and patriarchal power arrangements. The chapter concludes by considering how the practices of terrorism and counter-terrorism contribute to a broader heteronormative hegemony that reinforces gender hierarchies and the stereotypes which mask the variety of roles men and women perform in relation to political violence and terrorism.

## Introduction

In the past, when the subject of 'gender and terrorism' has arisen, discussion has often been limited to a small selection of women who join armed movements or engage in political violence in non-state groups (see, for example, McCafferty 1981; Blee 1991; Adele 1993). In particular, the cases of the Palestinian woman, Leila Khalid, and of the German women, Gudrun Ensslin and Ulrike Meinhof, are frequently cited. More recently, there has been a growing literature on female suicide terrorism (see Victor 2003; Zedalis 2004; Bloom 2005; Schweitzer 2006; Ness 2008). Less frequently discussed, however, is the involvement of women in relation to state terror or the use of women in justifying rescue narratives. In this chapter, we seek to address this imbalance by including in our study the cases of Lynndie England and Jessica Lynch, both soldiers in the US military. We will also look at how masculinity contributes to the production of violence, both in the war on terrorism and within a terrorist organization – the Irish National Liberation Army (INLA). The issue of gender-based terrorism, through a discussion of a rape camp in Bosnia, is also explored.

The approach taken here marks something of a departure from two broader tendencies within the disciplines of IR, politics and traditional terrorism studies. The first is the tendency to ignore issues of gender altogether, especially in relation to political violence (Sjoberg and Gentry 2007). The second is to focus solely on non-state terrorism to the exclusion of state terrorism and violence. Where gender is mentioned in the IR literature, the assumption is often made that the issue of gender is relevant to women, who 'have gender', whilst (genderless) men are 'the norm'. Of course, gender (and feminism) is as much about men and masculinity as it is about women and femininity. As we will argue, political violence and terrorism are shaped and formed by gender dynamics: the former simply cannot be understood without acknowledging the importance of the latter. This is evident in the predominance of men in combat roles, whether in non-state armed groups or in the institutions charged with countering terrorism on behalf of the state. Where women take up arms, they are most often depicted as the exception that proves the rule that women are inherently peaceful and less prone to violence by their very nature than men. As Sjoberg and Gentry (2007) show, they are typically represented in both the media and academia as either deviant women or victims to be rescued (see also Hunt and Rygiel 2006). With these authors, we argue that the roles played by women and men in political violence, and the ways in which they are represented, help to maintain gender formations and hierarchies. As such, they are an essential element in the maintenance of the status quo and therefore an expression of problem-solving theory; it is knowledge *for* something.

## Key terms and concepts

Until relatively recently in the social sciences, the term 'gender' was primarily understood to refer to the socially constructed identities associated with biological 'sex'. It referred to 'masculinity' in the case of men and 'femininity' for women (Connell 2009). These two genders were, in turn, associated with gender stereotypes, whereby men and masculinity was associated with strength, power, stoicism, action, toughness, and so on. Women and femininity were associated with weakness, powerlessness, passivity, gentleness, emotionality and softness. Whilst 'real' men and women are usually a mixture of these qualities, social norms exist whereby feminine men and masculine women are viewed as deviant – as somehow failing to be 'proper' men and women.

The politics of gender, like the politics of race and class, order categories of people into a hierarchy. In the case of **gender hierarchies**, supposedly masculine qualities tend to be socially and economically privileged and men tend to have more power and autonomy in social, economic and political life than women. Furthermore, gender hierarchies, which are ubiquitous, usually ensure that the men who comply best with gender norms and **heteronormative** standards have more power and resources than men who do not. Nonetheless, even non-compliant men tend to have more power and resources than women.

More recent approaches to gender are particularly useful in examining the connections between gender and political violence such as terrorism. Judith Butler (2006) sees gender as 'performative' – as something that we *do* in relation to others, rather than something we *are*. Understood in this way, one's gender emerges as part of an ongoing **social performance**. Importantly, it is something that is open to change and is therefore never fully fixed. Yet, we are relegated into categories of men and women in the service of the reproduction of heterosexuality, which is institutionalized as the norm. Those who do not fit easily within the categories of men and women, and who fail to conform to the norm of heterosexuality, attract social sanctions. Heterosexuality – sexual desire and relationships between men and women – is regarded as normal, while other forms of desire or relationship are regarded as deviant and lesser. This privileging of binary gender roles for men and women, and the legitimization of heterosexuality, is referred to as heteronormativity. Therefore, the roles we play in our working and private lives are implicated in the social construction of gender, of what it is to be a man or a woman. In turn, we are 'gendered', classified as more or less masculine or feminine, according to the way our performance fits in with ideals of masculinity and femininity – what 'proper' men and women should do and how they

> ## Key Points
>
> - Gender is often ignored in the literature on terrorism and political violence, as it is in IR and politics more generally.
> - Where gender is addressed, it is most often assumed to be about women's actions and behaviour; men are not considered to be gendered.
> - Political violence and terrorism, like all aspects of politics, can be said to be gendered in a number of important ways.
> - This gendering serves to maintain a gender hierarchy and reinforce essentialist stereotypes of women as peaceful and powerless, and men as war-like and powerful.
> - Typically, women are seen as victims of political violence, and men as perpetrators.

should behave. When individuals stray away from the ideal, they are frequently punished in subtle or overt ways.

Such explanations are necessary in order to uphold the dominant view of 'feminine' women as 'naturally' less violent, more peaceful and peace-loving, than men. This stereotype has promoted a simplistic, dichotomized equation of women with peace and men with war: men are the perpetrators of violence and women are their victims. However, as we shall see later, this is not necessarily borne out in practice.

## Masculinity, hypermasculinity and political violence

The concept of gender outlined above can help to draw out important issues that are frequently absent from orthodox discussions of terrorism. Importantly, for critical scholars committed to emancipation, an increased awareness of the role played by gender in the roots or causes of political violence can point to more effective alternatives to violence and to ways of ending or mitigating its damaging effects.

As mentioned, masculinity is the social and physical characteristic associated with being a man and is stereotypically linked with strength, emotional stoicism, power, dominance, and the like. Empirically, men are far more frequently the perpetrators of violence and are also victimized more often by targeted violence, including terrorism. For example, 91.1 per cent of those killed in the Northern Ireland conflict were male. Thomas Scheff (2006), among others, has suggested that a 'pumped-up' form of masculinity – what might be called 'hypermasculinity' – characterized by a lust for power, repression of vulnerable emotions and high tolerance of aggression, is an important factor in violence, especially when it is combined with certain forms of alienation. At the same time, super-feminine women and hyperfemininity encourage hypermasculinity in men where women emphasize their own helplessness, look to men for protection and admire their hypermasculine behaviour. This can be true for all forms of violence, not only political violence and terror. A gendered perspective on the causes of violence can thus provide an important baseline for a gendered approach to terrorism studies.

More specifically, Susan Jeffords (1989) has suggested that a 're-masculinisation of war' occurred after the Vietnam War. She describes how soldiers were (and still are) defined through acts of heroism, bravery and sacrifice and held to be the protectors and defenders of the nation. The remasculinization of war glorifies macho aggression and sharply polarizes images of the enemy. Moreover, new technologies of war permit a sanitized form of killing where the killers are distant from their victim, such as sitting at a computer remotely operating a drone, as if playing a computer game (Der Derian 2009). This facilitates greater emotional distance from the blood and mess of violence, rendering ever more brutal forms of killing less difficult and discriminate. At the same time, the victims of violence are often marginalized, described as 'collateral damage'; and where women are included, they are usually in passive or silent roles such as that of victim. Paradoxically, some of these features are also true of the suicide attack, where only the emissary delegated to kill and be killed comes close to the intended victim.

In insurgent populations, such as amongst Palestinians or Nationalists in Northern Ireland, resilience, toughness and the ability to protect one's family and community is part of the dominant masculine stereotype (see Box 4.1). Communities under siege operate with the expectation that 'the men' will protect their community and avenge attacks on it. In societies where adult males are humiliated by, for example, military occupation or political detention and imprisonment, adult role models can appear emasculated to a younger generation of males. Adolescent males can regard the previous generation of men as 'not hard enough', and may see increased militancy and the escalation of levels of violence as a way to both overthrow the oppressive presence of the enemy and recapture their own masculinity. This can lead adolescent males to assume the role of community protector as a route to adult status and to the enhanced status of a militant.

Alison (2004), in a study of Northern Ireland, has shown how the use of small arms and light weapons is gendered – to the extent that they are more easily carried by women and children. She points to a certain 'romanticism and sexualisation' attached to the possession of guns, and notes that armed men who are involved with Loyalist paramilitaries have a certain prestige in the community (see also Feldman 1994). At the same time, some women are attracted to this and obtain

## Box 4.1 The 'hard man' in Northern Ireland

The INLA in Northern Ireland was the subject of a study by anthropologist Allen Feldman (1994). The Irish Republican Socialist Party (IRSP) and its military wing, the INLA, were established in 1974 following a split from the official Sinn Fein and the Official IRA. The INLA was the most radical armed Republican group in the Northern Ireland conflict, espousing socialist politics and a proletarian revolution. During its active years, the INLA carried out bombings, kidnappings, extortion, robberies and high profile assassinations, such as that of loyalist paramilitary, John McKeague, and jailed loyalist paramilitary leader, Billy Wright.

Feldman studied working-class culture in the communities in which the INLA operated and identified the ideology of the 'hard man'. The hard man is a fist fighter, the tough, masculine man who was resistant to subjugation and adept at the use of violence. His manliness was assured by his track record as a tough, unsubdued actor within his own community, capable of defending that community and the women and children in it. The hard man relied on his fists and the strength of his body. With the advent of weapons in the conflict, however, men without physical strength could attain the status of pseudo-hard men, using weapons instead of physical prowess to intimidate others. Thus, although joining a paramilitary group was a method of attaining status and power, it was equally linked to, and helped reinforce, the older conceptualization of the 'true' hard man.

a vicarious status by associating with these men. On the Republican side, however, women's roles as paramilitaries tend to be more active – as armed combatants, as well as participating in the transporting, maintenance and storing of weapons.

However, women's involvement in this hypermasculinized culture raises other issues. How do female combatants operate in a hypermasculine paramilitary environment? What form of gender relations

## Key Points

- While masculinity is a culture of 'manliness' hypermasculinity is an extreme version of masculinity characterized by aggression and stoicism.
- New technologies of warfare have changed the nature of warfare, remasculinizing it in important ways.
- Hypermasculinity, especially in combination with other forms of alienation, can be an important factor in the production of violence.
- Certain forms of hypermasculinity can be found in armed organizations and can be associated with carrying weapons.

pertain within armed groups? How can hypermasculine culture survive and proliferate with women participating in the organization? We address these questions in the following sections.

## Heteronormativity and the sexualization of terrorism

The process of 'othering' the enemy and the humiliation of enemy combatants and populations during war has often involved representing them in propaganda material in homophobic and sexually graphic and humiliating ways. Carlson (2006), for example, has documented the use of sexual torture of males during the wars in former Yugoslavia. And in the war on terrorism, we have seen the sexual humiliation of detainees in Abu Ghraib (Antiwar.com 2006), as well as a range of homosexualized and sexualized imageries of Osama bin Laden (see, for example, www.mraceman.com/WTC/binladen_empire state1.jpg) and the sexual queering of the war on terror itself (see www.meeus-d.be/guerre/MakeLoveNotWar.jpg).

Puar (2007) argues that the increased tolerance for homosexuality and other 'queer subjects' in Western liberal contexts depends on a shifting of the heteronormative boundaries to include identities historically excluded from narrow racial, sexual and national ideals. At the same time, 'orientalised terrorist bodies' who constitute the 'other' are excluded from these. Puar proposes that through the use of what she calls 'homonationalisms' – the incorporation of heteronormativity into national politics – distinctions are drawn in society between acceptable 'properly hetero' (and latterly 'properly homo') American patriots and a population of suspected terrorists, such as Muslims and Sikhs, who are perversely sexualized and racialized. These ways of marking identities, in turn, make certain people appear identifiably 'other' and thus eligible for pernicious practices such as detention, deportation and rendition. Puar's work is useful for highlighting the ways in which sexuality is deployed within the field of terrorism, not only to replicate heteronormative practices, but also to marginalize and humiliate suspects and denigrate their cultures and beliefs. Nor is this limited, in her view, to dominant discourses; Islamophobia is becoming an increasing trend within queer movements.

Sexualization is a persistent theme in popular discourses about terrorism. It is vivid, for example, in homophobic representations of bin Laden as a 'queer' 'other'. There is a wealth of aggressive and sadistic material on the internet and elsewhere depicting him suffering practices such as anal rape, which is the ultimate humiliation for the masculine heterosexual man. In this homophobic reading, not only is bin Laden an evil terrorist, but he is also sexually deviant and deserves to be violated, which compounds his perversity. The sexualization of bin Laden and others associated with the 'enemy' thus positions or frames 'the other' as sexually perverse, thereby reinforcing the boundary between deviants and our 'natural' and 'normal' sexuality and peaceful way of life.

Paradoxically, anti-war propaganda that included depictions of bin Laden performing sex acts on President George W. Bush also worked to reinforce this heteronormative logic, in part by presenting America, through Bush, as passive and vulnerable to (sexual) predators. Here, the implication is that America must take a more 'manly' – that is, aggressive – stance on countering terrorism. As some scholars have argued (Puar and Rai 2002), the heteronormative, white, masculine nation turns to queer sexualities in order to distinguish clearly between terrorists and their victims. However, here too, matters are complicated. Queer 'others' are simultaneously marginalized and excluded from the heteronormative nation – although they may also collude with that nation and support the war on terror when it claims to liberate Iraqis or Afghans from sexually repressive and homophobic (Islamic) regimes. Once again, this emphasizes the barbarity and primitiveness of the terrorist, even though, in the West, homophobic and sexually abusive practices are rife in, for example, the military, as the case of Lynndie England clearly shows (see Box 4.2).

The prisoner abuse scandal at the Abu Ghraib prison in Iraq offers a graphic illustration of a number of these themes. Most immediately, it shows how the sexualized images discussed above linked with actual security practices in US prisons and holding centres. For example, interrogation policies in Iraq and elsewhere were influenced by a book on Arab culture and society called *The Arab Mind* (Patai 1973) which many senior administration officials had consulted. The book includes a long chapter on Arab attitudes towards sex, concluding that sexual subjects are a cultural taboo invested with shame in Arab society. This view of Arab sexuality was then deliberately used to fashion the sexual humiliation strategies vividly portrayed in the Abu Ghraib photographs (Hersh 2004: 38–9). The sexualization of the war on terrorism, therefore, did not only take place in the cartoon and internet images of political leaders. It was also visited upon the bodies of prisoners by soldiers who used sex as a weapon of domination and humiliation.

In the outcry that followed the release of the pictures from Abu Ghraib, the emphasis was on the treatment of prisoners as 'torture'; the sexual dimension of the humiliation was largely sidelined. If it was mentioned, it was in relation to the sexual repression of Muslims and the heightened significance of nakedness or sexual behaviour to them, implicitly leading to the conclusion that the sexual abuse of prisoners was mainly a problem for the prisoners and not a reflection of heteronormativity in Western societies. It was only later and in limited circles that the legality and morality of the use of inhuman and degrading

## Box 4.2 Women in the United States military: Lynndie England and Jessica Lynch

Two women soldiers in the US military illustrate in different ways how stereotypical gender roles are reinforced. On the one hand, the case of Lynndie England (b. 1982), a former United States Army reservist, seems to run against the stereotype of women as less aggressive than men. England was convicted on six of seven counts involving prisoner mistreatment and sentenced to three years in prison for her role in the abuse of Iraqi detainees in Abu Ghraib. In 2004, photographs of her and other US soldiers torturing and sexually humiliating detainees at the prison were widely circulated across the world's media.

However, in much of the press coverage, England was depicted as a victim and a dupe of Military Police Specialist, Charles Graner, who was both older than England and male. England's explanation of her abuse of the detainees was 'we were doing what we were told', portraying Graner as the ringleader in her trial defence. This defence drew on the popular stereotype of women as either victims or subordinate accomplices of male aggression and violence.

The case of Jessica Lynch also illustrates the ways in which representations of women's participation in violence can reinforce heteronormative notions of women as victims and men as heroes. Lynch was a 19-year-old private in the United States Army who was injured in an ambush in Iraq in 2003. She was taken to the local Iraqi hospital, which was full of fedayeen, where she remained for eight days. The Pentagon claimed that a dramatic rescue by US troops saved Lynch, who had stab and bullet wounds and had been ill-treated, according to Pentagon reports. A US military film released to the media depicted a 'daring' assault and rescue under fire in enemy territory, and Lynch quickly became a cult hero at the centre of a media storm. As the US spokesman in Doha put it: 'some brave souls put their lives on the line to make this happen, loyal to a creed that they know that they'll never leave a fallen comrade'.

However, it later emerged that Lynch's injuries had been sustained in a road traffic accident, and the doctors who had attempted to deliver her to her base failed because US troops had fired on them. Local reports confirmed that the Iraqi military had long fled the hospital by the time of the 'rescue', the US troops had met no opposition and had 'made a show – an action movie like Sylvester Stallone or Jackie Chan, with jumping and shouting, breaking down doors'. The Pentagon declined to release the unedited tape of the rescue or to discuss either the type of Iraqi resistance they met or Lynch's injuries. In her April 2007 evidence to the US Congress, Jessica Lynch accused the media and the military of lying. Jessica Lynch was therefore used to propagandize the heroic masculine behaviour of men at war and the way they protect 'their' women, who remain vulnerable and in need of rescue, even when they are armed soldiers.

*Sources*: Thomas 2004; Kelly 2008; Schmitt 2004; Kampfner 2003.

---

**Key Points**

- In pro-Western images, terrorists are frequently represented as 'sexually perverse'.
- At the same time, in anti-war propaganda the war on terrorism is often represented in terms of homosexual sex or exploitation.
- The 'queering' of the terrorist is also evident in the sexual humiliation and abuse of prisoners in Abu Ghraib.
- Such representations serve to depict both the terrorist and the war-mongers as aberrant, revealing the underlying sexualization of the war on terrorism and reinforcing wider social norms of heterosexuality and masculinity.

---

treatment by US troops became the focus of discussion in Western discourse. In this way, the West emerges from this episode as an ordered, secure, heterosexual space that must be defended against the onslaughts of sexually repressed and deviant terrorists. Thus, the war on terror is fought, in part, to uphold dominant heteronormative standards.

## Female combatants: pawns, victims or agents?

Historically, women have been active in a range of armed non-state organizations in a variety of roles. These include founder members and political thinkers such as Gudrun Ensslin (Box 4.3), participants in resistance movements such as Shirley Gunn of Umkontho We Sizwe in South Africa, well-known female volunteers such as Mairéad Farrell in the IRA (Box 4.4), couriers for arms and ammunition, honey-traps who lure male enemy combatants into a trap, intelligence agents, and spokespersons. Women have been militarily active in terrorism in a variety of armed organizations, including participating in acts of state terrorism whilst serving as members of state armed forces. It is estimated that in many armed groups women comprise more than 30 per cent of the fighting force and now make up a significant proportion of suicide bombers in places such as Chechnya, Palestine, Iraq, Afghanistan and elsewhere (Ness 2008: 2). There have also been a number of all-women armed organizations, including an all-women right-wing Norwegian organization (Fangen 1997), and women's wings of armed organizations, such as the Vituthalai Pulikal Makalir Munani (Women's Front of the Liberation Tigers) and Cumman na mBan, the women's IRA.

Sjoberg and Gentry (2007: 26–57) describe three narratives that are frequently used by academics and the media to depict women partici-

## Box 4.3 High-profile female militants

Leila Khalid (b. 1944), a Palestinian woman, an alleged member of the Popular Front for the Liberation of Palestine (PFLP), and a member of the Palestinian National Council, came to prominence in August 1969 when she participated in the hijacking of an aeroplane from Rome to Athens. There were no casualties, but the aeroplane was blown up following the disembarkation of the hostages. Khalid's photograph was widely circulated and she underwent plastic surgery in order to be able to continue carrying out operations without being recognized. In September 1970, she and a Nicaraguan man attempted to hijack an Israeli aeroplane on a flight from Amsterdam to New York as part of a series of PFLP hijackings at Dawson's Field, Zarka, Jordan. The Israeli air marshalls aborted the attack, but not before Leila Khalid's Nicaraguan accomplice shot one of the plane's crew. The Nicaraguan man was killed and Leila Khalid was disarmed and detained. She was taken into custody in London where the plane landed. She was released by the British government a month later as part of a prisoner exchange. Lina Makboul's film, *Leila Khaled Hijacker*, won the Best Film award at the Tri Continental Film Festival in India in 2007.

German woman Gudrun Ensslin's activism led to her death in a prison cell. A founder member of the Red Army Faction (RAF), along with Andreas Baader, his girlfriend Ulrike Meinhof and others, her feminist and leftist views shaped the RAF's political programme. She moved to West Berlin in 1965 as a PhD student, becoming politically active in the anti-nuclear movement. She gave birth to a son in 1967 (whom she left with his father in 1968 and who was later given up for adoption) shortly after she met Andreas Baader and then took to violent political action. In April 1968, an arson attack in Frankfurt led to four members of the RAF, including Ensslin and Baader, being arrested and sentenced to three years in prison. They breached parole following a failed appeal, but Baader was re-arrested. With Ulrike Meinhof and two other women, Gudrun Ensslin freed Baader, and the group was subsequently dubbed the Baader–Meinhof gang. They carried out a range of violent activities over the following two years before their arrest in Hamburg in 1972.

The trial that followed was the longest and most expensive in German history. Various attempts were made to free the RAF members from Stammheim Prison, but in October 1977 Gudrun was found hanging in her cell and the other RAF members were also found dead, shot in their cells. The suspicion at the time was that the killings were carried out by the German authorities. Gudrun Ensslin's life and that of other RAF members has been fictionalized in the film, *Die Bleierne Zeit* (1981), *Marianne and Juliane* (*The German Sisters* in the UK), in Rainer Werner Fassbinder's *The Third Generation* (1979) and in Uli Edel's *The Baader–Meinhof Complex* (2008).

*Sources*: Abdallah 2003; Dugdale-Pointon 2007.

pants in armed violence: those of the 'mother', the 'monster' and the 'whore'. In these portrayals, issues of identity and security are heavily bound together and women's participation in violence is depoliticized (see also Rajan forthcoming). In some cases, female combatants are represented as motivated by 'an intense and desperate link to motherhood' which is assumed to warp them and their capacity to think rationally (ibid.: 31), unlike their male counterparts who are viewed as rational actors motivated by political rather than personal concerns. In others, they are depicted as evil and lacking in femininity, or as sexually depraved. These narratives 'both represent the continuation of subordinating images of women in global politics and are complicit in that continued subordination' (Sjoberg and Gentry 2007: 56). Or, as McDonald (1992) put it more baldly, women terrorists are often seen as 'too mad, too bad and too hairy' – as 'failed women', in other words.

In addition, a certain mystique sometimes surrounds the female terrorist. Some counter-terrorism experts have characterized these women as especially ruthless and, sometimes, as more efficient than the men against whom they fight. MacDonald titled her book, *Shoot the Women First* – advice purportedly given to the marksmen in Germany's anti-terrorist squad, because 'female terrorists are less likely to hesitate when faced with danger and are more likely to harm anyone that challenges them' (2001: xiv). Christian Lochte, the head of Germany's internal anti-terrorism unit, opined that 'women have much stronger character, more power, more energy' than men (ibid.: xiv). Taylor (2000: 301), similarly, observed that women display ruthlessness, dominance and calm under pressure. In some cases, MacDonald (2001: xix) argues, 'not only do such women take on a masculine role – aggressive, predatory, political – they also appear to become more attractive as women by doing so'. She cites the example of Leila Khalid (Box 4.3), an attractive young Palestinian woman whose activities were avidly followed by the media around the world (ibid.: 91), and Ulrike Meinhof, one of the founders of the West German RAF (see Box 4.3), whose funeral attracted thousands of admirers (but no family members) and who was 'eulogized as one of the most significant women in German politics at her grave site' (Griset and Mahon 2003: 162).

Some armed organizations, such as the FLN, the Liberation Tigers of Tamil Eelam (LTTE), the Patiya Karkeren Kurdistan (PKK) and Hizbollah, have made the most of the tactical advantage to be had from gender stereotypes, relying on the 'invisibility' of women and the relative ease with which they can negotiate check-points or security procedures. They can also lessen the suspiciousness associated with male operatives by posing as a girlfriend, mother or wife. In more socially conservative and less militarized societies, reluctance to

---

### Box 4.4  Female militants in the IRA: Mairéad Farrell and Rose Dugdale

Two women activists in the republican movement illustrate how women are represented as feminist heroes and role models for a generation of militant Irish nationalist women, or in mainstream accounts as the epitome of depraved terrorism. They also illustrate the diversity of motivations and backgrounds of women who choose to join such organisations. Irishwoman **Mairéad Farrell** (1957–1988) was a member of the Provisional IRA, controversially shot dead by British Special Air Service (SAS) soldiers in an operation in Gibraltar designed to preempt an IRA bombing. She was from a middle class family in Belfast, joined the IRA in 1976, and she, along with two others, bombed a hotel in the suburbs of Belfast. One of her accomplices was shot dead by the police and Mairéad Farrell was arrested and sentenced to fourteen years in Armagh women's prison, where she led a range of prison protests, including a hunger strike and a no-wash protest.

She was released in 1986, and in 1988 she and two other IRA volunteers, Sean Savage and Danny McCann, travelled to Gibraltar on an IRA mission which the security forces had under surveillance. Here, she and her two colleagues were shot dead, although witnesses alleged that Farrell and McCann were surrendering at the time. No bomb or weapons were found on the bodies or in their car. The European Court found that the three had been unlawfully killed in breach of Article 2 (the Right to Life) of the European Convention on Human Rights, and the court criticised the authorities for the excessive use of force in the arrest operation.

→

---

subject women to intimate searches can also be exploited in the planning of clandestine operations. Women have, for example, worn suicide belts beneath their clothes, passing it off as pregnancy (Malji 2008).

The popular perceptions of ruthlessness and deviancy on the part of women can also be a tactical advantage exploited by terrorist groups. This perception can increase the fear with which an armed group is regarded by a target society. That is, 'when women are included in the commando group at the center of a terrorist organization, they may inspire greater fear than do men because their actions are so far outside the traditional behavior expected from women' (Griset and Mahon 2003: 159–60). An attack carried out by a woman may also attract greater publicity than that carried out by a man, due to the fascination with which female terrorists are regarded. Female suicide bombers, for example, tend to attract greater media attention then their male equivalents (Ness 2008). This is appealing to terrorist groups, as publicity is often central to their ability to communicate their demands.

**Rose Dugdale** (b.1941–) provides a strikingly contrasting example. An English former debutante, with an upper class education and PhD in economics, Dugdale worked for the British government as an economist before her radicalisation in the 1968 student protests and in Cuba. Unlike Farrell, she was not exposed to Irish nationalism in her family or class background. Her radicalism led her to forgo her privileges and she resigned her job in 1972, sold her house and distributed the proceeds and her inheritance to charity. She and her lover burgled the Dugdale family home to raise money for the IRA. She was also part of a raid on the home of Sir Alfred Beit, from which nineteen Old Masters paintings were stolen, for which they demanded half a million pounds and the release of IRA prisoners. Dugdale was arrested and sentenced in 1974 to nine years imprisonment (Coogan, 2002a: 406; Bell 2008: 407). She gave birth to fellow activist Eddie Gallagher's son in Limerick Prison. In 1975, Gallagher went to prison for the kidnapping of industrialist Tiede Herrema and in 1978, Gallagher and Dugdale married inside Limerick Prison. Rose Dugdale was released from prison in October 1980, and unlike Farrell, has survived her involvement in the republican movement.

In 2010, Óghra Shinn Féin, the youth wing of Sinn Féin, said of her: 'Rose remains a personification of revolution. She had the option of a comfortable life ... Yet she followed her instinct and threw her lot in with the revolution ... [W]hen we honour the female activists who have participated in our struggle, we salute Rose Dugdale, as one of the very finest of that company. A revolutionary to her very core.'

*Sources*: Relatives for Justice n.d.; Coogan 2002a; BBC News Online 2008; *TIME* 1974; Bell 2008; Harvey 2009; Óghra Shinn Féin 2010.

However, discussions about the tactical advantages of deploying women in these roles sometimes mask the assumption that this advantage is sufficient to explain the presence of women within armed organizations. In this way, women are portrayed as little more than passive recruits 'used' by men like pawns or dupes who have been manipulated into working for the group, often through their relationship with male members (Sjoberg and Gentry 2007). As such, they are again seen as lacking political intent and agency of their own, reinforcing the gendered stereotypes with which this chapter began (see also Rajan forthcoming).

In fact, Alison's (2009) study of women in the LTTE and armed organizations in Northern Ireland shows that overall, women made the decision to join armed organizations for much the same reasons as men (see also Sjoberg and Gentry 2007; Ness 2008; Rajan forthcoming). Women's motivations to join such groups include: adherence to a particular political ideology, such as nationalism; grievance and concern with injustice; avenging personal bereavement; a desire to improve one's social status; and a desire to change society for the better.

Women usually must overcome greater obstacles than men in order to join, so could arguably be seen as more highly motivated. Some women join organizations with left-wing or liberationist ideologies and egalitarian/emancipatory aspirations – organizations, according to Alison, typically more open and accommodating to women's involvement than pro-state paramilitaries. Alison also found that many of these women were happy to be described as feminists and that some were keenly aware of the barriers to women in the armed organizations to which they belonged. In short, as Nacos (2008: 217–18) puts it: 'there is no evidence that male and female terrorists are fundamentally different in terms of their recruitment, motivation, ideological fervor, and brutality'.

Cynthia Enloe (2000) emphasizes the danger of focusing on women combatants when studying war; and the same issue applies to terrorism: whilst some women perform a role as combatants, most do not, and an overconcentration on women combatants distorts the picture by overemphasizing women's roles. Conversely, an exclusive focus on women as victims of political violence, ignoring their other roles, provides a similarly incomplete account.

As the Jessica Lynch case suggests (Box 4.2), victimhood in terrorism and political violence is also frequently heavily gendered. There is a common perception that women are particularly vulnerable to political violence and are mainly its victims. Indeed, women (and children) are specifically protected in international law in situations of war by Articles 76 and 77 of Protocol 1 of the Geneva Conventions (International Committee of the Red Cross 2007). However, under humanitarian law, women are not deemed to be especially vulnerable by virtue of simply being women, although women's vulnerability in certain circumstances, such as pregnancy or responsibility for young children, is recognized. Children, on the other hand, are regarded as vulnerable by virtue of their immaturity and dependency on adults. The general view in international organizations such as the International Committee of the Red Cross is that women are not more vulnerable than men in situations of armed conflict or war, although they are now being targeted as civilians more frequently than before. Men, on the other hand, are more likely to be detained, go missing and be wounded or killed, since combatants are predominantly male. Around 96 per cent of those detained in armed conflict and 90 per cent of missing persons are male.

Nonetheless, women's roles as victims in war, however prevalent, are still deployed in propagandistic ways. The victims of the 11 September 2001 attacks were used by politicians to justify the invasion of Afghanistan and Iraq (Box 4.5), and their supposed sensitivities were also deployed by the Anti-Defamation League in the attempt to prevent

---

## Box 4.5  Seeing gender in the war on terrorism

From the outset, men and masculinity were on show in what was to become the war on terrorism. Western manhood was presented as severely tested by the scale of the attack by the foreign enemy, and men were called upon to avenge the attacks. Across the world, men declared their unflinching solidarity with President George W. Bush, who grew in stature as he squared up to the enemy and declared war in a national and international alliance among men as brethren. The media lauded the bravery of the heroic, uniformed men who put their own lives at risk, some dying in the attempt to rescue others. Fire-fighters, police officers and rescue workers – overwhelmingly male – became national heroes.

Women, on the other hand, were frequently portrayed as weeping widows, relatives passively awaiting the fate of their missing loved ones or mourning mothers. Other women were portrayed as oppressed victims under fundamentalist regimes and requiring rescue. Such a rescue, supported by some Western feminists, was part of the justification for the 2001 invasion of Afghanistan. When the war began, other women were the wives of soldiers, anxiously bidding farewell to their heroic soldier husbands, awaiting their return or hearing the dreaded news of death in combat.

The perennial pronouncements by government about the level of threat of terrorist attack and the consequent counter-terrorist practices cast the government in a fatherly protective role, defending citizens against the evil, irrational, fanatical and misogynistic terrorists. Media representations largely ignored others who complicated this account – the widowers who lost their wives, the women emergency workers, the gay men who lost their partners in the World Trade Center. The war on terrorism is thus largely represented as a morality tale of good pitted against evil, where heroic men rescue terrified, weeping, women victims; where the grave male leaders in Western governments defend their women and children, rescue Muslim women and maintain civilization. Gayatri Spivak (1999: 284) has described such narratives as 'white men saving brown women from brown men'.

*Sources*: Lorber 2002; Silberstein 2002; Mann 2006; Spivak 1999.

---

the building of a Muslim Community Centre in Manhattan near the site of the World Trade Center (Anti-Defamation League 2010). In Northern Ireland, one group of victims has campaigned to exclude others from being considered as victims by using the concept of 'innocent victims' (http://victims.org.uk/s08zhk/).

---

**Key Points**

- Women join armed organizations for much the same reasons as men and perform a large range of roles, from leadership to combat.
- Women are sometimes portrayed as more ruthless, more motivated and more feared than men.
- Females in armed organizations are sometimes used tactically in ways that exploit gender stereotypes.
- Women members of armed groups are often conscious of the obstacles facing female participation in such groups and some call themselves feminist.
- The war on terrorism has been constructed and portrayed in ways that uphold the view of women as victims of violence in need of protection by men.

---

## Gender-based violence: sexual terror and rape as a war crime

The use of rape as a weapon of war has a long history, yet the recognition of gender-based terror and war crimes is relatively recent. This recognition dates back to 1993–94 when rape and sexual violence were specifically identified as a crime in the statutes of the International Criminal Tribunals for the Former Yugoslavia (ICTY) and the International Criminal Tribunals for Rwanda (ICTR). This legal recognition and the prosecutions that followed provide the basis for the punishment of war crimes and sexual terrorism that take the form of rape and sexual violence.

In what sense is the use of rape and sexual violence a form of terrorism? Among many other cases, the war in the Democratic Republic of Congo (DRC) shows that rape is a prominent feature of the ongoing fighting. Rebel groups and militias often mark their victories by systematically raping women, children and men in the dominated territory. Some estimate the number of victims in six figures, with victims often raped multiple times. The consequences of these practices include sexually transmitted diseases such as HIV, pregnancy and social exclusion from their community, as well as psychological damage. The use of rape has been described by aid agencies in the DRC as sexual terrorism (Pratt and Werchick 2004), because it is employed as a means of terrorizing and humiliating populations and exerting domination over them. Furthermore, where pregnancy is a risk or an outcome of such rape, the 'contamination' of a blood line or the subverting of the racial or ethnic integrity of the next generation of enemy children is a factor in genocidal sexual violence, as was the case in Bosnia (Box 4.6).

---

## Box 4.6 Rape as a war crime: the Kunarac case

At the ICTY in 2000, the first international trial focusing on rape as a war crime and a crime against humanity, the court heard evidence from 16 Bosnian Muslim women who testified about systematic sexual abuse during the 1992–95 war. The women testified against those charged with rape in Foca, in south-east Bosnia, where an estimated 50,000 girls and women were raped during the war. They told the court that almost nightly in the summer and autumn of 1992, Serb soldiers came to the detention centres and selected victims. The women were sexually assaulted, forced to parade naked and to undertake demeaning tasks. Some were retained as sex slaves by soldiers who were their former neighbours and whose wives and families were known to their victims. The soldiers taunted the women that they would bear Serb babies as a result of the rapes. The prosecution argued that the rapists thus sought to humiliate, demoralize and terrorize the entire Muslim population.

The distinguishing characteristic of rape in the Bosnian conflict was its systematic, widespread manner, supported by official encouragement. The prosecutors argued successfully that rape was used in Bosnia as a mechanism of 'ethnic cleansing' and obtained the convictions of six participants who were sentenced to a total of 128 years imprisonment. This so-called Kunarac case was a landmark in judicial history, marking the first convictions for the war crime of rape.

*Source*: Mertus 2001.

---

The sexual enslavement of women and girls in war is also a form of sexual terrorism (Sharlach 2007), and was widely practised by Japan and Germany during World War II.

Rape has also been described as terrorism by the prominent Harvard lawyer, Alan Dershowitz, who asserted in 2007 that a group of Palestinian terrorists claiming to act in retaliation against Israel had been raping young teenage Israeli girls (Dershowitz 2007). The perpetrators claimed that the rapes were politically justified and saw their behaviour as justified acts of political revenge for Israel's military actions: 'we are raping Jews because of what the Israel Defense Forces is doing to the Palestinians in the territories.' Dershowitz thus argued that the use of rape by those he considers terrorists constitutes the use of rape as a terrorist weapon.

A third connection between rape and terrorism can be found in Jessica Stern's (2010) book, *Denial*, an autobiographical account of her own rape, which she says resulted in an emotional numbing that equipped her to conduct research on terrorism. Stern, a recognized terrorism expert, attempts in *Denial* to understand the mindset of her rapist, in the same way as she did in her previous work with those involved in terrorism. She concludes that there is a common theme in both – experiences of humiliation, particularly sexual humiliation, which either the rapist or terrorist (although they are distinct) turns against his victims. Other victims of rape have pointed to the ability of rape to terrorize populations, particularly populations of women (Sharlach 2008). As with the use of sexual humiliation in war, rape can be seen as part of a patriarchal and heteronormative system of domination, resting ultimately on the power of the threat of rape and other forms of violence to intimidate and pacify.

However, sexual violence and terrorism has often been dismissed as an inevitable consequence of violence and militarization. Here it has been conceptualized more as an offence to the father or husband of a sexually abused woman than an offence against the woman herself, since women historically have been seen as chattels in war (see, for example, Wood 1998). The rape of enemy women has been regarded in some military institutions as an additional benefit for the victorious combatants. At the same time, the rape of women has been seen as both the motivation for armed attack and the reason for revenge attacks and the prevention of such rape, thereby acting as a reason for, or cause of, political violence. Perversely, men who are fighting to protect 'their' women have also proved capable of raping the women of the enemy.

Importantly, while the use of rape and sexual humiliation has tended to be portrayed by feminists as a manifestation of patriarchal oppression and male violence, women can also, if more rarely, be complicit in sexual terror (Box 4.2). The existence of male victims does not fit easily with the heteronormative framework we have described or with maintaining cultures of masculinity and hypermasculinity.

In the end, a gender perspective, as it is advanced here, allows us to see rape and sexual violence as a deliberate terrorizing strategy. This is particularly evident in the use of rape as a war crime in the former Yugoslavia and elsewhere, where it can be seen as state terrorism (Box 4.6), but also in other areas such as in counter-terrorism or repressing political opposition (see, for instance, the case of Pakistan in Sharlach 2008: 98–100). Increasing international recognition of the gendered nature of war, political violence and terrorism has led to the prosecution of the perpetrators and ultimately to the recognition of rape as a war crime.

## Conclusion

A critical approach to terrorism argues that attempting to understand both terrorism and the conditions that give rise to it 'must take account of gender, of gendered stories, and of the interaction between

## Key Points

- Rape and sexual abuse, humiliation and enslavement in armed conflict can be considered a form of sexual terrorism.
- Sexual terrorism is used to demoralize and humiliate an enemy, to destroy the (perceived) racial or ethnic integrity of a target group, or to 'collect' the spoils of war.
- Although men are the most frequent perpetrators of gender-based terror, women have also participated in such terror as perpetrators and men have also been victims.

actual and sensationalist stories of gender to create the dominant narratives' (Sjoberg and Gentry 2007: 205). As such, a gender perspective opens up new and important questions and potential avenues for research. Although acknowledged rarely in the terrorism field until quite recently, it is clear that women play various roles in political violence – as combatants in armed groups and state armies, and as victims of both. Moreover, women's involvement in non-state armed groups is not evidence of their deviance from a 'normal' female passivity. Rather, it is evidence of women exercising a form of political agency in the same way that men routinely do, and for the same reasons as men.

A critical approach to gender and terrorism, however, must go beyond a focus on women and deviations from the stereotypes of femininity to look at the issue of masculinity and the role of hypermasculinity in the production of violence in general and terrorism in particular. We have seen both how representations of terrorism and gender roles therein are deployed to reinforce stereotypical notions of masculinity and femininity and how these also contribute to sustaining a dominant heteronormativity. This is the case for non-state and state actors alike that have employed terrorism and is an essential part of the ongoing war on terrorism.

In addition, critical scholars must also look at the way in which women are represented in discourses about terrorism, particularly those that are used to justify violence. Images of the woman who needs rescuing, or representations of the oppression of women as a group in need of liberation, are often deployed as the justification for violent intervention or counter-terrorism campaigns. Finally, the use of sexual terrorism in the form of rape, which now falls into the legal category of a war crime and is also considered an example of genocide, is a relatively recent development, and one which signals an increasing trend to recognize and address the issue of gender in a field that has traditionally been rather gender-blind.

## Discussion Questions

1. How has gender been treated as a subject in IR and traditional terrorism studies?
2. How have women and violence typically been portrayed in the media?
3. What stereotypical gender roles can be observed in the practices of terrorism and counter-terrorism?
4. How do gender roles in terrorism reinforce or undermine gender hierarchies?
5. Why do women join terrorist groups?
6. How does the concept of hypermasculinity assist in explaining terrorist violence?
7. In what ways are certain forms of political violence gender-specific?
8. In what sense can rape and sexual violence be seen as a method of terrorism?
9. What political function does the 'women as victims' narrative play in maintaining a gender status quo in terrorism and political violence?

## Recommended Reading

Alison, M., 2009. *Women and Political Violence: Female Combatants in Ethno-national Conflict*, London: Routledge. A book based on fieldwork in Sri Lanka and Northern Ireland examining the motivation, roles and outcomes of women's involvement in armed political movements.

Hawthorne, S. and Winter, B., eds, 2002. *September 11, 2001: Feminist Perspectives*, Spinifex. A collection of essays written after the attack on the World Trade Center in 2001 by a wide range of feminist activists, scholars and writers.

Hunt, K. and Rygiel, K., eds, 2006. *(En)gendering the War on Terror: War Stories and Camouflaged Politics*, London: Ashgate. An examination of the role of gender, race, class and sexuality in the war on terror, covering issues such as masculinity, the headscarf debate and white femininity.

McDonald, E., 1991. *Shoot the Women First*, London: Random House. A journalistic account of interviews with women involved in armed non-state groups.

Ness, C., ed., 2008. *Female Terrorism and Militancy: Agency, Utility and Organisation*, London: Routledge. An edited collection examining some of the main factors that influence why women participate in terrorism, how their involvement in violence is represented, and how states have attempted to deal with them.

Puar, J., 2007. *Terrorist Assemblages: Homonationalism in Queer Times*, Duke University Press. A sophisticated and demanding queer analysis of terrorism, this book provides an analysis of how configurations of sexuality, race, gender, nation, class and ethnicity are being recalibrated in contemporary processes of securitization, counter-terrorism and nationalism.

Sjoberg, L. and Gentry, C., 2007. *Mothers, Monsters, Whores: Women's Violence in Global Politics*, London: Zed. A powerful scholarly analysis of women's involvement in violence in global politics, including torture, the Chechen Black Widows, genocides in Bosnia and Rwanda, and female suicide bombers in the Middle East, and how this involvement is stereotypically represented to deny women's political agency.

Sylvester, C. and Parashar, S., 2009. 'The Contemporary "Mahabharata" and the many "Draupadis": Bringing Gender to Critical Terrorism Studies', in Jackson, R., Breen Smyth M. and Gunning, J., eds, *Critical Terrorism Studies: A New Research Agenda*, London: Routledge, pp. 178–93. One of the first articles to try and think through how a gender perspective can be incorporated specifically into the critical terrorism studies approach.

## Web Resources

UN Women Watch: *www.un.org/womenwatch/*
  The central gateway to information and resources on the promotion of gender equality and the empowerment of women throughout the UN system, part of a joint UN project to support implementation of the 1995 Beijing Platform for Action.

The International Committee of the Red Cross (ICRC) Women and War Project: *www.icrc.org/eng/women/*
  A Red Cross project concerned with sexual and other forms of violence visited upon women and femal children in conditions of armed conflict.

ICRC Report 'Women in Armed Opposition Groups': *www.icrc.org/web/eng/siteeng0.nsf/html/women-war-011006/*
  A useful Red Cross report on women's participation in armed groups.

Leila Khalid: *www.leilaKhalid.com/leila_frames.html*
  An online documentary about the Palestinian militant.

Gudrun Ensslin: *www.historyofwar.org/articles/people_ensslin.html/*
  An online article about the German militant.

American women and terrorism: *www.adl.org/main_Terrorism/american_women_terrorists.htm*
  An Anti-Defamation article on recent cases of alleged involvement in terrorism by American women.

# Part II
# Key Issues

# Chapter 5

# Conceptualizing Terrorism

## Chapter Contents

- Introduction
- The definitional quagmire
- Common mistakes in defining terrorism
- The politics of labelling
- Some characteristics of political terror
- The ontological limits of terrorism
- Conclusion

## Reader's Guide

Terrorism is a highly contested concept and no agreement can be found as to what its definition should be. In both the scholarly literature and official documents and laws there are literally hundreds of different definitions and conceptualizations of the phenomenon. In this chapter, we will explore why this is the case and what the problem of definition means for those who adopt a critical approach to the study of terrorism. We begin by exploring the historical, political and philosophical reasons that make reaching a consensual definition of terrorism so difficult and the reasons why scholars continue to search for a solution. The second section then examines a number of common problems encountered within traditional efforts to arrive at a universal definition. Following a discussion of the politics of labelling political violence, we demonstrate how a shift in focus from definition to description can help to highlight the core characteristics of terrorism, whilst avoiding many of the problems that accompany the term. The final section explores the ontological limits of terrorism. In it, we argue that remaining attentive to terrorism's unstable and unclear status encourages a healthy scepticism towards the use of this terminology, without requiring us to abandon it altogether.

## Introduction

As discussed in Chapter 1, although the term terrorism has been with us for over two hundred years, it was only in the late 1960s and early 1970s that it emerged as a major category within discussions of political violence. Before then, violent acts resulting in injury and death were routinely described as bombings, assassinations, hijackings and the like. Afterwards, however, the very same types of event were spoken of – and understood – quite differently: as acts of 'terrorism' or the actions of 'terrorists' (Zulaika and Douglass 1996: 46). In the intervening years, this dramatic language of terror has only rarely been absent from policymakers, media opinion formers and the equally powerful producers of popular culture.

In academic circles, the mushrooming of interest in terrorism lagged more than elsewhere. It was not until the attacks of 11 September 2001 that research on terrorism moved significantly beyond the outputs of a relatively small, but influential, coterie of experts – the 'terrorologists', as they were often known (George 1991b). Interestingly, although a relatively minor subdiscipline of Security Studies before those events, the work that did take place within Terrorism Studies was remarkably coherent in its focus and was centred on an identifiable set of core concerns. While discussions over the tactics, causes and appropriate responses to terrorism were all central to this common research agenda, one of the most prominent issues was the long-standing **problem of definition** (Schmid and Jongman 1988/2005; Jarvis 2009a; English 2009).

## The definitional quagmire

Many of the important words that we use to describe our social worlds are surrounded by controversy over their meaning. Concepts such as 'democracy', 'freedom', 'equality', even 'politics' itself, do not have universally accepted definitions. Instead, they are what W. B. Gallie (1955–56: 168) famously termed 'essentially contested', in that they lack 'one clearly definable general use … which can be set up as the correct or standard use'. As Gallie suggests, concepts such as 'freedom' are difficult to pin down, not only because of the complexity of that to which they refer, but because different people will have very different understandings – often equally plausible understandings – of the criteria by which they are to be identified and assessed. For reasons we will explain, 'terrorism' is also an essentially contested concept (see Gold-Biss 1994: 48–60).

In both the scholarly literature and the broader political discussions, it is simply impossible to find any agreement over the meaning of 'terrorism'. A major study from 1988, for example, surveyed over one hundred competing definitions of this term (Schmid and Jongman 1988). In the years since then, a successful resolution to this problem has remained elusive (Silke 2004c: 207–8). While numerous efforts have been made to such an end, the nature and value of these vary considerably, depending in part on the motivations behind them. Very broadly, definitions of terrorism produced by political elites (Box 5.1) tend towards over-generalization, even ambiguity, in order to offer the authorities and courts maximum flexibility in applying the term to different actors and situations. Academic definitions, such as those in Box 5.2, on the other hand, can suffer from the very opposite problem: building such complexity into the concept as to make it, for many, almost unusable (Badey 1998). While some scholars have responded to these concerns by arguing that we need to give up all hope of definitional agreement (Laqueur 1987: 11), others continue unabated in their quest for a consensual, even objective, solution to the definitional dilemma (Jackson forthcoming). The questions we need to ask, therefore, are: first, what specifically makes escaping this quagmire so difficult? Second, in light of these difficulties, why do so many scholars – both traditional *and* critical – remain firmly committed to the pursuit of definitional clarity?

## The challenges of universal definition

The first difficulty of defining 'terrorism' relates to the term's status as a highly pejorative label that carries with it assumptions about savagery, barbarism, even evil, when it is used (English 2009). Interestingly, this pejorative association was not always the case. In 1880, for example, the Russian revolutionary Nikolai Morozov offered the following call for arms in a pamphlet aimed at encouraging resistance against the Russian Tsarist regime:

> Terroristic struggle which strikes at the weakest spot of the existing system will obviously be universally accepted in life. The time will come when the present, unsystematic attempts will merge into one wide stream and then no despotism or brutal force will be able to stand up against them. (Cited in Laqueur and Alexander 1987: 77)

Morozov's words are not unusual in demanding violent struggle against what he deemed an unjust political order. Similar sentiments have been offered by an array of organizations both before and since those words were written. What is unusual, however, is his unapologetic use of the language of terrorism to describe the form of resistance he advocated. Such an embrace of this language is almost unimaginable today, although Osama bin Laden is unusual in also having employed it (BBC News Online 2001b).

## Box 5.1 Selected state definitions of terrorism

An act of terrorism means any activity that (A) involves a violent act or an act dangerous to human life that is a violation of the criminal laws of the United States or any State, or that would be a criminal violation if committed within the jurisdiction of the United States or of any State; and (B) appears to be intended (i) to intimidate or coerce a civilian population; (ii) to influence the policy of a government by intimidation or coercion; or (iii) to affect the conduct of a government by assassination or kidnapping.

(US Government Definition of Terrorism)

Terrorism is the unlawful use of force or violence against persons or property to intimidate or coerce a government, the civilian population, or any segment thereof, in furtherance of political or social objectives.

(US Federal Bureau of Investigation (FBI))

The calculated use of violence or the threat of violence to inculcate fear, intended to coerce or intimidate governments or societies in the pursuit of goals that are generally political, religious or ideological.

(US Department of Defense (DOD))

The term 'terrorism' means premeditated, politically motivated violence perpetrated against noncombatant targets ... by sub-national groups or clandestine agents, usually intended to influence an audience.

(US Department of State (DOS))

'Terrorism' involves serious violence against a person, or serious damage to property, that endangers a person's life (other than that of the person committing the action), creates a serious risk to the health or safety of the public or a section of the public, or is designed seriously to interfere with or seriously to disrupt an electronic system, where the use or threat of violence or damage is designed to influence the government or to intimidate the public or a section of the public, for the purpose of advancing a political, religious, or ideological cause.

(The Government of the UK)

A terrorist act means an action or threat of action where the action causes certain defined forms of harm or interference and the action is done or the threat is made with the intention of advancing a political, religious or ideological cause.

(Australian Government)

Any ... act intended to cause the death of or serious bodily injury to a civilian, or to any other person not taking an active part in the hostilities in a situation of armed conflict, when the purpose of such an act, by its nature or context, is to intimidate a population, or to compel a government or an international organization to do or to abstain from doing any act.

(UN 1999 International Convention for the Suppression of the Financing of Terrorism)

*Source*: Shanahan 2010.

Because of the connotations noted above, very few political actors willingly apply this label to their own actions. It is typically imposed from the outside – by others – as a means of condemning forms of violence seen as illegitimate or immoral. As Louise Richardson (2006: 19) puts it: 'terrorism is something the bad guys do'. So condemnatory is this language, indeed, that some of the world's largest news agencies have now taken an active stance against its use in their reporting. According to the BBC's editorial guidelines:

> Our credibility is undermined by the careless use of words which carry emotional or value judgements. The word 'terrorist' itself can be a barrier rather than an aid to understanding. We should try to avoid the term, without attribution. We should let other people characterise while we report the facts as we know them. (BBC n.d.)

A second, related difficulty concerns the frequent and promiscuous overuse of the language of terrorism in academic, media and political discourse. Because the word brings with it condemnation, its employment also triggers the feeling that something important and dramatic has happened when we hear it. In other words, the term 'terrorism' conjures up an impression not only of immorality, but also of the spectacular and exciting. For political actors searching for votes, and for media and cultural elites searching equally hard for consumers, it therefore offers a powerful tool to elicit and maintain the public's attention. Unfortunately, this power has encouraged its usage in a variety of contexts so diverse that the term has been stretched almost to the point of meaninglessness. Whatever we think of the environmentalist organization Greenpeace, for example, is it really legitimate to describe them as 'eco-terrorists' as did the leader of Japan's Institute of Cetacean Research (BBC News Online 2001a)? Similarly, does abortion really constitute 'terrorism with a human face', as a prominent Archbishop proclaimed (Pullella 2007)? With the language of terrorism regularly used to describe and denounce such a diversity of actors and practices, it is perhaps little wonder that a single, accepted definition has yet to be reached.

The third and arguably most serious obstacle towards achieving an accepted definition of terrorism is really an extension of the previous points. The use of the term to condemn organizations as diverse as Greenpeace and al-Qaeda not only reflects its value for denouncing one's political opponents, it also reflects the broader philosophical problem that the word is inherently subjective, as the well-known expression 'one person's terrorist is another person's freedom fighter' succinctly suggests. In other words, arriving at an acceptable definition of terrorism is not a case of the gradual uncovering of scientific facts through careful observation. Rather, its content and limits are fluid and changeable. The

## Box 5.2  A comprehensive academic definition of terrorism?

Two prominent researchers on terrorism – Schmid and Jongman (1988: 28) – created their own well-known definition of terrorism after analysing 109 competing definitions. Although more nuanced than many of its alternatives, this definition has been criticized for its over-complexity by some scholars:

> Terrorism is an anxiety-inspiring method of repeated violent action, employed by (semi-) clandestine individual, group or state actors, for idiosyncratic, criminal or political reasons, whereby – in contrast to assassination – the direct targets of violence are not the main targets. The immediate human targets are generally chosen randomly (targets of opportunity) or selectively (representative or symbolic targets) from a target population, and serve as message generators. Threat- and violence-based communication processes between terrorists (organisation), (imperilled) victims, and main targets are used to manipulate the main target (audience(s)), turning it into a target of terror, a target of demands, or a target of attention, depending on whether intimidation, coercion or propaganda is primarily sought.

meaning of terrorism is subject to historical and political trends on the one hand, and the perceptions, beliefs and values of the person defining it on the other. Terrorism – as with all its component parts, such as violence, threat, legitimacy and communication – is not an ontologically stable phenomenon. It cannot be defined objectively by appeal to the evidence or facts and no amount of laws or international conventions can remove it from the subjective realm (compare Halliday 2002: 48). Indeed, even the staunchest of allies, such as the USA, the UK, Australia and Canada, have different lists of proscribed terrorist organizations, in spite of employing what appear to be very similar definitions of the term (Silke 2004a: 5; Freedman 2010). While this does not mean we can put our words to whatever uses we want, critical scholars argue that it highlights the impossibility of speaking objectively about the 'things' that make up our social worlds, particularly when those things are as emotive and politically charged as terrorism.

A final factor to note concerns the considerable transformation of meaning undergone by the word 'terrorism' since its invention. It may be surprising to learn that the term was originally constructed not to describe the actions of non-state actors such as al-Qaeda, ETA or the Fuerzas Armadas Revolucionarias de Colombia (FARC) to whom we are instinctively drawn when we now hear it. Rather, it was created at the time of the French revolution to refer to the actions undertaken by the state against dissidents and dissenters in their own populations (Halliday 2002: 72; see also Thorup 2010). Moreover, in its original usage it lacked the negative, pejorative connotations that are now inherent to the term. Indeed, even in the aftermath of World War II, when the term became attached to anti-colonial struggles in Asia, Africa and elsewhere, it lacked, for many, the sense of illegitimacy we now frequently attach to it (Rapin 2009).

These changes in the meaning of terrorism are important for two reasons. First, by highlighting the relationship between historical context and meaning, they remind us once again that terrorism is a social construction: it is impossible to separate the term from the conditions in which it is used and understood (Toros and Gunning, 2009: 96). Second, they also draw our attention to the very real linkages between the political labels we use and the lived realities of global political life. Because understandings of terrorism can and frequently do shift so dramatically, so too do understandings of who the terror*ists* are in any historical or political context. Four Nobel Peace Prize winners – including Nelson Mandela – for example, were once labelled terrorists by those condemning their campaigns!

In summary, arriving at a universally accepted definition of terrorism is made difficult by a range of political, historical and philosophical factors. Given the scale of these obstacles, the relentless return to this question of definition appears rather curious. Yet, as noted above, of all the issues with which 'experts' on terrorism grapple, it is this one that still commands their attention. It will be useful to consider some of the reasons why scholars continue to seek a route out of this quagmire.

## Reasons to pursue a definition of terrorism

The first academic motivation for solving the problem of definition is that, for many in this field, our ability to understand, explain and perhaps even predict acts of terrorism is impeded by the lack of a single, accepted conception of the term. According to this logic, if we cannot agree on the basic character of what we are studying, our ability to formulate the models, theories or typologies of terrorism which could form the building blocks of a rigorous scholarly discipline is severely diminished (English 2009). If we are serious about advancing our knowledge of terrorism, it is imperative we begin with some consensus over its essence. As Merari's (1993: 214) reflections suggest, this argument builds on a popular understanding of knowledge as a process of accumulation:

> Achieving a consensus on the meaning of the term 'terrorism' is not an important end in itself, except, perhaps, for linguists. It is necessary, on the other hand, to differentiate between various conditions

of violence and to distinguish between diverse modes of conflict, whatever we name them, if we want to gain a better understanding of their origins, the factors which affect them, and how to cope with them.

A second policy-based motivation focuses rather more narrowly on the formulation of counter-terrorist strategies. From this perspective, our inability to define terrorism translates directly into an inability to tackle this phenomenon in the dangerous real world of global politics. If no consensus can be achieved on what terrorism is, the task of those legislators and strategists charged with preventing an already complex threat becomes even more complicated (English 2009). As Cooper (2002: 9) argues, if we are serious about establishing mechanisms capable of dealing with terrorism, we need to first navigate a route out of the definitional log-jam: 'we seek to define terrorism so as to be better able to cope with it. We cannot begin to counter effectively that which we are unable to fully comprehend or agree on as to its nature'.

These two arguments have obvious appeal for the student of terrorism. Better understanding within the academy, and better security beyond it, are both noble motivations. If we think more carefully about these aims, however, it becomes clear that they involve a very specific and troublesome problem-solving understanding of how the study of terrorism should proceed (Cox 1996: 88–9). Both arguments share the assumption that terrorism exists as a tangible, objective phenomenon that the observer is capable of accurately defining, if only he or she tries hard enough. And where the second argument goes further in tying this quest for definition to the formulation of security policies, it poses the very real danger of reducing terrorism scholarship to an instrumental, deeply conservative activity aimed at improving the functioning of existing institutions and power relations. As such, arguments of this type are at once emblematic of, and justifications for, a broader trend within terrorism research that tends 'to focus on a "short-term, immediate assessment" of "current or imminent threats" as defined by state elites, without placing them in their wider social and historical context, or questioning the extent to which the state or the status quo have contributed to these "imminent threats"' (Gunning 2007a: 366). By assuming that an accurate definition of terrorism is both possible and desirable, such arguments impose serious constraints on what the study of this phenomenon should look like and what it should offer (see Box 5.3).

Before we abandon all hope, however, let us turn to a third explicitly political reason for seeking to resolve the definitional problem. This argument, which is perhaps most strongly associated with the writings of Noam Chomsky (1991, 2002), follows a very different normative trajectory to those discussed above. Rather than seeking a better con-

---

## Box 5.3 Why define terrorism?

**Academic reasons:**
Resorting to analytical tools is perhaps no more than a philosopher's means of despair, yet it is vital to understanding current events and appropriately influencing future ones ... A canonical and consistent definition of 'terrorism' can and should be pursued by theorists, and particularly by philosophers. Such definitions and their corresponding normative codes, which are desirable for legal systems and the states they represent, are absolutely essential for moral philosophers if they are to contribute anything at all to modern affairs. If lawyers require definitions, moral and legal philosophers cannot do without them.

(Meisels 2006: 465–6)

**Policy reasons:**
As long as there is no agreement as to 'what is terrorism?' it is impossible to assign responsibility to nations that support terrorism, to formulate steps to cope on an international level with terrorism, and to fight effectively the terrorists, terror organizations and their allies.

(Ganor 2005: 2)

**Political reasons:**
If one keeps searching for acts of terrorism without defining terrorism itself, then its denunciation is encouraged more than its understanding by confusing the reasons for an action with its explanation, definition and support. In place of proper definitions we have to cope with descriptions of terrorist behaviour, which is more a social judgement than the comprehension of a global phenomenon.

(Sorel 2003: 370)

---

ceptualization of terrorism as a step towards advancing our scholarship and security, this reason directs our attention to the possibility of contesting its selective, often wilful, misuse by actors seeking to advance partisan interests. From such a perspective, accepted understandings of terrorism should not be approached as universal or objective truths spoken by experts, politicians, policymakers and the like. Instead, they need to be thought of as particular knowledge claims or the social products of specific political contexts, power struggles and competing interests. Here, critically oriented scholars have a responsibility not only to reflect on these contexts and interests in order to challenge the use and abuse of political labels like terrorism, but also to think carefully about their own uses of such labels. In other words, a continuous process of revisiting our understanding of terrorism has the potential to prevent elites from manipulating the language of terrorism as an instrument of propaganda aimed at condemning their enemies or obscuring

---

**Key Points**

- Following decades of effort, no universally accepted definition of terrorism has been produced by scholars or political elites.
- Key obstacles preventing such a definition from emerging include the term's pejorative connotations, promiscuous overuse, its subjective status and inconsistent employment.
- Despite these obstacles, many scholars remain keen to escape this definitional quagmire for a range of reasons: some academic, some policy-related and others more radically political.
- Critical arguments for revisiting the definition of terrorism encourage us to approach accepted understandings of this phenomenon as inherently social: as knowledge claims rather than objective truths.

---

their own violence. As we shall see below, this does not necessarily mean we have to abandon the language of terrorism altogether.

## Common mistakes in defining terrorism

In the previous section, we explored some of the key obstacles and justifications that accompany efforts to define terrorism. Before reflecting on the contributions that critical approaches might make to these discussions, we need first to acknowledge a number of common mistakes made by those seeking a way out of this quagmire. To help us, let us turn to a tale offered by Donald Puchala (1971: 267) in an earlier study on international integration:

> Several blind men approached an elephant and each touched the animal in an effort to discover what the beast looked like. Each blind man, however, touched a different part of the large animal, and each concluded that the elephant had the appearance of the part he had touched. Hence, the blind man who felt the animal's trunk concluded that an elephant must be tall and slender, while his fellow who touched the beast's ear concluded that an elephant must be oblong and flat. Others of course reached different conclusions. The total result was that no man arrived at a very accurate description of the elephant. Yet, each man had gained enough evidence from his own experience to disbelieve his fellows and to maintain a lively debate about the nature of the beast.

Puchala's story contains two warnings for those trying to understand the world. First, it cautions against an unreflective approach to the observations we make and presuming that direct experience equates to accurate knowledge. In social scientific language, this is a warning about the limits of empiricist epistemologies. At the same time, it also reminds us of the need for caution in moving from particular examples to general or universal assertions: that viewing one, ten or ten million white swans – to mix our bestial metaphors – cannot alone prove that all swans are white. In social scientific language this is also a warning about the limits of **inductive reasoning**. And, if Puchala's tale was appropriate for discussions of international integration, it is equally so for attempts at defining terrorism.

The first and most serious error within many traditional efforts to define terrorism concerns the belief in the possibility of **objectivity** in this endeavour. Given the term's inherently subjective character, it is surprising how many scholars and policymakers remain confident that an objective definition can be found (see for example Jenkins 1986: 779–80; Garrison 2004). Critical scholars argue that the assumption that a neutral, value-free definition of terrorism (or indeed any other term) can be discovered is flawed for three main reasons. First, searching for objectivity in the definitions of our words propagates what social scientists call a rigid **subject/object** distinction. Very simply, this is the belief in a sharp divide between the world 'out there' (the object of knowledge) and the person observing that world (the subject of knowledge). This is a problem, initially, because it fails to account for the viewing subject's values, perceptions and beliefs about the world – all of which contribute fundamentally to the way the world's 'shape' or appearance is experienced. Moreover, it also presumes that the subject and object – the terrorologist and terrorism respectively, in this case – are both stable and unchanging over time. As we have already seen, this is empirically dubious in the context of political violence.

A second flaw is that the search for objectivity presumes the labels we use can be detached from their historical or cultural contexts. As Toros and Gunning (2009: 90) have argued, the current understanding of 'religious terrorism', for example, emerges from a particular European notion of 'religion' as an essentially irrational and private affair, so that those claiming religious motivation in politics come to be seen as not only abnormal but inherently threatening (whether or not they actually use violence). What this means is that the use of this language brings with it baggage – whether intentional and conscious or not – that cannot be wished away by a simple pledge to impartiality. This is true, of course, for all the concepts we use.

Finally, demands for objectivity also imply that the language we use is detached from the consequences of its employment. As we will see more fully below, this is almost as far from the case as could be when it comes to the term 'terrorism'. Because knowledge claims are always embedded in political structures of power, claims to 'objectivity' or neutrality typically work to reflect these structures, reproducing the world-view that these structures help to constitute and, at the same time, excluding critical, counter-hegemonic perspectives (Roy 2007). Of course, recognizing these problems should not be used as an excuse for sloppy research or polemics. Rather, it should encourage us to be as rigorous as possible and at the same time reflective and transparent about our own values.

A second error in the search for a definition concerns the surprisingly commonplace assumption that it is possible to generalize about terror*ism* as a singular phenomenon (Silke 2004b). This assumption, either explicit or implicit in efforts towards an objective definition, runs dangerously roughshod over the specificities of particular manifestations of violence and subsumes different historical and political contexts beneath '*a* causally coherent, free-standing phenomen*on*' (Jackson 2009a: 75, emphasis added). Whether terrorism is approached broadly as 'the use or attempted use of terror as a means of coercion' (Wellman 1979: 250), or more narrowly as 'the organized use of violence to attack non-combatants ... or their property for political purposes' (Coady 2004: 5), assumptions of generality make it very difficult to speak sensibly about the causes, motives and/or legitimacy of specific local decisions to engage in political violence. Either of the above definitions could legitimately be employed to describe the **Weathermen** bombings of 1970s America or the 1972 **Bloody Sunday** shootings, for example. Yet, whatever we think of these cases, their differences in motivation, tactics, alternative available strategies and so forth far outweigh any similarities they possess (Gunning 2007a: 381). To subsume different acts of violence under a generic understanding of terrorism – a 'Terrorism with a capital "T"' (Aretxaga 2001: 145) – is therefore as intellectually unsatisfactory as it is analytically unproductive. As Laqueur (2003: 8) – an orthodox terrorism scholar with a historian's respect for contextual difference – reminds us: 'there is no authoritative systematic guide to terrorism ... and perhaps there never will be one, simply because there is not one terrorism but a variety of terrorisms and what is true for one does not necessarily apply to others'.

A third error involves tying terrorism in advance to specific categories of actor. As evident in Box 5.1, this typically means approaching it as an activity perpetrated *exclusively* and *by definition* by non-state agents. Building on an established, yet particular, understanding of the modern state as the only actor that may legitimately employ the instruments of violence, these definitions construct a problematic distinction between the deaths and injuries caused by insurgents and the deaths and injuries caused by states. Definitions of this sort are problematic for two obvious reasons. In the first instance, they perpetuate a viciously distorted understanding of modern world history, one that incites us to ignore the reality that the most devastating acts of terrorism have been conducted by states and their apparatuses. Anyone familiar with the murderous regimes of Nazi Germany, Mao's China, Amin's Uganda or Kampuchea will know this already. Less well known, though, may be the use of this tactic by Western liberal democracies, whether openly under the guise of the 'national interest' such as the British bombing of Dresden, or more covertly as in the USA's counter-insurgency programmes throughout Latin America (Blakeley 2009). These agent-specific accounts therefore encourage us to forget such 'wholesale' uses of terrorism (Chomsky 1991) and present the modern state primarily as the innocent victim of this phenomenon (Herman and O'Sullivan 1991: 43). Second, this approach also encourages onlookers to identify any act by a group labelled 'terrorist' as automatically and necessarily a terrorist action. It does so because by encouraging onlookers to see terrorism as something tied to specific organizations, anything those organizations do can therefore be viewed through this lens – whether or not their actions accurately fit the definition being employed.

A final problem concerns efforts which explicitly denounce and condemn this phenomenon within the act of definition itself. Typical examples of this include those which position terrorism rather simplistically as an a priori 'atrocity' (Malik 2000: 6–7) and, less explicitly, those which present this phenomenon as an illegitimate violence against 'innocents' (Goodin 2006: 6–30). Although not necessarily a problem for scholars who argue that 'you are forced, if you are intellectually honest, to the conclusion that whatever label it might bear, terrorism is a bad thing' (Cooper 2002: 4), this approach is rather less useful than it is appealing for two main reasons.

First, there is a danger of circularity entering these types of definition. If we wish to argue that terrorism constitutes a form of illegitimate violence, we need to do more than simply reverse the terms and define illegitimate violence as terrorism. We need to establish the criteria upon which a particular action such as a bombing may be condemned. In other words, we need to think carefully about the types of moral argument that can be presented to condemn terrorist violence, arguments that may focus on the characteristics of such violence, their consequences or both (see, for example, Primoratz 2004a; Held 2008; Shanahan 2010). Second, these types of definition also work to obscure questions over who decides when and where violence is illegitimate or otherwise. Who, for example, has the authority to determine whether a target was 'innocent', and what they were 'innocent' of? And, similarly, from where does their authority to make such decisions originate? This is not, of course, to suggest that terrorism cannot be – perhaps should not be – always condemned. Rather, it is to argue that these discussions cannot be secreted away beneath what masquerades

---

**Key Points**

- Traditional efforts at resolving the definitional quagmire are characterized by a number of common, and important, mistakes.
- Major definitional mistakes include: claims to objectivity which ignore the subjective baggage which shapes our understanding; over-generalizations which ignore historical and geographical specificity; actor-specific definitions; and failing to separate the description and condemnation of terrorism.

---

as a neutral and objective definition. As noted below, one of the strengths of critical approaches to terrorism is the open and explicit call it makes for acknowledging the inherent ethical questions at the heart of knowledge and research on terrorism.

## The politics of labelling

Having reached this stage, readers will now be familiar with the considerable complexities surrounding the enduring struggle to define terrorism. We have discussed the difficulties encountered by those seeking to solve this problem and some of the main reasons for continuing in the quest. We have also noted a number of serious limits common to efforts at navigating a route out of this quagmire. With this behind us, we are now in a position to start unpacking what a distinctively critical approach to the problem of definition might entail. We begin by reflecting on the politics of labelling in this context, taking our cue from the search for objectivity discussed above.

As we have argued, the search for an objective definition of terrorism fails to recognize the partiality and subjectivity of the concepts we use to understand the world. Terms such as terrorism should not be thought of as neutral words we employ to refer to an independent realm of existence. Rather, they are lenses that shape or co-construct the world around us, giving it order and meaning *as* we engage in the act of observation (Box 5.4; see also Gold-Biss 1994). At the same time, of course, these words also help to constitute our own identities and interests as we engage in the act of observing. Because of this, the words we select to describe political violence, or any other social phenomenon, and the meanings we give to those words, are never inevitable and their use is not determined or 'given' in advance. They are, instead, something we impose on the world through choices we make in particular historical and social contexts. In this sense, those words – such as terrorism – must be thought of as *political* labels for two related reasons.

## Box 5.4 Labelling our worlds

One of the most famous statements on the dynamic process of labelling comes from Michel Foucault. In the passage cited here, Foucault (1984: 127) argues that we need to approach the practices through which we give meaning to the world as a form of violence: as an imposition on, not a neutral reflection of, an underlying reality:

> We must not imagine that the world turns towards us a legible face which we would have only to decipher; the world is not the accomplice of our knowledge; there is no prediscursive providence which disposes the world in our favour. We must conceive discourse as a violence which we do to things, or in any case as a practice which we impose on them.

First, whenever we use language to understand a process or event, we *necessarily* exclude alternative languages – and thus alternative understandings – of the same occurrence. If a politician, for example, employs the language of terrorism to describe a bombing, he or she simultaneously eschews alternative vocabularies of criminals, freedom-fighters, revolutionaries and the like that were equally available. Any of these labels, of course, would both highlight and camouflage rather different aspects of the bombing to the chosen vocabulary, thereby shaping or constructing it as a very different type of occurrence. More than this, if our labels appear valid (or even inevitable) in a particular situation – if they are taken up by other actors and accepted as self-evident – they can actually foreclose the possibility of alternative understandings even emerging; different labels and understandings simply may not surface as legitimate options for us to consider. As a number of scholars have shown (Jackson 2005, forthcoming b; Croft 2006; Jarvis 2008, 2009b), the widespread representation of 9/11 as an act of terrorism, for example, was not a necessary or inevitable product of those attacks. Alternative interpretations of the events as criminal acts rather than terrorist or military attacks would have been equally valid, and possibly even more desirable than the dominant framing which emerged. Yet, alternative understandings were consistently marginalized by the repeated description of the attacks as the start of a new war on terrorism: a description propagated by political elites, undoubtedly, but quickly accepted and reproduced far beyond the Bush administration (Croft 2006).

Second, as the above example suggests, the labels we employ also bring with them considerable social and political effects in the 'real world' itself. This is particularly evident in the case of terrorism which is so heavily emotive and laden with historical baggage. The contemporary understanding of terrorists as inherently evil, for example, functions to legitimize particular forms of counter-terrorist response at the same time as it delegitimizes others. Once someone is labelled an evil-doer and depicted as lacking an identifiable political agenda, reasoning or negotiating with them becomes taboo: instead, they need to be pursued aggressively and quickly. Similarly, popular accounts of terrorism as an imminent, exceptional threat facing Western civilization also work to legitimize equally exceptional – and frequently brutal – measures aimed at preventing this threat from materializing. As former US Vice President Cheney (2009) recently argued in discussing the CIA's use of **water-boarding** to interrogate suspected terrorists:

> We had a lot of blind spots after the attacks on our country. We didn't know about al-Qaeda's plans, but Khalid Sheikh Muhammed and a few others did know. And with many thousands of innocent lives potentially in the balance, we didn't think it made sense to let the terrorists answer questions in their own good time, if they answered them at all.

By describing an individual as a 'terrorist', then, it becomes far easier to justify treating them in ways that would otherwise be considered unacceptable, even if consistency between words and actions is not always maintained. As such, the words we use and the definitions we give them are of profound importance, particularly in contexts of political violence. For critical scholars, this means that we need to remain highly sensitive to the politics of labelling and continuously explore the silences and consequences that follow discussions and designations of terrorism. As we shall see in the next section, however, this does not mean we have to abandon the language of terrorism altogether. Rather, it requires us to rethink how and why we employ it.

## Key Points

- Our words and the definitions we give them are not neutral reflections of reality; rather, they are lenses that help co-construct the reality we purport to be describing.
- The lenses or labels we adopt are inherently political in at least two senses: first, they are political because their usage prevents us from exploring alternative understandings of the thing being described; and second, they are political because they have very real (and often harmful) social and human consequences.

## Some characteristics of political terror

Treating terrorism as a political label that can never be objectively captured suggests two possible routes out of the definitional quagmire. The first would be simply to abandon the language of terrorism altogether and to search for alternative frameworks of meaning – alternative discourses – offering a more neutral understanding of political violence (Bryan *et al.* forthcoming). Unfortunately, things are not quite that simple, as any substitute would encounter similar difficulties of history, context and subjectivity. In addition, any substitute would have to battle against the current dominance of the term 'terrorism' and therefore risk marginalization in the field. The second possibility, and one favoured by many critical scholars, would be to not abandon the language of terrorism altogether, but rather to abandon the quest for an *objective* scholarly *definition*. Such a strategy involves rethinking the purposes of scholarship away from the search for a neatly demarcated meaning on which we all agree and focusing our efforts instead on describing the characteristics of terrorist violence, whilst also reflecting on how these descriptions relate to dominant power structures and value systems.

This movement from definition to description is an important one, as it enables critical scholars to make a very different type of knowledge claim about terrorism. Definitions, as we have seen, represent attempts to speak the 'truth' about terrorism – to tidy the phenomenon (as a singular phenomenon) away inside a box with clearly defined boundaries that separate it from other kinds of political violence and/or communication. Descriptions, on the other hand, function as an exercise in interpretation that recognizes both the complexities of the phenomenon being discussed and the centrality of the interpretative process (English 2009: 22). Such an exercise involves identifying (time- and context-bound) regularities in human behaviours, such as political violence, and distinguishing between these on the basis of characteristics that are shared or otherwise (Toros and Gunning 2009: 92–3; see also Jackson forthcoming). Crucially, because acts of description involve an element of interpretive work by the describer – because descriptions are always from somewhere and for someone (Booth 2008) – they must necessarily be viewed as products of their social and historical contexts.

Descriptions of terrorism therefore should not be thought of as statements of fact based on perfect knowledge of the phenomenon. Instead, they are rooted in the particular conditions of their emergence and the interests and intentions of the analyst, and are tied to the purposes for which they were produced. In this respect, undertaking a description of terrorism helps critical scholars retain the word for the political reasons we have already noted. At the same time, it forces us to be a little more reflexive – a little more honest – about our own values as scholars of terrorism and the social and political structures that this term both shapes and reflects. In this respect, they help us maintain a **minimal foundationalism** between the subject (the researcher) and the object (terrorism) of research, and highlight the ways in which the two shape one another in a never-ending dialectical movement (Toros and Gunning 2009: 92). What, then, are some of the characteristics of terrorist violence in the context of terrorism studies at the start of the twenty-first century?

First, terrorism is ultimately a form of politically motivated violence. It is different, for example, from the criminal violence that accompanies the activities of those engaged in the transnational trafficking of illegal drugs, consumer products or humans for profit. It is also different from the extortion rackets, kidnappings and murders conducted by criminal organizations such as the Cosa Nostra. Although there are intense definitional contests over what constitutes a *political* motive, common examples include: publicizing a cause or grievance; intimidating a population to enforce compliance; forcing a change in government policy; instigating popular revolution or social disorder; providing an additional strategy to revolutionary or guerrilla struggle; eliminating rivals or opponents; or illustrating the weakness of the state as a keeper of law and order, among many others. Although groups that engage in acts of terrorism may also participate in acts of criminality, this is often as a mechanism for raising monies to continue their broader political struggle. In other words, terrorism is best understood as a form of violent or harmful activity or practice aimed at political change (English 2009). Certainly, it is emphatically not an ideology or a belief system. This characteristic suggests that any act of political violence which meets all the relevant characteristics may be thought of as terrorism, regardless of the agent perpetrating it (Jackson, 2009b: 13).

A second feature of terrorism is that it is a form of political communication – what the early anarchists famously termed 'Propaganda of the Deed' (Box 5.5). Terrorism is an act of exemplary or symbolic violence designed to send messages to a range of audiences, including: the wider society from which the targets were selected; the authorities; external observers; media representatives; and potential and actual supporters or members of the group itself. In this sense, the violence is part of a broader process of transmitting a political message and receiving a response (Tuman 2003: 17–24); it is symbolic action. In part, this explains why the vast majority of terrorist attacks are against property rather than people and most attacks do not result in any injuries.

For non-state actors, the easiest way of communicating a message is through the generation of maximum publicity via media coverage and the careful selection of symbolically-charged targets. It is for this reason that so many terrorist attacks are directed at sites of national or

---

## Box 5.5 Mikhail Bakunin on the Propaganda of the Deed

The notion of the 'Propaganda of the Deed' was a popular one in nine-teenth-century anarchist writings. Here, Mikhail Bakunin (1870) employs it to describe the communicative potential of acts of political violence:

All of us must now embark on stormy revolutionary seas, and *from this very moment we must spread our principles, not with words but with deeds, for this is the most popular, the most potent, and the most irresistible form of propaganda.* Let us say less about principles, whenever circumstances and revolutionary policy demand it – i.e., during our momentary weakness in relation to the enemy – but let us at all times and under all circumstances be adamantly consistent in our action. For in this lies the salvation of the revolution.

---

political significance, which amplifies both the importance of the message and the earnestness of the organization behind it. As Brian Jenkins (1975) famously argued, terrorists generally want a lot of people watching rather than a lot of people dead. For other actors, however, with an interest in camouflaging or hiding the origins of their violence – such as states and certain contemporary non-state groups – generating maximum publicity may not be as desirable or effective. In these instances, communication may involve targeting very specific audiences with a warning created through the disappearance or torturing of an individual, for example (Jackson 2009b: 13). As with more spectacular attacks, violent acts such as these are still intended to convey a message, and it is therefore misleading to describe terrorism as random and aimed solely at creating mass casualties.

Together, the above characteristics point to a third aspect of terrorism, namely, that it involves **instrumental** violence. That is, acts of terrorism are a means to an end, and not an end in itself; terrorists (or any other actors) do not tend to commit violence simply for its own sake. Unlike strategic military violence during a war, groups employing terrorism rarely try to capture territory, degrade the enemy's capabilities or physically dominate their opponent. Instead, they are usually focused on communicating the broader political struggle in which they are engaged (Jackson forthcoming). The Red Brigades in Italy, for example, often conducted their activities on Wednesdays and Saturdays because Italian newspapers had a wider circulation on Thursdays and Sundays, hence their message would reach far more people this way (Gerrits 1991: 51). Whether the victims of terrorist violence are selected deliberately or incidentally, they are always instrumentalized in pursuit of objectives other than simply murder or destruction. And this holds true, of course, for victims that are selected for their participation in state apparatuses, such as the armed forces or police, as much as it does for the non-combatant victims of much non-state terrorism.

This instrumentality, of course, returns us to the very important role the media plays in the calculations behind terrorist violence. Here, media exposure functions as an amplifier of terrorist violence, offering what ex-British Prime Minister Margaret Thatcher termed 'the oxygen of publicity' (Box 5.6) – although, as we demonstrated in Chapter 3, the relationship between the media and terrorism is much more complex than this phrase suggests.

To summarize, describing rather than defining terrorism involves highlighting key characteristics or regularities that separate these acts of violence from others. As we have seen, terrorism represents a form of politically motivated violence intended to communicate a message, in part by the instrumentalization of its victims. A descriptive approach to terrorism is useful, first, because it does not differentiate between the actors behind particular acts of violence: states and non-state groups alike can and do engage in activities that fit the above characteristics and should therefore be judged using the same standards. Second, it offers a far more productive route into exploring the ethics of terrorism. Although critical scholars argue that violence that instrumentalizes human life – all violence that treats humans as a means to an end – can and should be condemned, this approach is not grounded in assumptions about the evil or immorality of those engaging in terrorism. Instead, it presents us with a normative position for assessing the morality of terrorism that looks far more carefully at the contexts in which particular attacks take place, the consequences of those

---

### Box 5.6  The oxygen of publicity

The then British Prime Minister, Margaret Thatcher, memorably used the term the 'oxygen of publicity' to depict the relationship between terrorism and the media in a 1985 speech to the American Bar Association:

> We must try to find ways to starve the terrorist and the hijacker of the oxygen of publicity on which they depend. In our societies we do not believe in constraining the media, still less in censorship. But ought we not to ask the media to agree among themselves a voluntary code of conduct, a code under which they would not say or show anything which could assist the terrorists' morale or their cause while the hijack lasted?

## Key Points

- Describing terrorism helps to identify its key characteristics without repeating the mistakes of those searching for objective definitions.
- Terrorist violence is always politically motivated, undertaken for a diverse range of political goals and reasons.
- Terrorism is a form of political communication or symbolic action; it is an effort to transmit a message to an audience other than its direct victims.
- Because of this, terrorism is usefully thought of as a form of instrumental violence; it is a means to an end, rather than an end in itself.
- Such an understanding refuses to differentiate between the actors behind terrorist attacks and offers a more sophisticated normative position that is not based on absolute moral judgements about evil.

attacks for their direct and secondary targets, and the alternatives that were available to the actors engaging in violence. Lastly, critical scholars, in keeping with their commitment to disciplinary and methodological pluralism, would argue that research which focuses on providing richly textured 'thick descriptions' of terrorism can make a genuine contribution to our understanding of this form of political violence, without the necessity of a universally accepted definition.

## The ontological limits of terrorism

Thinking about terrorism as something better described than defined takes us much closer towards the status of this concept within a critical approach. Terrorism, as conceptualized here, needs to be approached not as a brute material 'fact' that exists 'out there' beyond the descriptions we produce and advance. What we may call terrorist violence does not possess ontological fixity; it does not exist *as* terrorist violence outside of the categories and theories we use to designate it as such. Instead, terrorism is better approached as a social fact that comes into being within, and is dependent upon, the contextual, historical and political dynamics that structure its interpretation thus (Jackson *et al.* 2009b: 222). Building on the idea of minimal foundationalism introduced above, terrorism only exists as the outcome of a complex, ceaseless dialectic between acts of violence and those witnessing, describing and interpreting those violences. In this sense, terrorism is characterized by ontological instability: it is a label whose meaning always contains the possibility of change and whose use always emanates from someone speaking from somewhere and for some purpose.

Approaching terrorism as an ontologically insecure political label is important for a number of reasons. First, it reminds critical scholars that they need to remain sensitive to the myriad of ways in which it is employed in concrete political contexts. In turn, this encourages a continual process of questioning and challenging the uses of the term. This is particularly important where the label is used in what appears to be a dispassionate or neutral sense; that is, when it is used as a reflection of, rather than creative engagement with, the material realities of political violence. Second, this approach forces us to take seriously the ways in which the term has changed throughout history and to investigate differences between understandings of political violence as they emerge within different generations of scholars and opinion-makers with their own interests and political agendas. Viewed as a social construction, terrorism does not need to be limited – indeed, it cannot be limited – to the actions of non-state actors. The violence of states and non-state organizations can be meaningfully read through this lens (Jackson *et al.* 2009b: 224). Such an understanding therefore opens up considerable space for expanding or broadening research on terrorism beyond its typical preoccupations.

Finally, such an approach goes some way to removing the very real, and unfortunate, fear of moral contamination that follows the term's status as a political and cultural taboo. Historically, the pejorative connotations of the label have hindered contact between terrorism researchers and their subjects – the 'terrorists' – so that very few scholars have actually engaged directly with the practitioners of political violence (Zulaika and Douglass 1996; Gunning 2007a). Unsurprisingly, this has greatly stunted our ability to answer adequately a range of important questions surrounding this phenomenon, not least precisely *why* some people and groups resort to terroristic tactics in their political struggles (Breen Smyth 2009). By conceptualizing terrorism as ontologically unstable and lacking any concrete essence, then, this approach helps to mitigate that sense of moral contamination and encourages researchers to proceed with a self-reflective, critical orientation towards those on – or, indeed, with – whom they are working. In other words, this approach helps us to avoid the absolutist and essentialist connotations that accompany uses of the label 'terrorist' to identify particular individuals and groups (Toros and Gunning 2009: 97). Understanding terrorism as a social fact and a political label means that we can move beyond ritualistic condemnations and instead focus on describing and assessing specific acts of violence in their concrete conditions of occurrence. The challenge, however, is to do this while maintaining a healthy scepticism towards the concept's unclear status and a commitment to transparency regarding one's own interests and values in the pursuit of knowledge about terrorism (Jackson *et al.* 2009b: 225).

---

### Key Points

- Terrorism, from a critical perspective, is characterized by ontological insecurity; it is a social fact, rather than a brute material reality.
- Approaching terrorism in this way enables critical scholars to employ the language of terrorism, while at the same time encouraging them to remain sensitive to its status as a political label.

---

## Conclusion

The problem of how to define and conceptualize terrorism is unlikely to disappear any time soon. As we outlined at the start of this chapter, many scholars feel that there exist very sound reasons – academic, policy-related and political – for continuing to pursue this long-standing question. Even less likely, however, is the discovery of a definitive resolution to this problem. However much we may desire it, the term's pejorative connotations and inherent political character are simply not going to vanish. Concepts as emotive and politically charged as terrorism cannot be as readily shorn of their historical, social and cultural baggage as those seeking detached scientific objectivity would sometimes have us believe.

In this chapter we have explored the difficulties that factors such as these pose for traditional conceptualizations of terrorism. More importantly, we have argued that a critical approach to political violence does not necessitate removing this vocabulary from our scholarship. Instead, we need to think a little more carefully about how and why we use the labels that we do in describing our worlds. Maintaining a healthy scepticism towards the term 'terrorism' – viewing it as an inherently unstable social and political construction – opens new possibilities and questions for scholarship that a rigid insistence on definition cannot sustain. In the chapters that follow we will show how such an understanding helps us to rethink the scale of the contemporary terrorist threat, the practitioners or agents of terrorism and their tactics, and the appropriate techniques or mechanisms for responding to political violence.

## Discussion Questions

1. Why is terrorism so difficult to define?
2. Are there any good reasons for continuing to search for a definition of terrorism?
3. What mistakes have been made in existing efforts at definition? Is it possible to overcome these?
4. How is language connected to politics?
5. What is the difference between definition and description?
6. Why might critical scholars of terrorism prefer description to definition?
7. What are some of the characteristics of terrorist violence in the context of terrorist studies at the start of the twenty-first century?
8. What do we mean by 'Propaganda of the Deed'?
9. What does it mean to speak of terrorism as a social, rather than a brute, objective fact?
10. Why might critical scholars approach terrorism as something characterized by ontological insecurity?

## Recommended Reading

*Behavioral Sciences of Terrorism and Political Aggression*, Special Issue: The Definition of Terrorism, January 2011. A collection of articles debating whether the concept of terrorism should be abandoned by scholars or if it can be adequately defined.

Goodin, R., 2006. *What's Wrong with Terrorism?* Cambridge: Polity. A philosopher's engagement with the problem of how to define terrorism in a manner consistent with the desire to condemn this kind of violence on moral grounds.

Jenkins, P., 2003. *Images of Terror: What We Can and Can't Know About Terrorism*, New York: Aldine de Gruyter. An analysis of how the concept of terrorism has been socially constructed over the years and how its meaning has changed and evolved in relation to political events.

Schmid, Alex, P. and Jongman, Albert, J., 2005. *Political Terrorism: A New Guide to Actors, Authors, Concepts, Data Bases, Theories and Literature*, Somerset, NJ: Transaction. An updated version of one of the most comprehensive surveys of the terrorism literature available.

Thorup, M., 2010. *An Intellectual History of Terror: War, Violence and the State*, Abingdon, UK: Routledge. A thoughtful analysis of the history and language of terrorism as seen through its relationship to the evolution of the state over the past few centuries.

## Web Resources

The National Consortium for the Study of Terrorism and Responses to Terrorism (START), hosted by the University of Maryland: *www.start.umd. edu/start/*
> The website includes the Global Terrorism Database (GTD), an open-source database including information on terrorist events around the world since 1970. The GTD includes systematic data on international as well as domestic terrorist incidents that have occurred during this time period and includes over 80,000 cases. For each GTD incident, information is available on the date and location of the incident, the weapons used and nature of the target, the number of casualties, and – when identifiable – the identity of the perpetrator.

Worldwide Incidents Tracking System (WITS) hosted by the National Counterterrorism Center: *www.nctc.gov/wits/witsnextgen.html*
> WITS is a major database on terrorism events around the world. The website allows the user to generate graphs, charts and maps on terrorist events according to different characteristics.

*www.opendemocracy.net/conflicts/democracy_terror/what_is_terrorism*
> An online article by Charles Townshend on the Open Democracy website discussing some of the political problems associated with defining terrorism.

*http://en.wikipedia.org/wiki/Talk:Definition_of_terrorism*
> The discussion pages on the Wikipedia entry for 'definition of terrorism' offer an interesting, evolving conversation around the difficulties of achieving consensus on the concept of definition.

*www.ict.org.il/ResearchPublications/tabid/64/Articlsid/432/currentpage/1/Default.aspx*
> An article by ICT Executive Director, Boaz Ganor, calling for a clearer definition of terrorism in the service of counter-terrorism ('Defining Terrorism: Is One Man's Terrorist Another Man's Freedom Fighter?').

# Chapter 6

# Reconsidering the Terrorism Threat

## Reader's Guide

In this chapter we examine the threat posed by terrorism. We start by looking at how the threat is popularly understood and how the widespread belief in its seriousness forms the basis for the vast efforts made by governments and scholars to understand and prevent further acts of terrorism. We then go on to explore different ways of assessing risks to public safety, before evaluating a range of evidence to see just how serious the threat really is. As we show, a rational evaluation suggests there is a serious gap between the perception and the reality of the terrorist threat in contemporary society: in fact, it can be reasonably argued that terrorism presents a very minor threat to public or personal safety. In the next section we explore some of the psychological, sociological and political reasons why the fear of terrorism has become so out of proportion to its actual risk in the world today. The chapter concludes with a consideration of the social costs of overreacting to the threat of terrorism and we suggest that the terrorist threat should be put into its proper context and responded to with greater sensibility and proportion.

## Introduction

In response to acts of international terrorism in the 1970s and 1980s, including a number of high-profile airline hijackings, but in particular following the 11 September 2001 attacks, a great many political leaders, scholars and media experts have described non-state terrorism as a serious threat to national and international security. As Box 6.1 illustrates, it is frequently argued by authoritative figures that terrorism poses a threat to individual safety, social stability, national and international security, the operation of democracy, the international system, and even Western civilization itself (Jackson 2005; Mueller 2006). Some of these actors argue that non-state terrorism is now an unlimited threat – terrorists could attack anywhere, at any time, and with any weapon – and it therefore poses an existential threat to our entire way of life. In many cases, this viewpoint is based on dire predictions (Box 6.1) and doomsday scenarios (Box 6.2). In turn, many of the arguments about the serious threat posed by terrorism have been spread across society by politicians, scholars, think-tanks and the media, including the entertainment industry which has produced numerous popular films, television shows, documentaries and novels based on plotlines of terrorists threatening to use WMD.

One result of these dynamics has been a rise in the public fear of terrorism in many Western countries. Since the 1980s, terrorism has consistently been one of the top fears and concerns noted in opinion polls, including during periods when there were no terrorist fatalities at all (Zulaika 2003). This level of fear has remained consistently high since 11 September 2001 (see polling data in Mueller 2005, 2006; Goodin 2006; Richards 2010). Over time, and particularly following the attacks on the Twin Towers, politicians and scholars have also come to accept the 'reality' of the terrorist threat, in part because their spectacular nature made the threat appear self-evident, in part because this fear served particular interests, but also because politicians are sensitive to public opinion and media pressure.

The widespread perception and acceptance of the terrorism threat is of more than academic interest; it has a multitude of real-world consequences. As we shall see later, the response of governments to this perceived threat has cost hundreds of thousands of lives and trillions of dollars in wars and counter-terrorist operations and led to major changes to the legal and security frameworks for responding to terrorism. Importantly, the field of terrorism research itself evolved in large part as a response to the terrorist threat. After the terrorist attacks on America, for example, a great many new scholars began to study terrorism, often because they wanted to help prevent other similar attacks.

## Box 6.1  Depictions of the terrorist threat

**Political leaders**

There are thousands of these terrorists in more than 60 countries ...
[Terrorism is a] threat to our way of life.

(President George W. Bush, 20 September 2001)

Today's terrorists can strike at any place, at any time, and with virtually
any weapon.

(Department of Homeland Security, 2002)

The threat of international terrorism knows no boundaries.

(Cofer Black, US Spokesman Coordinator for Counter-terrorism,
30 April 2003)

Countering terrorism has become, beyond any doubt, the top national
security priority for the United States ... The catastrophic threat at this
moment in history is ... the threat posed by Islamist terrorism – especially
the al-Qaeda network, its affiliates, and its ideology.

(The 9/11 Commission, 2004)

So let me be clear: al-Qaeda and its allies – the terrorists who planned and
supported the 9/11 attacks – are in Pakistan and Afghanistan ... For the
American people, this border region has become the most dangerous place
in the world. But this is not simply an American problem ... The safety of
people around the world is at stake.

(President Barack Obama, 27 March 2009)

**Terrorism experts**

A new type of terrorism threatens the world, driven by networks of
fanatics determined to inflict maximum civilian and economic damages on
distant targets in pursuit of their extremist goals. Armed with modern
technology, they are capable of devastating destruction worldwide.

(Marc Sageman, 2004)

[Terrorism is] one of the most significant threats to the Western world in
general and U.S. national security in particular.

(S. Mishal and M. Rosenthal, 2005)

Rather than being degraded ... al-Qaeda is very much sticking with its
classic playbook of simultaneous, spectacular strikes against even hardened objectives. In other words, we have more to fear from this resilient
organization, not less.

(Bruce Hoffman, 20 February 2007)

## Box 6.2 Doomsday predictions

The conjunction of technology and terrorism makes for an uncertain and frightening future ... Nuclear terrorism is a distinct threat, and will remain one far into the future.

(Walter Laqueur, 1999)

And the possibility of the two coming together – of terrorist groups in possession of WMD, even of a so-called dirty radiological bomb is now, in my judgement, a real and present danger. And let us recall: what was shocking about September 11 was ... the knowledge that had the terrorists been able to, there would have been not 3,000 innocent dead, but 30,000 or 300,000.

(Tony Blair, 18 March 2003)

The attack on our country forced us to come to grips with the possibility that the next time terrorists strike, they ... might direct chemical agents or diseases at our population, or attempt to detonate a nuclear weapon in one of our cities ... No rational person can doubt that terrorists would use such weapons of mass murder the moment they are able to do so.

(Vice President Richard Cheney, 9 April 2003)

The Commission believes that unless the world community acts decisively and with great urgency, it is more likely than not that a weapon of mass destruction will be used in a terrorist attack somewhere in the world by the end of 2013.

(The Report of the Commission on the Prevention of WMD Proliferation and Terrorism, 2008)

I would say there is a greater risk of [a] nuclear terrorist attack upon the US today than there was on 9/11 ... When I think of nuclear terrorism, I think of a nuclear mushroom cloud enveloping an American city or some other great city of the world, devastating its heart. So think of a nuclear bomb exploding in New York City or Philadelphia or Boston or Washington.

(Graham Allison, 11 September 2008)

However, in recent years an increasing number of scholars, including many critical scholars, have started to question this widespread perception of the terrorist threat (Mueller 2006; Lustick 2006; Sprinzak 1998). At the same time, some human rights activists, lawyers and critical scholars have begun to question whether governments have misused the fear of terrorism to enhance their own power, control dissent and criticism, and pursue other political projects only tangentially linked to terrorism, such as immigration reform and identity cards (Cole 2003, 2007; Jackson 2007a; Kassimeris 2007).

## Assessing the terrorism threat

The aim of this section is to offer a systematic evaluation of the evidence and arguments made for considering terrorism to be a serious threat. However, in order to make a reasoned assessment, we first need to know how risks and dangers should be measured and understood, in part because there are an incalculable number of potential threats to human life and well-being and there is no objective way of identifying and prioritizing between them. Apart from all the known risks of war, crime, natural disasters, diseases, meteors and accidents, there are also unknown risks associated with climate change, genetic engineering, new technologies and a great many other human activities, including terrorism. A central question therefore, is: How should we approach this world of infinite risk, especially in terms of those dangers that have not yet become manifest?

### Determining social risks

There are three broad approaches commonly used to measure and assess social risks. The first and most widely used approach involves collecting data and making statistical comparisons. For example, governments and insurance agencies typically collect statistics on the causes of fatalities – the number of people killed by types of diseases, traffic accidents, criminal activity, alcohol abuse, suicide, lightning strikes, natural disasters and the like. The data can then be used to rank risks according to their statistical probabilities. For insurance companies and governments, these rankings can be used to determine the allocation of resources and the estimated costs of insurance. Using such statistics, it is well-known that driving a car is far more dangerous than taking a flight, for example, and death from suicide is more likely than being killed in the commission of a crime. Employing this approach to evaluate the threat of terrorism, therefore, would entail comparing the number of people killed in terrorist attacks with other causes of death and calculating the probabilities of dying in a terrorist attack compared to other dangers.

A second related approach involves combining statistical data with the analysis of past behaviour patterns and human psychology as a way of predicting future behaviour. For example, statistics show that 18–24 year-old males are involved in more car accidents than any other group; the analysis of the behavioural patterns and psychology of this group shows that this is because they tend to engage in more risky activities, such as driving too fast and driving under the influence of alcohol. This kind of evidence, then, allows insurance companies and governments to focus activities and resources on groups or activities which have shown a higher risk. Employing this approach to assess the risk of terrorism would involve combining statistical data on terrorist attacks and groups with the analysis of terrorist group behaviour and psychology.

The third approach originated in the field of environmental science and is based around the **precautionary principle**. Originally designed to deal with the potential effects of climate change, this approach states that governments have a responsibility to try and mitigate the effects of climate change even if there is no scientific certainty of its exact consequences. At its heart is the view that if a particular risk has potentially high or catastrophic consequences, we should exercise caution and take measures to mitigate possible effects, even if it statistically improbable. This principle has also long been at the heart of anti-nuclear and counter-proliferation activities which assume that, even if the likelihood of nuclear accidents or nuclear war is extremely low, the consequences would be so devastating that we have an obligation to try and prevent such an occurrence. In terms of terrorism, this approach suggests that even if terrorists are highly unlikely to launch a catastrophic WMD or conventional attack, the likely consequences of such an attack means that the authorities should take all preventative measures. Importantly, the common assessment of **WMD terrorism** – attacks with nuclear, chemical, biological or radiological weapons – is based partly on the assumption that a devastating terrorist attack would result in serious social dislocation and breakdown.

A final issue of relevance here concerns the question of resource allocation. Given that there are an infinite number of potential risks and dangers, but society only has finite resources, how should scarce resources be allocated between preparations for high-probability, low-impact events, like the thousands of annual deaths from influenza, and low-probability, high-impact events like meteor strikes? While there is no objective way of deciding such necessary trade-offs, it would be sensible to try and limit the influence of precautionary thinking, as this could lead to greater levels of anxiety about the unknown threats we face and a massive waste of resources preparing for an endless list of potential catastrophes. In any case, in assessing unknown risks that have no evidentiary basis, there is no way of making objective assessments; it is simply a matter of individual imagination, which is, in turn, shaped by people's subjectivity, interests and their cultural-political context. One person might believe that the threat of a catastrophic meteor strike on earth warrants the construction of a space-based protective shield, while another would rather screen every single airline passenger for evidence of disease to prevent the outbreak of a global pandemic. From this perspective, it could be argued that this approach is the least useful for evaluating the terrorism threat, although it is commonly used by experts and governments, partly because failure to act in a precautionary way can lead to public recriminations if a ter-

> ### Key Points
>
> - There is an infinite number of potential risks and dangers to human life and well-being; societies have to decide how they will assess and respond to these dangers, especially in cases of uncertainty.
> - There are three main approaches commonly used to assess risks: the use of statistical information, the analysis of past behaviour and the precautionary approach.
> - The precautionary approach is probably the least useful for evaluating the danger posed by terrorism: it cannot be tested against observed evidence, it might increase public anxieties, and it could result in an enormous waste of resources.

rorist attack does occur and the government is perceived as not having done enough to prevent it.

## Evaluating the evidence

Given that precautionary thinking offers no testable means of evaluating the threat posed by terrorism, it makes more sense to look at statistical data and the past behaviour of terrorist groups. Fortunately, there is a reasonable amount of data and evidence on non-state terrorist attacks and groups that we can use in making our assessment – although we can never be completely certain about the trends discussed below due to the political nature of defining terrorism, differences in datasets, the problems of measuring terrorism, and incomplete and distorted information. The statistical profile of the terrorist threat illustrated in Boxes 6.3 and 6.4, along with other studies, however, does highlight some important and surprising facts.

First, the data from all major studies on terrorism suggests that the vast majority of terrorist attacks around the world are actually directed against property rather than people and most do not result in any fatalities at all, although the media obviously gives most attention to lethal attacks. Second, the vast majority of attacks occur in a small number of countries clustered in four main regions: Western Europe, South America, South Asia and the Middle East. Third, the statistical record suggests that the total number of recorded terrorist attacks is not increasing annually but, according to some counts, may even be declining slightly (although the average lethality of attacks is increasing). Fourth, out of the tens of thousands of terrorist attacks recorded since the 1960s, only 20 or so have involved more than a hundred fatalities (Box 6.4). In other words, high casualty terrorism is actually extremely rare. Fifth, terrorist attacks outside of warzones like Iraq and Afghanistan are on average responsible for little more than a few hundred deaths over the entire world per year, even when high casualty attacks such as 9/11 are included. Sixth, in comparison to other causes of death around the world, terrorism ranks extremely low, particularly in relation to deaths caused by government, disease, crime and suicide. Lastly, on the basis of this kind of comparative data, it can be shown that the statistical probability of an individual living in a Western country being killed in a terrorist attack is miniscule. In comparison to other risks, statisticians have calculated it as ranking somewhere near the risk of being killed by lightning, drowning in the bathtub or being killed doing DIY. Even in Israel, which has experienced a great deal of terrorism over a sustained period, the chances of being killed in a car accident are still far greater than the chances of being killed in a terrorist attack (for data on these points, see Barker 2002; Jackson 2005; Hough 2004; Goodin 2006; Mueller 2006).

In addition to data on terrorist attacks, we must also add an analysis of past terrorist behaviour. What we know about terrorist behaviour from many years of study is that it most often forms part of wider political struggles, which is why most terrorism takes place in locations with ongoing conflict such as Israel, Kashmir, Pakistan, India, Algeria, Colombia, Chechnya and others. Of the 192 countries that are members of the UN, most have experienced little or no terrorism at all (Barker 2002). We also know from studies on terrorism that terrorists tend to strike at symbolic targets in cities of major importance, usually as a way of generating maximum publicity (Sprinzak 1998). In other words, even in those countries where significant numbers of attacks occur, people who live outside of city centres are generally safe from attacks (unless the terrorist attacks occur in the context of a guerrilla or civil/ethnic war). Finally, the analysis of terrorist behaviour shows that many groups are quite sensitive to public opinion and will try to avoid civilian casualties or discriminate more carefully if they start to lose their support base. Examples of this include the IRA's practice of telephone warnings and the PKK's abandonment of its suicide campaign in the 1990s (Pape 2005). In summary, the analysis of past behaviour shows that the terrorism threat is most often quite limited and fairly predictable in terms of its frequency and targets.

In response to the evidence presented above, it is sometimes argued that the only reason why these statistics are so low is because the authorities have taken the threat seriously and are working behind the scenes to prevent more attacks. This argument is difficult to evaluate because it is based on events that may or may not have occurred and because it is usually accompanied by claims by the authorities that they have access to secret information. However, there are some possible avenues for making an assessment.

For example, we can try objectively to compare the relative strengths and resources of terrorists and the government security agencies trying

## Box 6.3  Mortality causes and probabilities in global perspective

Mortality causes

*Terrorism:*

| | |
|---|---|
| 3, 547 | Total global fatalities from international terrorism outside of warzones in 2001 |
| 300–700 | Approximate annual fatalities caused by international terrorism outside of warzones, 1968–present |

*Other causes:*

| | |
|---|---|
| 100 | Approximate annual fatalities in accidents caused by deer in USA |
| 100 | Approximate annual fatalities caused by peanut allergies in USA |
| 320 | Approximate annual fatalities by bath drowning in USA |
| 5,000 | Approximate annual fatalities from infections in NHS hospitals, UK |
| 10,116 | Fatalities caused by firearms in the USA, 2007 (estimated at nearly 1 million since 1965) |
| 30,000 | Approximate number of suicides annually in USA |
| 32,000 | Approximate annual fatalities from adverse reaction to prescription drugs in USA |
| 40,000 | Estimated *daily* global fatalities from poverty-related causes |
| 150,000 | Estimated annual global deaths from disease caused by global warming |
| 500,000 | Estimated global fatalities by small arms per year |
| 536,000 | Estimated total global fatalities from complications in pregnancy, 2005 |

→

to stop them. Most terrorist groups have few resources, little training and must continuously try to avoid detection, which is why the vast majority of terrorist campaigns and groups fail within one year and are mostly ineffectual (Schneier 2007; Jones and Libicki 2008). It is also why the majority of terrorist plots fail. A potential terrorist group in the USA, for example, will be up against hundreds of thousands of highly trained and well resourced agents from the Department of Homeland Security (DHS), the FBI, the Bureau of Alcohol, Tobacco, Firearms and Explosives (ATF), local law enforcement and private security contractors – among others. Thus, for any terrorist plot to succeed, three conditions must be met: an individual or group must have the real intention to undertake the action required and not change

→

| | |
|---|---|
| 700,000 | Approximate annual fatalities from heart disease in USA |
| 1.0 million+ | Estimated annual global fatalities from malaria |
| 1.7 million | Estimated annual global fatalities from tuberculosis |
| 2.0 million | Estimated annual global fatalities from automobile accidents |
| 2.1 million | Estimated annual global fatalities from diarrhoeal diseases |
| 3.0 million | Estimated annual global fatalities from HIV/AIDS (estimated at 23 million since 1981) |
| 3.9 million | Estimated annual global fatalities from influenza |

**Mortality probabilities**

| | |
|---|---|
| 1 in 236 | Estimated probability of death from falling down (USA) |
| 1 in 325 | Estimated probability of death by firearm (USA) |
| 1 in 80,000 | Estimated probability of death from international terrorism (USA) |
| 1 in 80,000 | Estimated probability of death from asteroid or comet (USA) |

From 0.0000607 to 0.0000711: increased probability of dying by homicide in USA in 2001 following 9/11 attacks

From 0.0000024 to 0.0000128: increased probability of dying in an air crash in USA in 2001 following 9/11 attacks

From 0.0000291 to 0.0000395: increased probability of dying from an accidental or intentional injury at work in USA in 2001 following 9/11 attacks

*Sources*: Rummel 1994; Barker 2002; Hough 2004; Jackson 2005; Goodin 2006; Mueller 2006; FBI 2007; WHO n.d., 2008; CDC n.d.; Global Terrorism Database n.d.; Live Science n.d.

their minds at the last minute; they must have the skills, capabilities and resources to make the plot a reality; and they must avoid detection from authorities, friends, family and others they interact with on a daily basis. The achievement of all three of these conditions is actually far harder than is often assumed, especially by those in the media, who are given to sensationalism. While this could be interpreted as evidence that counter-terrorism efforts are effective in terms of decreasing the risk of attack, it also suggests that the argument that ever-greater counter-terrorism efforts are needed to deal with an ever-increasing terrorist threat are questionable.

Related to this, we can analyse those plots which have been uncovered by the authorities and examine the extent to which the plotter's

## Box 6.4   The terrorist threat in empirical context

Death by government

| | |
|---|---|
| 30,000 | Estimated enforced disappearances in Argentina 1976–83 |
| 200,000 | Estimated number of civilians killed in East Timor by Indonesian state 1975–99 |
| 500,000 | Estimated number of suspected communists killed by Indonesian state 1965 |
| 750,000 | Estimated number of class enemies killed by Ethiopian regime 1974–79 |
| 800,000 | Estimated number of Tutsi and opponents killed by Hutu regime 1994 |
| 1 million | Estimated number of Ibos killed during Biafran war 1966–70 |
| 1.9 million | Estimated number of Nuer, Nuba and Dinka killed during Sudan Civil War 1983–present |
| 2 million | Estimated number of Cambodian class enemies killed by Khmer Rouge 1975–79 |
| 2 million | Estimated number of class enemies killed by North Korean regime 1949–present |

170–200 million Estimated number of deaths caused by governments against their own citizens in the twentieth century outside of war

Terrorist attacks by geographical distribution

| | |
|---|---|
| 17,145 | Incidents globally from 1970–2007 (against people and property) |
| 256 | Incidents in North America |
| 1,078 | Incidents in Southeast Asia |
| 1,398 | Incidents in Central America/Caribbean |
| 1,577 | Incidents in sub-Saharan Africa |
| 2,325 | Incidents in Western Europe |
| 2,659 | Incidents in South American |
| 3,239 | Incidents in South Asia |
| 4,109 | Incidents in Middle East |

*Sources*: As Box 6.3.

intentions matched their capabilities. In most cases, such as the plot to destroy the Brooklyn Bridge with a blow-torch or the plot to blow up British airliners with liquid explosives in August 2006, the terrorists lacked both the technical skills – and a sense of realism – to achieve their goals, and even the basic ability to avoid continuous monitoring by the police (Schneier 2007).

Lastly, as shown in Figures 6.1 and 6.2 and Box 6.5, we can examine the data on the number of terror suspects arrested, charged and convicted, and the nature of the convictions. This gives an indication of the scale of the threat in terms of how many terrorists are likely to be operating at a given moment. What such an analysis shows for the UK and the USA is that around two-thirds of those arrested for terrorism are eventually released without charge, and, of those remaining, most are convicted of minor charges relating to immigration or other criminal offences. In addition, despite the arrest of thousands of suspects and intense searching for more than five years, the FBI has been unable to find evidence for the existence of a single sleeper cell operating in the USA, strongly suggesting that none in fact exist (Mueller 2006; Cole 2007). It is reasonable to conclude from this publicly available data that, outside of war contexts, terrorism is largely the activity of a relatively small number of people (rather than the many thousands claimed by the authorities), with most of these being rank amateurs who lack the training or resources to mount serious attacks.

**Figure 6.1**   *The 20 most lethal terrorist events since 1960 (total fatalities)*

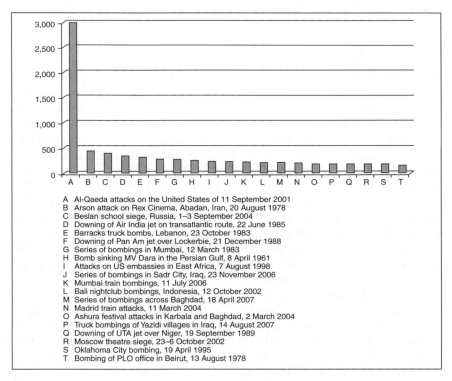

A  Al-Qaeda attacks on the United States of 11 September 2001
B  Arson attack on Rex Cinema, Abadan, Iran, 20 August 1978
C  Beslan school siege, Russia, 1–3 September 2004
D  Downing of Air India jet on transatlantic route, 22 June 1985
E  Barracks truck bombs, Lebanon, 23 October 1983
F  Downing of Pan Am jet over Lockerbie, 21 December 1988
G  Series of bombings in Mumbai, 12 March 1983
H  Bomb sinking MV Dara in the Persian Gulf, 8 April 1961
I  Attacks on US embassies in East Africa, 7 August 1998
J  Series of bombings in Sadr City, Iraq, 23 November 2006
K  Mumbai train bombings, 11 July 2006
L  Bali nightclub bombings, Indonesia, 12 October 2002
M  Series of bombings across Baghdad, 18 April 2007
N  Madrid train attacks, 11 March 2004
O  Ashura festival attacks in Karbala and Baghdad, 2 March 2004
P  Truck bombings of Yazidi villages in Iraq, 14 August 2007
Q  Downing of UTA jet over Niger, 19 September 1989
R  Moscow theatre siege, 23–6 October 2002
S  Oklahoma City bombing, 19 April 1995
T  Bombing of PLO office in Beirut, 13 August 1978

*Source*: Guelke 2008.

**Figure 6.2**   *Statistics on terrorism-related arrests, indictments and convictions in the UK (11 September 2001–31 March 2008)*

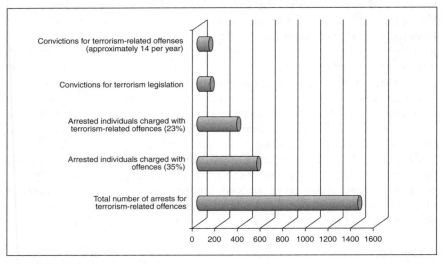

*Source*: United Kingdom Home Office 2009.

## Assessing the risk of WMD terrorism

Even before the attacks on the Twin Towers in 2001, a number of politicians, scholars and media experts had predicted that it was only a matter of time before a major terrorist attack employing chemical, biological, radiological or nuclear weapons would take place. Since then, concerns about WMD terrorism – sometimes called 'super-terrorism' (Sprinzak 1998) – have risen to new heights (see Box 6.1), and there are now a great many academic and security programmes devoted to its study and prevention. Proponents of this view point to the 1995 Tokyo underground sarin gas attack, the 9/11 attacks and the 2001 anthrax attacks as evidence of a growing determination by terrorists to employ WMD and achieve maximum civilian casualties. Needless to say, the entertainment industry has stoked such fears among the public with numerous films and television shows depicting an imaginative array of apocalyptic scenarios.

In assessing this claim, a number of scholars have argued that, although it cannot be categorically ruled out, terrorists are highly unlikely to use weapons of mass destruction because the risks are simply too great. More importantly, the use of such weapons is largely unnecessary: terrorists do not need to use WMD when conventional attacks are equally effective and less costly. Most terrorist groups simply do not have any intention to use WMD, even if they could

## Box 6.5 Statistics on terrorism-related arrests, indictments and convictions in the USA after 11 September 2001

| | |
|---|---|
| 693 | Defendants publicly associated with terrorism |
| 228 | Defendants charged under terrorism statute |
| 465 | Defendants charged with other crimes |
| 72% | Conviction rate per resolved trial on terrorism charges |
| 93% | National average for any felony charge |
| 19% | Dismissed or mistrial per resolved trial on terrorism charges |
| 6% | National average for dismissal or mistrial for any felony charge |
| 14 | Number of convicted terrorism defendants alleged to be associated with al-Qaeda |
| 58% | Percentage of defendants with no known alleged terrorism affiliation |
| 93,000 | Estimated number of Arabs and Muslims registered, finger-printed, interviewed or held in the USA after 9/11 |
| 0 | Convictions for terrorism as a result of Arab and Muslim questioning in the USA |
| 0 | Total number of al-Qaeda 'sleeper cells' found in the USA since 9/11 |
| 100,000 | Estimated total number of individuals detained in war on terror (Iraq, Afghanistan, Guantánamo Bay, and other undisclosed sites) |

*Sources*: Mueller 2006; The Center on Law and Security 2008.

acquire the capabilities to do so (ibid.; Jenkins 1998). Several frequently overlooked arguments are pertinent to this assessment.

First, these kinds of weapons are much more difficult to obtain and deploy effectively than is commonly believed. They require a level of scientific and technological knowledge, and often hard to access materials, which are beyond the capabilities of most terrorist groups. They are also extremely unstable weapons, liable to be as dangerous to the user as to the target, and in most cases they are less effective than a similar conventional attack (O'Neil 2003; Bunn and Wier 2005; Mueller 2006, 2009). Notwithstanding dramatic media portrayals and myths surrounding the chemical attacks of World War I, in reality literally tons of toxic materials, favourable weather conditions and effective dispersal methods are required to cause mass casualties using such weapons. Even so-called 'dirty bombs' – which are the easiest to assemble among the various WMD options – are still difficult to operationalize and are limited in the destruction they can cause.

Second, in using such weapons, the risk of all-out and debilitating retaliation by the target state is extremely high. Terrorist groups know that they risk total defeat and extermination if they violate the WMD taboo. Related to this, the use of such weapons would undoubtedly undermine the support and sympathy on which such groups often depend (Sprinzak 1998). We know from years of studying terrorist behaviour that they are most often rational actors who carefully calculate the consequences of their actions.

Third, as the Gilmour Commission – established by the US government to examine terrorist threats – concluded, rogue states are very unlikely to provide WMD to terrorist groups because the risk of losing control of the situation is too high (Mueller 2006, 2009). The risk that any WMD attack would be traced back to the contributing state, or that the weapons might be used against the contributing state itself, are simply too great for the leaders of such states to contemplate (Jenkins 1998).

These arguments appear to be backed up by important evidence. For example, despite the existence of thousands of terrorist groups throughout history and tens of thousands of terrorist attacks over the past 40 years, there have been no more than a handful of attacks using WMD, most of them by amateur religious cults rather than professional terrorist organizations. In fact, no established ideological or nationalist terrorist group has ever made an attempt to use WMD, although al-Qaeda is known to have considered but then rejected it in the case of the 9/11 attacks. Moreover, such attacks have resulted in far fewer victims than attacks with conventional weapons; every mass casualty terrorist attack (see Figure 6.1) has been conventional in nature. The example of the Japanese religious cult, **Aum Shinrikyo**, is illustrative of the real-world obstacles to WMD terrorism. Despite having at their disposal billions of dollars, around 30 trained scientists, several state-of-the-art laboratories and a strong determination to cause large-scale devastation, the group succeeded in only one of many attempts, and even then only managed to kill a dozen people on the Tokyo underground in 1995 – although thousands were injured, many of them seriously (Kaplan and Marshall 1996).

A final related argument we need to consider is the insistence from some politicians and scholars that a large-scale terrorist attack, particularly if it involved WMD, would cause social breakdown and chaos. In the first place, a great many studies have shown that similar devastating events almost never lead to such outcomes. In fact, societies are far more resilient than they are usually assumed to be (Mueller 2006; Jones et al. 2006), as demonstrated by the blitz in London during World War II, the atomic attacks on Japan, the long-term terrorist

| Key Points |
| --- |

- A more rigorous assessment of the relevant statistical evidence and past terrorist behaviour shows that terrorism ranks extremely low as a threat to human life and well-being.
- The available evidence suggests that, outside warzones, those seeking to perpetrate terrorist attacks are few in number and mostly lacking in the necessary capabilities.
- It is highly unlikely that terrorists would engage in WMD terrorism due to the inherent challenges of using unstable materials and the potential for counter-productive outcomes such as retaliation by the authorities and loss of constituent support.
- Even if terrorists were able to mount a large-scale WMD attack, there is little evidence that it would cause social breakdown and widespread chaos.

campaign in Israel and the 9/11 attacks, among many others. Therefore, it seems likely that even if a major WMD attack by terrorists occurred, the affected society would continue to function normally. Additionally, although modern terrorism has been around for decades, no country has ever been seriously threatened by major terrorist attacks, although importantly a number of states have experienced severe instability when violent counter-terrorist campaigns have undermined the social and political order (Wolfendale 2007) or states have used widespread terror against their own citizens.

## Explaining the terror of terrorism

Every death caused by terrorism is a great tragedy and should not be minimized. It is also true that serious terrorist attacks such as 9/11 and the Bali, Madrid and London bombings do occur occasionally in the context of political conflict; terrorism is a real material threat to some societies. Nonetheless, it is clear that by any rational assessment terrorism poses a relatively minor risk to human life and well-being, particularly in comparison to other common dangers. Certainly, it cannot be credibly described as an existential threat or even as a serious national security concern. What this points to is a large and somewhat surprising gap between the widely accepted perception and the reality of the terrorist threat. The question is: Why do so many people fear terrorism more than they fear automobiles or lightning for example, and why do societies expend such vast resources to try and deal with a risk that equates to the threat posed by DIY accidents?

The answer to this puzzle lies in a complex combination of several different phenomena. In the first place, psychological studies make it clear that at the individual level people fear violence from fellow human beings, particularly if it seems random and uncontrollable, more than they do the violence of accidents or seemingly 'natural' processes. In part, it is a question of the perception of control: individuals feel in control of a car, but cannot control where and when a terrorist attack will occur. This is the reason why people fear flying (where they are not in control) more than they fear driving (where they feel in control), despite the fact that driving is far more likely to result in death or injury. Such fears of seemingly random violence by fellow human beings are enhanced by the continuous and graphic coverage of terrorist events by the media. The global spread and constant repetition of the images from the 9/11 attacks intensified the psychological vulnerability that people, particularly in Western societies, felt. Of course, we must take care not to exaggerate the psychological effects of terrorism, nor can we assume that individual psychology is the limit of the explanation for the fear of terrorism. Studies suggest that terrorism rarely causes long-term traumatic stress, nor does it cause an actual state of terror; more accurately, it leads to increased anxiety for a relatively short period of time until other concerns take over (Rapin 2009).

A second explanatory factor is what sociologists have called the 'culture of fear' that has developed in Western societies over the past few decades (Glassner 1999; Furedi 2002; Altheide 2002, 2006; Robin 2004). What they have discovered is that, despite the fact that people in these societies have never lived longer, more safely and more securely than at any time in human history, they have become much more anxious than previous generations. Sociologists note a range of social fears and **moral panics** which periodically obsess society, including fears of crime, paedophiles, youth delinquency, global pandemics, immigrants, genetically modified organisms, mobile phone towers, flesh-eating diseases, killer bees, sharks and terrorism – among others (Guelke 2008). In many cases, these fears and moral panics are stoked by exaggerated and sensationalist media coverage, and opportunistic politicians. From this perspective, the fear of terrorism is simply part of this broader culture of fear. In particular, it feeds off the widespread fear of crime which is similarly concerned with the possibility of sudden violent death.

Another important perspective in explaining this perception–reality gap comes from an analysis of the actors and institutions who directly benefit from the widespread fear of terrorism and who therefore might have an interest in encouraging and maintaining it (whether done consciously or unconsciously, or for self- or other-serving motives). In other words, as critical scholars, we need to ask probing questions such as: Who benefits from the fear of terrorism? For whom does this accepted knowledge of the terrorist threat work? Which actors and interests are served by it? There are a number of actors and interests who can be identified as benefiting directly from the acceptance of the terrorist threat argument.

At the political level, governments and politicians have at times tried to exploit the public's fear of terrorism as a way of ensuring re-election, silencing their critics, controlling dissent, creating a more docile public, distracting the public from more entrenched and difficult social problems, and pursuing other kinds of political projects that are not necessarily related to terrorism, such as the introduction of identity cards, restrictions on immigration, increasing financial regulation and limiting civil liberties (Oliverio 1998; Glassner 1999, 2003; Mueller 2006; Kassimeris 2007; Jackson 2007a). The fear of terrorism has also been useful to politicians pursuing foreign policy objectives, such as regime change, expanding a military presence to new countries, increased military aid to allies and changing the terms of overseas aid and development assistance. President George W. Bush and Prime Minister Tony Blair both argued that the threat of Iraq-supported terrorism against the West warranted the invasion of Iraq in 2003. Politicians are able to get away with these kinds of actions in part because, as studies have shown, the more afraid people are of terrorism, the more willing they are to sacrifice civil liberties for order and security (Davis and Silver 2004).

A great many other parts of government also have vested interests in the fear of terrorism. The military and the security services, for example, can all claim greater resources, greater freedom of action and more respect in an atmosphere where terrorism seems to pose an immediate danger (Sprinzak 1998; Mueller 2006). In most Western countries, there has been a massive increase of funding for such actors since 2001, as well as the lifting of restrictions on some of the activities in which they can engage. In the UK, **MI5** has doubled in size since 2001, while in the USA, the FBI and the Central Intelligence Agency (CIA) have had restrictions on their surveillance activities lifted. The DHS in the USA is tasked with countering the terrorist threat, which means that its 184,000 personnel have direct career interests in ensuring that terrorism continues to be treated as a serious threat for the foreseeable future. It is not surprising then that agencies like MI5 and the DHS regularly release dire warnings of impending terrorist attacks and contribute to the perception that terrorism poses a real and present danger. This is not necessarily done in bad faith. But it is important to reflect on the interests that are served, wittingly or unwittingly, by heightening the fear of terror.

Beyond government, there are a number of other social institutions and actors who also benefit directly from the fear of terrorism. The media in particular has benefited greatly for several decades (Zulaika and Douglass 1996; Nacos 2002) through greater viewing figures and profits from terrorism-related stories, documentaries, films, television shows, books, articles and the like. In fact, given the way terrorism depends on media coverage for publicity, and the way the media depends on terrorism for dramatic stories, some have suggested that they exist in a symbiotic relationship (Farnen 1990; Nacos 1994; Chapter 3). Academics and experts who study terrorism also have a direct interest in the continued fear of terrorism, as they are awarded greater funding for research, sell more books and receive greater recognition as a consequence. Hundreds of millions of dollars have been awarded to academics studying terrorism since 2001 by the US and the UK governments, hundreds of new books have been published, and dozens of new think-tanks have been established from which resident terrorism experts provide advice to the media and government agencies. In other words, there are now many professional careers that depend directly upon terrorism's continued salience as a major threat, including, up to a point, this book's authors.

At a material level, there are numerous private firms, many of them but not all linked to the **military-industrial complex**, which profit directly from the widespread fear of terrorism. A partial list of such actors includes: the private security companies who provide screening at airports and security on public buildings; the pharmaceutical companies who provide vaccine stocks and decontamination suits; the military contractors who resupply the military and security services; the firms who supply CCTV equipment to local councils; the makers of X-ray machines; the companies contracted to supply identity cards; and many more. A study by the Washington Post identified some 1,271 government bodies and 1,931 private contractor companies working on counter-terrorism in the USA, employing nearly a million people and costing the taxpayer tens of billions of dollars (Pilkington 2010). Such immense profits would be threatened if there was a widespread recognition that the terrorism threat had been exaggerated. In other words, a number of powerful actors in society have a vested interest in making sure that the terrorism threat remains highly visible; it is therefore unsurprising that many of these same actors continue to argue that it poses an existential threat to our societies (although, again, not necessarily in bad faith).

In addition to psychological, social and political-material reasons for the persistence of this perception–reality gap, there is another useful perspective to consider, namely, that the terrorism threat has become a dominant discourse, or a regime of truth, in Western societies. In other words, the narrative about the existential terrorist threat has been repeated so many times by so many authoritative actors in society, and has then been acted upon as if it were indeed true, that it has gradually become an unquestioned truth. In addition, through the daily enactment of counter-terrorism by a myriad of social institutions such as the police, airline officials and the military, it has taken on an external reality which can be seen and touched, and which then confirms or reifies the narrative. In part, this is due to the authority of those actors who claim that terrorism is a major threat and who then invest vast amounts of resources to counter it. The public are inclined to assume that the government would not spend so much money and effort trying to counter something that was not as threatening as presented. Certainly, the terrorism threat-level warnings are real, as are the security checks at airports. Terrorist attacks are of course equally real, but far less widespread or prominent. One of the consequences of this established truth regime about terrorism is that it is extremely difficult to counter, because alternative arguments seem to contradict accepted commonsense. This is why all the publicly available evidence and perspectives on the terrorism threat presented above are not widely known or discussed, and why authoritative figures often genuinely believe their own narratives, despite contrary evidence.

To summarize, the explanation for the paradoxical gap between the accepted perception that terrorism is a significant threat and the actual risk it poses involves a number of interlinked levels and explanatory factors. The psychology of terrorism means that individuals are likely to fear it more than other kinds of risks, and this fear is intensified by the broader culture of fear which has grown up in Western societies and the media's sensationalist approach to public fears and moral panics. Feeding into this process, a great many powerful actors with vested interests have, for a complex range of reasons, deliberately encouraged the perception of the terrorist threat. As government agencies and social institutions have accepted, reproduced and acted upon

## Key Points

- Explaining the gap between the popular perception and the reality of the terrorist threat involves a combination of factors and levels of analysis.
- At a psychological level, terrorist violence is more frightening to people than accidents or natural phenomena such as disease or natural disasters.
- At a social level, the threat of terrorism is part of a broader culture of fear which affects Western societies.
- A political analysis shows that there are a great many vested interests in the popular perception of the terrorism threat, including politicians, the security forces, the media, academics and sections of the economy.
- The terrorism threat has come to be accepted as a dominant discourse or regime of truth, which makes it extremely difficult to counter.

this narrative, it has taken on an external 'reality' which seems to confirm it as truth and commonsense. Interestingly, this is not the first time this has happened. During the Cold War, similar beliefs about the threat of communism resulted in embedded vested interests and a dominant truth regime which sought to continue the conflict as long as possible.

## Conclusion

A critical approach to terrorism does not take popular arguments regarding the terrorism threat at face value simply because they are widely accepted or because authoritative figures claim or believe them to be true. Instead, it rigorously examines the evidence and arguments and ask questions about who benefits from, and whose interests are served by, the fear of terrorism? As we have demonstrated in this chapter, a reasoned evaluation of the relevant evidence suggests that terrorism is, in reality, a relatively minor security threat. Certainly, it is not credible to claim that terrorism is a serious or existential threat or that a major terrorist attack, even in the unlikely case of a WMD attack, would lead to chaos and social breakdown. The reason why the terrorism threat is given such prominence and is so widely believed is because it is now a dominant regime of truth in which a number of powerful actors are deeply invested, and because it accords with the existing culture of fear that characterizes many Western societies.

However, a critical approach must go beyond the most obvious level of analysis to examine some of the direct social and political consequences of the widespread acceptance of the terrorism threat narrative. In Chapters 10 and 11, we look at this question in more detail when we critically examine different kinds of counter-terrorism and the war on terrorism after 11 September 2001. Here it will suffice to note that at the sociological level, the acceptance of the 'reality' of the terrorism threat has led to a condition of almost permanent anxiety about the next terrorist attack – the creation of a society always 'waiting for terror' (Zulaika and Douglass 1996; Zulaika 2003). At the political level, it has impacted upon, and in many cases distorted, almost every area of domestic and foreign policymaking – diverting resources, changing priorities and complicating processes. For example, funding earmarked for community health programmes has been diverted to stockpiling vaccines in preparation for bioterrorism; immigration and asylum programmes have been adjusted to include special checks on terrorism involvement; and banking regulations have been made more complex in order to accommodate new rules designed to prevent terrorist financing (Amoore and de Goede 2008). Legally, the response to the threat of terrorist attack has seen accepted principles and practices,

## Box 6.6  Assorted expenditures on counter-terrorism measures after 9/11

**1. US defence spending**

| | |
|---|---|
| $370 billion | Defence Budget, 2000 |
| $513 billion | Defence Budget, 2009 |
| 39% | Percentage increase in defence spending, 2000–09 |
| $16 billion | Average defence expenditure increase per year (excluding contingency payments for Iraq and Afghanistan) |

**2. Homeland Security spending**

| | |
|---|---|
| $300 billion | Cost spent on improving US homeland security, 2001–06 |
| $737 million | Department of Justice (DOJ) budget for counter-terrorism activities, 2001 |
| $417 million | Increase in FBI funding for counter-terrorism enhancements and investigations, 2005 |
| $3.6 billion | DOJ budget for counter-terrorism activities, 2006 |
| $50 billion | Annual budget for DHS |
| £300 million | Estimated annual budget for MI5 |

**3. Other spending**

| | |
|---|---|
| $47.7 million | Research funding awarded for terrorism-related projects by the National Science Foundation, 2001–05 |
| $50 billion | Estimated annual spending on private security in USA |
| $132 billion | US budget for scientific research, mostly on defence and counter-terrorism, 2006 |

**4. Opportunity costs of Homeland Security spending: expenditure per life saved**

| | |
|---|---|
| $200,000 | Typical cost per life saved via smoke alarm spending |
| $1–10 million | Typical cost per life saved, measurement used by US Federal Agencies |
| $64.2–617.3 million | Estimated cost per life saved by Homeland Security spending |
| $15 billion | Estimated annual cost to the US economy of extra half-hour spent at airports due to security measures |
| 1,000 | Estimated additional road fatalities in the USA between 11 September and 31 December 2001 due to the fear of air travel following 9/11 attacks |

*Sources*: Mueller 2005; Lustick 2006; Stewart and Mueller 2008; Sharp 2009; US Department of Justice 2009.

## Box 6.7  A comparison of the costs of the 9/11 attacks and the war on terrorism

### 1. Comparative casualty rates

| | |
|---|---|
| 2,975 | Deaths caused by 9/11 terrorist attacks |
| 4,730 | Coalition troops killed in Iraq, March 2003–July 2010 |
| 1,457 | Estimated private contractors killed in Iraq, March 2003–July 2010 |
| 1,947 | Coalition troops killed in Afghanistan, October 2001–July 2010 |
| 97,082–105,855 | Estimated civilian deaths from violence in Iraq according to Iraq Body Count |
| 654,965 | Estimated civilian deaths in Iraq by July 2006 according to Burnham *et al.* 2006 in the medical journal, *The Lancet.* |

### 2. Comparative economic costs

| | |
|---|---|
| $500,000 | Estimated cost of al-Qaeda's 9/11 operation |
| $50 billion | Estimated cost of damage caused by 9/11 attacks |
| $888 billion | Cost to US Government of 'Overseas Contingency Operations', 2001–09 |
| $50 billion | Estimated annual spending on homeland security in USA |
| $2 trillion | Estimated inclusive costs of Iraq war to US government and society |

*Sources*: Barker 2002; Mueller 2005; Iraq Body Count 2010; http://antiwar.com/casualties/.

such as habeas corpus and the absolute prohibition on torture, attacked and modified – on the grounds that the threat is so great that such protections must be suspended for the sake of security (Cole 2003).

More concretely, responding to the terrorism threat has been immensely costly in human and material terms. As Boxes 6.6 and 6.7 demonstrate, trillions of dollars have been invested in new institutions and measures (such as the Iraq war) to deal with the terrorism threat. This is in addition to the almost immeasurable opportunity costs involved in putting scarce resources into counter-terrorism measures instead of road safety, poverty alleviation, health care and other pro-grammes which could demonstrably save lives and improve human well-being. As well, the military interventions of the war on terrorism have cost hundreds of thousands of casualties and caused immense material, political and psychological damage. Arguably, it has also encouraged and emboldened terrorist groups who perceive that they have been taken far more seriously than their capabilities warrant.

What this demonstrates is that the response to terrorism is often far more costly and damaging than the terrorist attacks themselves, and over-reacting to terrorism can be far more dangerous than the terrorism it is designed to deal with (Wolfendale 2006; Mueller 2006). Certainly, as Box 6.7 clearly shows, the response to 9/11 has been far more damaging and costly than the initial attacks. In fact, throughout history, the response to acts of terrorism has almost without exception been far more damaging and deadly than the terrorism itself.

What such an analysis calls for is a more self-critical assessment of the terrorism threat and a more measured response to countering it (Mueller 2005, 2006). Some scholars have argued that while governments cannot be seen to do nothing in response to acts of terrorism, they should expend much greater effort in seeking to reassure the public about the size and nature of the threat, rather than exaggerating it (Goodin 2006). They could also treat it as a form of criminality and deal with it through community policing and the criminal justice system, rather than treating it as a form of warfare and a serious national security threat. As we explain in Chapter 10, options for responding to terrorism that do not involve costly overreaction include political and social reforms, direct negotiations, amnesties, and other political measures. In the process of trying to engender a more measured response to acts of terrorism, critical scholars have a responsibility to try and deconstruct the distorted assessment and overreaction to the threat it poses. They can do this by exposing both the many fallacies at the heart of popular perceptions of terrorism, and the embedded interests that are invested in its continuation.

## Discussion Questions

1. What different ways are there to assess risks to human life and well-being?
2. What is the best way to assess risks to society, and why?
3. What evidence should we use to evaluate the risk that terrorism poses to Western societies today?
4. Is the precautionary principle a useful way of evaluating risk?
5. In your view, is terrorism a serious threat to personal or national security?
6. Why do people fear terrorism?
7. Who benefits from the widespread fear of terrorism?
8. What are the main costs and consequences of over-reacting to terrorism?
9. How can governments respond to the threat of terrorism in a more measured and proportionate manner?

## Recommended Reading

Altheide, D., 2006. Terrorism and the Politics of Fear, Lanham, MD: Alta Mira Press. An analysis of the relationship amongst the media, the government and the existing culture of fear, and how the political and media elite have stoked the public's fear of terrorism for political advantage.

Kassimeris, G., ed., 2007. Playing Politics with Terrorism: A User's Guide, New York: Columbia University Press. A collection of case studies tracing some of the ways in which governments around the world have manipulated the threat of terrorism for political advantage.

Lustick, I., 2006. Trapped in the War on Terror, Philadelphia, PA: University of Pennsylvania Press. An analysis of how politicians and society have become trapped in a costly over-reaction to terrorism after 9/11.

Mueller, J., 2006. Overblown: How Politicians and the Terrorism Industry Inflate National Security Threats and Why We Believe Them, New York: The Free Press. An analysis of the ways in which the terrorism threat has been exaggerated by the government and the terrorism industry, the costs of over-reacting to terrorism and suggestions for a more measured approach.

Mueller, J., 2009. Atomic Obsession: Nuclear Alarmism from Hiroshima to al-Qaeda, Oxford: Oxford University Press. A powerful deconstruction of the alarmism surrounding the threat of nuclear terrorism.

Oliverio, A., 1998. The State of Terror, New York: State University of New York Press. An analysis of how terror and the construction of terrorism has been integral to the hegemony of the state.

Robin, C., 2004. Fear: The History of a Political Idea, Oxford: Oxford University Press. An analysis of the central role of fear in the Western political tradition.

Social Research, 71(4), Winter 2004. Special issue on 'Fear: Its Political Uses and Abuses'. The issue contains useful articles on terrorism and the politics of fear.

## Web Resources

The US Department of Homeland Security: *www.dhs.gov/index.shtm*
Provides information on the terrorism threat level and counter-terrorism activities.

The British Security Agency, MI5: *www.mi5.gov.uk/output/terrorism.html*
Explains the nature and extent of the terrorism threat facing the UK.

The UK Home Office's current 'Terrorism Threat Level' webpage: *www.homeoffice.gov.uk/counter-terrorism/current-threat-level/*
Contains information on the current threat level and how to respond appropriately.

The website for 'Top Secret America': *http://projects.washingtonpost.com/top-secret-america/*
Report by the Washington Post on a two-year investigation into the massive national security build-up in the USA after the 9/11 attacks. It details the vast sums being spent on countering the terrorism threat and the private actors who have benefited.

The RAND Database of Worldwide Terrorism Incidents (RDWTI): *www.rand.org/nsrd/projects/terrorism-incidents/index.html*
Codes and documents over 36,000 incidents of terrorism.

## Chapter 7

# Types of Terrorism

---

## Chapter Contents

- Introduction
- The categories of terrorism studies
- Evaluating categories of terrorism
- Is the new terrorism really new?
- How religious is religious terrorism?
- Conclusion

## Reader's Guide

A great many categories have been used by researchers to try and bring analytical order to the diverse range of agents and behaviours associated with terrorism. In this chapter, we examine the main examples used in the field and some of the key problems associated with them. We begin by looking at common distinctions between domestic and international terrorism, state and non-state terrorism, different types of ideological terrorism, and methods-based categories such as suicide terrorism. Next, we examine some of their advantages and limits, including their potential to obscure important differences between groups; their tendency to assign causal power to factors like ideology or organization; the lack of empirical verification for many of the cases included in certain categories; and the political consequences of constructing categories and assigning groups to them. The next two sections critically interrogate two of the most popular contemporary categories, namely, 'new terrorism' and 'religious terrorism'. Here we argue that 'new terrorism' is a dubious and ideologically dangerous construction, and that notions of 'religious terrorism' might not be very helpful at all. In the conclusion, we reflect on the value of critical approaches towards categorization in the context of political violence.

## Introduction

Although terrorism is typically portrayed as a singular, unitary phenomenon, the term actually encompasses an eclectic and diverse array of actors and behaviours. Despite their very different aims, organization, methods, histories and contexts, groups such as al-Qaeda, the IRA, the LTTE, the Red Brigades, Aum Shinryko, the Iranian Revolutionary Guards and the Animal Liberation Front, as well as a number of lone individuals like Theodore Kaczynskithe, the so-called 'Unabomber', have all regularly been included under this label. Similarly, a great many different activities have been categorized as 'acts of terrorism', including: aerial bombings; hijackings; suicide attacks; assassinations; kidnappings; insurgency; guerrilla warfare; propaganda; fundraising; drug trafficking; credit card fraud; sabotage; vandalism; computer hacking; downloading of internet material; and writing poetry – among others.

As the terrorism studies field emerged in the late 1960s and early 1970s, it began to develop a series of typologies in an effort to impose a degree of order on the complex empirical realities of contemporary political violence. The social scientific purposes of categorization are to highlight similarities and differences, shed greater light on the specific characteristics of each class of group or activity, and allow for shorthand description. As such, developing typologies is a standard approach to building knowledge of a phenomenon and one that occurs in virtually every field of research. However, as we have argued throughout this book, the process of constructing knowledge is not an objective or neutral process, nor is it without political or ideological consequence. As critical scholars, we therefore need to think carefully about how categories of terrorism are constructed, how useful they are and how they function ideologically in society.

The purpose of this chapter is to assess critically the main categories used in terrorism research. This is important for a number of reasons. First, categories play a significant role in constructing the phenomenon of terrorism as a form of political violence distinguished from other types of violence. Second, while categories can help to draw out differences, they can also function to decontextualize specific cases from their environment and obscure important differences between groups identified as similar. Treating Hamas as a 'religious terrorist' group in the same category as al-Qaeda, for example, obscures the impact of the context created by the Israeli occupation of Palestine on Hamas's behaviour, the important role of Palestinian nationalism and the impact of participation in Palestinian politics. Third, categories create the impression that the factors used to differentiate groups are important elements in explaining their behaviour. Describing a group as a case of left-wing terrorism, for example, implies that the group's

Marxist ideology is at least partially responsible for its violent actions. Finally, rather than being neutral and objective, categorizations are products of particular power structures and have serious political implications, not least for how societies respond to terrorism. Categorizing a group as 'religious terrorists', for example, implies that they have other-worldly aims and are more fanatical and implacable than political groups with negotiable goals.

Importantly, questioning the practice of categorization does not lead critical scholars to deny that ideology, goal or organizational structure influence a group's behaviour. Nor does it imply that critical scholars refrain from using categories altogether. Rather, critical approaches question the positivist assumptions underpinning the practice of categorization and, in particular, its pretension to universal applicability. In short, critical approaches question the universality of categories, emphasizing instead the historical and geographical specificity of actors. They also seek to problematize the boundaries between categories, look for traces of the category's opposites and question the causal implications of categorizations. Finally, they work to highlight the political and normative implications of using categories in social research.

## The categories of terrorism studies

Any overview of the terrorism studies field reveals a proliferation of types and categories in contemporary research; Schmid and Jongman (1988), for example, identified at least 50 typologies and ten common bases for classifications for terrorism. Some categories are binary, consisting of two opposites, such as state versus non-state; others describe a spectrum along which different groups fall, such as those which differentiate groups according to ideology. This diversity of categorizations in part mirrors the almost infinite number of variables which can be used to differentiate groups. For example, distinctions can be made between groups in relation to the type of actor they are, the ideology they espouse, the methods they employ, the targets they choose, their organizational characteristics, the types of goal they pursue, the group's relationship with wider society, and any combination of these and other factors. Here, we discuss some of the most common approaches to categorizations and the categories they produce.

### International versus domestic terrorism

One of the first and most common binary distinctions used in the terrorism literature is that between national or domestic terrorism and international or transnational terrorism. Domestic terrorism is defined as campaigns of political violence that take place primarily inside the boundaries of a state. International or transnational terrorism refers to campaigns that take place across national boundaries, involving at least two states. This means that groups like the IRA, ETA and Hamas are usually classified as domestic terrorism, despite sometimes operating across state boundaries, while the PLO and al-Qaeda are considered quintessential examples of international terrorism. This binary categorization is prevalent in both official circles and in the broader terrorism studies literature, and in part reflects the continuing influence of IR in the field. Interestingly, it is only in recent years that the category of domestic terrorism was even included in the main empirical databases on terrorism.

## Actor-based categories

Another common distinction made in both the traditional and the critical literature is between state and non-state terrorism, or, to use Noam Chomsky's (1991) provocative phrase, 'wholesale' versus 'retail' terrorism. The logic behind this binary opposition is that state and non-state organizations are believed to have very different aims and motives, and are subject to very different constraints and opportunities. State apparatuses tend to have far greater resources at their disposal than non-state organizations, and unlike the majority of non-state organizations involved in terrorism (as opposed to, for instance, guerrilla warfare), they have to maintain control of a territory. They are also assumed to enjoy greater levels of legitimacy, although this is not always the case in practice, and they can be said to be subject to different sets of internal and external dynamics. For instance, they have to contend with other states and international fora to a far greater extent than non-state organizations. However, because the vast majority of orthodox scholars have focused on non-state rather than state terrorism (Jackson 2008), this is more a delineational device, serving to delineate what is being studied, than a formal scholarly categorization of subjects studied.

A related distinction that is sometimes made in the literature is between individual terrorism – otherwise termed 'lone wolf' or 'amateur' terrorism – versus group terrorism. Prominent examples in the former include Timothy McVeigh, Theodore Kaczynskithe (the Unabomber), Richard Reid (the Shoe Bomber) and Umar Farouk Abdulmutallab (the Detroit Christmas Day bomber). However, as before, this is often more a delineational device than a subject category. Similar to the state/non-state distinction, this binary typology simply seeks to highlight the different capabilities, motivations and constraints facing individuals in comparison to groups and states.

## Method-based categories

Categories of terrorism are sometimes based on the methods employed by terrorists. For example, as we noted in Chapter 6, there is a rapidly growing literature on WMD terrorism, which is contrasted with conventional terrorism (see, among many others, Falkenrath *et al.* 1998; Simon and Benjamin 2000; Allison 2004). WMD terrorism is conceived as terrorist activities involving the threat or use of chemical, biological, radiological or nuclear weapons. Research on this category seeks to understand the conditions under which terrorist groups might use WMD, the kinds of attacks they might launch and their likely consequences, and how to counter the threat. The primary example of WMD terrorism is Aum Shinryko's sarin attack on the Tokyo subway in 1995.

Another method-based category is that of 'cyber-terrorism', which also has a growing literature (see, among many others, Alexander and Swetnam 1999; Arquilla and Ronfeldt 2001; Colarik 2006). A controversial term, 'cyber-terrorism' refers to attacks on computers, networks and information systems designed to cause panic in the pursuit of political, ideological or religious objectives. In large part, research on this category explores possible scenarios and the vulnerabilities of computer systems, as there have been very few cases of actual terrorist groups employing this method of attack. Interestingly, it is a form of activity sometimes connected to the 'new terrorism' (discussed below), but also to state actors, most prominently, Russia.

Perhaps the most important method-based category in use today is suicide terrorism. It is fast becoming a stand-alone topic, attracting a very large and growing specialist literature (Reuter 2004; Pape 2005; Bloom 2005; Gambetta 2005; Pedahzur 2005, 2006; Skaine 2006; Falk and Morgenstern 2009). Scholars studying suicide terrorism argue that the attacker's expectation of death differentiates it sufficiently from other types of terrorism to warrant its own separate category. Research on suicide terrorism seeks to understand the conditions under which groups and individuals adopt the tactic, the reasons for its rise and spread, its aims and how to counter it.

## Ideological categories

Categories based on ideological orientation are probably the most widely used in the terrorism literature. The most frequent type includes broad categories ranging from left-wing or revolutionary terrorism, to right-wing terrorism, nationalist/separatist terrorism and religious terrorism (Table 7.1). An additional category not included in Table 7.1, but which is increasingly used by law enforcement agencies and the media, is 'eco-terrorism'. This refers to acts of terrorism, violence or

**Table 7.1**  *A categorization of terrorist groups by ideology*

| Leftwing/ revolutionary | Right-wing | Nationalist-separatist | Religious |
|---|---|---|---|
| Red Brigades (Italy) | Aryan Brothers (USA) | Provisional IRA (Ireland/Northern Ireland) | Aum Shinrikyo (Japan) |
| Baader Meinhof Gang (Germany) | New Order (Italy) | ETA (Spain/ Basque Country) | Army of God (USA) |
| Shining Path (Peru) | Self Defense Forces of Columbia | EOKA (Cyprus) | Egyptian Islamic Jihad |
| FARC (Colombia) | Russian National Unity | Tamil Tigers (Sri Lanka/Tamil Eelam) | GIA (Algeria) |
| Unified Communist Party of Nepal | UNITA (Angola) | Fatah (Palestine/ Israel) | Al-Qaeda |
| Naxalites (India) | | | Hamas (Palestine/Israel) |
| Symbionese Liberation Army (USA) | | | Lord's Resistance Army (Uganda) |

sabotage directed against people or property in support of ecological, environmental or animal rights causes. However, there is no significant academic literature on this category to date and there is real debate about whether such groups should be studied under the rubric of terrorism. Similarly, there is only a very small historical literature on the wave of 'anarchist terrorism' of the late nineteenth century.

Research has focused on each of these categories in an effort to understand better their different origins, causes, motives and manifestations. For example, there is a large and growing literature on the category of 'religious terrorism', which we examine below. In addition, there have been a number of studies which try to compare the differences between ideological groups, allowing scholars to make a number of interesting observations. Left-wing groups, for instance, appear to be more likely to attract members from the more educated and middle classes, at least initially. Right-wing and reactionary groups, in contrast, are more likely to attract those from less privileged socio-economic classes, especially males (Weinberg and Davies 1989: 84–96). Reasons proffered for this discrepancy include the argument that left-wing ideologies tend 'to stress economic and social equality as goals', while reactionary groups 'commonly emphasize military values and the traditional role of women in society' (ibid.: 92–3). However, as

Weinberg and Davies have noted, these distinctions do not hold universally. Right-wing/reactionary groups in 1970s Italy, for example, were much more likely to come from the middle classes, whereas left-wing groups recruited successfully from among the working classes. The reason for this, Weinberg and Davies argue, is that, for historical and structural reasons, the working classes were far more susceptible to 'revolutionary appeals' in Italy than in Germany or Japan, for example. The result was that the working classes came to be seen as a serious threat to the status quo, causing members of the middle classes to mobilize in defence thereof (ibid.: 91–2). In Germany, by contrast, the working classes were 'largely indifferent to revolutionary appeals', facilitating greater association of the working classes with the status quo (ibid.: 94).

A more nuanced comparative schema by Daniel Masters (2008) divides these broad categories into 'mixed' subsets: right-wing religious, right-wing religious/ethno-national, left wing/ethno-national and left wing. The right-wing religious category contains the subsets of fundamentalist, racial or ethnic superiority, and cult. The right-wing religious/ethno-national category is given two subsets of fundamentalist and social domination, while the left wing category has a subset of nihilist. He further recognizes that each subset has both domestic and international manifestations, breaking up the 'international' section into those 'globalizing local issues' and those with an 'emphasis on global issues' (Figure 7.1).

**Figure 7.1**   *A typology of ideological terrorism*

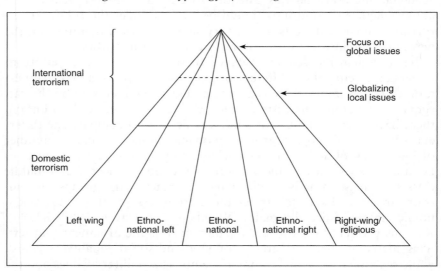

*Source*: Adapted from Masters 2008: 403.

Having defined these categories, Masters then searched for statistical correlations between ideological subset and group behaviour and characteristics. Contrary to common arguments about 'religious terrorism' (see below), he finds that the groups with the highest average casualty rate per attack are those who subscribe to an ethno-nationalist ideology – whether left wing or right-wing religious. He also finds that ethno-nationalist groups are more lethal than right-wing religious groups without an ethno-nationalist aspect to their ideology. However, his research also suggests that the right-wing religious/Ethno-nationalist fundamentalist category (which does not include al-Qaeda) has a higher average casualty rate than its left wing/Ethno-nationalist counterpart (ibid.: 408). However, without further contextualization – for example, whether the attacks were carried out in the context of a wider war, state repression or political liberalization – it is impossible to say exactly what role, if any, ideology played in 'producing' these differences in behaviour.

## Other categories

There are a number of other categories of terrorism that either do not fit into any of the broad approaches described above or cut across several of them. For example, the category of 'criminal terrorism' and/or 'narco-terrorism' is used to describe the involvement of terrorist groups in drug-trafficking and other criminal activities. Some distinguish between the broad orientation of different groups, separating revolutionary and conservative terrorism. Others take a historical perspective and distinguish very broadly between ancient and modern terrorism or 'new' and 'old terrorism' (see below). Some other residual descriptive categories include single issue terrorism and high-casualty terrorism. In most cases, these are delineational categories which simply describe the kind of groups or actions the researcher wants to study, rather than systematic classificatory schemas.

### Key Points

- Typologies of terrorism can be constructed in a number of ways, by reference to the nature of the actors, their methods, their ideology, their aims and goals, or their organizational characteristics.
- Some commonly employed categories in terrorism studies include international versus domestic terrorism, state versus non-state terrorism, suicide terrorism and new terrorism.
- The most widely used categories in terrorism studies differentiate between groups according to their ideology, including left-wing, right-wing, nationalist and religious terrorism.

## Evaluating categories of terrorism

In the previous section, we discussed some of the main typologies used in the terrorism studies field and gave examples of research based on common categories. Of course, constructing typologies and categories can be simultaneously useful and profoundly problematic. Traditionally, categorization has been considered 'one of the most basic functions of living creatures' (Mervis and Rosch 1981: 89). As human beings, we use it to make sense of a chaotic and limitless world, and to do so quickly and simply. Or, as psychologist Tania Lombrozo (2009) observes, quoting Rosch, 'category representations are typically posited in the service of inferential utility: they provide "maximum information with the least cognitive effort"'. In other words, categories are a form of shorthand for clusters of information which are believed to pertain to a particular type of object or activity. By invoking a category, we immediately conjure up a set of 'typical' characteristics concerning the causes of the object, its shape, its behaviour and the like. This is part of the reason why the employment of ideal types and categories is also an established practice within social science, and why it can be useful for understanding complex realities and uncovering salient aspects of a particular phenomenon.

From a Critical Theory perspective, with its emphasis on context and its critique of generalizing theories (see Toros and Gunning 2009), categorization is useful insofar as it encourages us to pay close attention to local detail, thereby acting as a counter-balance to the positivist temptation towards generalization. For example, if categorization leads analysts to differentiate between predominantly localized groups with local goals, networks and constituencies, on the one hand, and predominantly transnational groups with transnational goals, networks and constituencies, on the other, the analysis is more likely to reveal how contextual differences affect the behaviour of different groups. Categories can also draw attention to particular characteristics or dynamics which might otherwise be overlooked in the multitude of possible observations. Categorizing groups according to organizational structure, for instance, underlines the potential impact of structure on decision-making processes, goals and tactics. A socially embedded organization is more likely to take public opinion into account than a socially isolated group.

Additionally, a Critical Theory framework, unlike some post-structuralist approaches, does not automatically reject the notion of human regularities, as long as these are treated as historically and geographically situated, and not as timeless, abstract, universal categories. As Cox (1986: 244) observed, 'regularities in human activities may indeed be observed within particular eras, and thus the positivist approach can be fruitful within defined historical limits, though not with the uni-

versal pretensions it aspires to'. The key difference is that within a critical framework (and among those traditional scholars who meticulously historicize their subject), the categories are treated as
contextually situated and thus as both fluid and specific – changing
over time, according to the particularities of a context. Similarities
across time and space are thus certainly possible, and categorization
can help to identify these. The crucial point is that a Critical Theory
framework does not make a priori assumptions in the absence of a
meticulous analysis of contextual differences and other factors. In
short, as long as the categories are treated as historically and geographically bounded, categorization is an acceptable practice within critical
approaches to terrorism.

However, there are also a number of problems with categorization
which both critical and orthodox scholars have noted and to which we
must remain sensitive. In particular, there are at least four main problems with the typologies and categories commonly used in terrorism
research: (1) the problems of essentialism, homogeneity and universalism; (2) the implication of causality; (3) problems of empirical verification; and (4) issues relating to knowledge and power.

## Essentialism, homogeneity and universalism

The first problem with the practice of typologizing terrorism is that it
can function to obscure real and important differences between actors
or behaviours within one category, fostering the illusion that they represent an essential, homogenous and universal phenomenon. That is,
by creating a universal category, one risks taking groups out of their
specific context and highlighting only those aspects that 'fit' the
general label. In this way, characteristics emphasized by the typology
are liable to be exaggerated, while others may be overlooked or down-
played. Categorizing a group as 'religious terrorists', for example,
encourages the researcher to focus primarily on the group's religious
aspects and hence to neglect its secular or political dynamics (if we can
make such a sharp distinction between 'religious' and 'political').
Similarly, once a group is typologized under the rubric of 'new terrorism', analysis tends to focus on its transnational characteristics, the
presumed fanaticism of its members, its religious goals, and so on,
while any characteristics it may share with 'old terrorism' are relegated
to the background.

A related problem is that by creating general categories, one risks
producing an impression of homogeneity when real and significant differences could be more important. The Italian Red Brigades and the
German Baader–Meinhof group, for instance, both had left-wing ideologies and are frequently included in the same ideological category,
but in reality they differed greatly in their goals, tactics and member-

**Table 7.2**    *A comparison of two leftist groups*

|  | Italian Red Brigades | Baader–Meinhof Group |
|---|---|---|
| Goals | Primary focus on Italy | More global, anti-imperialist focus |
| Tactics | Kidnappings (18%) Factories prime target | Few kidnappings (4%) Factories hardly targeted |
| Membership | Cross-class | Predominantly middle class |

*Sources*: Porta 1995b; Weinberg and Davies 1989.

ship profiles (Porta 1995b). Some of the important differences between these two groups can be seen in Table 7.2. In short, echoing Michel Foucault, typologizing 'deliberately ignores all differences and all identities not related to the selected structure' (1970: 140).

Paradoxically, at the same time as they obscure differences, categories can also function to obscure similarities. The widely accepted distinction between state and non-state terrorism, for example, is rooted in the assumption that they are so dissimilar as to constitute separate types of the terrorism phenomenon. This preconception then functions to obscure all the many and important similarities between acts of state terrorism and acts of non-state terrorism (Jackson 2008). The analytical blindness brought about by these separate categories can then be an obstacle to the knowledge that could potentially be gained by considering them together.

## The implication of causality

A second key problem with typologies is that they tend to slip from pure description – 'this group is inspired by religion' – to causal inference – 'this group is violent *because* it is religious' – even if such an explanation is not supported by empirical evidence. According to George Lakoff, such inference 'is based on the common idea of what it means to be in the same category: things are categorized together on the basis of what they have in common' (1987: 5). In other words, classification according to a particular criterion creates the impression that that criterion is the key factor influencing the group's behaviour. By differentiating groups according to ideology, for example, one implies that ideological differences can account for many, if not most, of the differences in behaviour between types of group. However, in reality, not only do groups sharing ideological views behave very differently, but ideology is often not the key factor determining their behaviour; organizational dynamics, political expediency or structural changes also affect opportunities, tactics and motives.

A related situation in which categorization becomes problematic is when a particular instance of a category is taken as typical of that entire category. Thus, if al-Qaeda, which is frequently classified as 'religious', carries out a mass-casualty attack, the inference is made that all groups in the 'religious terrorism' category are likely to carry out mass-casualty attacks. From there it is but a small step to assume that religion is the 'cause' of such behaviour, without need of further proof. In reality, there are countless instances of actors categorized as 'religious' which have not carried out mass-casualty attacks, just as there are secular actors such as the LTTE who have been responsible for such attacks.

## Problems of empirical verification

A third key problem for the broad categories commonly used in terrorism research is that even the simplest binary categories break down and appear to lose their analytical utility under close empirical examination. Take, for example, the simple distinction between international and domestic terrorism. Is it sufficient for groups to operate across state boundaries to qualify as 'international terrorism', which would mean that many groups otherwise primarily national in focus would qualify? Or, should a group also have international goals and an international membership? The PLO, for instance, was viewed as the quintessential international terrorist group in the 1970s and 1980s when it carried out armed operations across Europe and the Middle East, had bases in numerous countries and was part of a web of alliances crossing national borders. However, it is debatable how international the PLO really was. Its goal – the liberation of Palestine – was decidedly national. Its members were similarly overwhelmingly Palestinian. Its web of international alliances, moreover, was not substantively different from the alliances of other national groups such as the IRA. Numerous national groups similarly carry out activities across state boundaries, cooperate internationally and have international references within their ideologies.

Al-Qaeda, meanwhile, while international in its aims, membership and operations, also possesses a number of characteristics frequently identified as typical of national groups (Pape 2005). Many of those who consider themselves part of the global al-Qaeda network have very domestic goals, such as the establishment of an Islamic state in Algeria (al-Jama'ah al-Islamiyah al-Musallaha (GIA)) or in Indonesia (Jemaah Islamiyah (JI)). Their members are often drawn primarily from one national group, such as Algerians (GIA) or Philippinos (Abu

Sayyaf). Even some of al-Qaeda's core aims, such as the establishment of an Islamic Caliphate in the Arabian Peninsula, can be said to be nationalistic, if the **ummah** (the world-wide community of Muslim believers) or, in this case, the Arab part thereof is seen as the nation in question. Nations, after all, are 'imagined communities' (Anderson 1983). In other words, applying the label 'international terrorism' even to such an ostensibly international network as al-Qaeda is not, upon close scrutiny, without problems.

The contestability of categories and blurredness of their boundaries becomes even more apparent when groups have mixed characteristics, as they invariably do in the real world. How does one classify a group which has goals inspired by both nationalism and religion, for example, or a group whose religious beliefs make it nationalistic? Where should one file away a group made up of both non-state and state actors? David Rapoport's (2004) famous 'four waves of terrorism' model suggests that the boundaries between the 'anarchist', 'anticolonial', 'new left' and 'religious' waves are clear and describable. However, the boundaries between these waves are profoundly blurred, as Rapoport (2004: 47) acknowledges:

> Nationalist organizations in various numbers appear in all waves, for example ... The Anarchists gave them tactics and often training. Third-wave nationalist groups displayed profoundly left-wing aspirations, and nationalism serves or reacts to religious purposes in the fourth wave.

In reality, many of Rapoport's anticolonial groups were shaped by religious beliefs and structures, as were many nationalist groups, while some of the left-wing groups outdid their religious counterparts in fanaticism and extreme worldviews (Gunning and Jackson forthcoming).

Similarly, the analytical lines between ideological categories do not always hold up for real-world cases, and a number of groups fall between categories. Hamas, for example, can be classified as both religious and nationalist-separatist. Russian National Unity is both right wing and nationalist (though not separatist), with a heavy emphasis on religion in its identification with the Orthodox Church. The Army of God is similarly both right wing and religious in its orientation, while the Tamil Tigers was both nationalist-separatist and left wing, with a heavy emphasis on religious symbolism.

The use of categories as a means of describing or explaining differences in behaviour between terrorist groups is also problematic in real-world cases. When terrorist groups are classified on the basis of their overarching ideology (such as left wing, right wing, nationalist and religious), the conclusion routinely reached is that so-called Islamist groups are the most lethal. This is then commonly explained with reference to a group's extreme ideology which divides the world starkly into believers and unbelievers and purportedly sees violence as a divine duty (Juergensmeyer 2000; Stern 2003).

However, empirical research by Piazza (2009) shows that a group's lethality cannot be predicted by its overarching ideology. A much better predictor, he argues, is the group's goal type, in particular whether its goals are 'universal-abstract' with unbending, utopian goals, or 'strategic' with limited (and typically territorial) aims. Specifically, once one disaggregates groups that have universal-abstract goals from those with strategic goals, one finds that Islamist groups with strategic goals, such as Hamas and Hizbullah, are not significantly more lethal than nationalist-separatist groups, whereas all groups with utopian-abstract goals, whether secular or religious, nationalist or leftist, exhibit far greater lethality. One reason for this is that groups with strategic goals are more likely to be embedded in local constituencies than groups with universal-abstract goals: a group which has a large social infrastructure and has to contend with others for popular support is more likely to modify its behaviour to achieve short-term strategic goals than groups that lack such infrastructure and political presence (see also Sageman 2004; Gunning 2007b).

## Knowledge, power and politics

Finally, as we have argued throughout this book, the production of knowledge is never neutral or objective; rather, knowledge and power are intimately connected. At the broadest level, the construction of categories of terrorism functions to impose and maintain a particular political order in society. In other words, typologies can be seen as problem-solving tools, used to classify problems and suggest solutions aimed at protecting the status quo. Similarly, the proliferation of terrorism categories over the past few years to include new categories such as eco-terrorism, narco-terrorism or cyber-terrorism reflects efforts to deal with challenges to the authority of states. By categorizing a particular problem as a form of 'terrorism', states can then deal with it using extraordinary measures.

More specifically, when typologies are presented as universally applicable, without recognition of the specific power-knowledge structures in which they emerged and which sustain them, they can function as a tool of ideology. The categories 'national' and 'international', for example, make little sense beyond the context of the modern state system which divides the world into separate, sovereign states with clearly defined borders. Because this system has become the dominant global mode of political organization, it is possible to apply the terms 'national' and 'international' globally. But to elevate them to the status of a universal category suggests not only that everyone accepts the division of the world into states, but also that this system is natural and inevitable, rather than socially constructed and historically specific.

In addition, by using typologies that have emerged in a specific context universally, without further reflection, we can end up imposing our normative commitments on others. The national/international typology, for example, privileges the state as a political organization over other indigenous modes of governance. Or, when we apply the category of 'religious terrorism' (see below), we privilege a particular understanding of religion, developed in the context of the so-called 'wars of religion' and the subsequent birth of the Westphalian state, as a private set of beliefs which should be kept separate from the political realm. Within such a normative framework, 'political religion' is seen as inherently problematic and a threat to the secular order of the state (Thomas 2005; Gunning and Jackson forthcoming).

From a post-structuralist perspective, the practice of classification is problematic because of its assumptions of 'sameness' and 'otherness' and its reliance on presumed essences and binary differences. Michel Foucault's *The Order of Things* (1970) was crucial in this respect. It was inspired by his encounter with an ancient Chinese categorization of animals which looked so arbitrary to him that he began to question the basis of any method of classification. He asked: on what basis do we establish sameness and otherness? On what basis do we select which characteristics are to be noticed and privileged, which ignored or marginalized? If categories are so arbitrary, do they perhaps say more about the categorizers and the systems of meaning in which they are embedded than the categorized? Recognition of the fundamental arbitrariness of our systems of classification has therefore led some post-structuralists to adopt a wholly anti-essentialist position, arguing that there is no 'essential' characteristic to any object, let alone human behaviour. What we consider essential or similar or different is therefore merely an artificial (and violent) construct – a figment of language and the prevailing power structures.

Whilst recognizing the importance of these criticisms, Critical Theory-based approaches to terrorism adopt a minimal foundationalism which accepts the existence of observable characteristics, limited regularities and a normative framework for their analysis (Toros and Gunning 2009). What distinguishes critical theorists from traditional positivists is that they do not view their categories as timeless or universal, but as products of a particular set of power structures and their regimes. Categories may be useful as shorthand descriptors; one could even argue they are unavoidable. However, they are not to be treated as self-evident 'truths'. Instead, they should be continuously interrogated, their boundaries, dichotomies and causal implications problematized, and their political and ideological effects exposed.

---

## Key Points

- Categories can be helpful in organizing complex information about the real world and creating shorthand descriptions.
- The practice of categorization can be problematic due to its essentializing, homogenizing and universalizing tendencies.
- The factors used to create categories are problematic when they are assumed to have a causal influence on behaviour.
- Many of the commonly used categories in terrorism studies break down under close empirical scrutiny.
- Categories are not neutral or natural but deeply ideological in the way they contain and reproduce hidden values.

---

## Is the new terrorism really new?

One of the most important typologies in use today is the distinction between 'new' and 'old' terrorism. According to proponents (see, among many others, Laqueur 1999; Lesser *et al.* 1999; Simon and Benjamin 2000; Hoffman 2006), a new form of terrorism emerged from the early 1990s which differs fundamentally from its predecessors in terms of organizational structure, personnel, beliefs and aims, and attitude towards the use of violence. Organizationally, and in contrast to the nationally based, hierarchical groups of the mid-twentieth century, the new terrorism is thought to be transnational and comprised of loosely linked networks, making it harder to detect or counter. In terms of its personnel, the new terrorism is believed to draw more heavily on amateurs than 'professionals', making it less dependent on state support. Ideologically, it is said to be driven by a fanatical and absolutist interpretation of religion, characterized by blind hatred and a disregard for concrete political aims. Finally, the new terrorism is said to be more indiscriminate in its selection of targets and intent on causing mass casualties, possibly through the use of WMD.

Al-Qaeda is often described as the archetypical example of a 'new terrorist' network (Neumann 2009). It is a transnational 'network of networks', drawing in a number of 'amateur' or self-radicalized operatives. Ideologically, al-Qaeda is portrayed as having fanatical, otherworldly, non-negotiable aims, rather than concrete political goals such as national liberation. Moreover, it has been responsible for the highest single mass-casualty attack by non-state actors to date, killing nearly 3,000 in the infamous attacks of 11 September 2001. This is on top of a number of other mass-casualty attacks, such as the 1998 embassy bombings in Kenya and Tanzania, and the 2004 Madrid attack.

However, an increasing number of orthodox and critical scholars alike have shown that much of that which is considered 'new' about 'new terrorism' was exhibited by the so-called 'old terrorism' (Copeland 2001; Tucker 2001; Duyvesteyn 2004; Spencer 2006; Crenshaw 2008). For example, the transnational and networked organizational structures thought to distinguish new terrorism can also be found among the anarchist terrorists of the late nineteenth century, as well as the secular left-wing groups of the 1970s. Similarly, the presence of 'amateurs' can be found among both 'new' and 'old' terrorist groups. The assertion that the 'new terrorism' is primarily motivated by religion is also largely unsupported by the evidence, as is the assertion that they are irrational fanatics who mindlessly slaughter innocent civilians.

In fact, virtually all of the so-called 'new terrorist' groups demonstrate strategic rationality in their choice of tactics and strategies. They often show great care in articulating not just theological but also political justifications for their actions, responding to criticism of certain kinds of attacks and readjusting their methods following doctrinal and strategic review (Wiktorowicz and Kaltner 2003). Mass-casualty attacks are also not unique to 'new terrorists' and their increase since the 1990s has arguably been driven by technological changes, globalization and changes in the media and the public's receptivity, rather than the emergence of a new breed of actor. The use of WMD, meanwhile, has been markedly absent from the arsenal of so-called 'new terrorism', despite the worst case scenarios that continue to be drawn up by analysts.

A close analysis of al-Qaeda – the quintessential 'new terrorist' group – illustrates the limitations and distortions of this category. For example, al-Qaeda's organizational and strategic characteristics suggest that it is as easily explained within classic theories of terrorism developed by nineteenth-century Italian anarchists as by the 'new terrorism' thesis (Sedgwick 2004). Similarly, al-Qaeda's public statements reveal a clear political analysis and set of political goals, such as: support for the establishment of a Palestinian state; ending US military occupation of the Arabian peninsular and its ongoing support for Israel; overthrowing corrupt and oppressive Arab regimes; supporting local insurgencies in Iraq, Kashmir, Chechnya, the Philippines and elsewhere; and the expulsion of Western forces from Iraq and Afghanistan (Lawrence 2005). On this basis, Jason Burke concludes that al-Qaeda's 'grievances are political but articulated in religious terms and ... the movement is rooted in social, economic and political contingencies' (Burke 2004: xxv–xxvi; see also Bergen 2001; Pape 2005: 104; Ayoob 2005; Holmes 2005).

In summary, the category of 'new terrorism' is therefore unhelpful in the analysis of real world cases, serving to obscure and distort rather than illuminate. Aside from these analytical shortcomings, however, critical scholars also draw attention to the political agendas served by

---

**Key Points**

- The category of 'new terrorism' posits a difference from 'old terrorism' in terms of organizational structure, personnel, beliefs, aims and attitude towards the use of violence.
- A growing body of research, including studies on al-Qaeda, indicates that the 'new terrorism' category is an inaccurate and analytically unhelpful category.
- Critical scholars note that the 'new terrorism' category is ideologically loaded and can be used to justify extraordinary counter-terrorism measures.

---

this category. For instance, the 'new terrorism' label can be used to justify extraordinary counter-terrorist measures, such as torture, rendition and targeted killing, on the grounds that an identified group's lethality and irrationality represents an extraordinary threat to security. In addition, lessons from past conflicts, such as the importance of dialogue and reform, may also be ignored on the grounds that the threat is 'new'. Thus, the UK government can argue that the effects of draconian counter-terrorist legislation on the Irish community in the 1970s have nothing to teach us about the impact of counter-terrorist legislation on British Muslims during the 2000s, while the US government can similarly claim that nothing can be learned from previous terrorism campaigns in Europe and elsewhere.

## How religious is religious terrorism?

Directly related to the idea of 'new terrorism' is the category of 'religious terrorism', one of the most widely used and accepted categories in terrorism studies today. It is also popular with both politicians and the media. Following David Rapoport's influential article on religion and violence (1984), and in reaction to the events of 9/11, an increasing number of widely cited scholarly works have sought to establish the primary claims about the nature and causes of 'religious terrorism', particularly as it relates to contemporary 'Islamic' or 'Islamist terrorism' (see among many other examples, Ranstorp 1996; Laqueur 1999; Juergensmeyer 2000; Stern 2003; Byman 2003; Wiktorowicz 2005).

This literature argues that 'religious terrorism' is uniquely different from other types because it is aimed 'not at clearly defined political demands but at the destruction of society and the elimination of large sections of the population' (Laqueur 1999: 81). It is argued that 'religious terrorists' are more lethal and indiscriminate, less willing to compromise, more radical and more fanatical than their secular counterparts, in large part because they are inspired by extreme religious beliefs which see it as their divine duty to kill God's adversaries. That is, to the 'religious terrorist, violence is ... a sacramental act or divine duty executed in direct response to some theological demand' (Hoffman 2006: 88) or an effort to destroy society altogether, as opposed to a tactical means to a political end. In other words, the purpose of religious terrorism is 'not to achieve a strategic goal but to make a symbolic statement' (Juergensmeyer 2000: 125).

As a consequence of this label, it is assumed that when it comes to negotiating concrete political demands, religious terrorists 'don't want a seat at the table, they want to destroy the table and everyone sitting at it' (Morgan 2004: 30–1). This necessarily implies that there are limited options for dealing with religious terrorism. In relation to al-Qaeda, for example, Daniel Byman suggests: 'because of the scope of its grievances, its broader agenda of rectifying humiliation, and a poisoned worldview that glorifies jihad as a solution, appeasing al-Qaeda is difficult in theory and impossible in practice' (2003: 147). The logic of this description implies that bringing such religious terrorists 'to justice can only take the form of extirpation – root, trunk and branch' (Barber 2002: 246).

However, as with 'new terrorism', the category of 'religious terrorism' poses a number of key problems. First, the notion of 'religion', particularly as it is contrasted with 'secular', is neither straightforward nor uncontested (Gunning and Jackson forthcoming). Simply put, it is extremely difficult in practice to make a clear distinction between the two, as almost every area of life is infused with ritualism and symbolism. In addition, many political ideologies have religious characteristics in terms of their underlying assumptions and beliefs, while all religions are political insofar as they deal with questions of morality and social existence. The fact is that our understanding of religion – and therefore the concept of 'religious terrorism' – comes out of a particular historical context in which religion is defined as a private, nonpolitical concern. In reality, religion and politics are deeply enmeshed and cannot be so easily disentangled.

A related problem is that it is unclear exactly what factors or characteristics make a group 'religious'. Is it sufficient that its ideology is infused with religious symbolism and beliefs? If so, then how should we categorize those whose rhetoric contains both religious and nationalist or other secular elements? Should leaders identify themselves as religious or should the organization be recognized as such by its adherents or by established religious authorities? Do its targets and goals have to be religious? If so, how does one distinguish between a religious and a political target or goal, given the difficulties in defining religion highlighted above? Apart from the fact that there are few groups which exhibit the characteristics 'typical' of 'religious terrorists', it is also unclear how important religious elements are when other political factors are also present.

The case of Hamas perfectly illustrates this problem: its leaders are predominantly 'secular' professionals elected in internal elections, its ideology is heavily influenced by nationalism, its targets are not typically religious, and its operational logic resembles that of other 'secular' groups. At the same time, its leaders derive their authority in part from religious sources, while piety and involvement in the mosque all serve to enhance a leader's symbolic capital. However, even this 'religious' capital has 'secular' qualities. 'Religious' knowledge, for instance, is primarily valued if it concerns knowledge of Islamic law – which in Palestine, where Islamic law is a central source of legislation, is a 'secular' as well as a 'religious' good. Piety, similarly, is associated in the popular imagination with incorruptibility, while mosque involvement implies administrative and social networking skills and social status (Gunning 2007b). In other words, in the case of Hamas – often depicted as a quintessential 'religious terrorist' group – distinguishing the religious from the political is not only difficult but is also potentially misleading.

Similarly, many 'secular' groups display 'religious' characteristics. For example, both the German RAF and the Italian Red Brigades pursued a radically different world order, painted their conflict in terms comparable to 'cosmic war', and described their enemies in similar eschatological terms to al-Qaeda. Much of their violence was 'symbolic' or 'redemptive' rather than 'strategic', and the level of loyalty demanded from members was as total as that of the most exacting religious cult. By the late 1970s, they had virtually lost their earthly constituency and one could say that violence had become almost a 'sacramental act' in response to a teleological imperative (Porta 1995b).

This leads to a third serious problem with this category, namely the implication that 'religion' can be causally linked to the group's behaviour, particularly its level of violence. Even if it could be clearly demonstrated that 'religious' groups were more lethal than secular groups, and this is itself debatable (Piazza 2009; Gunning and Jackson forthcoming), it is not at all clear that religious beliefs are the main reason for increased lethality. That is, by classifying groups on the basis of their beliefs, one makes the simplistic, and often misleading, assumption that beliefs are the main determinant of behaviour. The RAF and the Red Brigades, for instance, had a very similar set of ideological beliefs, but evolved and behaved very differently, due to a complex combination of other factors (Porta 1995a, 1995b). At an individual level, research suggests that joining (or leaving) a violent organization does not necessarily involve conversion to a particular belief system. Individuals become involved in violent activity for a range of reasons, from familial or friendship ties, to a search for social acceptance, reaction against police brutality or securing access to otherwise unavailable goods and services, including protection (Sageman 2004: 99–135; see also Porta 1995b; Bjørgo 2005a, 2009).

Fourth, many of the arguments put forward about religious terrorism – that it is more lethal and unconstrained, that religious terrorists have cosmic, other-worldly aims, and that they are not amenable to political compromise, for example – are not supported by empirical evidence. Many of the groups labelled 'religious terrorists' do not behave like this in practice and have clearly identifiable this-worldly goals and constituencies. Many also rationally weigh up cost–benefit calculations (within their own cognitive frameworks), and regularly demonstrate political pragmatism (Gunning 2007b). Compared to 'secular' groups like the FARC, LTTE and PKK, for example, Hamas and Hizbullah have been far less lethal, more restrained and shown greater willingness to negotiate and compromise. At the same time, even the most lethal 'religious terrorist' groups do not come close to the level of destruction meted out by some secular state apparatuses, such as Nazi Germany, Stalin's Soviet Union or Mao's China, or secular rebel movements of the past few decades, such as the Revolutionary United Front (RUF) in Sierra Leone or the Khmer Rouge in Cambodia.

In the end, it is clear that, like 'new terrorism', the category of 'religious terrorism' is inaccurate and analytically unhelpful, and in most cases it serves to obscure and distort rather than illuminate. Also, as with 'new terrorism', critical scholars would argue that it is an ideologically loaded term that can be employed to further particular political interests and reinforce the status quo.

---

## Key Points

- 'Religious terrorism' is one of the most widely used categories in terrorism research today. It is assumed to be more lethal and indiscriminate, less willing to compromise, more radical and more fanatical than other kinds of 'secular' terrorism.
- There are compelling arguments and a great deal of evidence to suggest that the category of 'religious terrorism' is analytically unhelpful and misleading, especially the assumed causal connection between religious belief and behaviour.
- Critical scholars argue that the category of 'religious terrorism' is deeply ideological and functions to justify harsh counter-terrorism measures and reinforce the status quo.

## Conclusion

The phenomenon of terrorism encompasses a vast array of different actors and behaviours. Typologies and categories can potentially be a useful aid to our understanding of the complex realities of terrorism and may help in uncovering its salient aspects. However, many of the categories commonly employed in the terrorism studies field have been more often a hindrance than a help to rigorous research. In some cases, such as 'new terrorism' and 'religious terrorism', they have worked to sustain a series of misleading and inaccurate myths about the nature, causes and solutions to contemporary terrorism. As such, they have functioned as an example of problem-solving theory and have been used ideologically in the service of existing power structures.

As we have tried to argue throughout this book, critical approaches are important because they interrogate every part of the knowledge production process and ask crucial questions about what kind of knowledge is being produced, for whom it works and what kinds of effects it has on society. In this chapter, we have asked these questions about the categories of terrorism: What kind of knowledge do terrorism categories produce? In whose interests does the knowledge of particular categories work? What are the effects of this knowledge on society? At the very least, asking these kinds of questions can help to prevent the adoption of ideologically loaded, inaccurate and misleading typologies and categories, and can thus help to prevent dangerous and misleading over-simplifications. More importantly, it can reveal how knowledge and power work together in terrorism research and the areas in which we need to be reflexive about our research.

Although some critical scholars would reject the use of categories in social research altogether, terrorism categories can be useful as long as they are constantly problematized in terms of their historical origins, their effect on our understanding and their relationship to existing power structures. In practice, this means reflecting on a category's underlying (often hidden) assumptions – for example, that religion 'ought' to be a private affair, or that the state is a 'natural' entity whose interests 'ought' to trump those of individuals or groups – and acknowledging that these assumptions, and the interests they serve, have an effect on how we understand the phenomenon thus categorized. In addition, it means questioning a category's boundaries, looking for traces of its opposite or characteristics that do not fit – such as 'secular' actors acting irrationally or 'new terrorists' acting in 'old' ways. Third, it means challenging the notion that the existence of a typical characteristic necessarily implies a causal explanation (indeed, the very notion of causation needs to be revisited; see Chapter 10). Finally, it means acknowledging that typologies cannot adequately capture the rich, and often contradictory, web of motivations and meanings that underpin human behaviour (which in turn has implications for any causal explanation).

## Discussion Questions

1. What are the main dimensions along which terrorism is differentiated into separate categories?
2. Why are essentialism, homogeneity and universalism in terrorism categories so problematic?
3. What are the problems associated with the causal implications of categorizations?
4. To what extent do common terrorism categories hold up under close empirical scrutiny?
5. What issues of knowledge and power are raised by the practices of categorization?
6. What are some of the problems and dangers involved in treating suicide terrorism as its own special category?
7. What are the main problems with the category of 'new terrorism'?
8. What are the main problems with the category of 'religious terrorism'?
9. What characterizes the critical approach to the practice of categorization in terrorism research?
10. What are the advantages of taking a critical approach towards categories and types of terrorism?

## Recommended Reading

Duyvesteyn, I., 2004. 'How New is the New Terrorism?', *Studies in Conflict and Terrorism*, 27(5): 439–54. This article challenges the claims of the 'new terrorism' literature by highlighting continuities with the 'old terrorism' and calls for historical comparative research which goes beyond sterile typologies.

Foucault, Michel, 1970. *The Order of Things: An Archaeology of the Human Sciences*, London: Tavistock Publications. This seminal book looks at the way the human sciences have produced knowledge, in part through the construction of categories and typologies.

Piazza, J., 2009. 'Is Islamist Terrorism More Dangerous? An Empirical Study of Group Ideology, Organization, and Goal Structure', *Terrorism and Political Violence* 21(1): 62–88. An important study which statistically interrogates the notion that Islamist groups are more lethal than non-Islamist groups.

Weinberg, L. and Davies, P., 1989. *Introduction to Political Terrorism*, New York: McGraw-Hill. A classic textbook providing a highly accessible introduction to the various typologies of groups and actors found in the traditional terrorism literature, but also offering a number of counter-examples to show that the typologies can be problematic.

## Web Resources

START: *www.start.umd.edu/start/*
Website of START, hosted by the University of Maryland. The website includes the GTD, an open-source database including information on terrorist events around the world since 1970. The GTD includes systematic data on international as well as domestic terrorist incidents that have occurred during this time period and includes over 80,000 cases. For each incident, information is available on the date and location of the incident, the weapons used and nature of the target, the number of casualties, and – when identifiable – the identity of the perpetrator.

WITS: *www.nctc.gov/wits/witsnextgen.html*
The webpage for WITS, hosted by the National Counterterrorism Center. WITS is a major database on terrorism events around the world. The website allows the user to generate graphs, charts and maps on terrorist events according to different characteristics and types.

# Chapter 8

# Understanding State Terrorism

---

## Reader's Guide

In this chapter we examine the frequently neglected issue of the use of terrorist violence by states. It begins with a discussion of why state terrorism has remained largely unstudied within the broader terrorism studies field, and some of the ideological consequences of this silence. The next section offers a definition of state terrorism. It demonstrates how certain forms of state violence clearly fit the definition of terrorism and interrogates some of the most common arguments that have been used against the concept. This is followed by a brief overview of the nature and extent of state terrorism over the past two centuries and some examples of contemporary state terrorism. This overview reveals that state terrorism is a far more serious and destructive form of political violence than non-state terrorism. The final section analyses the reasons why states employ terrorism, as well as the main actors, methods and outcomes of state terrorism. In the conclusion, we reflect on the implications of including forms of state violence within the study of terrorism and try to suggest a way forward for further exploration of this important issue.

## Introduction

In terms of human and material destruction, state terrorism has typically been a far more serious problem than non-state terrorism. Over the past century, governments have killed hundreds of millions of their own citizens outside of war (Rummel 1994; see also Table 8.1), a considerable amount of which violence can be described as terroristic. In comparison, the actions of non-state terrorists have killed in the order of tens of thousands of people over the same period (see Chapter 6). As we demonstrate below, states continue to kill and injure far more of their own and other states' citizens than do non-state terrorists. In part, this is simply because most states have far greater coercive resources than any non-state group, even in today's globalized world.

Despite this disparity in destructive power, critical scholars have noted that the orthodox terrorism studies field remains almost solely focused on the subject of non-state terrorism. It rarely acknowledges or studies the problem of state terrorism in any systematic manner – unless the violence is carried out by so-called 'rogue states' in support of terrorist groups (Jackson 2007e). A survey of articles in *Terrorism and Political Violence* and *Studies in Conflict and Terrorism*, the terrorism field's two flagship journals, found that less than 2 per cent of articles between 1990 and 1999 focused on state terrorism (Silke 2004c: 206). This trend has remained largely unchanged since then. Similarly, only 12 of the 768 pages in Crenshaw and Pimlott's (1996) *Encyclopedia of World Terrorism* examined state terrorism in any form (quoted in Goodin 2006: 55), while a more recent *Dictionary of Terrorism* discusses state terrorism on only 8 of its 308 pages (Thakrah 2004). These findings confirm the observation that within terrorism studies 'there is a conspicuous absence of literature that addresses itself to the much more serious problem of state terrorism' (Schmid and Jongman 1988: 179–80; see also Walter 1969: 3; Jackson 2008).

This is not to say that state terrorism has not been studied at all. Different kinds of state violence, such as repression, human rights abuses, genocide and state crime, many of which arguably contain terroristic aspects, have long been studied in fields such as law, history, political science, criminology, sociology, anthropology and others. There is also a relatively small but very important body of research on state terrorism which developed out of some of the critical approaches to terrorism described in Chapter 2 (see for example, Herman 1982; Stohl and Lopez 1984, 1986; Duvall and Stohl 1988; Stohl 1988, 2006; Perdue 1989; Chomsky 1991; George 1991a; Sluka 2000; Gareau 2004; Stokes 2005; Becker 2006; Grosscup 2006; Blakeley 2009). However, on the whole, it is fair to say that research on state terrorism which utilizes the concepts, theories, methods and insights of the established terrorism studies field remains relatively rare.

The reasons why terrorism scholars have generally been reluctant to include state actions in their research is something of a puzzle, especially given that 'terrorism' was originally a term used to describe a particular kind of state violence. Reasons for this state of affairs probably include: the state-centric and problem-solving character of the broader terrorism studies field as it has evolved; the tendency of some terrorism scholars to follow powerful states in defining terrorism solely as actions undertaken by non-state groups; the challenges involved in studying state terrorism, such as obtaining reliable information and intimidation by state officials; and the challenges of researching an immoral and arguably illegal form of state behaviour when scholars are embedded within institutions and societies which frequently view the state as a generally positive force.

As we explained in Chapter 2, a critical approach begins by questioning the relationship between knowledge and power and seeks to ascertain how certain kinds of knowledge function in society. In this case, we need to ask: What are the ideological consequences of the failure to study – or the 'silence' on – state terrorism within the wider terrorism studies field? Who benefits from these silences and whose voices become marginalized as a consequence?

At the broadest level, the silence on state terrorism works to maintain the fiction that terrorism is largely the activity of dissidents, while states are primarily the victims of terrorist violence. This has a distorting effect on knowledge and research on terrorism, not least because it creates the wholly misconceived impression that it is more important to understand and deal with non-state terrorism than with state terrorism. Related to this, the silence functions to reinforce the myth that states by definition cannot engage in terrorism, regardless of what they do, and that they are essentially good or at least benign actors in the world. This has the effect of reinforcing state power and authority, in part by immunizing the state from particular kinds of criticism, but also by allowing states to create anti-terrorism legislation for use against non-state actors which are not applied to their own actions (Jackson 2008). In Western societies, this widely accepted view of the state promotes the dangerous idea that democratic states are immune to abusing their power and that their counter-terrorism measures are therefore inherently legitimate.

In response to this situation, critical scholars have argued that there is a genuine and pressing need to 'bring the state back in' to terrorism research (Blakeley 2007; Jackson *et al.* 2009c) and that a major effort to understand the nature, causes and responses to state terrorism is urgently needed to end the imbalance and distortion in the existing field. The purpose of this chapter is to explain the concept of state terrorism, outline its nature and extent, describe its main aims, actors, methods and types, and to make some suggestions for future research on the subject.

## Conceptualizing state terrorism

State terrorism can be conceptualized or described as the intentional use or threat of violence by state agents or their proxies against individuals or groups for the purpose of intimidating or frightening a broader audience (Jackson *et al.* 2009c: 3; see also Box 8.1). The direct victims of the state's violence are not necessarily the main targets, although the state may want to eliminate them in any case because they are seen to pose a threat of some kind. Instead, as with non-state terrorism, the victims are instrumental to the primary goal of frightening an audience who are intimidated through the communicative power of exemplary and symbolic violence. The intended effects of the violence are the achievement of specific political or political-economic (as opposed to private or criminal) goals, such as undermining political opposition to the government, enacting a new political programme, protecting a set of economic arrangements or influencing the policies of another state. In these aims, state terrorism includes the use of open or clandestine violence against domestic opponents, as well as the direct or indirect involvement in terrorism against foreign or external enemies. In practice, state terrorism involves a range of violent actions from the use of bombs on airliners and in public places to political murder, kidnapping, enforced disappearances, torture and the like. From this perspective, in terms of motivations and tactics, state terrorism is remarkably similar to non-state terrorism, except of course that it is undertaken by a different type of actor with different types and quantities of resources.

Although it would seem to be a relatively straightforward and uncontroversial proposition that terrorism is a violent *strategy* which any actor – including states – can employ, there are in fact several common objections to the concept of 'state terrorism' which are sometimes heard from terrorism scholars (Jackson *et al.* 2009c; Jackson forthcoming a). It is important that we deal with these objections before we proceed.

First, it is argued by some scholars that one of the core defining features of 'terrorism' is that it is a form of political violence practised solely by non-state actors and that states cannot engage in terrorism because they have the legitimate right to use violence – in contradistinction to non-state actors who have no such right. This objection, which is based on an actor-based definition of terrorism, can be easily dismissed, however. As we have already noted, terrorism is first and foremost a strategy of violence utilized to achieve political aims, somewhat akin to the strategies employed in insurgency and **guerrilla warfare**. Therefore, to suggest that the engagement of state agents in the very same strategies as non-state terrorists – such as the hijacking or blowing up of civilian airliners or the planting of a series of bombs

---

## Box 8.1   Conceptualizing state terrorism

[State terrorism is] the policy of using acts inspiring great fear as a method of ruling.

(Nagengast 1994)

[State terrorism is] a method of rule whereby some groups of people are victimized with great brutality, and more or less arbitrarily by the state, or state-supported actors, so that others who have reason to identify with those murdered, will despair, obey or comply. Its main instruments are summary arrest and incarceration without trial, torture, political murder, disappearances, and concentration camps.

(Bushnell *et al.* 1991)

State terrorism should be understood as a threat or act of violence by agents of the state that is intended to induce extreme fear in a target audience, so that they are forced to consider changing their behaviour in some way.

(Blakeley 2009)

The ultimate strategic purposes of terrorism are either to maintain a regime or create the conditions for a new one ... For a regime the terror is a message of strength, a warning designed to intimidate, to ensure compliance without the need to physically touch each citizen ... [The] purpose of terrorism is to create or enforce obedience, either of the population at large or within the ruling party.

(Stohl 1979)

Terrorism by states is characterized by official support for policies of violence, repression, and intimidation. This violence and coercion is directed against perceived enemies that the state has determined threaten its interests or security. Although the perpetrators of state terrorist campaigns are frequently government personnel, and directives do originate from government officials, those who carry out the violence are also quite often unofficial agents of the government.

(Martin 2003)

---

in public places – ceases to be terrorism, is logically unsupportable. In effect, maintaining this position entails arguing that the 1988 Lockerbie bombing was *not* an act of terrorism because it was undertaken by state agents, while the bombing of an Air India flight in 1985 *was* an act of terrorism because it was undertaken by Sikh militants.

Related to this, the suggestion that states have a legitimate right to use violence while non-state actors do not, is, in fact, not so clear-cut (Valls 2000). It is a misrepresentation to suggest that all state violence is legitimate while all non-state violence is illegitimate. The state's right to use violence is highly circumscribed by national and international legal frameworks and does not include the right to commit genocide, ethnic cleansing, war crimes or other illegal acts such as kidnapping or torture. In addition, many states lack legitimacy precisely among the constituencies that support armed insurgencies, calling into question the former's 'right' to use violence on behalf of those constituencies. There is also a long-standing moral principle that non-state actors may use political violence against highly repressive and genocidal states as a last resort when other methods have failed or other states fail to intervene. Throughout history, states and international organizations have recognized and supported violent non-state groups, some of whom have practised terrorism, including: the resistance to Nazi occupation during World War II; the PLO, the African National Congress (ANC), the South West African People's Organization (SWAPO) and other UN-recognized movements; and the Contras, anti-Castro groups, the Uniao Nacional para a Independencia Total de Angola (UNITA), the Mujahaddin and other groups who received extensive military and political support from Western states. In the end, an academic, as opposed to a political, approach would adhere to the procedure of identifying acts of terrorism according to the characteristics of the violence, not the (politically or otherwise) privileged nature of the actor employing the violence.

A second frequently heard objection to the concept of state terrorism is that state repressive violence is very different from non-state terrorism because its victims are not randomly chosen (they are all opponents of the state) and individuals know what they can do to avoid state violence (unlike in cases of non-state terrorism). A simple answer to this argument is that state agents do engage in random acts of violence such as bombing civilian airliners or public places and, in those cases at least, there can be no doubt that they are engaged in acts of state terrorism. In addition, the reality is that quite a few non-state terrorist groups choose their victims very specifically, rather than randomly. Both ETA and the IRA, for example, have over a long period targeted soldiers, police officers and state officials rather than randomly chosen civilians. Their violence may have been designed to be unpredictable, but their victims are very rarely selected arbitrarily (Neumann 2009: 37). The key point here is that terrorism is not defined by the choice of victims, but by the instrumentalization of the victims, whether they are chosen randomly or deliberately, in order to communicate a message to an audience.

A related point is that states can never physically eliminate *all* of their opponents, so they will frequently target particular opponents in order to intimidate both the wider opposition movement and the state's own supporters. In addition, states may also have more than one objective to their terroristic violence. For example, they may want to eliminate particularly troublesome opponents while simultaneously sending a message to other real or potential opponents. In 'terror states' such as Nazi Germany, Stalin's Soviet Union, Pol Pot's Kampuchea and Pinochet's Chile, the entire population lived in fear precisely because no one could be sure that they were completely safe; even faithful party members could inadvertently fall victim to state terror.

A third objection to the concept of state terrorism suggests that state repressive violence is not terrorism because state agents do not seek publicity but rather try to hide their involvement – unlike non-state terrorism which is aimed at maximizing publicity (Nacos 2002). This argument mistakes publicity for communication. It is communication to an audience which is one of the key elements of terrorist violence, not necessarily publicity (Duvall and Stohl 1988: 239–40). For non-state actors who lack the means to reach the whole society, publicity is the easiest way to communicate. But this is not necessarily the case for states, as their violence will not always require publicity to reach their intended audience. In reality, when an individual in a terror state is kidnapped and then forcibly 'disappeared', returned following torture or their corpse is left mutilated in a public place, the local observers know exactly who the intended audience is, what the message is intended to convey and from whom it has been sent. The lack of publicity and denial of any state involvement in the violence is usually aimed at external audiences in order to maintain a good international reputation or for domestic constituents whom the state relies upon for support. For example, the European settler community in South Africa were largely kept unaware of the violence meted out by the state to its non-white population.

A fourth objection is that what is called 'state *terrorism*' is already covered by terms like 'repression' and 'human rights abuses', and that acts of state terrorism are already circumscribed in international law and do not require new legal or analytical concepts. This is a political or pragmatic argument which ignores the scholarly principle of including all the cases that fit the criteria in order to retain analytical consistency. It also ignores the fact that the same argument can be applied to non-state 'terrorism': all the acts and activities performed by non-state terrorists are also already circumscribed in law and there exist a range of useful terms – violence, murder, hijacking, bombing, assassination and many more – to describe their actions. It can also be argued that state (or non-state) actions are never solely and exclusively 'terrorism', 'human rights abuses' or 'repression'. They can be – and by definition always are – both acts of 'terrorism' and 'human rights abuses' at the same time, and there is no contradiction in describing them using either or both terms. Critical scholars tend to take the position that terrorism, whether conducted by state or non-state actors, involves a number of specific moral wrongs (beyond unjustified killing and harm), such as the instrumentalization of human suffering, the intention to cause widespread fear and the betrayal of the duty of care towards fellow human beings (Goodin 2006: 102). These wrongs are not limited by the nature of the actor but are the result of the act, whichever actor performs it.

A fifth common objection is that although states may engage in terrorism which is far more destructive than that of non-state actors, their violence is qualitatively different in aims, modes and outcomes and there is little analytical value to be gained in studying state violence and non-state violence under the same label (Hoffman 2006). In response, critical scholars argue that, given that the term 'terrorism' was first used to describe a form of state violence, terrorism committed by the state represents perhaps the purest and most original form of the phenomenon and therefore has much to tell us about its causes and effects. Certainly, in an empirical sense, state terrorism comes closest to generating real 'terror' in a broad population; acts of non-state terrorism rarely result in widespread 'terror' (Rapin 2009) and are in a sense little more than a poor imitation of state violence. Moreover, as we have shown above, state and non-state actors engage in many of the same acts of political violence – kidnap, extra-judicial killing, bombing, torture and the like – and have very similar aims – intimidation of an audience to achieve political aims, either revolutionary or conservative. It is therefore contestable that state terrorism is so different from non-state terrorism that it requires a different concept and research field, although differences in scale, resources and processes do complicate comparisons. Besides, there is no reason why state terrorism cannot be studied as one type of terrorism, just as civil war is studied as one type of war.

Lastly, it is sometimes argued that accepting that 'states can be terrorists too' would make the field of terrorism studies too broad and unfocused because it would then have to include a vast array of actors and actions that it has previously chosen not to study, potentially including most state violence and coercion. This objection is rooted first and foremost in a misunderstanding of the specific characteristics of terrorist violence. Employing the description of terrorism we have advanced in this book (see Chapters 2 and 5), it is clear that not all (or even most) state violence would fit the analytical label of terrorism. It is also rooted in a pragmatic desire to limit the focus of study, instead of a desire to remain theoretically consistent. In reality, the same argument could be made against concepts such as elections, wars or nonstate terrorism, which are also broad terms describing a vast array of events, actions and actors. Having a broad concept does not undermine research in these areas, however, as few scholars focus broadly on elections, war or terrorism, but instead concentrate on specific aspects of their subject. The same is true for the study of (state) terrorism.

To conclude, critical scholars would add that there are a number of important ethical-normative reasons for retaining the term 'state terrorism'. For example, due to the powerful connotations of the 'terrorism' label today, its retention as a descriptor of certain forms of state violence could be an important means of advancing a progressive political project aimed at protecting or emancipating marginalized and vulnerable populations from indiscriminate and oppressive forms of state violence, whether they occur under the rubric of war or counter-terrorism (Primoratz 2004b). That is, at the most basic level, employing the concept and identifying the criteria of 'state terrorism' can have the effect of delegitimizing any and all forms of violence that seek to instrumentalize human suffering for the purpose of sending a message to an audience. In the present context, where state counter-terrorism campaigns are causing mass suffering around the world (Wolfendale 2007), and where states are oppressing groups and individuals in the name of counter-terrorism, demonstrating that 'states can be terrorists too' could have a powerful normative effect of constraining state excesses and promoting genuine human security. In summary, following Robert Goodin, critical scholars would argue that the objections raised to the concept of state terrorism 'cannot change any logical or deontological facts of the matter. If what [states] do is otherwise indistinguishable from what is done by non-state actors that we would deem to be terroristic, then the acts of the state officials doing the same thing would be morally wrong for just the same reasons' (Goodin 2006: 56).

## Key Points

- State terrorism can be understood in the same way as non-state terrorism as a strategy of political violence which instrumentalizes victims in order to send a message to an audience for the purposes of influencing their behaviour.
- Objections to the term 'state terrorism', including the argument that terrorism is an inherently illegitimate form of non-state violence, can be shown to be illogical and inconsistent.
- In addition to analytical reasons, there are also compelling normative reasons for retaining the concept of state terrorism, most importantly because it could delegitimize certain forms of destructive state violence.

## An overview of state terrorism

The history of state terrorism begins with the French revolution when the term 'terror' was first coined to describe the counter-revolutionary violence of the new regime against its opponents (Perdue 1989; Thorup 2010: 88–101), although political rulers have employed exemplary forms of violence for thousands of years as a way of subduing and controlling subject populations. The use of state terror has been so frequent and extensive since then that any overview will necessarily be partial and incomplete. As such, and keeping in mind the issues raised in Chapter 7 about the dangers of categorization, it is helpful to consider the phenomenon under some broad periods and categories.

First, from a historical perspective, political elites used terrorism extensively as a means of forcibly incorporating different regions and peoples into a single polity during periods of state consolidation in Europe and elsewhere, as the French revolutionary period illustrates. Following this, and parallel to it, empires and states employed terrorism for the purposes of pacification across the world during the age of imperial expansion (Perdue 1989; Barker 2002: 61–4; Blakeley 2009; Thorup 2010: 115–18). In North and South America, Africa, Asia, Australasia and elsewhere, imperial powers used overwhelming forms of violence to subdue and control indigenous populations, clear land for settlers and incorporate indigenous people into extractive economies as slaves and labourers. In countless instances, the imperial powers slaughtered and burned entire towns and villages, hanged people in public places, amputated hands, whipped and imprisoned people, and visited numerous other atrocities on entire populations, most often as a means of exemplary and symbolic punishment designed to communicate the message to the rest of the subjected population that they should not oppose imperial rule. In the Belgian Congo, for example, King Leopold's officials amputated the hands of African workers as a method of maintaining productivity and preventing resistance in the rubber plantations. Similarly, in what is now modern day Iraq, British colonial officials bombed rebellious villages with poison gas, while in the Americas, European settlers used overwhelming violence against native peoples, including the deliberate spread of diseases like smallpox (Campbell 1998; Barker 2002: 61).

Another wave of state terrorism occurred in the early part of the twentieth century when the rise of fascism in Japan, Germany, Spain and Italy led to a number of notorious 'terror states' who used the full coercive power of the state to terrorize their own and other populations during expansionary wars across Asia, Africa and Europe (O'Kane 1996; Johnson 2000; McLoughlin and McDermott 2002). The use of terror by Japan in China and Korea, by the Italians in

Ethiopia, and by the Nazis across Europe is well known and documented. In all these cases, torture, extra-judicial killing, mass rape, imprisonment in concentration camps and a great many other forms of exemplary violence were used to terrify populations into submission and undermine resistance.

At the same time, and following this, the rise of communist totalitarian states in the Soviet Union, China, Cuba, North Korea, Vietnam, Cambodia and elsewhere also relied greatly on the use of terror as a means of regime consolidation and the enforcement of national programmes of economic and political reform. In China and the Soviet Union, for example, tens of millions of people were killed, tortured, exiled to Siberia, incarcerated in re-education camps and subjected to a great many other forms of violence in an effort to eliminate enemies, control opposition, reform economic systems, enforce compliance with state policies and change individual behaviour. In the Kampuchean 'killing fields', the Khmer Rouge murdered up to three million people during a campaign of social engineering and regime consolidation (Chandler 2000).

The use of terrorism as a method of state rule and consolidation was then adopted by a great many right-wing, populist and other postcolonial states. Among numerous examples, despots in Uganda, the Central African Republic, Ethiopia, Haiti, Indonesia, Turkey and Chile, as well as South Africa and Rhodesia's apartheid regimes, all employed state terror in an effort to destroy opposition and maintain power (Van Bruinessen 1996; Barker 2002). In Indonesia, the state killed 500,000 suspected communists in 1965 in an effort to destroy the communist party and discourage opposition, while Idi Amin killed over 200,000 Ugandans in an attempt to cling onto power. During the 1970s and 1980s, human rights organizations documented many thousands of cases of enforced disappearance, torture, extra-judicial murder, imprisonment and **politicide** across dozens of states in Africa, South America, Asia, the Middle East and Europe, the vast majority of which clearly fit the definition of state terrorism (see the annual reports by Amnesty International). In a great many of these cases, the regime was supported and assisted by either the USA or the Soviet Union as part of their broader rivalry in the still ongoing cold war. Table 8.1 summarizes some selected cases of **genocide**, politicide and state terror campaigns to illustrate the extent of the violence.

Over this entire period, Western liberal states also engaged in the extensive use of terrorism, sometimes to genocidal levels. Following the eras of imperialism and colonialism when Western powers like Britain, America, France, Spain, Portugal and the Netherlands used massive state terrorism in their colonies resulting in the deaths of millions of indigenous people, the period of decolonization again saw Western states use terror in an effort to combat nationalist movements and

Table 8.1    *Selected genocides, politicides and campaigns of state terrorism*

| Regime/conflict | Victims | Years | Estimated deaths |
|---|---|---|---|
| Turkey | Armenians | 1915–17 | 1,500,000 |
| USSR (Lenin) | Class enemies | 1917–22 | 750,000 |
| Nationalist China | Communists | 1927–49 | 3,500,000 |
| USSR (Stalin) | Class enemies | 1928–53 | 49,500,000 |
| Nazi Germany | Jews, Slavs | 1933–45 | 16,500,000 |
| Communist China | Class enemies | 1949–76 | 35,000,000 |
| North Korea | Class enemies | 1949–present | 2,000,000 |
| North Vietnam | Class enemies | 1954–75 | 1,000,000 |
| Pakistan | Bengalis | 1958–87 | 1,500,000 |
| China | Tibetans | 1959–present | 1,600,000 |
| Guatemala | Left-wing opponents | 1960–96 | 100,000 |
| Indonesia | Communists | 1965 | 500,000+ |
| Nigeria | Ibos | 1966–70 | 1,000,000 |
| Uganda | Regime opponents | 1971–79 | 500,000 |
| Ethiopia | Class enemies | 1974–79 | 750,000 |
| Cambodia (Khmer Rouge) | Class enemies | 1975–79 | 2,000,000 |
| Indonesia | Timorese | 1975–99 | 200,000 |
| El Salvador civil war | Left-wing opponents | 1977–92 | 100,000 |
| Sudan | Nuer, Nuba, Dinka | 1983–2007 | 1,900,000 |
| Burundi civil war | Tutsi, Hutu | 1988–present | 100,000+ |
| Rwanda | Tutsi, Hutu opponents | 1990–94 | 800,000+ |

*Source*: Adapted from Hough 2004.

resist popular pressures for independence. In Algeria for example, the French extensively employed torture and assassination as a method of intimidation against the nationalist movement, the Portuguese authorities employed brutal repression in the African colonies of Angola and Mozambique, and the USA waged a bloody counter-insurgency campaign in the Philippines. Similarly, during World War II, the Allies employed the strategy of 'terror bombing' against civilians in Japan and Germany, including the use of atomic attacks on Hiroshima and Nagasaki, in an effort to demoralize the civilian population (Garrett 2004; Grosscup 2006). Later, during the height of the cold war, Western states engaged directly in, and sponsored, many acts of terrorism in **pro-insurgency** and counter-insurgency campaigns in Latin America, Vietnam, Malaya and elsewhere (Chomsky 1979; Chomsky and Herman 1979; Herman 1982; Klare 1989; Klare and Kornbluh 1989; Perdue 1989; Barker 2002; McSherry 2002; Gareau 2004; Menjívar and Rodríguez 2005; Stokes 2005; Esparza *et al.* 2009). More specifically, in counter-terrorism campaigns in places like

Northern Ireland and the Basque region, British and Spanish state forces frequently engaged in the use of torture, **extra-judicial killings** and other 'dirty war' tactics (Boxes 8.2 and 8.3; see also the case studies in Sluka 2000).

A few important examples of contemporary state terrorism (see Jackson *et al.* 2010) include the widespread use of so-called 'extraordinary rendition' (a euphemism for kidnapping), torture, targeted killings, death squads, support for warlords and private militias, and widespread human rights abuses in the global war on terrorism (Foot 2005; S. Grey 2006; Blakeley 2009). In addition to well documented acts of state terrorism in Iraq, Afghanistan and other parts of the Middle East by Western states and their allies (see, among others, Gareau 2004), a number of other countries have used the excuse of fighting terrorism to engage in their own campaigns of state terrorism in countries like China, Russia, Uzbekistan, India, Pakistan, Saudi Arabia and Egypt. Other prominent examples of state-directed terror aimed at regime opponents or particular ethnic groups include ongoing violence in Chechnya, Kashmir, Darfur, Zimbabwe, Colombia, Tibet, Myanmar, Turkey and Indonesia. In fact, human rights organizations continue to report the

---

### Box 8.2  A case study in state terrorism: Operation Condor

Operation Condor was a highly secretive programme of state terrorism that emerged in the context of the cold war. Formally established in 1975, Condor presented a coordinated international response to the perceived threat of communists, dissidents and revolutionaries within Latin America and beyond; with Argentina, Brazil, Bolivia, Chile, Ecuador, Peru, Paraguay and Uruguay all key participants, supported by external allies including the USA. The initiative combined the cross-border sharing of intelligence information with 'counter-terrorist' techniques of repression, torture and targeted assassinations. Alongside the hundreds of individuals that were 'disappeared', the programme also involved the killing of high-profile political opponents to the right-wing regimes in power in many of these states. Prominent amongst these were the leader of the Chilean Christian Democrats, Bernardo Leighton, and Bolivia's former president, Juan José Torres. Condor's reach, however, extended far beyond the Latin American borders. As the FBI's attaché in Buenos Aires made clear in a cable that was sent in 1976, 'Operation Condor involves the formation of special teams from member countries who are to travel anywhere in the world to non-member countries to carry out sanctions up to assassination against terrorists or supporters of terrorist organisations from "Operation Condor" member countries' (Scherrer, cited in Blakeley 2007).

widespread use of torture, enforced disappearances, extra-judicial killings, incarcerations and other abuses by states around the world (see the links to human rights organizations at the end of the chapter).

A somewhat controversial case involves state terrorism by the Israeli state in its conflict with Palestinians and surrounding Arab states. Since the founding of the state of Israel in 1948, the Israeli government has used attacks on civilians, collective punishments, torture, targeted killings, kidnapping, the use of human shields during military operations, attacks on civilian infrastructure, the sponsorship of private militias and other forms of suppressive violence. These tactics have been employed to clear the way for Jewish settlements on Palestinian land, intimidate the Palestinian population and other Arab states, and prevent and control opposition to Israeli occupation and policies (Perdue 1989; Amnesty International 2002; Kapitan 2004; Araj 2008; Nasr 2009; Hamilton 2009). These actions are defended by Israel and its supporters, including the USA, as necessary and proportional responses to Palestinian terrorism (Pappe 2009), and therefore as acts of counter-terrorism, not state terrorism.

---

## Box 8.3  Death squads

*Definition*
'Death squads are clandestine and usually irregular organizations, often paramilitary in nature, which carry out extrajudicial executions and other violent acts (torture, rape, arson, bombing, etc.) against clearly defined individuals or groups of people. Murder is their primary or even sole activity ... Death squads operate with the overt support, complicity, or acquiescence of government, or at least some parts of it. In many cases, government security forces have participated directly in the killing.'
(Campbell 2000)

*Extent of death squad activity*
Death squad activity has been reported by human rights organizations in dozens of countries over several decades, and on every continent. Death squads have been responsible for the deaths of at least 200,000 to 300,000 people in the past few decades. Such activity reached its height during the cold war, often in right-wing states struggling to contain left-wing opposition, when tens of thousands were killed or disappeared every year, but also in communist states as a means of liquidating opponents.
(see Sluka 2000)

*Contemporary examples of death squad activity*
Death squads continue to operate today in Colombia, El Salvador, Chechnya, Sudan, the Republic of Congo, Iraq, Thailand, the Philippines, the Israeli occupied territories, Côte d'Ivoire, India and Sri Lanka.

## Key Points

- States and empires have employed terror as a form of governance for centuries, although the term 'terrorism' was first used to describe state counter-revolutionary violence during the French Revolution.
- Waves of state terrorism accompanied imperialism and the colonial era, the rise of fascism and communism in the twentieth century, the struggle for decolonization and the cold war conflict.
- There are numerous examples of contemporary state terrorism today, a number of which are taking place under the rubric of the war on terrorism.
- Western states, including Israel, have under certain circumstances arguably engaged in the use of state terrorism.

## State terrorism: aims, methods and types

Like non-state terrorism, state terrorism is practised by a wide variety of actors, in the context of both war and peace, employing many kinds of methods, and for a great many different reasons. In this section, and keeping in mind the limits and dangers of imposing categories, we will briefly discuss the main actors, types, modes, tactics, motives, aims, causes and outcomes of state terrorism (see Jackson 2009d).

### State terrorism: actors

As explained above, terrorism has been employed by many different kinds of states, which suggests that the motive or capability to use terror is not limited by any essential characteristic related to state size or political system (Stohl 2005). From the world's only remaining superpower to small and impoverished states like the Central African Republic, and from military dictatorships such as Pakistan to liberal democracies such as Britain and Australia, terrorism has been, and continues to be, employed by almost every kind of state (see the variety of cases examined in Jackson *et al.* 2009c). This confirms our conception of terrorism as a violent political *strategy* which can be employed by any actor, whether individuals, groups, weak states, strong states, authoritarian states, liberal states and, theoretically at least, international organizations. Importantly, this means that, as with non-state terrorism, every case of state terrorism occurs in a unique context of power capabilities, political interests, culture, history and institutional and agential configurations. In turn, this highlights the limitations of applying broad generalizations about the nature and causes of state terrorism and the necessity of retaining a strong sense of context.

Interestingly, it contradicts the popular truism that terrorism is primarily a 'weapon of the weak'; historically and on aggregate, powerful actors like states have employed terrorism far more extensively than weak actors like terrorist groups.

The human agents of state terrorism include, first, individuals and groups acting in their official capacity as representatives of the state, such as military and security personnel, the police, the intelligence services, prison officers and other state employees. In other cases, state terrorism is carried out by state employees acting in an unofficial (but tacitly approved) capacity, such as off-duty police or military personnel. Lastly, the agents of state terrorism frequently involve a variety of private non-state groups and individuals acting on behalf of the state or with the state's approval (or actors within the state apparatus), whether tacit or explicit. At the formal end of the scale, this can include private security actors subcontracted by the state, such as private military companies (PMCs) and private security companies (PSCs). More frequently, it includes private militias, death squads (Box 8.3; see also Campbell and Brenner 2000; Sluka 2000), vigilantes, lone assassins, para-military organizations, gangs, mobs, non-state terrorist groups and other informal actors.

## State terrorism: types, modes, tactics

State terrorism comes in a variety of forms and can be divided into various categories according to factors such as its intended victims or its primary methods – although, within a critical framework, it is important to reiterate that these categories are time- and place-specific and only make sense within a particular set of conceptual and material power structures. Two broad initial types are, first, limited state terrorism, such as one-off operations designed for a specific outcome, and, second, more generalized, governance-based or 'wholesale' state terrorism where a state seeks to intimidate an entire society, large sectors of society or another state over an extended period of time (Chomsky 1991; Blakeley 2009).

Limited state terrorism involves exactly the same actions as those perpetrated by non-state terrorist groups, such as civilian-directed bombings, assassinations and kidnappings, or direct involvement in or sponsorship of acts of non-state terrorism. Some examples of this form of state terrorism include: the so-called Lavon affair when Israeli agents planted bombs in Cairo; the black-flag operations by the Italian government in the 1980s designed to discredit the leftist movement (Ganser 2005); the Lockerbie bombing by Libyan agents; the Korean Airline bombing by North Korean agents in 1987; the US sponsorship of anti-Castro terrorist attacks; the mining of Nicaraguan ports by US agents; and the bombing of the *Rainbow Warrior* in Auckland harbour by French agents. In some instances, limited state terrorism involves acts of **coercive diplomacy**, such as threatened or actual military actions against another state, in order to achieve particular policy outcomes, such as the USA's actions in the Mayaguez operation against Cambodia in 1975 (Stohl 1988: 174–5). Coercive diplomacy can also take place during war, such as the atomic attacks on Japan and the saturation bombing of German residential areas during World War II (Grosscup 2006), the Christmas bombing of Hanoi in 1972 and Israel's attack on Lebanon in 2006 (Hamilton 2009).

Wholesale state terrorism, on the other hand, involves a range of state actions and actors beyond those seen in non-state terrorism that function collectively to coerce and intimidate a large population (Duvall and Stohl 1988; Chomsky 1991). As noted above, wholesale state terrorism is employed by many states and involves an imaginative array of specific tactics, including: extra-judicial killing and political assassination; kidnapping, **extraordinary rendition, enforced disappearances** and detention; **pogroms** and mass killings; torture and prisoner abuse; mass rape and sexual violence; indiscriminate attacks on civilian populations during war or counter-insurgency; using civilians as human shields during military operations; harsh and politicized forms of counter-terrorism; the deliberate and exemplary destruction of people's livelihoods during counter-insurgency operations; collective punishments and revenge attacks; and the construction of punitive and brutal forms of incarceration. As noted, these actions may be undertaken directly by state agents or indirectly through proxy actors. In practice, they typically involve a mix of state and non-state groups acting in concert, such as the coordinated use of private militia and Sudanese military forces to attack civilians in Darfur (Mickler 2009).

In addition to limited and wholesale categories, state terrorism can also be divided into direct and indirect, domestic and international, and overt and covert forms (Martin 2003; Stohl 2005). Direct state terrorism involves the use of violence by officials of the state, while indirect state terrorism employs proxies, such as death squads, private individuals, other states or non-state terrorist groups, to commit the violence. Another form of indirect state terrorism occurs when a state or states provide support, assistance or a role model to other states who are then more able and willing to employ their own forms of state terrorism. This has been described as **surrogate state terrorism** (Stohl 2005). Domestic state terrorism is employed within the territory of a state against internal opponents, while international state terrorism involves actions outside of the state's borders against either state or non-state opponents. Overt state terrorism is intended to convey a clear message about the perpetrator of the violence and includes the use of coercive diplomacy, terror bombing or the widespread and official use of torture. Covert state terrorism occurs when a regime wishes to conceal its use of terror from a particular audience (such as international human rights monitors or an allied Western state), in which case the use of secret state-directed death squads or other proxy groups might be employed.

A final commonly discussed type of indirect state terrorism involves the sponsorship of terrorist groups who then act as a proxy. **State-sponsored terrorism** comes in a variety of forms, from joint operations, military training, financing, equipping and directing of terrorist groups, to indirect forms of political, ideological or diplomatic support, to passive support when the state turns a blind eye to the group's activities (Martin 2003; Byman 2005). The US State Department publishes annual reports on state-sponsored terrorism, although it does not recognize cases of its own sponsorship of non-state terrorist groups. Examples of state sponsorship include, among others: US sponsorship of the Nicaraguan Contras and Cuban anti-Castro groups, Iranian and Syrian sponsorship of various Palestinian groups, Israeli sponsorship of Christian militias during Lebanon's civil war, British sponsorship of Loyalist paramilitaries in Northern Ireland, and Sudanese sponsorship of the Lord's Resistance Army (LRA).

In the end, as we argued in relation to types and categories of non-state terrorism (Chapter 7), any attempt to define types of political violence must avoid over-generalization and essentialism. As with non-state terrorism, every act of state terrorism occurs in its own unique context and there is little value in treating all acts of state violence, or all states, as essentially the same.

## State terrorism: motives, aims, causes

Like non-state actors, states may choose to employ terrorism for broadly conservative or revolutionary ends. More often, their specific aims and goals include: isolating, demoralizing, and terrorizing individuals and groups who voice opposition under colonialism, dictatorship, military occupation or post-revolutionary rule; rendering social movements impotent; attempting to gain psychological advantage over an adversary in counter-insurgency, counter-terrorism, war or interstate rivalry; securing access to resources; maintaining economic privilege or the enforcement of labour flows; punishment, revenge and the restoration of national pride; population expulsion and ethnic cleansing; and the intimidation or deterrence of foreign adversaries.

The key point is that state terrorism has a rational basis – it is purposive and directed towards particular ends – and is sometimes a highly successful policy, at least in the short and medium term, for the elites who enact it (Terry 1980: 99). In Latin America, for example, state terrorism by regimes in El Salvador, Chile, Guatemala, Paraguay and Argentina during the cold war successfully undermined the emergence of a great many progressive and reform-oriented social movements which might have threatened elite rule (Raphael 2009; Blakeley 2009). Similarly, US state-sponsorship of the Contras succeeded in undermining and eventually overturning the Nicaraguan regime, while Western sponsorship of the mujahideen in Afghanistan contributed to a humiliating defeat for the Soviet Union and its eventual collapse.

Duvall and Stohl (1988: 253–62) have outlined an 'expected utility' model which suggests that states employ terrorism under two broad conditions: (1) when they calculate that it will achieve their goals more effectively than other policies (it has lower production costs than the alternatives); and (2) when they anticipate that the response costs of using terrorism will be lower than the costs of other strategies. Other contributory factors include: the presence of violent cultural values in a given context; the ease with which victims of state repression can be dehumanized; and the degree to which violence becomes part of bureaucratic routine (Stohl 1986: 207–34). Similarly, Ted Gurr suggests that the decision to use terrorism by a ruling elite is the result of specific calculations based on: (1) situational conditions relating to the nature of the group threatening the state and the state's resources for countering the threat; (2) structural conditions relating to the position of the elite and the state in relation to other social actors and the wider international system; and (3) dispositional variables – factors which affect the orientation of the elite, such as norms of violence or learning experiences (Gurr 1986: 62–7; see also Stohl 2005: 205). As is clear from this chapter, there are many different contexts in which states have made, and continue to make, exactly these calculations in deciding to employ terrorism in pursuit of specific political or political-economic goals.

Importantly, states will often calculate the potential costs of employing terrorism in relation to the external support they receive from other (usually powerful) states or, alternatively, their ability to compensate for any external anticipated or unanticipated costs (Lasslett 2009). In other words, state terrorism is frequently enabled, at least in part, by the military, economic and diplomatic support, tacit approval or even simply the calculated indifference they receive from influential, international actors. This has been described as surrogate state terrorism by great powers (Stohl 1988: 192). Such surrogate state terrorism has, in contemporary times, been practised in particular by Western states bolstering client states in the global south, and must be seen against the political and economic interests the former (believe they) have in maintaining their power and ability to extract valuable resources (Blakeley 2009). Alternately, the use of state terrorism can be enabled by the fact that powerful states can absorb or deflect any externally imposed costs of employing terrorism. The international context therefore – the presence of external patrons or the ability to compensate – is an important determinant (enabling cause) of state terrorism.

At the same time, an important internal condition for the decision to employ state terrorism are those situations in which the state or its ruling elite perceive that they are facing a potentially serious challenge to their authority or continued rule. This occurs more often in fragile and institutionally weak states – states that are still trying to consolidate their monopoly on the instruments of violence and their institutional reach, often following periods of revolutionary change or decolonization (Duvall and Stohl 1988: 241–3). However, it can also occur in strong, established states when political leaders perceive that an opposition movement which employs terrorist tactics, for example, poses a serious threat to the stability of the nation. In both cases, the use of exemplary or symbolic violence against opponents appears as a readily available, psychologically satisfying and efficient response, certainly in comparison to the much more difficult and uncertain options of political dialogue or social reform. In this sense, state terrorism is in part a reflexive strategy rooted in the accepted doctrines and practices of sovereignty, particularly the notion that the state should have a monopoly on the means of violence and the legitimate right to employ both punitive and defensive violence. In fact, it is only recently that states have begun to accept limits on the forms and types of violence they may employ, and there is still controversy over whether the state can legitimately use 'any means necessary' (including, massive and indiscriminate terror) if it faces a 'supreme emergency' or a direct threat to the continuation of its sovereignty.

## State terrorism: consequences

One of the most commonly noted aspects of state terrorism relates to its consequences and effects on individuals and communities. There is a wealth of information from human rights organizations, lawyers, criminologists, psychologists, truth commissions and scholars from different disciplines which document the physical, psychological, cultural and political harm resulting from state terrorism (Suarez-Orozco 1987; Corradi *et al.* 1992; Hayner 2002; Kornbluh 2003; Gareau 2004; Menjívar and Rodríguez 2005; Agger and Jensen 2006; Wright 2006; Esparza *et al.* 2009; see also annual reports from Human Rights Watch and Amnesty International, and the United States Institute of Peace (USIP) Truth Commission Reports). No one can doubt that state terrorism is immensely destructive to individuals, communities and entire societies, and has a myriad of negative consequences for democratic participation, institutional legitimacy, human rights, human and social well-being, law and order, security, the rule of law, social trust, community cohesion, social capital, the positive functioning of civil society, intercommunal relations, and a number of other aspects of political, social and cultural life (Stokes 2005; Jackson *et al.* 2009c). On the other

---

**Key Points**

- State terrorism is not limited to any particular kind of state, and a great variety of official and unofficial actors are often involved in its perpetration.
- State terrorism can occur in limited forms, as a comprehensive strategy and through the direct or indirect sponsorship of non-state groups.
- State terrorism occurs when elites calculate that its potential benefits will outweigh its costs and when they receive support from external actors. Their political motives can be conservative or revolutionary.
- State terrorism can have devastating consequences for individuals, groups, communities and whole societies. It frequently results in the deaths of thousands or, more rarely, hundreds of thousands of people.

---

hand, relatively undocumented to date are the effects of state terrorism on diplomacy, law, norms, institutions and the wider processes of international politics, especially when it is perpetrated by the major powers who function as opinion leaders and norm setters (Stohl 1988: 158).

In the end, it is precisely because the destruction of state terrorism vastly outweighs that caused by non-state terrorist groups, and because some forms of state terrorism occur in the context of counter-terrorism campaigns (Stokes 2006) and can be responsible for triggering acts of non-state terrorism (Gurr and Goldstone 1986; Araj 2008), that critical scholars argue that the study of terroristic and other forms of state violence should have a central place in any study of terrorism.

## Conclusion

A central aim of critical approaches to terrorism involves rebalancing the wider field to give equal attention to the far more widespread and destructive forms of terrorism perpetrated by states. There are both analytical and normative reasons for taking this stance. Analytically, terrorism occurs in its original and purest form as exemplary state violence, and, not infrequently, it is inextricably linked to reactive campaigns of non-state terrorism (Araj 2008); there is, therefore, much to be gained by its systematic study. Normatively, the study of state terrorism can contribute to efforts aimed at holding states that employ such forms of violence to account. It also works to deconstruct the dangerous idea that liberal states are exceptional and essentially benign in their relations with other regions (especially the global south) or that Western states are primarily the victims of terrorism and never its perpetrators, whether directly or indirectly (Blakeley 2009).

At present, research on state terrorism is hampered somewhat by the lack of theoretically oriented analyses of the processes, causes, outcomes and termination of state terrorism. It is also hampered by the problem of selective coverage; for example, while wholesale state terrorism and so-called state sponsorship of terrorism has received relatively solid coverage, the practices of coercive diplomacy or the use of terrorism during war has been largely ignored – with only a small number of notable exceptions (see, for example, Stohl 1988; Grosscup 2006). Similarly, while state sponsorship of terrorist groups by Middle Eastern countries has been extensively documented, state sponsorship of right-wing groups by Western countries and their allies has been far less frequent. In short, as we argued in Chapter 2 in relation to non-state terrorism, there is a real need to *broaden* the study of state terrorism to new topics and cases, to *deepen* the study of state terrorism to develop more rigorous theories, and to make *emancipatory praxis* the normative heart of the research enterprise.

More specifically, there are a number of topics which are in need of further detailed and systematic study, including: the silences and gaps within the terrorism studies field on state terrorism; theoretical and conceptual aspects of state terrorism; the research practices and ethics for research on state terrorism; the causes of state terrorism – the reasons why elites choose to employ it at particular moments and the specific contexts within which it occurs; the many cases of state terrorism being enacted within the broader practices of the global war on terror; and how state terrorism ends.

## Discussion Questions

1. How should state terrorism be conceptualized or described? What are its core characteristics?
2. Why has the study of state terrorism been neglected in the broader terrorism studies field, despite its greater extent and destruction?
3. What are the primary objections to the concept of state terrorism, and how valid are they?
4. What are the main forms, actors, strategies and outcomes of state terrorism?
5. Explain how and when torture, disappearances and extraordinary rendition can sometimes fit the descriptive characteristics of state terrorism.
6. How might coercive diplomacy fit the description of state terrorism?
7. Can state terrorism occur during war, and what forms might it take?
8. What are the main causes of, or reasons for, state terrorism?
9. Why do Western states engage in state terrorism?
10. What positive normative effects might the greater study of state terrorism have?

## Recommended Reading

Blakeley, R., 2009. *State Terrorism and Neoliberalism: The North in the South*, Abingdon: Routledge. An important theoretical and empirical study of the concept of state terrorism and its use by powerful Western states as a strategy of hegemony in the global south.

Chomsky, N., 2002. *Pirates and Emperors, Old and New: International Terrorism in the Real World*, London: Pluto. A provocative collection of Chomsky's essays on state terrorism.

George, A., ed., 1991a. *Western State Terrorism*, Cambridge: Polity Press. The classic volume on Western state terrorism during the cold war and the role of terrorism scholars in its legitimation.

Grosscup, B., 2006. *Strategic Terror: The Politics and Ethics of Aerial Bombardment*, London: Zed Books. A fascinating study of aerial strategic bombing as a tactic of state terrorism employed during colonialism, in war and as part of humanitarian intervention.

Jackson, R., Murphy, E. and Poynting, S., eds, 2009. *Contemporary State Terrorism: Theory and Cases*, Abingdon: Routledge. A collection of theoretical chapters and contemporary cases which attempts to defend the concept and study of state terrorism and to suggest a future research agenda.

Sluka, J., ed., 1999. *Death Squad: The Anthropology of State Terror*, Philadelphia, PA: University of Pennsylvania Press. A volume of case studies on state terrorism, particularly in the use of death squads.

Stohl, M., ed., 1988. *The Politics of Terrorism*, 3rd edn, New York: Marce Dekker.

Stohl, M. and Lopez, G., eds, 1984. *The State as Terrorist: The Dynamics of Governmental Violence and Repression*, Westport, CT: Greenwood Press.

Stohl, M. and Lopez, G., eds, 1986. *Government Violence and Repression: An Agenda for Research*, Westport, CT: Greenwood Press. The foundational studies from Stohl and Lopez that continue to be a key source for understanding state terrorism today.

## Web Resources

The Political Terror Scale: *www.politicalterrorscale.org/*
This 'measures levels of political violence and terror that a country experiences in a particular year based on a 5-level "terror scale"', and covers the period 1976–2007.

The Project on Extrajudicial Executions: *www.extrajudicialexecutions.org/*
Provides research and fact-finding on state killings which supports the United Nations Special Rapporteur on extrajudicial executions.

Amnesty International: *www.amnesty.org/*
An important source for regular factual reports on state violence, repression and human rights abuses, including acts of state terrorism.

Human Rights Watch: *www.hrw.org/*
Another important source for regular factual reports on state violence, repression and human rights abuses, including acts of state terrorism.

The United States Institute of Peace Truth Commissions Digital Collection: *www.usip.org/resources/truth-commissions-digital-collection*
Contains documents from over 35 truth commissions and related commissions of inquiry. The documents contain numerous details on state violence and repression, including acts of state terrorism.

Chapter 9

# The Causes of Non-State Terrorism

## Chapter Contents

- Introduction
- Thinking critically about causation
- Some prevalent myths
- Macro-level explanations
- From macro- to meso- and micro-explanations
- Explaining and understanding suicide bombing
- Conclusion

## Reader's Guide

The question of what causes terrorism is one of the most important and hotly debated topics in terrorism studies. This chapter introduces the reader to the main issues and questions surrounding this topic, exploring how we might think critically about causation. We begin by exploring the different ways in which causation has been approached in the traditional terrorism studies and IR literatures, before outlining the key concerns raised by critical scholars. This is followed by a discussion of some of the prevalent myths about the causes of terrorism, such as that it is caused by poverty, psychopathy and religion. Next, we look briefly at some of the macro-level factors, or 'root causes', discussed in the literature, before concluding that a macro-approach cannot adequately explain why, how and where violence occurs. We then discuss an alternative approach rooted in social movement theory which looks at the interplay between macro-, meso- and micro-dynamics. In the final section, we put this approach to the test by applying it to a short study of the tactic of suicide bombing.

## Introduction

Why do some people turn to terrorism? Why do more people not turn to terrorism, given that many of its apparent causes such as religion and poverty exist in places where no terrorism occurs? Is there a 'terrorist profile'? How do theories about the causes of terrorism inform counter-terrorism policies? Is it helpful to talk about cause and effect, given the complexity of human behaviour? Or is the search for identifiable – and thus manipulable – causal perspectives part of the problem? Numerous causes have been suggested for terrorism, ranging from mental illness and religious indoctrination to poverty, state repression, grievance and political exclusion. In this chapter we will be exploring explanations such as these and what they tell us about all of the above questions.

Critical approaches to terrorism do not have a unified stance on the causes of terrorism. While some critical scholars are sceptical of the entire notion of causation, regarding it as too embedded in positivist, problem-solving perspectives, others accept it but are wary of mono-causal explanations. What they all share is a sceptical approach to accepted explanations and an acute awareness of the way causal explanations can be used to depoliticize terrorists and to legitimate specific counter-terrorism policies. If, for instance, terrorists can be shown to be mentally ill or motivated solely by greed or 'religion', there is no need to take their political demands seriously. This, in turn, can legitimize coercive counter-terrorist responses and militate against the use of non-violent alternatives.

## Thinking critically about causation

In the past, it was somewhat controversial to try and understand the political causes of terrorism, because 'to many people, any focus on underlying causes, motivating factors, and grievances, implies a kind of justification' (Lia and Skjolberg 2005: 7). Instead, it was commonly argued that terrorism was a product of psychological illness or brainwashing, rather than political dynamics. This served a very political purpose: ignoring the possibility that violence might have been caused by systemic problems, such as political exclusion or discrimination, meant depoliticizing those engaged in it, thus preventing any reflection on how the status quo might have contributed to the problem. Terrorism research has changed drastically since those early days, and efforts to understand the causes of terrorism are now one of the mainstays of the field. But the temptation to downplay the political causes of this type of violence and to absolve the status quo from any responsibility is still with us.

Of course, understanding a phenomenon necessitates neither exonera-tion nor justification, and a rich body of research has emerged on the causes of terrorist violence. Here, we outline some of the main approaches to causal analysis in the literature and discuss some key issues and questions about the nature of causality in terrorism research.

## Different ways of approaching causation

Causes, or those factors that can be said to produce an effect or event (in this case, 'terrorism'), have been broadly divided into two types: permis-sive or background conditions that make political violence more likely, and proximate or immediate causes that trigger particular acts of vio-lence (Crenshaw 1981). Without a set of enabling, background condi-tions, a crisis or trigger event is less likely to lead to a sustained campaign of terrorist violence than if such enabling conditions are present. Similarly, without a trigger event or catalyst, a set of enabling back-ground conditions is less likely to evolve into sustained political violence.

Broadly, research on the causes of terrorism has tended to focus on three distinct levels of explanation: the macro- or systemic level, the micro- or individual level, and the meso- or organizational level (McLean Hilker *et al.* 2009; see also Figure 9.1). Macro-explanations seek a causal link between violence and structural factors like the type of political system or levels of socio-economic or ethnic inequality – what are often referred to as 'root causes'. Such explanations are premised on a particular understanding of individuals, usually a mixture of the **frustration-aggression thesis** made popular by Ted Gurr's (1970) 'relative deprivation model' and **rational choice** models (Crenshaw 1981). Micro-level analyses focus on individuals and their beliefs systems, psychological states and personality characteristics. The notion that 'terrorists' are psychopaths or driven by psychological deviances has now largely been debunked by psychologists, and most micro-explanations today focus on factors such as individual motiva-tions and beliefs, the effects of misperception and miscalculation, and small group dynamics (Silke 1998; Horgan 2003). Meso-explanations focus on groups and organizational dynamics. Focusing on this level can obscure the impact of other factors, such as state repression or non-ideological individual motivations such as a need for acceptance or protection from rival groups. But the more comprehensive type of meso-explanation can help to explain how similar macro-dynamics give rise to very different types of political violence.

Another division in the literature is between those who emphasize the role of grievances in the decision to turn to violence and those who focus on opportunity structures, arguing that while grievances are everywhere, violence is not. This suggests that opportunity is indeed a key factor. However, to ignore grievances and their formulation is

**Figure 9.1** *The causes of terrorism: macro-, meso- and micro-levels of analysis*

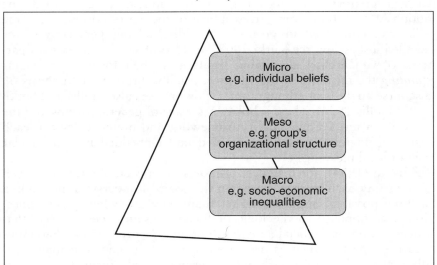

equally wrong-headed, as the existence of opportunities does not necessarily explain what type of violence is adopted by whom and against whom, while the interpretation of opportunities is as significant as the 'reality' of those opportunities (Kurzman 1996).

Lastly, in thinking about the nature of causality, it is crucial to keep in mind the agency–structure distinction (Wendt 1987). Simply put, structural explanations approach political violence as the outcome of the conditions or contexts in which it occurs. This suggests that structures – social, political, economic, including cultural conditions – shape and limit the choices that human agents make, thereby predetermining their behaviour. Agential approaches, in contrast, argue that such accounts are over-deterministic, and that human beings can act autonomously. They argue that humans are not simply cogs in a machine, but active agents capable of rational decisions, but also affected by emotions, false consciousness, cultural values and the like. Agency-based approaches examine the attitudes and behaviour of both elites and their followers and suggest that, because political violence is a human activity, it is within humans that its origins lie. The critical approach we take in this book looks at both structural and agency-based explanations, situating agents within their structural contexts while recognizing that these contexts are, in part, shaped by the actions of those agents (in the context of explaining war, see Suganami 2002: 321).

## Critical approaches to causation

Critical terrorism scholars do not have a unified stance towards the notion of causation. Some are sceptical of the entire notion, regarding it as too embedded in positivist, problem-solving perspectives (for detailed discussion, see Kurki 2008). Instead of seeking to *explain* patterns of violence by identifying regularities, their focus is on *understanding* the meaning of the violence, usually through an emphasis on discourse analysis or ethnographic fieldwork (see also Hollis and Smith 1991; Hollis 1994). These scholars are wary of generalizations and the quest for a unified explanatory framework and prefer to look at each instance of violence as self-contained and embedded in a particular web of local meanings.

Zulaika (1984), for instance, proposes an epistemological approach to the study of 'terrorism' based on this logic of understanding (rooted in 'how possible' questions rather than 'why' or 'what causes' questions), as opposed to the logic of linear causality. He suggests that when we approach social activities that involve ritualized and communicative aspects – such as organized forms of violence – it may actually make little sense to ask 'why' questions at all. Instead, it is more useful to seek to understand the historical roots, political antecedents, ritual dimensions, social functions and 'deep **cultural grammar**' (Johnston 2008) expressed by these forms of social activity – to provide a theoretically and empirically 'thick description' of the phenomenon under study (see also, Jabri 1996; Brass 1997; Ellis 2001; Kaufman 2001).

To understand violence as a social activity beyond its rational-strategic dimensions, Zulaika argues, we need to learn to 'read' the cultural language that it simultaneously expresses and constructs – to understand the actors' own subjectivity. This means, first, refusing to divorce acts of 'terrorism' from their wider context of historical movements and struggles; second, recognizing that social movements and groups evolve in a dynamic, iterative process of interaction with their surrounding state and society; and third, that one has to be extremely careful about generalizing across cultural contexts. In other words, before attempting to compare 'terrorisms' across cases, we need to understand it fully according to its own cultural grammar – and not simply the cultural grammar of the (usually) Western scholar.

Scholars from a Critical Theory background tend to be more accepting of the notion of causation and acknowledge there exist human regularities on which tentative causal generalizations may be made. But they reject the positivists' desire to turn these tentative generalizations into 'objective' laws and insist on taking both local meaning and their own (scholarly) subjectivity into account (Kurki 2008; Toros and Gunning 2009).

However, all critical scholars share an acute awareness of the way causal explanations can be used to depoliticize terrorists and legitimate specific counter-terrorism policies – an effect of the relationship between knowledge and power. A critical approach thus involves a call to greater reflexivity concerning the interests that scholarly causal explanations serve and the way they inform policy. In particular, it challenges the problem-solving approach to causality which uses causal explanations to construct counter-terrorism policies without adequate consideration of the possibility that terrorism is in part 'caused' by the institutions and injustices of the status quo and thus not separate but profoundly intertwined with it. A poignant example of this is the way counter-terrorism agencies use social network analysis to neutralize militant organizations without addressing underlying 'root causes' and in the process decapitating the political leadership of an entire section of the population (Mac Ginty 2010).

## Quantitative explanations and terrorism databases

If one rejects the idea that there is an objective, ontologically stable form of violence called 'terrorism', which exists independently of one's normative framework and its local context, then the notion of drawing causal conclusions from a set of quantitative empirical data becomes highly dubious. Yet, this is precisely what much of the macro-level literature seeks to do: it tries to find causal links by uncovering statistical correlations between instances of violence and structural factors. There are four main problems with such an approach.

First – and this is a critique many traditional scholars share – establishing a statistical *correlation* between violence and a particular factor (meaning that, statistically, they are likely to occur together) does not necessarily provide evidence of a *causal* link. Religiously inspired actors may be statistically more violent than their secular counterparts, but that in itself does not prove that religion is the cause of this violence. In short, critical scholars are critical of both the practice of boiling a complex situation down to a small set of measurable, independent, causal factors and of the practice of drawing causal conclusions from observed regularities.

Second, because the very notion of 'terrorism' is politically and conceptually contested so too are most of the databases commonly used by quantitative scholars. Databases tend to include all acts of violence perpetrated by groups labelled 'terrorist'. However, not all the acts perpetrated by a group labelled 'terrorist' are the same, let alone 'terrorist' acts. Attacks on Israeli soldiers by Hamas inside the Gaza Strip, for example, differ markedly from sending a suicide bomber into a pizzeria inside Israel. The first act falls more squarely within the paradigm of guerrilla activity, while the second is a classical example of what is usually understood as 'terrorism'. Yet both acts would normally be recorded in a database as 'terrorism', with potentially serious implications for any subsequent causal conclusions that are drawn.

Third, because entry into a database is determined by an action's nature, rather than its context, statistical databases tend to decontextualize the violence they record – again, with potentially serious implications for causal analysis. Hizbullah's 1983 attacks on the US embassy in Beirut, for instance, took place in the middle of a vicious civil war – in which the USA was seen as having taken sides – and in the wake of a bloody invasion by Israel which had devastated the South of Lebanon, one of Hizbullah's heartlands. Hizbullah's violence cannot be properly understood outside this context – yet this is precisely what databases do by grouping extremely diverse sets of incidents together. Similarly, when scholars argue that 'Islamic terrorists' are more violent than 'secular terrorists', they typically do so by comparing conflicts such as those between the Red Brigades and the Italian state with conflicts such as those between the Armed Islamic Group and the Algerian military. The latter operated for long periods of time in the midst of a full-blown war within a severely weakened state, whereas the former 'secular' group operated in peace time in a relatively stable state with considerably enhanced opportunities for political participation. Critical scholars would question whether one can meaningfully compare these situations without meticulously situating them in their very different contexts.

---

### Key Points

- The causes of terrorism have been approached in numerous ways, including: background versus trigger conditions, macro-, micro- and meso-level explanations, top-down versus bottom-up explanations, grievance- versus opportunity-focused explanations, demand-side versus supply-side explanations, monocausal versus multicausal explanations, and structural versus agential explanations.
- Critical scholars are sceptical of monocausal explanations, value multicausal explanations, and are wary of linear positivist causal reasoning. Instead, they prioritize 'thick description', understanding over explanation, historical and cultural context, subjectivity, and the dynamic interaction between actors, factors and meanings.
- Critical scholars are acutely aware of the uses to which causal explanations can be put in the construction of counter-terrorism policies.
- Critical scholars caution against quantitative databases on the grounds that the inclusion or exclusion of data is profoundly political, data is often decontextualized and observed correlations are too readily interpreted as causal relationships.

A final related problem with quantitative analysis is that it tends to use country-wide statistics – a legacy of its origins in the state-centric traditions of strategic studies. Yet, violence tends to be highly contextual, influenced not just by national factors but also by local or transnational factors. This becomes particularly problematic in countries with high levels of internal differentiation. Much of the 'terrorist' violence that took place in Egypt, for instance, occurred in Upper Egypt, which is both poorer than Lower Egypt and characterized by different types of local political structures (McLean Hilker *et al.* 2009). The use of country-wide data wholly misses these internal differences. Similarly, if violence is influenced by transnational factors, such as the presence of actively organized diasporas, country-wide statistics fail to capture these dynamics.

## Some prevalent myths

If part of the remit of critical approaches is to interrogate accepted knowledge claims, a good place to start is to identify some prevalent myths about what is popularly proclaimed to cause terrorism. Three myths are particularly dominant, in part because they are persistently repeated by the media, political leaders and some academics. Critical scholars are not alone in questioning these myths; indeed, much of the research they draw on has been carried out by critically minded traditional scholars. The first myth – that poverty causes terrorism – has become particularly popular since the attacks of 9/11. In 2002, US President George W. Bush told a UN development summit that 'poverty and hopelessness, lack of education and failed government ... often allow conditions that terrorists can seize' (*The Independent*, 23 March 2002).

The causal link between poverty and terrorism is far from clear. If anything, quantitative research suggests that people living in poverty are less likely to turn to terrorism and poorer countries are less likely to experience terrorism. Numerous studies have found that those involved in terrorism are more often well-educated and middle class than poorly educated and poor. Studies of the Italian Red Brigades, the Baader–Meinhof group, Hamas, Hizbullah and militant Israeli settlers all suggest that those responsible for violence are usually better off than their compatriots (Weinberg and Davis 1989; Krueger and Malec̆ková 2003). Popular support for terrorist tactics in the latter three cases was also found to be particularly high among the better off and more highly educated (Krueger 2007; Gunning 2007b). This, in itself, is not surprising since political activism in general tends to attract members of the educated middle classes.

However, dynamics are different where larger movements are concerned, particularly if they are engaged in a civil or guerrilla war. In this context, a group's 'foot soldiers' are often recruited from the poorer sections of society. Lack of job opportunities in particular can be a motivation for young men to join up, as can the status derived from group membership. The PIRA in Northern Ireland and the LTTE in Sri Lanka, for example, both had relatively high percentages of 'foot soldiers' from poorer backgrounds (Heiberg *et al.* 2007). But in these conflicts we are moving away from 'terrorist' tactics to situations where a plethora of tactics is used, many falling within the guerrilla warfare category.

Leaving aside the fact that activists are more likely to come from middle-class, well-educated backgrounds, one could argue that poverty provides a background condition which either motivates terrorists or which they can exploit. The argument here is not that those carrying out the violence are poor, but that they are motivated to turn to violence on behalf of their poorer brethren. However, this argument is also unsupported in the research. Quantitative studies have found no statistically relevant link between a country's poverty level and levels of terrorism (Piazza 2006; Krueger 2007), although there is some evidence to suggest that when economic inequality overlaps with ethnic divisions, there is an increased possibility of activists turning to violence (Stewart 2008). In short, levels of poverty alone cannot explain why terrorism occurs, which is not to say that poverty should not be tackled in its own right. Poverty, as Yunus (2006) points out, 'is the absence of all human rights', and according to World Bank figures, 1.4 billion people, almost a quarter of the world's population, lives below the so-called poverty line – less than US$1.25 a day (Shah 2010). Yet, these statistics in themselves further support the argument that poverty in itself is not a primary cause of terrorism: if the majority of the world's population lives in poverty, why is there so little terrorism?

There are of course political reasons for politicians' efforts to reiterate a link between poverty and terrorism. Yemen, for instance, has benefited greatly from an increase in development aid as a direct result of the war on terrorism. Since the country has become a region of concern over the presence of al-Qaeda supporters, development aid has grown exponentially, driven in part by the notion that development can help stem terrorism (DFID 2010). This notion is not just about the presumed link between poverty and terrorism. The UK's Department for International Development, for example, is very clear that poverty per se does not cause terrorism (DFID 2005: 11). Rather, its decision to prioritize development aid to Yemen was motivated by a complex set of other reasons. If state failure, or the absence of strong state structures, is a factor in facilitating terrorism, as many argue, strengthening the state through development may help to limit terrorism. Development can also strengthen communities, which, in turn, is believed to help prevent terrorism. Thus, poverty can have an indirect effect on factors such as state strength or level of civil society activism, which affect the occurrence of terrorism more directly.

Moving from the macro- to the micro-level, a second prevalent myth is that psychological deviance causes terrorism. This myth has taken on various guises. Some have argued that terrorists are irrational; others that terrorists are psychopaths or suffer from psychological disorders. A variation is that terrorism is caused by brainwashing – echoes of which are still present in some of the current radicalization literature. In all cases, the intent, or at least the effect, is to locate the cause of the violence in the perpetrator's mental state or personality, while ignoring the political and social context within which the act is perpetrated.

This myth is chillingly encapsulated in the following quote from Jerrold Post (1990: 25), one of the exponents of the notion of 'psycho-logic': 'political terrorists are *driven to commit* acts of violence *as a consequence of psychological forces* ... their special psycho-logic is constructed *to rationalize acts* they are *psychologically compelled* to commit. Thus ... individuals are drawn to the path of terrorism in order to commit acts of violence' (emphasis added). By the 1990s, this rather crude explanation of terrorist psychopathy had been replaced by explanations involving more 'subtle' forms of 'deviance', such as narcissism, splitting and paranoia (Horgan 2005: 48; for examples, see Post 1990; Pearlstein 1991). However, as Horgan and others have noted, the evidence for these arguments is flimsy at best and methodologically dubious. The datasets on which the research is based tend to be small and idiosyncratic, and the inferences drawn are often speculative and not consistently supported of this narcissistic interrelationship (Horgan 2005: 59). In addition, studies are often based on interviews with those who have been imprisoned, thus making it difficult to establish whether any apparent psychological traits were a cause or a consequence of engaging in violence.

The consensus of more recent research – or rather, what Silke terms 'most serious researchers in the field' – is that those engaged in terror tactics 'are essentially normal individuals' (Silke 1998: 53). Like any population group they will be diverse – which is why it is problematic to try to arrive at a single psychological profile. In fact, there are strong strategic reasons for not employing activists with psychological problems. For example, while psychopaths may be drawn to violence as 'an outlet for aggressive tendencies' unburdened by remorse, Horgan (2005: 51) rightly points out that they lack 'some of the required characteristics sought after by terrorist leaders ... high motivation, discipline and an ability to remain reliable and task-focused in the face of stress, possible capture and imprisonment'. Acknowledging that those who engage in terrorism do so for tactical and strategic reasons, it soon becomes clear that psychological deviance is usually a hindrance, rather than an asset, to any group seeking to employ terrorism strategically.

One of the reasons for the prevalence of the psychological deviance myth is what psychologists term 'the **fundamental attribution error**'. According to this, we 'tend to explain other people's behaviour with reference to dispositional features (e.g. personality, what they are "like"), while we might attribute situational features to our own (e.g. it was the type of company I was in that night that made me behave in that way)' (ibid.: 47–8). This tendency is particularly strong when we are caught up in the emotions of an event. Another reason for its prevalence is that it is easier to explain terrorism by reference to abnormality, thereby absolving us of any moral or political responsibility for the occurrence of an attack (Zulaika and Douglass 1996).

A final prevalent myth is that religion is a primary cause of terrorism, and that when people are inspired by religion, they are more violent, more radical and less willing to compromise. From Laqueur (1999) to Juergensmeyer (2000) and Hoffman (2006), it is argued that we are currently experiencing a new form of religiously inspired terrorism, which is more lethal and more threatening to Western interests than anything that came before. Religion, in this view, is seen as a cause of violence, rather than an intervening factor. Hoffman (2006: 88–9), for instance, explicitly links the assumed tendency of 'religious terrorists' towards greater violence to their religious perspective and, in particular, the notion that God has both sanctioned and commanded the violence. In this, the literature on 'religious terrorism' is part of a long – and problematic – tradition within Western social science linking religion causally to violence (see p. 109; Hasenclever and Rittberger 2000; Cavanaugh 2004). In addition, scholars have assigned a causal role to religion on the basis that, taken together, 'religious terrorists' appear to have been more violent than their secular counterparts (Gurr and Cole 2000: 28–9; Hoffman 2006: 85–8).

We have already discussed some of the contradictions within this view and the lack of conclusive evidence supporting it. To recapitulate briefly, although on aggregate those labelled 'religious terrorists' have caused more deaths than their secular counterparts, a closer look at individual cases identifies numerous secular groups (mostly ethnonationalist) which have been far more violent and uncompromising than many 'religious' groups. In addition, even in cases where religiously inspired militants have been more brutal than secular militants, it is far from clear that it is religion that was the causal factor, rather than the fact that the violence was carried out in the context of a civil war, for example (Cavanaugh 2004: 13, 28–9).

More broadly, the relationship between beliefs and behaviour is far from clear (Gunning forthcoming). Beliefs, for instance, do not necessarily *cause* people to act, but can instead be the *effect* of activism which people may embark upon for non-ideological reasons (Ferree and Miller 1985). Activists have been found to join movements for a

---

## Key Points

- The myth that poverty causes terrorism has largely been discredited by terrorism research, but continues to be propounded by politicians.
- The myth that those engaging in terrorism are psychologically abnormal has largely been discredited by psychologists, but it lives on, less explicitly, in some of the radicalization literature.
- The myth that religious belief causes terrorists to be more violent is beginning to be critiqued, but the notion that ideas, *on their own*, cause behaviour is still prevalent.

---

variety of reasons, including peer pressure, a longing for social standing or a desperate search for protection from the violence of states or rival groups (Porta 1995a; Bjørgo 2005a, 2009). Groups, meanwhile, do not necessarily act out their ideological views, preferring at times compromise to marginalization (Gunning forthcoming). Religion, or ideology more broadly, can act as a primary motivation – but it does not do so automatically. In short, although religious identity, beliefs, networks and institutions can play an important role in how conflicts are perceived and the resources available to protagonists, the notion that religion is a primary causal factor is empirically dubious and should be approached with caution (Gunning and Jackson forthcoming).

Nonetheless, governments and counter-terrorism practitioners often argue that religious beliefs, particularly extreme or radical views, are a primary cause of terrorism. The UK's Prevent strategy (see p. 228), for instance, accords radical religious ideology a central place in the process of radicalization and sees nurturing alternative religious voices as a key tactic in the fight against terrorism (HM Government 2008). Radical religious beliefs, rather than religion per se, are thus singled out as a core driver of terrorism, replicating the logic of the 'religion-inspires-violence' thesis. Politically, such views are popular because they allow states to ignore the political grievances and demands of the terrorists or the accusation that foreign policy is a key driver of violence.

## Macro-level explanations

Much of the terrorism literature focuses on macro-level explanations – or 'root causes' – and covers a variety of perspectives (Bjorgo 2005a). Some are based in the Marxian notion that ideology and behaviour are products of political and socio-economic structures; others are driven by a Weberian focus on sociological and institutional factors and how these influence behaviour and beliefs. Critical scholars cautiously welcome the shift away from individual level explanations which focus overly on psychological or religious explanations towards existing structural conditions. After all, the crucial task of a critical analyst, following Cox (1981), is to stand aside from the status quo and to consider its emergence and role in contributing to the conditions for political violence. A focus on macro-level factors is thus a fundamental part of any critical enterprise.

However, the 'root causes' approach can also be deeply problematic to the extent that it decontextualizes macro-level factors and treats them as mechanistic manifestations of 'universal categories' obeying 'universal laws'. In such a framework, local meanings and dynamics can be lost, leading to a truncated and often flawed analysis. From a critical perspective, a focus on local context is crucial, since events and behaviour only make sense within their local meaning and context, even if this is influenced by global and transnational dynamics. Critical Theorists thus often advocate a multi-level approach to causation which looks at the dynamic interaction between macro-, meso- and micro-factors and marries explanation with understanding of subjective meanings.

Broadly speaking, macro-level factors suggested in the literature can be subdivided into political, socio-economic, cultural-social and geographical factors (see Table 9.1). Quantitative studies use these factors to focus their analysis, looking for correlations with the outbreak of terrorist violence. However, not only can one usually find (at times starkly) contradictory outcomes across different quantitative studies, but individual cases do not necessarily correspond with the predictions of quantitative studies.

Take the example of democratization. Some studies have found statistically that an increase in democratization leads to an increase in terrorism (Li and Schaub 2004). Others have found that democratization diminishes the chance of terrorism occurring, at least after an initial period where violence is more likely (Kurrild-Klitgaard *et al.* 2006). The problem lies in part with the complexity of democratization and the way it affects grievances and opportunities to mobilize. On the one hand, greater political participation can lead to a reduction in oppositional violence by providing institutional avenues to address grievances non-violently (Eckstein and Gurr 1975; Rummel 1995; Gissinger and Gleditsch 1999; for discussion, see Lia and Skjolberg 2005: 34). On the other hand, greater levels of freedom and greater restrictions on governments can lead to an increase in terrorism by making it easier to mobilize and formulate grievances and less costly to use violence (Wilkinson 1986; see also Lia and Skjolberg 2005: 38).

**Table 9.1**   *Widely cited macro-level factors in the causation of terrorism*

| Political | Socio-economic | Social | Geopolitical |
|---|---|---|---|
| Democratization | Inequality/relative deprivation | 'Youth bulges' and (under)-employment | Globalization |
| Political exclusion, lack of political opportunities | Rapid, uneven economic development | Type and expansion of education | Western foreign policy |
| State repression | Modernization and urbanization | Migration (e.g. into cities) | Migration and diasporas |
| Lack of state legitimacy | Lack of welfare provision | | International aid organizations and non-governmental organizations (NGOs) |
| Historical legacies | | | |
| Weak civil society | | | |
| 'Weak' or 'failed' states | | | Transnational crime |

Directly related to this, during the early part of the war on terrorism, it became something of an accepted view that there was a link between so-called failed states and terrorism (The 9/11 Commission Report 2004; Rotberg 2005). Officials and some scholars suggested that the absence of democracy and profound institutional weakness created space for terrorist activities, and there was therefore a need for Western security intervention to rebuild failing states and encourage democracy in countries like Afghanistan, Somalia and Yemen. However, as a macro-level factor, studies have not found sufficient evidence that failed states in any way cause or generate terrorism (Hehir 2007; Jackson 2007e). In fact, failed states more often pose serious challenges for terrorists, as not only are individuals and groups more vulnerable to military counter-terrorism measures in failed states, but such environments also tend to be inhospitable and dangerous for foreigners (Menkhaus 2007).

Similar discrepancies can be found in relation to other macro-level factors. Quantitative studies on the link between repression and oppositional violence (including terrorism), for instance, are inconclusive, with some finding that an increase in repression triggers a violent response (Lichbach and Gurr 1981), others that oppositional violence is lowest where repression is either high or largely absent (Muller 1985; Muller and Weede 1990; see also Lia and Skjolberg 2005: 37).

---

> ### Key Points
>
> - Quantitative studies tend to focus on macro-level factors to explain political violence, ranging from political and socio-economic to socio-cultural and geopolitical factors.
> - Quantitative studies of macro-level factors are useful in isolating factors that may contribute to violence by highlighting those more likely to be present where violence occurs. They cannot, however, prove causality.
> - Quantitative studies often produce contradictory or inconclusive findings, which, according to critical scholars, is because they do not take meso- and micro-dynamics into account.

The link between terrorism and education, inequality, youth bulges and diasporas, to name but a few, is similarly contested. Education, for example, has been argued to enhance political participation, grievance reduction and social status – thus reducing violence. At the same time, it has been argued to lead to a greater likelihood of violence by improving skills and opportunities for mobilization while increasing awareness of status inequality (Li and Schaub 2004: 237; Thyne 2006).

Quantitative analyses of macro-level factors are useful in highlighting possible causal factors by showing which conditions are more often in place when violence occurs. But they cannot explain *why* certain macro-factors correspond to an increase, a decrease or no change at all in violence in particular cases. They also cannot explain causal mechanisms; if a factor is statistically more likely to be present when violence occurs, this does not necessarily mean that it causes the violence. Similarly, if it is found to be statistically insignificant, it may still play a role, whether direct or indirect, in particular conflicts. For instance, inequality and lack of education can play a background role in the way militants formulate their grievances, even if they are not statistically relevant. Finally, quantitative analyses say nothing about the way macro-level factors are understood by those carrying out the violence. Whether an opportunity is perceived as an opportunity is, after all, dependent on one's perception (Kurzman 1996), just as is whether inequality is interpreted as an injustice which can be remedied or a mere fate to be borne (McAdam 1982).

## From macro- to meso- and micro-explanations

One way around the problem of contradictory and inconclusive findings in quantitative studies is to look not just at macro-level factors, but at the dynamic interplay between macro-, meso- and micro-dynamics (Figure 9.1) and the ways in which individuals and groups interpret macro-factors. Greater political participation can, for instance, lead to the isolation of hardliners among protest movements if it reduces the need for mass protests. If this is the case, hardliners may resort to terrorist tactics in an attempt to regain the initiative, restart mass protests and punish those who opted for compromise. But whether this is the case depends in turn on internal group dynamics and how these are affected by the interaction between militants, the state and wider society.

Porta (1995a, 1995b) observed this dynamic in Italy, where increases in violence coincided, first, with the end of the mass protest cycle of 1968–73, and, subsequently, with the rapprochement between the Communist Party and the Christian Democrats. By the mid-1970s, the New Left had come to feel betrayed by the Communist Party and the trade unions, leaving it isolated and seemingly bereft of political options. Unemployment and housing shortages were still acute in the eyes of the New Left, and the Communist Party's alliance with the Christian Democrats (whom the New Left blamed for the inequalities of Italian society) left the militants feeling embattled against a state and society which it began to see as a monolithic enemy. A hardening of police tactics against protesters and the increasing criminalization of protest by the law had led activists of the New Left to go underground, severing them from wider society and triggering a 'spiral of encapsulation' in which radical measures came to be seen as increasingly acceptable. Within this enclosed and embattled environment, justifications for violence in communist ideology were brought to the fore and acted upon, which in turn helped to forge a strong group identity. The experience of defending themselves from attacks by the police and the Italian Right, meanwhile, had created a cadre of experts in the use of violence who began to compete against each other for supremacy within the broader New Left movement.

It is thus in the interplay between these various factors – greater political participation leading to an alliance between the Left and the Centre Right, greater police brutality, isolation from wider society, the activation of existing ideological justifications for violence, evolving expertise in violence and competition between groups – that the explanation for terrorist violence must be sought, and not simply in an analysis of macro-level factors.

In a similar vein, whether inequality leads to violence depends on whether (and how) this inequality is perceived, who is blamed for it, and whether people believe it can be changed. These beliefs, in turn, are affected by organizational dynamics and how movements interpret the situation and the responses available to them. Hafez (2003: 9–19), for instance, shows that an analysis of macro-socio-economic factors alone cannot explain the different protest trajectories of Algeria and

Tunisia. Both countries have comparable statistics for the period 1980–92 regarding changes in average gross national product (GNP) per capita, population growth, urban growth, rural–urban migration, unemployment, urban poverty and inequality. Yet, while Algeria experienced a long and bloody civil war during the 1990s, Tunisia experienced little oppositional violence. To explain the different trajectories, Hafez argues, we need to look at the particular way the different political systems were organized, the attitudes of the elite towards repression, the relative strength of opposition movements vis-à-vis the state, the way they interpreted the situation, and so on.

One method for capturing this complex web of interactions is to adopt a **social movement theory** framework (Figure 9.2). Within this framework, behaviour is analysed as an outcome of the interaction between four factors: long-term *socio-economic processes* (e.g. urbanization or an expansion of tertiary education); changes in the *political opportunity structure* (e.g. a shift from autocracy to democracy); *internal movement dynamics* (e.g. changes in a movement's leadership structure or its relationship with the wider society); and *movement framing* or how the movement interprets the conflict, its own behaviour and the behaviour of its opponents. Importantly, social movement theory emphasizes the temporal and interactive nature of behaviour through the notion of protest cycles, capturing how movement behav-

**Figure 9.2**   *A social movement theory framework for explaining movement behaviour*

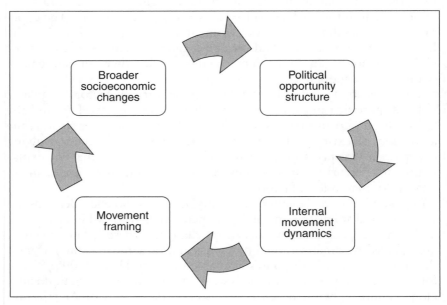

---

**Key Points**

- A focus on the interaction between macro-, meso- and micro-factors, including how participants perceive the conflict, their behaviour and their opponents' behaviour, can help us to understand particular outbreaks of terrorist violence.
- One useful way of capturing these dynamics is to adopt a social movement theory framework which focuses on the *interaction* between macro-, meso- and micro-factors.

---

iour is influenced by its own behaviour and the responses of its opponents (Gunning 2009). By focusing on the meso-, as well as the macro- and micro-levels, it can show how individual beliefs change as a result of participation in group dynamics and macro-level changes.

## Explaining and understanding suicide bombing

One of the tactics that has baffled terrorism researchers most is that of suicide bombing, or 'self-martyrdom operations'. Why do activists choose to kill themselves? Are they driven primarily by beliefs, psychological trauma, poverty, political exclusion or military occupation? The literature on this provides a good illustration of some of the themes discussed above: the inability of poverty, psychopathy and religion to explain the phenomenon; the importance of merging macro- with meso- and micro-explanations; and the importance of marrying explanations drawn from structural analysis to an understanding of the subjective meanings that participants assign to their situation and behaviour.

Although often linked by politicians and terror experts to poverty, psychopathy and religion, none of these can adequately explain suicide terrorism. Neither quantitative nor qualitative studies of the characteristics of known suicide bombers have found a significant link between either poverty or psychological abnormalcy and suicide tactics (Krueger and Malečková 2003; Horgan 2003; Pape 2005: 17–19; Hafez 2006: 10–11). Suicide bombers are both rich and poor and display roughly the same psychological range of profiles as the general population. If anything, suicide bombers are more likely to be better educated than the general population and less likely to be psychologically impaired.

The relationship between religion and suicide bombing is more complex. Those scholars who privilege cultural explanations rightly emphasize that, while other factors, such as group rivalry, military occupation and differences in military strength between militants and their opponents are important, religious beliefs play a motivational and framing role for those militants who draw their inspiration from religion (Israeli 1997; Post 2005; Hoffman 2006). But this does not explain why the group most active in suicide bombings is the secular, anti-religious Tamil Tigers or why non-religious beliefs (such as loyalty to one's nation or strategic calculations) play an equally central role. Nor does it explain why many conflicts involving religiously motivated militants do not experience a turn to suicide tactics. Hizbullah, which pioneered the tactic in the Lebanese–Israeli conflict of the 1980s, ceased suicide bombing in the 1990s, even though Israel's occupation of Southern Lebanon continued until 2000. Similarly, Hamas did not begin carrying out suicide bombings until 1993, nearly 50 years after the creation of Israel and more than 20 years after the occupation in 1967.

One popular macro-level explanation is that formulated by Pape (2005). Following a statistical analysis of suicide tactics over the past three decades, Pape concluded that suicide tactics are most likely to occur when a democracy occupies a population of a different religious persuasion than the occupying force. Religion can thus play a role as a source of identification and differentiation, and it can render a conflict more intense by presenting it as an existential, zero-sum or even cosmic struggle between Good and Evil (see also Hasenclever and Rittberger 2000). But suicide tactics become 'plausible' primarily in the context of asymmetric conflicts, where the opponent is militarily stronger yet dependent on maintaining popular consent. In this context, targeting civilians can appear an 'attractive' option, particularly if military targets are better protected.

Pape touches on meso- and micro-factors to corroborate his rational choice explanation, but cannot explain why not all conflicts involving democracies occupying people of a different faith experience suicide tactics, or why militants cease carrying out such tactics while conflict continues. Nor does he adequately explain the importance of suicide tactics beyond their supposed utility, for instance at an emotional level or in terms of the way they are made to resonate with a society's 'deep cultural grammar'. To explain this, we have to turn to meso- and micro-dynamics: to the processes by which organizational elites decide to employ the tactic; the way organizations socialize their recruits and align individual motives with organizational strategies; the interaction between militant organizations and wider society and its cultural norms; and the way macro-factors affect people's lived experiences (Pedahzur 2005: 22–42; Hafez 2006: 9–15).

Bloom (2005), Hafez (2006) and Gunning (2007b) have all shown in the context of the Israeli–Palestinian conflict – which involves a militarily stronger democracy occupying a population of a predominantly different faith – that the turn to suicide tactics was a function of inter- and intrafactional rivalry, changes in tactical know-how and a changed political opportunity structure which affected both wider society and the political arena.

For example, at an organizational level, the adoption of suicide tactics in 1993 can be traced to an increase in contact between Hamas and Hizbullah which had pioneered the tactic in the 1980s, following the expulsion of 415 Islamist leaders to Lebanon in 1992. Before this expulsion, Hamas had undergone intensive reorganization, resulting in an ever more professionalized, hardened and separate resistance wing, led by a younger generation of activists who were less cautious than their elders, radicalized by the violence of the intifada and externally funded. Organizationally, Hamas was thus more open to the adoption of such a tactic than it had been previously. This (forced) contact with Hizbullah provided Hamas with both practical know-how and ideological socialization, a process facilitated by the fact that Hizbullah's ideas and beliefs overlapped closely with those of Palestinian society at the time. Here, notions of martyrdom, individual defensive jihad and self-sacrifice were readily available in Hamas's 'cultural grammar', needing only decoupling from the stigma of suicide. Ritual chants, such as 'with our soul, with our blood, we sacrifice for you, o martyr' (Hafez 2006: 42), resonated as strongly in 1990s Palestinian society as they did in Lebanon.

At a macro-level, the political opportunity structure had also begun to change following the end of the first intifada and the rapprochement between Hamas's main rival, Fatah, and the Israeli government in the context of the Madrid and Oslo peace processes. By 1993–94, Hamas feared the dual prospect of political marginalization and an end to violent struggle. Mass support for violent resistance had waned as the first Palestinian intifada had ground to a halt and people were rallying behind Fatah and the Oslo peace process. Hamas was thus looking for a way to reignite the struggle, undermine Fatah and Israeli public support for the peace process, and consolidate its own political influence. At the same time, the Israeli army was beginning to withdraw from Palestinian town centres, forcing Hamas to look for new ways to engage the enemy.

However, even though Hamas adopted the tactic from 1993 onwards, it used it relatively sparingly during the 1990s and it was not until the 2000s that its suicide operations multiplied dramatically. To explain this, we have to look at changes in the political opportunity structure and in Hamas's organizational response to those. The breakdown of the Oslo Peace Process and the subsequent outbreak of the al-Aqsa intifada in 2000 played a major part in this shift, as did the fact that the Palestinian Authority (PA) stopped preventing Hamas and others from carrying out such operations. But another important factor was a dramatic shift in popular support for the tactic which had not exceeded 50 per cent in the 1990s. Within a context of daily deaths, shocking violence and an apparent breakdown in political options, suicide bombing became socially 'acceptable' because society had become what Araj (2008) calls an 'insurgent society'.

An approach which looks at the interplay between macro-, meso- and micro-dynamics, and which takes subjective meanings as well as structural changes into account is, therefore, better able to explain the dynamics of suicide bombing than either culturalist explanations (with their narrow focus on culture and religion), individual-level explanations (with their preoccupation with psychology, ideology or individual socio-economic profile) or macro-explanations that ignore meso- and micro-factors. This type of explanation is more sensitive to the need to explain why particular cultural or religious themes become prevalent at a particular time. It draws on both macro- and micro-explanations and adds the meso-link between the micro- and macro-levels.

## Key Points

- Poverty, psychopathy and religion cannot explain the turn to suicide bombing. Suicide bombers can be rich or poor, religious or non-religious and are no different psychologically to the general population.
- Religion can play a role as a motivatory factor and in framing the conflict and providing institutional resources; but whether it does depends on many other factors.
- Macro-level analyses can provide some insight, but they cannot explain why suicide tactics are not adopted in all such situations.
- An integrated analysis which looks at the interplay between macro-, meso- and micro-factors and takes into account the meanings and interpretations assigned to these by participants is better able to explain why, how and when suicide bombing occurs.

## Conclusion

This chapter has shown that terrorism is a complex and multicausal phenomenon involving the dynamic interaction between structures, organizations and agents, between grievance-formation and opportunity structures, and between leaders and followers. It has also highlighted that there are different approaches to understanding causality and that a much richer understanding of the phenomenon can be achieved by eschewing a single methodological or disciplinary approach. In particular, we have suggested that the causes or roots of terrorism are local and historically contingent, and cannot be properly understood without understanding specific social, cultural, economic and political contexts. This means rejecting the tendency to decontextualize and dehistoricize terrorism that is prevalent in quantitative approaches, and adopting a more interpretive approach attuned to local context and its 'deep cultural grammar'. We have also shown that a macro-level approach, on its own, is insufficient because it does not take into account the interpretations and meanings actors assign to their situation. To understand this process, we need to look at the interplay between macro-, meso- and micro-dynamics and take participants' – and our own – subjectivities into account.

Finally, we have tried to demonstrate the importance of reflecting on how causal explanations inform policy. A critical approach cautions against taking accepted explanations at face value, particularly those which depoliticize terrorism. We touched on three common myths about the causes of terrorism, but there are countless other explanations which do not stand up to a sustained critical analysis. A more fundamental point concerns how explanations are used to combat terrorism. If they are used in a purely problem-solving manner to neutralize militant organizations, without simultaneously addressing the underlying structural inequalities and grievances that fuel a conflict, the outcome may be counter-productive in the long-run. By reinforcing the status quo, the explanatory model can then become implicit in upholding the very power structures that gave rise to the conflict in the first place.

## Discussion Questions

1.  What do we mean by the terms micro-, meso- and macro-levels of analysis for the study of terrorism?
2.  Why are critical scholars wary of monocausal explanations of terrorism?
3.  How do individuals' perceptions of themselves, others and their environment feed into terrorist violence?
4.  What are the major limitations of quantitative approaches to the question of causation in the context of terrorism?
5.  Why do efforts to link terrorism to poverty, religion or psychological deviance concern critical scholars?
6.  What are the advantages of the social movement theory framework for understanding the causes of terrorism?
7.  Is suicide bombing an exceptional form of terrorism and where do its causes lie?
8.  What kind of approaches and assumptions do critical scholars make in their approach to the roots or causes of terrorism?
9.  What are some of the political and ideological issues involved in the study of the causes of terrorism?

## Recommended Reading

Bjorgo, T., ed., 2005b. *Root Causes of Terrorism: Myths, Reality and Ways Forward*, London: Routledge. A collection of articles on macro-level explanations for terrorism and an assessment of the state of the literature.

Crenshaw, M., 1981. 'The Causes of Terrorism', *Comparative Politics*, 13(4): 379–99. A seminal article which examines the main causes of terrorism.

Krueger, A., 2007. *What Makes a Terrorist: Economics and the Roots of Terrorism*, Princeton: Princeton University Press. A powerful examination of the root causes of terrorism by a leading economist.

Pape, R., 2005. *Dying to Win: The Strategic Logic of Suicide Terrorism*, New York, NY: Random House. A classic study on the nature and causes of suicide.

Zulaika, J., 1984. *Basque Violence: Metaphor and Sacrament*, Reno, NA: University of Nevada Press. The classic study of Basque terrorism using a cultural approach to understand the roots and expression of the violence.

## Web Resources

International Summit on Democracy, Terrorism and Security: *http://english. safe-democracy.org/causes/*
> Website for the summit held in Madrid, 8–11 March 2005. The summit brought together leading experts to examine the causes of terrorism and develop an agenda for action. The Commission's report on the causes of terrorism can be found here.

Exploring Root and Trigger Causes of Terrorism: *www.transnational terrorism.eu/tekst/publications/Root%20and%20Trigger.pdf*
> A useful report published by the European Commission under the Transnational Terrorism, Security and the Rule of Law (TTSRL) Research Program.

Causes of Terrorism: An Expanded and Updated Review of the Literature: *http://rapporter.ffi.no/rapporter/2004/04307.pdf.*
> A very useful overview and discussion of the literature on the causes of terrorism published by the Norwegian Defence Research Establishment.

Chapter 10

# Responding to Non-state Terrorism

## Chapter Contents

- Introduction
- Counter-terrorism approaches
- Key issues in contemporary counter-terrorism
- A critical assessment of counter-terrorism
- Conclusion

## Reader's Guide

In this chapter we explore some of the central issues concerning state responses to acts of non-state terrorism. We begin with a discussion of the impact of 9/11 on policymakers' perceptions of how terrorism should be countered. We then explore the social and political impact of post-9/11 counter-terrorism policies. This is followed by a brief description of some of the main counter-terrorism approaches and tools in use by governments today and a short analysis of their evolution. The next section discusses four important issues facing contemporary counter-terrorism: the question of how counter-terrorism policies can be properly evaluated; the debate over tensions between liberty and security; the question of the efficacy and morality of torture as a counter-terrorism method; and the issue of conflict resolution and the ways in which terrorism ends. In the final section, we put forward a series of principles and perspectives which critical scholars typically adopt for understanding and evaluating counter-terrorism. In the conclusion, we reflect on some of the key contributions a critical approach may make to counter-terrorism, including the important but neglected issue of how to respond to the much more serious problem of state terrorism.

## Introduction

The way in which different states and societies respond to terrorism and the prescriptions authorities attempt to apply in countering violent non-state groups are intimately linked to how terrorism is defined and constructed culturally and politically. As Ronald Crelinsten (2009: 19) puts it: 'how we conceive of terrorism determines to a great extent how we go about countering it and what resources – money, manpower, institutional framework, time horizon – we devote to the effort'. If terrorism is viewed as an expression of pathological evil, for example, states will simply try to eradicate it through any and all means. If it is conceived of as a type of criminal activity, it will likely be tackled through policing and legal measures. If it is seen as the result of oppression and political conflict, states may attempt to bring in reforms and negotiate with the leaders of militant groups. Alternately, if it is framed as a kind of war, the state may launch an expensive military-based 'war on terrorism' (Jackson 2005).

The events of 11 September 2001 are crucial for understanding contemporary approaches to counter-terrorism, not least because they were initially framed and understood as 'evil', as acts of 'war' and as an expression of the 'new', religiously inspired terrorism (ibid.; Jarvis 2009b). These widely held understandings of the nature and causes of the threat posed by the new terrorism have subsequently functioned to establish the main approaches and parameters of the global response to terrorism. The belief that the events of 9/11 amounted to 'acts of war' against Western societies for example, established the foundations for a global '*war* on terrorism' and the utilization of militaristic counter-terrorism measures, such as counter-insurgency operations, targeted assassination, the indefinite detention of prisoners and the trial of terrorist suspects by military commissions. Similarly, the scale of the 9/11 attacks was initially thought to indicate the dawning of a 'new age of terror' in which terrorists threatened massive destruction – that terrorism posed an existential threat to Western societies and their populations. The scale of the perceived threat, therefore, meant that the response needed to be on a global scale, involve the cooperation of all nations and entail the use of exceptional measures, including vast new investments in security measures and the suspension of legal protections for people suspected of involvement with terrorism. At the same time, the notion that 9/11 revealed that contemporary terrorists were irrational religious fanatics acting out of blind hatred for the West, and that they lacked a political agenda, meant that alternative approaches to countering terrorism, based on dialogue and reform, were automatically precluded from serious consideration.

Approaches to counter-terrorism and the ways in which societies respond to terrorism are critical subjects of analysis for some fairly obvious reasons. In the first instance, it is important that states take measures to protect their citizens from threats and dangers such as terrorism. At the same time, it is important that the counter-terrorism measures adopted are effective, proportionate, legitimate and do not result in more harm or make matters worse by intensifying violence and conflict. More recently, the counter-terrorism measures adopted across the world since 2001 have had a deep and pervasive impact on a great many areas of social, economic and political life. For example, counter-terrorism measures and priorities have become a major part of airline travel, public buildings and infrastructural protection, surveillance, policing, law, foreign policy, banking, education, the media, international aid, immigration and numerous other areas. There is probably no society or individual anywhere in the world who is not affected by the counter-terrorism measures brought in after 2001.

## Counter-terrorism approaches

Partly as a consequence of the way in which terrorism has been popularly understood as an exceptional form of extreme violence and a serious threat to security, it is commonly believed that there are very limited options for dealing with it and that the authorities must always respond forcefully to terrorist attacks. In reality, there are many different approaches and methods of dealing with terrorism. They range from domestically oriented to international measures, from coercive to persuasive measures, from reactive to proactive measures, from short-term to long-term measures, and from measures designed to suppress or control terrorism to those aimed at resolving the deeper causes of terrorist violence (Martin 2003; Crelinsten 2009). Historically, societies have responded in very different ways to campaigns of non-state terrorism. In Argentina and Algeria, for example, the authorities responded with brutal military crackdowns against suspected terrorist groups and their supporters. By contrast, in the Philippines the authorities opened direct negotiations with militant groups. States have also altered their response over time. In South Africa, Israel and Northern Ireland the authorities moved over the course of several years from trying to suppress terrorist groups violently to dialogue, negotiation and reform – with varying degrees of success.

In this section, we briefly outline some of the main counter-terrorism strategies and tools, and some of the different ways of approaching counter-terrorism. This is followed by a short outline of the evolution of counter-terrorism approaches by Western states since the 9/11 attacks. Our purpose here is to show that there are a wide variety of options for responding to terrorism, many of which do not necessitate the use of military force.

## Options for responding to non-state terrorism

A review of the literature and practice of counter-terrorism reveals a wide array of counter-terrorism approaches, strategies and tools (for very useful discussions, see Martin 2003; Crelinsten 2009). The plethora of possible responses to terrorism can be helpfully summarized under four main headings: the use of force; intelligence and policing; homeland security; and conciliation and dialogue. We summarize these different approaches in Table 10.1.

First, *the use of force* involves deploying the military and coercive apparatus of the state to destroy, disrupt, deter or prevent future acts of terrorism; capture wanted terrorist suspects; or retaliate against groups for particular terrorist attacks. Force-based counter-terrorism approaches range from full-scale war and major counter-insurgency campaigns designed to kill or capture terrorists, destroy their base of

**Table 10.1**   *Summary of counter-terrorism approaches*

|  | *Description* | *Underpinning conception of terrorism* | *Examples* |
|---|---|---|---|
| The use of force | The destruction, disruption, deterrence or prevention of terrorism via military force. | Terrorism as a special form of warfare. | Targeted killings; special forces operations; war on terrorism. |
| Intelligence and policing | Counter-terrorism via the state's security services. | Terrorism as a criminal activity and security threat. | Intelligence-gathering operations; psychological operations; community-based counter-terrorism policing. |
| Homeland security | Enhancing the state's resilience to, and protection from, terrorism. | Terrorism as a manageable security threat. | Critical infrastructure security measures; targeted immigration controls; counter-terrorism legislation. |
| Conciliation and dialogue | Non-violent efforts to address terrorism's 'root causes'. | Terrorism as the expression of socio-political grievances and conflicts. | Economic sanctions; public diplomacy initiatives; 'hearts and minds' campaigns. |

operations and disrupt or pre-empt their activities, to more limited covert military operations, including the use of special forces for kill-and-capture operations or hostage rescue. A force-based tactic which has received increasing attention in recent years is the **targeted killing** of terrorist suspects, frequently using unmanned aerial vehicles or drones. The force-based approach is based on a view of terrorism as a special form of warfare and relies largely on the military as the primary counter-terrorism actor.

Second, *intelligence and policing* involves deploying the broad range of the state's security services to gather information on terrorist groups and activities in order to interdict and arrest terrorist operatives either before or after they have acted. This will typically involve specific and general intelligence-gathering operations by the security services, cooperation with foreign intelligence organizations and the use of normal law enforcement and community policing methods. In some cases, it may also involve extraordinary and controversial measures such as **psychological operations (psych-ops)**, the use of torture or so-called 'enhanced interrogation' methods, establishing new organizations with special powers for dealing with terrorism, and the extraordinary rendition of terrorist suspects to and from foreign countries. In recent years, states have also invested major resources in attempting to track terrorist financing so as to cut off the source of their funding. The intelligence and policing approach is based on a view of terrorism as a serious security threat to the state, but which is nonetheless primarily a form of criminal activity rather than warfare.

Third, *homeland security* involves measures aimed at making society more resilient in the face of terrorism and improving the authorities' ability to respond effectively to terrorist attacks. Efforts to protect against terrorist attacks are sometimes called 'anti-terrorism' measures, in contrast to more proactive 'counter-terrorism' measures. At the broadest level, the homeland security approach involves measures to protect the country's critical infrastructure, providing greater security for places and events likely to be targeted by terrorists, preventing potential terrorists from entering the country, and improving emergency preparedness and crisis management in the event of a major attack. Typically, it involves the introduction of new anti-terrorist and security legislation which gives the police, courts and security services greater powers to investigate and punish people involved in terrorist activities and the establishment of new agencies tasked with keeping the country safe from terrorism. It may also entail new programmes aimed at involving ordinary citizens, private security companies, commerce, local police and other groups in community policing and security activities to complement the work of the police and security services, as well as programmes aimed at creating social resilience.

More controversially, this approach can involve the adoption of **pro-filing**, the extensive use of police stop-and-search powers, special restrictive measures aimed at specific groups, the preventive detention of individuals deemed to pose a potential risk, the issuing of **security certificates** against certain groups and individuals, the banning of certain groups, the use of special courts and tribunals for cases involving terrorism, and expanded programmes of surveillance. The homeland security approach is also based on a view of terrorism as a serious security threat to the state, but it assumes that the effects of terrorist attacks can be minimized through preventive and proactive measures.

Fourth, *conciliation and dialogue* involves the use of non-violent measures to try and deal with the so-called 'root causes' and underlying motivations of terrorists, or to change their behaviour through inducements or material sanctions. At the broadest level, states may try to engage in diplomatic initiatives or impose economic sanctions in order to resolve the issues driving the violence or persuade states from sponsoring terrorist groups. At this level, they may also try to engage in **public diplomacy** or propaganda campaigns, or in some cases so-called 'hearts and minds' approaches to counter-insurgency. More specifically, they may try to engage in dialogue and negotiations with violent groups, either directly or through intermediaries. This may be accompanied by the offer of amnesties to groups and individuals willing to give up terrorism and join the political process, the enactment of social and political reforms designed to deal with the group's grievances, or direct concessions on specific demands by the terrorist groups. In recent years, a number of states have engaged in different types of 'counter-radicalization' programmes designed to convince extremists to adopt more moderate views and join the legitimate political process. The conciliation and dialogue approach is based on the view that terrorism is an expression of legitimate political grievances and deeper social conflict, and that resolving these deeper issues will go a long way towards ending terrorist threats.

States often go through a series of stages in their response to campaigns of terrorism. Typically, they will first react with force-based approaches designed to suppress terrorist groups. This may be followed by homeland security measures, the introduction of new anti-terrorism laws and intelligence-led efforts to prevent further attacks. The state may eventually enter into dialogue with the terrorist groups and begin making reforms. In effect, at any given time, states will normally be engaged in an array of different strategies and approaches in their attempts to tackle terrorism. The UK government's CONTEST strategy combines several of the different approaches described above through its Pursue, Prevent, Protect and Prepare strands (Table 10.2), as does the global war on terrorism. It seems to be the case that while very small terrorist movements can sometimes be suppressed through

**Table 10.2** *The UK CONTEST counter-terrorism strategy*

|  | Overview | Key objectives |
|---|---|---|
| **Pursue** | Reducing the threat of terrorism through detecting and investigating terrorist networks and disrupting their activities. | Increasing capabilities of detection, investigation and prosecution.<br><br>Develop more effective non-prosecution actions.<br><br>Strengthen the coherence between counter-terrorism, counter-insurgency and capacity building work in Afghanistan, Pakistan and elsewhere. |
| **Prevent** | Stopping people becoming terrorists or supporting violent extremism, based on a better understanding of the causes of radicalization. | Challenge the ideology behind violent extremism.<br><br>Disrupt those who promote violent extremism and support the places where they operate.<br><br>Support individuals who are vulnerable to recruitment or have already been recruited by violent extremists.<br><br>Increase the resilience of communities to violent extremism.<br><br>Address the grievances which ideologues are exploiting. |
| **Protect** | Reducing national vulnerabilities to terrorist attacks. | To further reduce the vulnerability of the critical national infrastructure, crowded places, the transport system and the national borders. |
| **Prepare** | Mitigating the impact of terrorist attacks through emergency management and the strengthening of post-attack recovery. | To ensure that capabilities are in place to deal with a range of terrorist incidents.<br><br>To ensure there is continuity or swift recovery in critical national infrastructure following terrorist incidents.<br><br>To ensure central, regional and local crisis management structures are appropriately equipped, competent and trained. |

*Source*: http://security.homeoffice.gov.uk/counter-terrorism-strategy/.

the application of overwhelming military force, large-scale, sustained, terrorist campaigns tend to be controlled through a mixture of intelligence-based and law enforcement measures, and end only after substantial political progress on the central issues articulated by the terrorist groups and their constituencies has been made.

## Counter-terrorism after 9/11

Although it is a fairly blunt generalization with several exceptions, it can be argued that counter-terrorism approaches among many Western states and their allies began with force-based suppression campaigns from the late 1960s to the late 1980s. This period saw President Reagan declare the first 'war on terrorism' (Wills 2003; Jackson 2006), a campaign that saw military retaliation for terrorist attacks in Lebanon and Libya, and the invasion of Grenada, among other military measures and activities. It also saw the Spanish 'dirty war' against ETA, the British crackdown on terrorist violence in Northern Ireland (with a mixture of police and military forces), numerous Israeli military operations against Palestinian groups, a major counter-insurgency campaign against the LTTE in Sri Lanka, and many other smaller force-based operations against terrorist groups, some by police others by military forces, in Germany, France, Italy, Argentina, Guatemala and elsewhere (Crelinsten and Schmid 1993).

This initial response to terrorism was followed by a softening of counter-terrorism approaches in a number of important cases during the 1990s, and the fairly widespread adoption of conciliation and law-enforcement-based counter-terrorism strategies. Direct talks with terrorist groups and movements got under way in Northern Ireland, Spain, Israel, South Africa, Sri Lanka and elsewhere. In each case, significant political and social reforms were initiated to try and deal with the underlying roots of these conflicts. At the same time, counter-terrorism responsibilities were institutionalized in law enforcement agencies, and major terrorist attacks such as the Lockerbie and Oklahoma City bombings were pursued largely through law enforcement channels. Of course, there were notable exceptions in places, including Israel, Chechnya, Kashmir and Colombia, as well as President Clinton's use of cruise missiles in response to al-Qaeda in 1998, where the use of force-based approaches continued to dominate.

The events of 9/11 were a watershed in counter-terrorism, largely because they were interpreted as a clear and unambiguous indication of a new and more threatening form of terrorism, one that posed an existential threat to Western societies and the stability of the international system. The initial response to the attacks involved the marginalization of law-enforcement-oriented counter-terrorism approaches and, instead, the launching of two major wars, numerous smaller military

**Table 10.3**   *Selected new counter-terrorism legislation around the world after 9/11*

| State | Year | Legislation |
|---|---|---|
| Australia | 2004 | Anti-Terrorism Act, 2004 |
| Canada | 2001 | Anti-Terrorism Act, 2001 |
| India | 2002 | Prevention of Terrorism Act, 2002 |
| Ireland | 2005 | Criminal Justice (Terrorist Offences) Act, 2005 |
| Jamaica | 2005 | Jamaica Terrorism Prevention Act, 2005 |
| Netherlands | 2004 | Crimes of Terrorism Act, 2004 |
| New Zealand | 2002 | Terrorism Suppression Act, 2002 |
| South Africa | 2004 | Protection of Constitutional Democracy Against Terrorist and Related Activities Act, 2004 |
| Tanzania | 2002 | Prevention of Terrorism Act, 2002 |
| United Kingdom | 2001 | Anti-Terrorism, Crime and Security Act, 2001 |
| United States of America | 2001 | Uniting and Strengthening America by Providing Appropriate Tools Required to Intercept and Obstruct Terrorism Act of 2001 (USA Patriot Act) |

operations and interdiction and rendition programmes in an attempt to decapitate al-Qaeda, seen as the most important terrorist group, and to suppress terrorism globally. This was followed within a few years by major attempts to strengthen intelligence, policing and homeland security within key Western countries such as the USA, the UK and Australia, and to build a global cooperative counter-terrorism campaign through the UN and the EU. There was a rush of counter-terrorism legislation (see Table 10.3), much of it criticized for being draconian and restrictive towards human rights.

By 2010, several new counter-terrorism approaches were added to the war on terrorism, such as **counter-radicalization programmes**, **hearts and minds approaches** to counter-insurgency in Iraq and Afghanistan, moves towards dialogue with 'moderate' insurgent groups, and domestic community outreach programmes. Although this could be viewed as a move towards conciliation and reform-based counter-terrorism, the continuation of major counter-insurgency operations in the Afghanistan–Pakistan region, Iraq, the Horn of Africa, Yemen and elsewhere, as well as the continuation and intensification of targeted killing campaigns, suggests that force-based approaches continue to dominate counter-terrorism thinking in Western states. In fact, the Western force-based model of counter-terrorism seen in the global war on terrorism has been taken up – or used to justify already existing force-based practices – by numerous regimes around the world in their struggles against internal opposition.

---

### Key Points

- While it is commonly perceived that states have to respond forcefully to terrorism, there is in fact a very wide variety of potential strategies for dealing with terrorism.
- Responses to terrorism can be usefully considered under four broad approaches: the use of force; intelligence and policing; homeland security; and conciliation and dialogue.
- Before 9/11, a number of high profile terrorist campaigns were dealt with using conciliation and dialogue; after the terrorist attacks, force-based approaches became more widely used.

## Key issues in contemporary counter-terrorism

In considering the vast field that comprises counter-terrorism, critical scholars argue that four key issues in particular require sustained scholarly analysis. They are: the question of the effectiveness of counter-terrorism approaches and policies; the popular argument that countering terrorism involves an inevitable trade-off between liberty and security; the ongoing question of the legitimacy and effectiveness of torture as a tool of counter-terrorism; and the issue of how to resolve terrorist conflicts.

### The question of effectiveness

The question of how we might evaluate different counter-terrorism policies is critical, not least because, while there are currently a great many different ideas as to how to respond to terrorism, there is little systematic evidence for demonstrating what actually works and few transparent and rigorous methods for tracing and evaluating the specific effects of particular policies (Townshend 2002: 133). It is still not entirely clear how and why campaigns of terrorism end (Jones and Libicki 2008; Cronin 2009). For example, it is difficult to assess whether the decision by the al-Gama'a al-Islamiyya in Egypt to end its use of terrorism as a strategy of struggle was the result of Egyptian counter-terrorism measures or due to internal changes within the group itself – or indeed broader changes to the situation in the Middle East and international relations more generally. Similar questions can be asked about the decision of the IRA to negotiate an end to its violent campaign: was the decision to negotiate the result of internal, socio-economic and political changes, or due to the pressure on the organization from the British security forces – or a mixture of all of these?

Despite the difficulties of precisely tracing the effects of particular policies, there is a wealth of case study and anecdotal evidence to show that force-based counter-terrorism approaches are often ineffective and counter-productive, particularly in comparison to conciliation-based approaches (English 2009: 127–30; see also Hewitt 1984; Bryan and Conybeare 1994; Parker 2007; Jones and Libicki 2008; Crelinsten 2009; Cronin 2009; Nacos 2010). For example, there is no compelling evidence that, in isolation, the targeted assassination of terrorists has ever had an appreciable impact on the prevention of further terrorist attacks (David 2002: 8; Martin 2003: 350). In fact, there are reasons for arguing that it is counter-productive, in terms of fuelling revenge attacks and radicalizing the conflict (Araj 2008), eliminating the cadre of leaders needed to negotiate an end to the conflict, and undermining the social capital needed to rebuild society following the end of violence (Mac Ginty 2010). At the very least, it only addresses the symptoms of the conflict, fails to deal with its roots and can lead to the entrenchment of cycles of hatred, violence and revenge – as it has clearly done in the Israel–Palestine conflict, Chechnya, Kashmir, Sri Lanka, Spain, Algeria, Pakistan, Iraq and elsewhere. Similar studies have clearly demonstrated the failure and counter-productive results of employing torture against terrorist suspects (see below), and the self-fulfilling and counter-productive consequences of the 'war on terrorism' since 9/11 (Zulaika 2003, 2009).

In addition to being often ineffectual and counter-productive, force-based approaches have been consistently shown to be damaging to human rights, the rule of law, democratic accountability and social cohesion (Luban 2002; Mueller 2005; Cole 2007; Crelinsten 2009: 213; see also *New Internationalist* 2009). In virtually every case, the years following the end of violent repressive counter-terrorism campaigns have seen revelations of serious human rights abuses and abuses of power, such as torture and rendition, wrongful imprisonment and secret assassination programmes. Regular public revelations of abuses by the security services continue to emerge about the counter-terrorism campaigns in Northern Ireland, the 'dirty war' in Spain, Israel's actions in the Palestinian territories and the war on terrorism, among many others. These revelations are arguably very costly and destructive, as they undermine trust in government, leave a legacy of grievance and anger among targeted communities and damage the reputation of the institutions of law and order such as the police and judiciary (Martin 2003: 372–3). It is largely on the basis of this evidence that critical scholars question the arguments put forward by those who advocate force-based counter-terrorism policies as both necessary and effective (for example, Litwak 2002; Shultz and Vogt 2003).

Force-based tactics can and do change the cost–benefit calculations of those employing terrorism, and in this way they can contribute to creating conditions that are more favourable for (eventual) conciliatory tactics, for instance by making violence too costly for insurgents. But this tends to come at great cost to society and often prolongs the conflict by extending the cycle of revenge. In the Israeli–Palestinian conflict, for instance, targeted assassinations, rather than hastening Hamas's 2003 ceasefire declaration, apparently delayed it, and the tactic's continuation was one factor in the ceasefire's breakdown, fuelling a further two years of violence (Gunning 2007b).

More broadly, a small number of studies have demonstrated that anti-terrorism measures designed to prevent and protect societies have little impact in the long-term on the number of terrorist attacks, and in fact tend to produce a displacement effect (Enders and Sandler 1993). That is, when embassies or public buildings are made more secure, for example, terrorists change their methods and move onto other targets. In the end, it is one of the features of post-9/11 counter-terrorism approaches that new laws are regularly enacted by political elites without any evidence that they are at all effective (see Table 10.4).

## Liberty versus security

Politicians and some academics sometimes argue that terrorists exploit the freedoms and liberties of democratic countries to organize and perpetrate their attacks, and that securing society against terrorism therefore necessitates restricting the freedoms of citizens (Meisels 2005; Wilkinson 2006; Yoo 2010). Inherent to this view are a number of underlying assumptions about terrorism and security. For example, this argument is based on the belief that democratic societies are inherently vulnerable because they allow for, and protect, individual freedoms – as opposed to the argument that it is such freedoms that make them robust and strong or the alternative argument that it is the resources and skills of the security services that is the crucial factor. It is also sometimes based on the belief that terrorism is somehow motivated by a hatred of Western societies and a desire to turn the freedoms of these societies against themselves. Perhaps most importantly, it is based on the belief that restricting freedoms and campaigns of suppression and repression are effective and legitimate methods of responding to terrorism.

Critical scholars, as well as a number of orthodox scholars, question these taken-for-granted assumptions and reject the argument that any trade-off between liberty and security is necessary (Cole 2003, 2010; Waldron 2003; English 2009: 133–6). Based on a number of key arguments, they suggest that such a trade-off represents a false dichotomy. First, they point out that the evidence that terrorism is caused by democracy is deeply ambiguous and not at all conclusive. In many cases, terrorists are in fact part of a broader movement fighting for

**Table 10.4**   *The growth of UK counter-terrorism law since 2000*

| Act | Key measures |
| --- | --- |
| The Terrorism Act (2000) | • Consolidated and made permanent counter-terrorist legislation<br>• Defined terrorism<br>• Established permanent mechanisms for proscription of terrorist groups<br>• Created new offence of inciting terrorism abroad<br>• Expanded definitions of 'receiving or providing weapons training'<br>• Empowered police to establish cordons in counter-terrorist operations<br>• Established powers to detain suspects for up to 14 days |
| Anti-Terrorism, Crime and Security Act (2001) | • Freezes terrorist assets<br>• Promotes counter-terrorism information sharing ( Part IV)<br>• Allows indefinite detention in Britain of foreign nationals suspected of involvement in terrorism<br>• Proscribes incitement of religious and racial hatred and violence<br>• Provides for security of aviation and nuclear industries<br>• Consolidates security of dangerous substances<br>• Extends police powers to the British Transport Police and Ministry of Defence Police<br>• Makes UK meet international protocols on countering bribery and corruption |
| Prevention of Terrorism Act (2005) | • Established 12-month control orders, which could be made with the approval of a judge against any person suspected of terrorism<br>• These imposed a range of restrictions short of house arrest |
| The Terrorism Act (2006) | • New offences of:<br>  – committing acts preparatory to terrorism;<br>  – encouraging terrorism;<br>  – disseminating terrorist publications;<br>  – giving or receiving training in terrorist techniques<br>• Extends police power of entering and searching property owned or controlled by terrorist suspects<br>• Extended the permissible period of detention of suspects from 14 to 28 days<br>• Creates the capacity to proscribe organizations that glorify terrorism |

greater freedom and democracy; it is repressive policies, not democracy, that most often provokes violent opposition. This is why terrorist campaigns tend to occur in states with controversial policies (such as foreign occupation or internal repression) and less so in peaceful democracies where human rights and democratic values are fully respected.

Second, there is little conclusive evidence that the restriction of individual liberties is actually effective in enhancing security against terrorism, unless one adopts draconian measures such as building walls around 'suspect communities'. Certainly, there are no clear cases where terrorism was ended or significantly reduced through greater restrictions on individual civil liberties alone. On the other hand, there are plentiful examples where the restriction of individual freedoms as a counter-terrorism measure led to a greater sense of grievance among the targeted population and greatly enhanced the support of the terrorist groups (Jones and Libicki 2008). From this perspective, it could be argued that the balance of argument and evidence suggests that trading freedom for security is more likely to be counter-productive than effective.

In addition to the fundamental argument that security without liberty is an oxymoron (or at the very least, is based on a restrictive view of what 'security' entails), it is also unrealistic to assume that in a modern society, with all its infinite vulnerabilities, individuals could be sufficiently monitored and restricted to prevent them from ever engaging in a violent attack. Only in a hypothetical society, such as that envisaged by George Orwell in *Nineteen Eighty-Four* or in the film, *Minority Report*, could individuals be prevented from ever engaging in violent attacks (Weber 2007). In any case, attempting to restrict the ability of individuals to move about or organize only deals with the symptoms of terrorism; it does not deal with the reasons why individuals and groups would try to engage in a terrorist campaign in the first instance.

Third, as we demonstrated in Chapter 6, counter-terrorism measures can easily be manipulated by political elites for other purposes, and there are often powerful vested interests in their continuation. For example, restricting individual freedoms in the name of countering terrorism can be used as a cover for increasing executive power, restricting political opposition, targeting particular groups or communities, constructing more intrusive surveillance systems, the militarization of society, controlling immigration, expanding the powers of the security services, and the like. It may also directly benefit corporations and actors who are contracted to provide security services, such as surveillance equipment or financial monitoring. These kinds of manipulations and vested interests have emerged in numerous countries around the world under the cover of the war on terrorism.

Furthermore, as a consequence of the advantages which can accrue to political leaders from restricting human rights, it is frequently the case that emergency powers taken by the state in response to terrorism have tended to become the norm over time. As Table 10.4 demonstrates in the case of the UK, a number of measures which were once declared as temporary for dealing with the terrorism crisis in Northern Ireland have now become a permanent feature of the statute books. Moreover, they also tend to expand in their application to cover new types of actors and actions. Many post-9/11 counter-terrorism laws, for example, are now being used to restrict environmental activists – so-called 'eco-terrorists' (Sorenson 2009) – and counter-terrorism legislation has notoriously been used to deal with arms protestors, foreign banks with bad debts and many other activities unrelated to terrorism.

Finally, critical scholars, as well as many orthodox scholars, believe that there is a strong argument for maintaining the moral high ground in the response to acts of terrorism which the trade off of liberty undermines (Cole 2003, 2007; English 2009: 135). At the very least, it is argued that the maintenance of human rights and civil liberties is necessary for maintaining the legitimacy of state counter-terrorism programmes. Some of the main human rights concerns about counter-terrorism in the UK are summarized in Box 10.1.

## The question of torture

There is a long history of states employing torture during counter-terrorism campaigns. Algeria, Egypt, Pakistan, India, Russia, Uzbekistan, Argentina, Chile, Colombia, Guatemala, Spain, Northern Ireland, Sri Lanka, Saudi Arabia, Israel, Iraq, Afghanistan and a great many other states have systematically tortured terrorist suspects and regime opponents over many decades (Rejali 2007). However, the question of torture gained real impetus in the years following 9/11, particularly after the prominent Harvard lawyer, Alan Dershowitz, argued for its legalization as a counter-terrorism tool (Dershowitz 2002, 2010). It gained further currency following the revelations of torture at the Abu Ghraib prison in Iraq in 2004 (see pp. 81–3, 261). Since then, a great many investigations and reports have demonstrated the systematic and extensive use of torture by Western states and their allies in the war on terrorism (Danner 2004; Hersh 2004; Rose 2004; Greenberg and Dratel 2005; Greenberg 2006). The thousands of known cases of torture and abuse make it clear that 'torture has become a core tactic in the war on terror' (Bellamy 2006: 147). Other studies suggest that there is now a torture-supporting culture in several Western countries, which is, in part, the result of cultural and political processes related to the war on terrorism (Crelinsten 2003; Jackson 2007c). It remains to be seen whether President Obama's promise in 2008 to end the use of torture in America's struggle against terrorism will be kept.

Along with many orthodox scholars, critical scholars believe that there are a number of arguments which collectively make a powerful

## Box 10.1 Human rights concerns with UK counter-terrorism

| | | | |
|---|---|---|---|
| Association of human rights demands with subversion | The use of lethal force | The profiling and targeting of suspect communities | The treatment of prisoners/detainees |
| Interrogation techniques such as torture | Reliance on confessions as evidence | Interference with the relationship between the accused and their legal representatives | The use of informers, especially young or vulnerable people |
| The use of special courts and no jury trials (case hardening) | Miscarriages of justice | The impunity of security forces | The misuse of special/anti-terrorist legislation |
| The loss of certain rights, such as the right to silence/drawing adverse inference | The militarisation of the police | The independence of the police | Extradition treaties and operations |

case for maintaining an absolute prohibition on the use of torture as a tool of counter-terrorism. In the first place, from a normative perspective, it can be argued that torture is by its very nature a unique kind of moral wrong – it is a form of rape that perverts human relationships and agency – that cannot therefore be morally justified under any circumstances (Scarry 1985; Sussman 2005; Ramsay 2006). In addition, torture violates the principle of non-combatant immunity, which is an important reason why terrorism is often viewed as morally wrong by those condemning it (Shue 1978; Allen 2005). It is also known to result in permanent damage to both the tortured (Sussman 2005) and the torturer, who has to live with the knowledge of the pain he or she caused to a fellow human being (Rejali 2007). As David Sussman puts it, 'the agony of torture typically continues to reproduce itself in the lives of victims and those close to them long after the physical torments stop' (Sussman 2005: 12).

Directly related to these moral arguments, torture also involves a fundamental denial of an individual's non-negotiable human rights, as well as the state's duty of care towards its own and other states' citizens (Blakeley 2009). This is why it is absolutely prohibited under any circumstances in international law and in the legal systems of most countries of the world. As we have suggested above, counter-terrorism methods which surrender the moral high ground by violating human rights standards, as torture clearly does, should be questioned and resisted, not least because they are also likely to be ineffective and counter-productive. There is real evidence that the use of torture in the war on terrorism, and in other conflicts such as Israel–Palestine, Kashmir and Chechnya, has directly contributed to a greater sense of grievance and increased support for terrorist groups. If it is widely known that the authorities are employing torture against terrorist suspects, it can certainly lead to the withholding of information about suspected terrorists by friends and family members who fear for the safety and well-being of their friends and relatives.

A related argument here is that because the extreme pain of torture will often cause people to admit to anything as a way to end their suffering, and extreme pain interferes with cognitive processes like memory (in other words, there can be no 'science of pain'), torture is actually a very poor tool of intelligence-gathering (Rose 2004; Applebaum 2005; Rejali 2007). In reality, most professional interrogators reject the use of torture and coercion because they recognize that it frequently leads to poor quality or even misleading information. Another danger demonstrated by historical examples is that investigators who come to rely on physical coercion as a quick and uncomplicated way of generating information from suspects quickly lose their broader investigatory skills.

In making the case for the use of torture, scholars and politicians have often relied on the so-called 'ticking bomb' scenario in which a captured terrorist refuses to reveal the whereabouts of a ticking bomb which will kill many innocent civilians within a few hours, but the use of torture will lead to a confession about its whereabouts. A staple of popular films and television shows like *24*, the ticking bomb scenario has been shown to be a highly flawed thought experiment with virtually no real-world relevance (Scarry 2004; Luban 2005; Bellamy 2006; Brecher 2007). For example, it is highly unlikely that all the conditions of the thought experiment will be present in a given case – that the authorities will know for certain that the captured terrorist has the information they need, and that he or she will be vulnerable to revealing it under torture. In fact, if the terrorist knows where and when the bomb is going to explode, then he or she knows how long the torture needs to be resisted or where to send the investigators in order to lead them away from the bomb's location. As we've shown, because there is no science of pain, there is no guarantee that the torture will work in any case or that it will not simply result in poor quality information from an individual desperate to end his or her own suffering. In reality, most terrorist groups also have procedures to change their plans when one of their members is caught so that the information they have will quickly be out of date. In fact, despite the torture of tens of thousands of suspected terrorists over many decades in numerous countries, there are no clear examples of an actual real-world ticking bomb scenario where the torture of a terrorist resulted in the prevention of its explosion.

Finally, it can be argued that if torture was to be legally adopted, as Dershowitz (2002) and other scholars have advocated, it would entail moral practices that are incompatible with democratic norms and rights, such as torture-training for interrogators and doctors, medical support for torture sessions, research and development in non-lethal torture and the manufacture of torture equipment and facilities, among others (Wolfendale 2006). Even if it was reserved for exceptional cases, sociologically and historically, exceptions to the prohibition on torture have, in practice, always led to its widespread use in non-exceptional cases and have undermined the moral community and respect for human rights more generally (Allen 2005; Bellamy 2006). In other words, adopting torture as a counter-terrorism method also has a longer-term morally corrosive effect on society. Here, the adoption of torture for countering terrorism could be the start of a slippery slope in which it is also used to gain information about other imminent serious crimes.

## Conflict resolution and the end of terrorism

Ending campaigns of terrorist violence should be the fundamental, underlying aim of all counter-terrorism efforts (English 2009). However, critical scholars, along with many orthodox scholars, would argue that the way in which terrorism has been constructed and treated by the authorities and the terrorism industry, particularly in the years since 9/11, places major obstacles in the way of its peaceful resolution. For example, as we saw in Chapter 3, terrorism has been constructed as a unique kind of modern evil and cultural taboo, and terrorists are often now viewed as essentially savage and inhuman. A consequence of this is that terrorism is treated as an exceptional form of violence, completely separate from other forms like insurgency or war. As we saw in Chapter 7, terrorism today is also treated as 'new' and entirely different from the 'old terrorism' of the pre-9/11 era. This view assumes that contemporary terrorism is conducted by irrational, religious fanatics who lack a political basis or desire for negotiations, and who simply wish to slaughter innocent civilians and cause mayhem and destruction. It also automatically assumes that the historical lessons of dealing with terrorist groups like the IRA do not apply to current groups.

A practical consequence of this framework of terrorism is the vast complex of anti-terrorism laws and processes which mean that even associating with people or groups designated as 'terrorists' or viewing the materials they produce can result in attention from the authorities or even criminal prosecution (Cole 2003). In fact, in June 2010 the US Supreme Court upheld a law which allows for the prosecution of groups or individuals who offer assistance to designated terrorist groups, even if they are providing training or advice in non-violent conflict resolution (McGreal 2010).

Together, these factors make it extremely difficult to pursue peaceful conciliation and reform-based approaches to the resolution of terrorism and place real obstacles in the way of considering conflict resolution as a serious option for responding to terrorism. Critical scholars argue that this is self-defeating and counter-productive, because conflict resolution approaches have arguably had success in ending campaigns of terrorist violence in countries like Canada, South Africa, Northern Ireland and Israel. Perversely, in the current international atmosphere, while negotiation or even reconciliation can be pursued with rebel groups or states that have committed genocide or massive human rights abuses, such as in Rwanda, the former Yugoslavia or Sierra Leone, the question of negotiating or reconciling with terrorist groups is risky and problematic. Conflict resolution with terrorist groups is even more difficult to attempt in practice because of the risk of breaking any one of the multitude of laws which prohibit contact or support of any kind for designated terrorist organizations. In the Philippines, for example, attempts by the government to negotiate a peace agreement with certain Moro groups have been hampered by the Moro groups' inclusion on the US State Department's list of designated terrorist groups (Toros 2008). As a consequence, the Philippine government has had to lobby to get the groups removed from the list of terrorist organizations in order to facilitate face-to-face talks and avoid running foul of anti-terrorist sanctions.

Critical scholars therefore argue that as a form of political violence, terrorism should be de-exceptionalized and treated in the same way as other forms of political violence; it should not be singled out as a separate, special category of 'evil' violence. In part, this is because non-state terrorism actually causes far less suffering than other kinds of political violence such as war, occupation, genocide and repression. More importantly, the field of conflict resolution has long studied ways of ending political violence and can tell us a great deal about how to deal with the roots of political violence and terrorism. Taking emancipation seriously, critical scholars argue that much greater effort needs to be put into dealing holistically and peacefully with terrorism, instead of automatically responding in kind with even greater state counter-violence. They suggest that just as negotiation, mediation, conciliation, reform, reconciliation and other forms of conflict resolution have been effective in ending civil wars, insurgencies, coups, state repression and

---

### Key Points

- Although more systematic evaluation is required, there are good reasons for questioning whether force-based counter-terrorism approaches are effective.
- In responding to terrorism, the argument that there needs to be a trade-off between security and liberty is problematic and counter-productive.
- The absolute prohibition on torture should remain both on moral grounds and because it is an ineffective and counter-productive strategy in the struggle against terrorism.
- The field of conflict resolution has a great deal to teach us about how to resolve conflicts involving terrorism, although the construction of terrorism as evil and illegal makes it a difficult strategy to pursue in practice.

---

the like, there are good reasons for believing that such approaches can also be successful in helping to end campaigns of terrorism (Jones and Libicki 2008). At the very least, terrorism scholars ought to begin engaging seriously with the very large literature on conflict resolution for its application to terrorism (Toros 2008).

## A critical assessment of counter-terrorism

As we explained in Chapter 2, critical scholars, like many orthodox terrorism scholars, adopt an open normativity and reflexivity in their analysis of terrorism and counter-terrorism, and their evaluation is based on a number of key principles and perspectives. Specifically, in approaching questions of counter-terrorism, especially its evaluation, critical scholars adopt the following commitments and perspectives.

First, as we explained in Chapter 6, critical scholars question the commonly accepted view of terrorism as an existential threat requiring enormous efforts to control and counter it. They also reject the notion that terrorism creates a **state of exception** justifying extraordinary measures such as the suspension of normal legal safeguards for human rights. They argue instead that non-state terrorism is typically (and particularly outside war situations) a relatively minor risk to individual and national security, especially in comparison to other threats; that it in no way justifies a state of exception; and that the vast resources spent on counter-terrorism are wasteful and could be much more productively directed elsewhere. Moreover, there is a danger that once emergency laws are brought in, they tend to become permanent and expansive to other activities. In fact, given the human and material costs of the response to the initial 9/11 attacks in the decade since (as well as other costly counter-terrorism campaigns around the world), there is a strong argument for suggesting that doing nothing new or different from the usual response to 'ordinary' criminal violence might be a better overall counter-terrorism policy (McCauley 1991: 137). At the very least, doing nothing new in response to terrorism eliminates the risk of causing 'collateral damage', undermining human rights or wasting scarce resources on ineffective measures.

Related to this, critical scholars also argue that an empirical analysis clearly demonstrates that state terrorism poses a much more serious threat than non-state terrorism and that the international community should be expending much more effort in trying to end ongoing campaigns of state terrorism. Questioning the fundamental necessity of counter-terrorism measures, especially the argument to maintain a state of exception which justifies extraordinary measures, is an initial, crucial, first step in the critical evaluation of contemporary counter-terrorism.

Second, as we have alluded to, the adoption of a critical stance involves questioning commonly accepted ideas about the utility of force and violence as a rational tool of policy (English 2009). The inherently unpredictable consequences of violence – particularly its tendency to provoke further resistance and violence – means that force-based counter-terrorism is always a high-risk strategy with incalculable effects and costs. The 9/11 attacks for example, were part of an escalatory cycle of violence between al-Qaeda and the US government that went back to the early 1990s and which included al-Qaeda's East African embassy bombings, followed by the US missile attacks on Sudan and Afghanistan, followed by the 9/11 attacks. In another sense, they were an even longer-term unforeseen consequence of the US policy of supporting Afghan resistance to the Soviet invasion during the 1980s (Johnson 2004), although other factors played a part too. Israel and Palestinian groups similarly have been locked into a violent retaliatory cycle since at least the 1960s (elements of this cycle started in the 1920s) in which terrorist attacks are responded to with military force, followed by further terrorist attacks. In an analysis of force-based counter-terrorism, it is difficult to find any examples of clear successes, although it could be argued that force-based counter-terrorism can be a (deeply problematic) factor in preparing the ground for conciliatory processes. Violently repressive counter-terrorism campaigns have historically caused far more death, destruction and terror than the terrorism they were originally designed to counter. As Chapters 6 and 11 show, the war on terrorism launched after 9/11 has resulted in the death of hundreds of thousands of mostly innocent people compared to the less than 3,000 people killed in the initial terrorist attacks. At the very least, force-based counter-terrorism campaigns, such as the war on terrorism, leave a legacy of bitterness and anger at the heavy-handedness of the state's response. At worst, they can actually generate more terrorism.

In taking this approach, critical scholars reject the ahistorical argument that contemporary terrorism is 'new' and unrelated to the 'old' terrorism of the past. Instead, they prioritize context and history and seek to learn lessons from previous counter-terrorism campaigns. As noted, analyses of earlier responses to terrorism reveal important lessons about the limited effectiveness of military force-based strategies, for example, and the successes that have come from dialogue and reform-based responses to terrorism.

Related to questions about the fundamental utility of responding to violence with even greater violence, critical approaches also question the broader problem-solving approach which views terrorism narrowly as a pathological or unwarranted challenge to the status quo which is simply in need of a quick solution. They also question the argument that the role of terrorism scholars is primarily to help the authorities to solve better the problem of non-state terrorism, despite the fact that countering non-state terrorism is the *raison d'être* of the terrorism studies field which has a vast literature devoted to this issue. Instead, they ask alternative questions about the extent to which the status quo itself, in which Western states dominate the international system and millions suffer under conditions of structural violence, for example, might be implicated in the causes of terrorism (Rogers 2010).

Thus, rather than asking how terrorists who are opposed to Western foreign policy can be defeated, it might instead be asked how and why Western foreign policy provokes violent responses. In taking this approach, critical scholars challenge the view that Western societies are simply innocent victims of terrorism, suggesting instead that the best way to respond to terrorism might be to review and revise oppressive policies which provoke violent resistance in the first instance. Al-Qaeda has stated that its campaign is a direct response to American policies in the Middle East (Lawrence 2005), while Palestinian groups act, at least in part, in response to the oppressive status quo engendered by the occupation and territorial encroachment of Israel (Gunning 2007b). The terrorists who attacked London on 7 July 2005 similarly stated that they were acting in response to the UK's involvement in the Iraq war.

Third, critical scholars are openly committed to human security and a broad notion of emancipation, rather than a narrow commitment to orthodox notions of national security. In the context of counter-terrorism, this means the rejection of false choices between human rights and the rule of law, and security – the so-called liberty/security trade-off (see above) – and the rejection of arguments about the exceptional nature of the terrorist threat. At the same time, it means retaining a focus on and judging the effectiveness of counter-terrorism by the impact that it has on human rights, human well-being and social cohesion. This includes, but goes far beyond, arguments about saving lives through preventing terrorist attacks – which as Chapter 6 shows, are sometimes questionable in any case. In this respect, critical analyses of counter-terrorism pay close attention to the human, social, political and material costs of counter-terrorism policies. It asks questions about the impact and costs of new anti-terrorism legislation, military operations overseas, policing practices such as profiling and shoot-to-kill policies, surveillance programmes, the use of torture and enhanced interrogation, and other counter-terrorism practices on human rights protection and human well-being. For example, it is demonstrable that the policies and approaches of the war on terrorism has resulted in the construction of Muslims as a 'suspect community' (see pp. 256, 263; Hillyard 1993).

More broadly, critical scholars ask questions about the ways in which counter-terrorism is linked to projects of state hegemony and **governmentality** (Amoore and de Goede 2005, 2008); the way it is sometimes linked to efforts to control dissent, win support for anti-immigration policies, secure foreign policy objectives and bolster the power of elites; and perhaps most importantly the material interests that have come to be invested in its continuation. Countering the perceived threat of terrorism has resulted in the investment of hundreds of billions of dollars in new institutions, programmes and policies that are extremely lucrative and beneficial to key actors and sectors like the military–industrial complex, private security providers and state security institutions – while at the same time being of dubious effectiveness in preventing terrorism (Pilkington 2010). In the short time since 9/11, these actors have grown into a pervasive terrorism industry which has powerful material and political interests in maintaining counter-terrorism as a key government priority in order to secure the continued flow of resources. The existence of the terrorism industry has the potential to distort counter-terrorism approaches, because actors wanting to protect their interests will resist the discontinuation of counter-terrorism policies or programmes that come to be seen as ineffective or counter-productive.

In the end, critical scholars argue that the minimal test of any counter-terrorism policy or broader campaign is whether it meets the three tests of *proportionality, effectiveness* and *legitimacy*. In other words: Is the response truly proportionate to the threat or does it constitute an overreaction and disproportionate, heavy-handed response? Are the measures adopted really effective in dealing with the threat of further terrorism or are they ineffectual, counter-productive or far more costly than the terrorism itself? Is the response legitimate or does it contravene accepted moral principles and standards of behaviour? Although critical scholars recognize that such judgements are context-

## Key Points

- Critical approaches to counter-terrorism begin by rigorously questioning the assumption that terrorism represents an existential threat to states, societies or people.
- Critical scholars also question whether there is a 'new terrorism', arguing that lessons can be learned from previous counter-terrorism campaigns.
- Critical scholars dispute the utility of force as an effective response to terrorism, as well as the broader problem-solving framework from which it emerges.
- With a commitment to emancipation, critical scholars question the effects of current counter-terrorism policies in terms of their impact on suspect communities and their role in extending state power and vested interests.
- Critical scholars argue that counter-terrorism policies should be evaluated through the tests of proportionality, effectiveness and legitimacy.

specific and dependent on one's overall normative framework, they still maintain that, within a minimal foundational framework, these three tests offer a useful benchmark. Adhering to these minimal tests ensures that counter-terrorism does not morph into state terrorism by failing to distinguish between the innocent and the guilty, being highly disproportionate, aiming to terrify or intimidate the wider population or a particular community into submission or being co-opted to serve a political agenda (Goodin 2006: 69–73; Crelinsten 2009: 51; see also Crenshaw 1995). Maximally, critical scholars suggest that the test of counter-terrorism is whether it improves human security and well-being by both protecting them from physical violence and contributing to their emancipation, and dealing with the sources of political conflict which engender violence (English 2009).

## Conclusion

It is sometimes argued that critical approaches are good at criticizing government approaches to counter-terrorism, but offer little in the way of alternative practical advice to officials who have the day-to-day responsibility of protecting their citizens. In answer to this criticism, we would suggest that critical approaches have the potential to make real and important contributions to counter-terrorism policy and wider social debates on how to respond to terrorism in a number of ways. First, and most basically, critical approaches play an important role in suggesting a more realistic and balanced assessment of the nature of the terrorist threat. This can, in turn, greatly help to avoid unnecessary and costly overreactions by the state or the creation of self-fulfilling prophecies in which counter-terrorism promotes the terrorism it seeks to prevent (Zulaika 2009).

Second, critical approaches can provide rigorous and ethically oriented evaluations of counter-terrorism policies which, if acted upon, could also have the effect of helping to avoid ineffective or counter-productive policies like the torture of terrorist suspects, profiling or launching a 'war on terrorism'. The commitment to emancipation by critical scholars means that they approach counter-terrorism from a more holistic perspective than a concern with state security does, which can potentially have broader benefits for human security and well-being. Analytically, the commitment to emancipation also has implications for how scholars approach the question of how to measure the effectiveness of counter-terrorism measures and policies. It avoids narrow or limited approaches based on how many terrorists are killed or captured or how many plots are disrupted, and suggests that issues of moral principle, democratic participation, social justice, community cohesion, human well-being and conflict transformation should also be applied in assessing counter-terrorism policies.

Lastly, many critical scholars are committed to the serious exploration of peaceful alternatives to force-based forms of counter-terrorism, particularly in terms of the lessons and well-established approaches of the conflict resolution field. From this perspective, critical scholars can offer practical policy advice such as ending oppressive policies and initiating reforms to deal with grievances and social injustice, opening lines of dialogue with relevant groups and providing processes for meaningful political participation.

As a final note, critical scholars provide an alternative perspective to the questions raised in this chapter by maintaining that ultimately state terrorism has been a far more serious and destructive threat than non-state terrorism. However, the question of how to respond effectively to state terrorism has been greatly neglected as a topic of research, apart from a fairly small body of literature on how to deal with state sponsorship of non-state terrorist groups. We would argue, therefore, that efforts to devise counter-state terrorism policies and end campaigns of wholesale state terrorism should receive much greater scholarly attention than they currently do in the terrorism studies field. This perspective is so far outside the normal terrorism framework, however, that it is difficult to even begin conceptualizing what counter-state-terrorism approaches would entail. Critical scholars, however, would argue that the efforts of human rights campaigners and conflict resolution scholars and practitioners provide a potentially rich vein of knowledge and practical lessons for developing this perspective.

## Discussion Questions

1. What are some of the main strategies available for countering non-state terrorism?
2. How did the events of 11 September 2001 change the way in which states responded to terrorism?
3. What key principles and perspectives are adopted by critical scholars in their approach to counter-terrorism?
4. How should scholars contribute to the state's efforts to respond to terrorism?
5. By what minimal and maximal standards and principles should counter-terrorism policies be assessed and evaluated?
6. Is there a necessary trade-off between liberty and security when responding to terrorism?
7. Is the torture of terrorist suspects ever justified?
8. Why do critical scholars prioritize conflict resolution approaches to dealing with terrorism?
9. What are some of the main obstacles to applying conflict resolution approaches to terrorism?
10. How do counter-terrorism policies sometimes reinforce the power of the state?
11. Under what conditions can counter-terrorism become a kind of state terrorism?
12. In your view, what is the best approach for responding to terrorism?

## Recommended Reading

Brecher, R., 2007. *Torture and the Ticking Bomb*, London: Wiley-Blackwell. An incisive deconstruction and rejection of the popular ticking bomb scenario.

Crelinsten, R., 2009. *Counterterrorism*, Cambridge: Polity. A very thorough and intelligent overview and analysis of contemporary approaches to counter-terrorism and the strengths and weaknesses of different strategies.

English, R., 2009. *Terrorism: How to Respond*, Oxford: Oxford University Press. An eloquent and sophisticated argument based on a deep historical understanding about how modern societies should respond sensibly and effectively to terrorism.

Hillyard, P., 1993. *Suspect Community: People's Experience of the Prevention of Terrorism Acts in Britain*, London: Pluto. The classic study of the effects of counter-terrorism laws and police practice on the construction of the Irish community as 'suspect'.

→

Lustick, I., 2006. *Trapped in the War on Terror*, Philadelphia, PA: University of Pennsylvania Press. An analysis of how politicians and society have become trapped in costly overreaction to terrorism after 9/11.

## Web Resources

*www.powerbase.info/index.php?title=Counter-Terrorism_Portal*
A comprehensive portal with links, articles and analysis from a critical perspective on different aspects of counter-terrorism.

The National Counterterrorism Center (NCTC): *www.nctc.gov/*
The NCTC was established by Presidential order in 2004 as part of the key recommendations of the 9/11 Commission; its mission is to lead America's counter-terrorism efforts at home and abroad.

The US government's Office of the Coordinator for Counterterrorism:
*www.state.gov/s/ct/*
Established in 1994, the Office 'coordinates and supports the development and implementation of all US Government policies and programs aimed at countering terrorism overseas'.

Official Country Reports on Terrorism from the US Department of State:
*www.state.gov/s/ct/rls/crt/index.htm*
Annual reports on terrorism presented to Congress by the US Secretary of State.

The UK government's counter-terrorism strategy, CONTEST: *http://security. homeoffice.gov.uk/counter-terrorism-strategy/*
Resources include news on counter-terrorism activities in the UK, public guidance and other official documents.

The Anti-terrorism website of the UK's Metropolitan Police: *www.met. police.uk/so/at_hotline.htm*
Provides information and advice for the public.

*The Guardian* newspaper: *www.guardian.co.uk/commentisfree/series/a-z-of-legislation*
A summary of the main UK legislation related to terrorism.

The UN's efforts to combat terrorism worldwide:
*www.un.org/terrorism/*
Includes access to UN strategy, reports and resolutions directed towards combating terrorism.

The official website for the Bloody Sunday Inquiry: *www.bloody-sunday-inquiry.org/*
Includes access to the final published report. The inquiry was established to review one of the most controversial counter-terrorism actions in contemporary British history.

# Chapter 11

# Assessing the War on Terrorism

## Reader's Guide

The war on terrorism is the term used to describe the global counter-terrorism campaign that was launched in response to the attacks of 11 September 2001. In its scope, expenditure and pervasive impact on social and political life, the war on terrorism is comparable to the decades of the cold war. In an important sense, it represents the beginning of a new phase in global political relations and has important consequences for security, human rights, international law, cooperation and governance. In this chapter we critically examine this new conflict, beginning with an overview of its major military, intelligence, diplomatic, legal, domestic and discursive dimensions. Following a critical examination of this conflict's purported successes and failures, the chapter investigates its origins and evolution, and the ways the war on terrorism has become embedded and normalized across the world. Here, we argue that this new security paradigm is likely to be with us for some time, despite moves by some official actors to abandon the term. In the conclusion we reflect on the extent to which the war on terrorism is the logical outcome of the way in which terrorism has been constructed, studied and countered in Western societies in the twentieth century.

## Introduction

George W. Bush was sworn into office as the 43rd President of the United States of America on 20 January 2001. Despite CIA warnings of the threat then posed by al-Qaeda (Oliver 2007: 29), the extent to which his tenure would be dominated by a global confrontation with terrorism was at the time almost inconceivable. On 11 September 2001, however, following the devastating attacks on the USA, a new 'war on terrorism' was announced by the President (Silberstein 2002: 9; Jackson 2005: 9) and an administration that had been relatively uninterested in international affairs (Singh 2006: 14; Patman 2007: 56) thrust itself into the most extensive – and most expensive – global conflict since the cold war.

The global impact of the war on terrorism has been profound. In economic terms, it had cost the USA alone an estimated US$864 billion by 2008 – the equivalent of the Netherlands' annual GDP (Belasco, cited in Croft 2010: 192). In military terms, it has entailed two major conflicts in Afghanistan and Iraq, alongside smaller but nonetheless serious military operations in states such as Pakistan, Somalia, the Philippines, Georgia and Yemen. In human terms, in addition to hundreds of thousands of military-inflicted deaths, the war has caused large-scale refugeeism, the torture and rendition of thousands of suspected terrorists and insurgents, and other major violations of human rights and international law. In addition, since 2001, most countries around the world have introduced draconian legislation to counter the terrorist threat, with some, such as Russia, India, China and Zimbabwe, using the language of the war on terrorism to justify confrontations with internal dissidents (Jackson 2005: 13).

Understanding the origins and consequences of this new counter-terrorism paradigm is imperative for critical as well as orthodox scholars. Achieving this requires, in the first instance, returning to the relationship between power, knowledge and discourse to ask how the war on terrorism emerged as a possible, necessary and legitimate response to 9/11 (Zulaika 2009). Doing so involves uncovering dominant narratives of threat and war, tracking their consolidation across social and cultural sites, tracing the political and material interests behind these narratives and the practices they engender, and pointing to alternative ideas and practices the war on terrorism has obscured. Second, it involves uncovering and critiquing instances of political repression and violence within this new counter-terrorism paradigm, guided by the normative commitment to emancipation outlined in Chapter 2 (see also McDonald 2009). Finally, because critical scholars are also committed to the practical question of identifying possibilities for change within the realities of political life, we must try to understand the origins and consequences of this war as a vital first step in attempting to transform its practices by engaging with the power structures behind it (Toros and Gunning 2009).

## An overview of a global anti-terror campaign

The war on terrorism is a multidimensional campaign of almost limitless scope that has impacted on all of the world's regions. Here, we briefly sketch the different dimensions of this counter-terrorism campaign (summarized in Figure 11.1), before assessing their consequences in the following section.

### The military dimension

The war on terrorism's military dimension has been its most visible and controversial aspect, particularly in relation to the two major wars fought in Afghanistan and Iraq. The military campaign in the former began in October 2001 with the launch of the US-led **Operation Enduring Freedom**. Over 60 states joined the 'coalition of the willing' created to prosecute this war (Office of Public Affairs 2002), including traditional US allies such as the UK and Canada, strategically significant states such as Pakistan and Kazakhstan, and major global powers including France and Russia. By November 2001, the combination of Special Forces personnel, air strikes and a re-armed **Northern Alliance** had succeeded in collapsing the ruling **Taliban** regime and in dispersing al-Qaeda (McInnes 2003; Rogers 2009). An interim authority was established under future President Hamid Karzai in December

**Figure 11.1** *Dimensions of the war on terrorism*

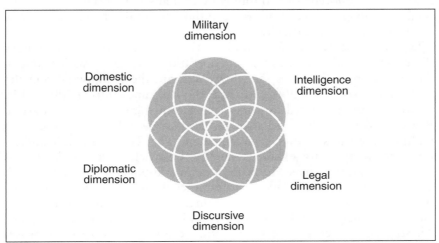

2001. With the establishment of US military bases in neighbouring countries and growing confidence in Afghanistan's transition to a pro-Western state, this military dimension then took a more controversial turn with the subsequent invasion of Iraq (Rogers 2009).

Using 9/11 to justify conflict with **Saddam Hussein's** Ba'athist regime had been proposed by key figures in the Bush administration immediately after the attacks took place (Woodward 2003: 79–92; Clarke 2004: 30). Although the war on terrorism's initial focus was on Afghanistan, a military invasion of Iraq was launched in March 2003 under the title **Operation Iraqi Freedom**. Despite continuing international concerns around the war's legality (Hancock and Valeriano 2006; Ryan 2006: 178–9; Miller 2007: 113–14) over 40 coalition states contributed. However, only the USA and the UK committed significant numbers of troops, offering 424,000 and 41,000 respectively (Garden 2003: 703; Rajaee 2007b: 162). As with the Afghanistan war, military victory arrived swiftly with Saddam Hussein's regime collapsing in three weeks. The newly established Coalition Provisional Authority (CPA) quickly found itself occupied with attempting to manage the looting, organized crime and violent resistance that began to fill the vacuum created by the collapse of Iraq's security infrastructure (Rathmell 2005).

Within a few months of the invasion of Iraq, an organized and effective resistance force emerged to fight the occupying Coalition forces, resulting in the deaths of more than 6,000 Coalition troops and private contractors by 2010 (see pp. 258–61). Similarly, in Afghanistan the Taliban regrouped in the years following 2001, and by 2008 Coalition forces were fighting a serious insurgency with more than 100,000 troops. By mid-2010, more than 2,000 Coalition troops and private contractors had been killed in Afghanistan. In both Afghanistan and Iraq, many hundreds of thousands of civilians have been killed in the ongoing violence (see Box 6.7), although establishing the precise number has proved difficult.

Beyond these two major conflicts, the war on terrorism's military dimension has also included covert operations such as assassinations of terrorist suspects in states including Pakistan, the Philippines, Somalia and Yemen (see Arkin 2002; Kibbe 2004; Rees and Aldrich 2005: 913), as well as the expanded targeted killing campaign in the Afghanistan/Pakistan region. It has also involved large-scale military assistance for willing supporters within this campaign. The Trans-Sahara Counterterrorist Initiative, for example, saw the USA help train Special Forces of African states such as Morocco, Algeria and Nigeria (van Wyk 2007: 132; see also R . Grey 2006). More targeted programmes included the provision of counter-insurgency training, funds and equipment to specific allies, such as the Philippines (Nankivell and Boutilier 2007: 117). These programmes, of course, all required and relied on vast increases in US military expenditure which had reached an enormous US$537 billion by 2005, amounting to 48 per cent of all global military spending (Williams 2008: 10). Many of these programmes have been continued and even expanded under the Obama administration.

## The intelligence dimension

A second key aspect of the war on terrorism is its intelligence dimension. At the domestic level in the USA, this involved institutional reorganization of the national intelligence services, assisted by dramatic increases in the funding available to them (see, for example, Aldrich 2004). As we noted in Chapter 6, a major study by the *Washington Post* identified some 1,271 government bodies and 1,931 private contractor companies working on counter-terrorism in the USA by 2010, many of them in the intelligence-gathering and analysis sector (Pilkington 2010). This aspect of the war on terrorism also involved the creation of dramatic new intelligence programmes, including the controversial and short-lived Operation TIPS programme which encouraged members of the public to report suspicious behaviour to the authorities (Jarvis and Lister 2010).

At an international level, the war on terrorism has been characterized by a global intelligence-gathering exercise involving increased cooperation between different national security agencies (Jackson 2005: 11). The CIA's rendition programme, for example, involved the abduction and forcible transfer of terrorist suspects to specialist facilities for interrogation and questioning. Many of the suspects picked up under this programme were taken to Camp X-ray at Guantánamo Bay in Cuba, where their designation as '**enemy combatants**' was used to deny them the protections of domestic and international law (Cole 2005: 39–43). Still more disturbing was the transfer and subsequent torture of those such as Maher Arar to other states with dreadful human rights records (see Box 11.1).

---

### Box 11.1 The rendition and torture of Maher Arar

The Syrian-born Canadian citizen Maher Arar was picked up by the United States Immigration and Nationalization Service (INS) at JFK airport in New York following a holiday in Tunisia in September 2002. After two weeks of questioning as a suspected terrorist in the USA, Arar was covertly transferred to Syria for further interrogation. Once in Syria, he was held in an underground cell of three feet, by six feet, by seven feet, and subjected to extreme physical, psychological and mental torture for prolonged periods. Arar was eventually released without charge and returned to his home in Canada one year after his initial detention.

*Sources*: Leung 2004; Mayer 2005; Mutimer 2007.

A final aspect of the intelligence dimension was the global campaign to track and intercept terrorist financing. This campaign, frequently hailed as this war's earliest success, saw the US government alone block over US$130 million in assets by 2004 (Josselin 2006: 168). It has also resulted in sanctions and black-listing by the UN for numerous individuals and organizations thought to be involved in terrorism-related activities.

## The diplomatic dimension

A third major aspect of the war on terrorism is its diplomatic dimension, which involves a concerted effort to maintain a global coalition of partner states and organizations in this conflict. Here, international diplomatic initiatives have included the increase of bilateral aid programmes to strategically significant states such as Jordan, Pakistan and Turkey (Woods 2005: 397–8; Josselin 2006: 169). In addition, the USA embarked on an extensive public diplomacy campaign to counter anti-Americanism in the Middle East and beyond. With former advertising executive Charlotte Beers appointed Under Secretary of State for Public Diplomacy and Public Affairs (Kennedy 2003: 317), the USA worked hard to revitalize its global **soft power**, in part by broadcasting Public Service Announcements and establishing radio and television stations to help restore the American global 'brand' (van Ham 2003; Nye 2004). Secretary of State Colin Powell even starred in a 90-minute MTV broadcast designed to help win this 'battle for hearts and minds' amongst younger audiences (Peterson 2002: 83)! However, many aspects of this programme have been controversial, such as revelations that the Pentagon planted stories in the Iraq media to counter the negative publicity generated by the deaths of civilians and the torture and abuse of detainees.

The public diplomacy dimension of the war on terrorism has been continued and expanded since the election of President Barack Obama, with a range of policy initiatives and measures directed at countering anti-Americanism. In June 2009 for example, President Obama made a major speech in Cairo aimed at rebuilding America's image in the eyes of the Muslim world and instigating a new era of mutual respect.

## The legal dimension

The war on terrorism's legal dimension involved the introduction of new and wide-ranging domestic counter-terrorism legislation in nearly every country around the world, as well as a number of new international conventions aimed at restricting transnational terrorist activities. Much of this activity was the direct result of **UNSC Resolution 1371**, which the UN Security Council unanimously adopted on 28 September

2001. The resolution required every member state of the UN to review their counter-terrorism legislation to ensure that it complied with international conventions on terrorism. As a consequence, nearly every state in the world adopted new, more extensive, counter-terrorism legislation (see p. 230), as did many of the major international organizations, including the UN, the EU, the Organization of American States (OAS), the African Union (AU), the Organisation of the Islamic Conference and the Association of Southeast Asian Nations (ASEAN).

That many states took this as an opportunity to strengthen law enforcement powers caused considerable concerns for human rights advocates. A number of African countries including Kenya, Nigeria and Ethiopia, for example, re-examined their anti-terrorism powers after 9/11, strengthening powers against terrorist financing, expanding the types of evidence that could be submitted in anti-terrorism trials and increasing the incarceration periods for those found guilty of terrorism-related activities (Harmon 2008: 131). Western European states and the USA similarly introduced dramatic new anti-terrorism powers relating, for example, to precharge detention, control orders, stop and search powers, and other similar measures. In the UK, for example, the 2001 Anti-Terrorism, Crime and Security Act initially allowed the Home Secretary the power to *indefinitely detain* foreign nationals suspected of terrorism without charge or trial, before it was successfully challenged by the House of Lords.

## The domestic dimension

This aspect of the war on terrorism comprised a sustained effort to shore up American national security against the threat of external and internal terrorism. Over thirty US states changed their terrorism laws after 9/11 and established new counter-terrorism agencies and measures (ibid.), while at a Federal level the **USA PATRIOT Act** of October 2001 brought about a range of new provisions, including: dramatically increasing the surveillance powers available to the US government; providing for the use of nationwide search warrants; enabling the deportation of immigrants accused of raising money for designated or suspected terrorist organizations; and empowering the Secretary of State to designate any foreign or domestic group as a terrorist organization without review (Cole 2003; Jackson 2005: 14). Other important legislative measures included President Bush's November 2001 military order which facilitated the use of military commissions to try non-US citizens suspected of involvement in international terrorism (Jackson 2007c: 356).

In addition, the domestic war on terrorism led to the creation of major new governmental institutions such as the DHS which centralized the functions of existing American agencies responsible for domestic security, as well as the involvement of thousands of private security companies in all aspects of counter-terrorism (Pilkington 2010). It has also involved the preventive detainment of thousands of terrorist suspects and the photographing, fingerprinting and interviewing of 80,000 men from Arab and Muslim countries under the government's Special Registration programme (Cole 2003: xxiii). Other domestic measures included the strengthening of emergency response procedures, increased security measures for airports, borders and public events, and a range of new programmes and strategies aimed at involving the public in the counter-terrorism enterprise. Similar domestic measures have been introduced in many Western states, such as the UK, Spain, Italy and Australia.

## The discursive dimension

A final, discursive, dimension of the war on terrorism concerns the commonsense view of terrorism and its solutions – the 'regime of truth' – that has been established since 9/11 (Jackson 2005; Croft 2006). This regime of truth relates, first, to the widespread international acceptance and use of dominant narratives about the 9/11 attacks as an act of war, and the exceptional threat posed by contemporary terrorism; and, second, to the widespread global construction of counter-terrorism policies that perpetuate this dominant understanding of the terrorist threat. Although the actual term 'war on terrorism' is now rarely mentioned, especially after President Obama announced that it would no longer be employed by his administration, the broader shared understanding of counter-terrorism it fostered remains embedded within the continuing practices of racial profiling, target strengthening, the surveillance of citizens and counter-terrorism generally (Jackson forthcoming b). As outlined below, this dominant truth regime makes the war on terrorism extremely difficult to either contest or escape, even as we see new political executives replacing those responsible for its emergence.

## Key Points

- On 11 September 2001, President George W. Bush announced that the USA had entered into a new global war with terrorism.
- The consequences of this war have been vast, extending far beyond the military conflicts in Afghanistan and Iraq to include intelligence, diplomatic, legal, domestic and discursive dimensions.
- The impacts of this war also stretch far beyond the US borders, with most countries having implemented new and wide-ranging anti-terrorism measures.

## Assessing the war on terrorism

Evaluating the success of any political project depends on our making two related choices. First, we must settle on the normative and political values against which to assess a project's desirability: are we more interested in its impact on security, equality, freedom or justice, for example (Dannreuther 2007: 7–10)? Second, we must also decide how to measure these values, asking how we might know if security, for instance, has been achieved in a particular context. These decisions, of course, cannot be settled objectively; they will always be shaped by one's political standpoint. To illustrate, this section outlines some of the ways that critical scholars have assessed and critiqued the US-led war on terrorism. Before that, let us briefly consider some of the war on terrorism's purported successes.

Broadly sympathetic accounts of the war on terrorism tend to focus on a set of relatively narrow strategic achievements. These include, in the first instance, the arrest of hundreds of terrorist suspects, often in conjunction with the new anti-terrorism powers noted above, and the successful conviction of several would-be terrorists, including those outlined in Box 11.2.

Second, from an American perspective, the war on terrorism could also be seen to have prevented further large-scale terrorist attacks on the US mainland, despite the efforts of individuals such as those in Box 11.2. Third, the two military conflicts in Afghanistan and Iraq both led to the toppling of brutal political regimes responsible for massive human suffering, with subsequent elections in each. Fourth, training camps used by al-Qaeda in Afghanistan have been shut down or rendered dysfunctional, and many of the movement's senior members, such as **Abu Musab al-Zarqawi**, have been either killed or captured since 9/11. Finally, the construction of the global war on terrorism has facilitated enhanced international cooperation in counter-terrorism efforts, a development that may have positive future spill-over effects for attempts at cooperation around other issues.

To gauge the importance of these apparent successes, it is first necessary to consider their efficacy by contextualizing them within and against their financial, human, social, political and other costs. Additionally, we need to evaluate the desirability of these 'successes' and other developments within the war on terrorism, which requires being explicit and reflective about our political values. Critical scholars, as well as many orthodox scholars, argue that the war on terrorism is problematic on both pragmatic and normative grounds. First, it has not been effective or efficient as a response to the 9/11 terrorist attacks and the nature of ongoing terrorist activities. Second, because of the value critical scholars attach to the notion of emancipation, this leads them to argue that the war on terrorism has been neither propor-

## Box 11.2   Some key arrests and convictions of suspected terrorists

| Case | Description |
|---|---|
| 'Shoe Bomber': Richard Reid | British citizen, Richard Reid, was arrested in December 2001 after attempting to ignite explosives hidden within his shoes while travelling on a flight to Miami. The 'shoe bomber' pleaded guilty to eight counts against him, including the attempted use of a WMD, and was sentenced to 110 years in prison in 2003. |
| The '20th Hijacker': Zacarias Moussaoui | The '20th hijacker', Zacarias Moussaoui, pleaded guilty in 2005 to conspiring with the 19 hijackers responsible for the 9/11 attacks on the USA. Moussaoui was sentenced to life imprisonment in 2006, despite prosecution calls for the death penalty, and remains the only individual charged in connection with 9/11 in the USA. |
| The '21/7' Bombers | Four men, all in their twenties, were sentenced to life imprisonment in 2007 following their failed attack on the London transport system of July 2005. The attempt caused widespread concern, arriving only two weeks after the successful '7/7' bombings in London. |
| The 'Detroit Bomber': Umar Farouk Abdulmutallab | The Nigerian Abdulmutallab was arrested after an alleged failed attempt to detonate a bomb hidden in his underwear while on a flight to Detroit on Christmas Day 2009. The so-called 'Detroit Bomber' pleaded not guilty to six charges in January 2010. |

tionate to the terrorist threat nor legitimate in its methods and outcomes.

More specifically, despite the vast sums of money and other resources poured into this conflict (Cox 2002; Josselin 2006; Rajaee 2007b), it can be argued that the war on terrorism has been largely ineffective in preventing the global spread of terrorist violence. Notwithstanding problems associated with statistical counts of terrorism, according to the US Department of State's own figures (which include terrorist attacks in warzones like Iraq), there were almost 12,000 terrorist attacks on non-combatants alone in 2008, in addition to over 29,000 in the two preceding years (see Figure 11.2). As Figure 11.3 further illustrates, these attacks led to over 15,000 deaths and more than 30,000 injuries, many of them within the context of the wars in Iraq and Afghanistan which were enacted as major fronts in the war on terrorism.

**Figure 11.2**   *Global incidents of non-state terrorism*

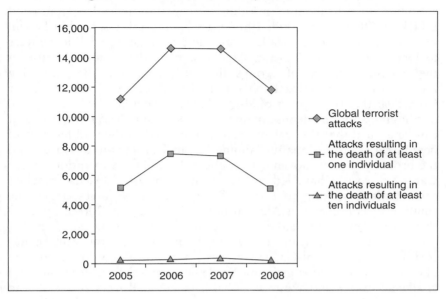

*Source*: US Department of State (2009).

**Figure 11.3**   *Global impacts of non-state terrorism*

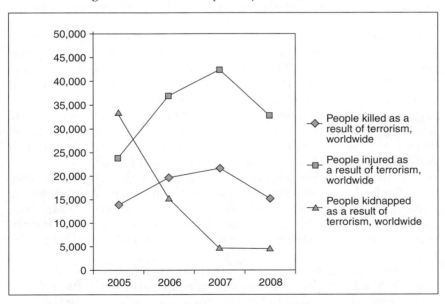

*Source*: US Department of State (2009).

In addition, al-Qaeda continues to exist as a globally relevant organization, despite the capture or killing of several of its leaders (Jones and Libicki 2008; English 2009: 106–7). Its figurehead, Osama bin Laden, moreover, continues to evade arrest, despite ongoing coalition efforts to locate him in the Pakistan–Afghanistan border region. Because of the nebulous nature of groups like al-Qaeda, and the increasing number of self-radicalized loner terrorists (Sageman 2008), it is far from clear that the capture of al-Qaeda leaders could ever be successful in bringing about its demise in any case (Neumann 2009). Moreover, it can be argued that the war on terrorism has led to the proliferation of new terrorist groups, many claiming ideological links to al-Qaeda and the broader jihadist movement. In effect, US military operations in the war on terrorism have led to the proliferation of al-Qaeda franchise organizations seeking to oppose Western military forces; from one small al-Qaeda group in Afghanistan in 2001 (Burke 2004), by 2010 there were new al-Qaeda-affiliated groups in Iraq, Pakistan, Somalia, the Maghreb, Yemen and elsewhere. Seen this way, the war on terrorism has elevated al-Qaeda's global status and importance, both by allowing this nebulous grouping to depict themselves as a meaningful challenger to US and Western global hegemony (Rogers 2009: 8), and by scattering and decentralizing the al-Qaeda network, making it even harder to counteract. By increasing rather than reducing the risk of terrorism around the world, the war on terrorism has become a self-fulfilling prophesy; the global counter-terrorism campaign has become implicated in promoting the behaviour it seeks to prevent (Zulaika 2009).

A second broad point is that the war on terrorism has also failed quite dramatically to deter 'rogue states' from either sponsoring terrorism or acquiring WMD. Two of the original 'axis of evil' – Iran and North Korea – have, if anything, become more belligerent in their resistance to American threats, and concerns continue over their respective nuclear weapons programmes. In the years since 9/11, North Korea has twice successfully tested nuclear weapons, with its launch of short-range ballistic missiles in 2009 indicating a capacity for their delivery. Critics also allege that President Ahmadinejad's regime continues to seek nuclear weapons, despite Iranian protests to the contrary. Indeed, the invasion of Iraq, and subsequent revelation that Saddam Hussein's regime did *not* possess a developed WMD programme, may even have encouraged states such as Iran to increase their efforts at acquiring non-conventional weapons to avoid a similar fate.

A third, normative, criticism of the war on terrorism relates to the massive human suffering it has engendered, particularly (though not exclusively) in relation to the major military operations in Afghanistan, Iraq and Pakistan. Despite American military sophistication and its 'virtuous war' (Der Derian 2009) claims to avoid 'collateral damage', the civilian casualties in each conflict have been enormous (see p. 146) – although it is possible to argue that the removal of the brutal regimes in Iraq and Afghanistan may have simultaneously served to save lives. Operations Enduring Freedom and Iraqi Freedom alone resulted in vastly higher death tolls than that of 9/11, and ongoing violence continues to produce large numbers of civilian casualties in each of these countries. By July 2010, the organization Iraq Body Count had estimated the total number of post-invasion civilian deaths in Iraq at between 97,082 and 105,855 (Iraq Body Count 2010), while an earlier study in the medical journal, *The Lancet*, suggested a civilian death toll of 654,965 by July 2006 (Burnham *et al.* 2006) from the war and subsequent violence.

Importantly, these deaths do not fully exhaust the total cost to human security of these two conflicts. By 2006, refugeeism had become a major concern in the Iraq conflict, with one million people having fled the state amid escalating violence (Miller 2007). Moreover, the destruction of national infrastructure and collapse of local security services in each country profoundly reduced public safety and living conditions for those left behind (Marsden 2003: 92; Rathmell 2005: 1023) – although reconstruction efforts in Iraq, and to a lesser extent in Afghanistan, are gathering pace at the time of writing. In Iraq, for example, the disbanding of the Iraqi armed forces meant reconstruction efforts were hindered not only by the lack of local forces capable of maintaining order, but also by the sudden creation of hundreds of thousands of well-armed, frequently embittered and newly unemployed young men (Tripp 2004: 552).

A fourth negative consequence has been the dramatic erosion of civil liberties and human rights that has taken place under the mantle of the war on terrorism. Among a great many other human rights abuses, the policy of extraordinary renditions discussed above has resulted in the torture of hundreds of terrorist suspects in recipient countries from Afghanistan, Algeria, Egypt, Jordan, Morocco, Syria, Thailand, Uzbekistan and elsewhere (*New Internationalist* 2009: 8). Further, in 2004 it was dramatically revealed that US soldiers had been torturing prisoners within Iraq's Abu Ghraib prison, a practice that had become widespread in global counter-terrorist operations (Jackson 2007c). Other serious human rights abuses associated with the war on terrorism include the operation of US-trained, Interior Ministry-based death squads in Iraq (Plumer 2005; Human Rights Watch 2006) and the use of a special assassination squad called Task Force 373 in Afghanistan (Davies 2010). Perhaps more damaging, however, has been the willingness of other states to use the war on terrorism to justify their own programmes of repression against internal dissidents and critics (see Box 11.3). The Russian leadership, for example, has argued that the continuing campaign of violence in Chechnya presents a contribution to the same war on terrorism being fought by the USA and UK (Buckley 2006: 58; Light 2007). As we noted above, sweeping new counter-terrorism legislation in states across the world has greatly undermined established civil liberties.

A sixth criticism concerns the damage brought by the war on terrorism to the functioning of the international system more broadly. Because of the wars in Iraq and Afghanistan, the increased American military presence across the globe, and the growth of repressive counter-terrorism campaigns, the Middle East, the Caucuses, the Horn of Africa and parts of Asia have all suffered increased regional instability (although other factors played a role too). The international community has experienced division and tension in relation to the fail-

---

## Box 11.3 The war on terrorism and global repression

The *New Internationalist* (2009: 9) identified the following examples of states using anti-terrorism as a justification for their own political repression, often either directly or implicitly sanctioned by the USA:

**Algeria**: torture; prolonged secret detention without trial; hundreds on death row on terror charges; security forces given legal immunity against charges of human rights abuses.

**Egypt**: widespread torture by State Security Investigation officials and police, and trials by military courts. According to official figures 1,500 people have been detained without charge; 10,000 according to other sources. Egypt is the second largest recipient of US aid.

**Iraq**: in 2008 US forces held 15,500 people without charge or trial for security purposes, and the Iraqi authorities held at least 26,000.

**Pakistan**: the Inter-Services Intelligence agency was responsible for numerous 'disappearances' with the Government admitting to 1,102 people disappeared in Baluchistan province alone. The problem was exacerbated by bounty offered by the CIA for terror suspects.

**Saudi Arabia**: 2,000 detained in secrecy on security grounds. The USA and Britain praised and promised to learn from a Saudi 're-education' programme that keeps suspects detained without charge or trial.

**Syria**: arbitrary and incommunicado detention widespread for people suspected of involvement in terrorist activity. Some 17,000 disappeared people, mainly Islamists, remain untraced.

For further information on global repression in the war on terrorism, see Suggested Websites at the end of the chapter.

ures of US diplomacy surrounding Iraq (Brown 2007: 30), with the integrity of global institutions such as the UN also damaged in the absence of a second United Nations Security Council (UNSC) Resolution relating to that conflict (Ryan 2006). The UN's credibility, moreover, has been further called into question in light of the widespread and global willingness to abuse human rights in the name of counter-terrorism (Evans 2006). Finally, anti-Americanism has spread throughout the world, fuelling further violence and resentment amongst traditional allies and opponents of the USA alike (see Table 11.1).

A further important consequence of the war on terrorism has been its construction of Islam and Muslims as a dangerous Other threatening Western lives and values (Jackson 2007d). Although political leaders frequently disassociated this campaign from any specific religion, Muslims around the world have suffered violence, stereotyping and suspicion because of the perceived link between Islam and terrorism. In the USA, tens of thousands of Muslims were investigated after 9/11, while in the UK thousands of Muslims have been subject to stop-and-search practices by the police every year. For some critics, this widespread suspicion has created a new 'suspect community' (Hillyard 1993), where much of the post-9/11 counter-terrorism legislation, policing practices and other measures have disproportionately impacted on Muslims (see for example, Bahdi 2003; Fekete 2004; Brzezinski 2007).

Finally, beyond its direct consequences, the war on terrorism has resulted in some significant opportunity costs. The vast resources ploughed into this war have inevitably been diverted from more pressing human security concerns such as poverty, disease and environ-

**Table 11.1**  *Europe responds to the USA: views amongst Europeans polled on the United States' involvement in matters of global security*

|  | *Positive* | *Negative* | *Neither positive nor negative* |
|---|---|---|---|
| On the USA increasing peace in the world | 23% | 55% | 18% |
| On the USA aiding the fight against terrorism | 37% | 43% | 16% |
| On the USA aiding the fight against poverty | 21% | 50% | 22% |

*Source*: Eurobarometer 66 (2007).

mental change that would have benefited from the international community's attention. As noted in Chapter 6, the damage brought on by these indirect or structural forms of violence vastly outweighs that caused by non-state terrorism. Here, it might be useful to remember General Dwight D. Eisenhower's famous criticism of the military-industrial complex in the USA's cold war experience:

> Every gun that is made, every warship launched, every rocket fired signifies, in the final sense, a theft from those who hunger and are not fed, those who are cold and are not clothed. This world in arms is not spending money alone. It is spending the sweat of its laborers, the genius of its scientists, the hopes of its children ... Under the cloud of threatening war, it is humanity hanging from a cross of iron ... Is there no other way the world may live?

In summary, critical scholars, and many orthodox scholars, argue that the war on terrorism's costs greatly outweigh any of its successes. From a normative perspective, it has been responsible for dramatic human suffering and insecurity across the globe and, as such, it cannot be viewed as either a proportionate or legitimate response to the events of 9/11. From a practical perspective, it has failed to achieve all of its major goals, including: arresting the spread of terrorism; curbing the attraction of WMD; and deterring rogue states from threatening regional or international order. Indeed, so disproportionate and punitive has this conflict been, that some have argued that aspects of it may have crossed the line into a form of state terrorism itself (Goodin 2006: 69–73; Crelinsten 2009: 51).

---

### Key Points

- The successes of the war on terrorism include the arrests and convictions of terrorist suspects, disruptions to al-Qaeda, the toppling of brutal regimes in Afghanistan and Iraq, and some developments in international cooperation.
- Critics argue that the failures of the war on terrorism far outweigh its successes, and that it has been ineffective, illegitimate and self-defeating.
- Major criticisms of the war on terrorism relate to the vast resources spent on this conflict, the human suffering it has caused, the damage it has done to human rights and civil liberties, its destabilizing impacts on the international system, and its opportunity costs.

## Explaining the war on terrorism

Notwithstanding the devastating impact of the 9/11 attacks, it is still something of a puzzle how a counter-terrorism operation initially directed at a small group in Afghanistan grew into the extensive global war on terrorism we have described above. In this section, we explore the psychological, political, historical and discursive origins of the war on terrorism, and try to explain how it became such a powerful influence within American and global political life.

Perhaps the most common explanation for the emergence of the war on terrorism is the psychological impact of the 9/11 attacks on the American public and political elites. This deeply traumatic experience shattered assumptions about US hegemony and invulnerability. The Bush administration was obliged to respond forcefully and swiftly to the attacks, in part due to public demands to take decisive action. The restructuring of US strategic capabilities and political institutions to counter a new and dangerous threat thus appeared somewhat inevitable. As the official 9/11 Commission Report (The 9/11 Report 2004: xvii) suggested: 'we learned that the institutions charged with protecting our borders, civil aviation, and national security did not understand how grave this threat could be, and did not adjust their policies, plans, and practices to deter or defeat it'.

Second, political leaders, and American presidents in particular, often come to be known by a set of core principles that capture their understanding of domestic and international politics, the goals they set for themselves and the methods through which they will achieve these aims (Buckley and Singh 2006: 1). President Bush's time in office, including the events surrounding the 9/11 attacks, was marked by one such set of principles that has come to be known as the **Bush Doctrine**. Although the term was never used by the president or key administration figures (ibid.: 3), the doctrine's four pillars (Jervis 2003) were prominent in official discussions of the war on terrorism and in key strategic documents such as the 2002 National Security Strategy of the United States of America (see Box 11.4). Investigating the Bush Doctrine helps us to understand both why the war on terrorism was initiated and how it took shape.

The first pillar of the Bush Doctrine built on the administration's belief that the post-9/11 era was one where terrorists and rogue states seeking to acquire WMD posed an exceptional, existential threat to the USA and its allies. Because of the unconventional and fanatical character of this threat, traditional methods of deterrence were no longer seen as adequate for ensuring American and global security, hence **preventive wars** (such as in Iraq) would be required to confront emergent threats before they were fully formed. In addition, because consensus for preventive war is often difficult to achieve, the USA would need to employ **unilateralism** when necessary – to 'go it alone' if efforts at coalition building proved unsuccessful. The Bush Doctrine went on to place strong emphasis on the internal political organization of other countries, viewing strong democracies as more stable and less likely to spawn terrorist violence than authoritarian regimes. Finally, to help facilitate the spread of democracy and freedom, to confront new threats as they emerged, and to resist opposition to unilateralism, the USA needed to maintain its position as the world's pre-eminent power.

---

## Box 11.4 The Bush Doctrine and the war on terrorism

In September 2002, the White House released the National Security Strategy of the United States of America. This important strategic document offered the then fullest version of the Bush Doctrine that came to characterize the war on terrorism, with each of its four pillars readily identifiable:

**Preventive war**
'The United States has long maintained the option of preemptive actions to counter a sufficient threat to our national security. The greater the threat, the greater is the risk of inaction – and the more compelling the case for taking anticipatory action to defend ourselves, even if uncertainty remains as to the time and place of the enemy's attack. To forestall or prevent such hostile acts by our adversaries, the United States will, if necessary, act preemptively.' (p. 15)

**Unilateralism where necessary**
'While the United States will constantly strive to enlist the support of the international community, we will not hesitate to act alone, if necessary, to exercise our right of self defense by acting preemptively against such terrorists, to prevent them from doing harm against our people and our country.' (p. 6)

**Idealism**
'America must stand firmly for the nonnegotiable demands of human dignity: the rule of law; limits on the absolute power of the state; free speech; freedom of worship; equal justice; respect for women; religious and ethnic tolerance; and respect for private property ... We will champion the cause of human dignity and oppose those who resist it.' (pp. 3–4)

**Maintaining American hegemony**
'It is time to reaffirm the essential role of American military strength. We must build and maintain our defenses beyond challenge. Our military's highest priority is to defend the United States. To do so effectively, our military must: assure our allies and friends; dissuade future military competition; deter threats against U.S. interests, allies, and friends; and decisively defeat any adversary if deterrence fails.' (p. 29)

A third explanation views this conflict as an exercise in **American imperialism**. Although the precise meaning of imperialism and its applicability to the war on terrorism is much debated (Hirsh 2002; Ignatieff 2003; Kaplan 2004; Colás and Saull 2006; Ferguson 2008; Lake 2008; Nexon 2008; Saull 2008; Spruyt 2008), this account emphasizes the vast American superiority over its competitors according to virtually every indicator of power. For example, the post-9/11 period witnessed a dramatic extension of US military power across the globe, with 860 military installations located in 46 foreign countries, and – by March 2004 – around 350,000 active-duty US military personnel deployed overseas (MacDonald 2009: 55). As Figure 11.4 indicates, the USA alone is responsible for nearly 46 per cent of total global spending on defence – a figure that dwarfs the *combined* defence expenditure of other major international powers, including Britain, France, China, Japan, Germany, Russia and India. In terms of economic strength, US GDP accounted for approximately 31.2 per cent of global GNP in 2002 (ibid.). And, despite the growth of anti-Americanism throughout the world, the USA still enjoys considerable influence through its soft power resources, including the global consumption of American popular culture.

From this perspective, the unrivalled pre-eminence enjoyed by the USA allowed the Bush administration to embark on the war on terrorism as a way of consolidating and extending its national interests. By expanding its overseas military presence, coercing or cajoling other states to join its campaign and attempting to install supportive regimes

**Figure 11.4**   *Global defence expenditure*

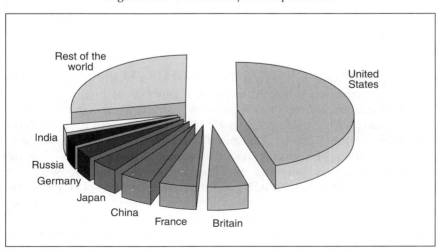

*Source*: Sapolsky *et al.* (2009: 15).

in Afghanistan and Iraq, the war on terrorism represents the exercise of authority over subordinate states and regions with a view towards spreading American ideas and ideals. This exercise in hegemony is motivated in part by geopolitical objectives – including, perhaps, greater access to the world's dwindling oil reserves (Harvey 2005: 1–25) – and in part by the pursuit of enhanced national security through an extended zone of influence. Although dissimilar to earlier imperialist exercises, because the USA has not sought to annex foreign territory directly (Cox 2004, 2005), the war on terrorism is seen here as something more than solely a security response to 9/11 attacks.

A fourth explanation focuses on a specific interest group that came to prominence in American politics after 9/11, namely the **neoconservatives** or 'neocons'. Neoconservativism describes a broad group of individuals with a shared intellectual and political project (Ikenberry 2004; Williams 2005: 310; Brown 2006: 696). Intellectually, it combines a critique of modern liberal societies and their celebration of self-interested individualism, with an embrace of free-market economics and conservative moral values such as civic responsibility, patriotism and self-sacrifice (Williams 2005). This intellectual platform manifests itself politically in a desire to reassert American national greatness, in part through the construction of an outward-looking, value-led, foreign policy. As one leading neoconservative scholar summarized it, neoconservativism involves:

> a concern with democracy, human rights, and more generally the internal politics of states; a belief that U.S. power can be used for moral purposes; a scepticism about the ability of international law and institutions to solve serious security problems; and finally, a view that ambitious social engineering often leads to unexpected consequences and often undermines its own ends. (Fukuyama 2006: 4–5)

This group's role in the war on terrorism is much contested. The Bush administration certainly included a number of high-profile neoconservatives, including: Paul Wolfowitz, Deputy Secretary of Defense; Lewis Libby, Vice President Cheney's Chief of Staff; and Richard Perle, Chairman of the Defense Advisory Board (Singh 2006: 16). In addition, there were important neoconservative lobby groups like the American Enterprise Institute, the Washington Institute for Near East Policy and the **Project for the New American Century** (PNAC) that had been forcefully demanding a more aggressive foreign policy approach long before 9/11. PNAC, in particular, had become increasingly prominent in US Republican politics in the 1990s and included amongst its participants key figures from the subsequent Bush administration such as Dick Cheney, Donald Rumsfeld and Paul Wolfowitz (Patman 2007:

54). Members of this group wrote to President Clinton in January 1998, arguing that 'if Saddam acquired weapons of mass destruction, he would pose a threat to American troops in the region, Israel, to the moderate Arab states, and to the supply of oil' (ibid.: 55). Interestingly, a PNAC report in 2000 alluded to the possible value of a 'new Pearl Harbor' for revitalizing American global hegemony. While these sentiments appear alarming with hindsight, other scholars argue that it is difficult to think of many of the government's key figures, including the President and his Secretary of State Colin Powell, as neoconservative (Singh, 2006: 16). Nevertheless, the combination of the 9/11 events with US hegemony and the presence of powerful neocons and their ideas about foreign policy at that moment in history may help to explain the subsequent evolution of the war on terrorism.

A fifth, domestic, perspective on the war on terrorism argues that it is less new or distinctive than is often assumed; in fact, it is simply a recent incarnation of much older American political traditions and ideologies (Campbell 1998; Leffler 2003). Here, scholars such as the historian John Lewis Gaddis (2004) have pointed to the longevity of ideas about pre-emption, unilateralism and hegemony within US Foreign Policy, identifying a lineage stretching back almost 200 years. Others have pointed to the war on terrorism as an expression of powerful American political myths such as American 'exceptionalism' and '**Manifest Destiny**' (Smith 2006: 5; see also Hughes 2003), which refers to the idea that the USA has a unique mission to spread its values and expand its global authority. In other words, the war on terrorism has grown out of, and builds upon, existing truth regimes about the nature of security threats in the international system and the identity and role of US leadership.

These efforts to locate the war on terrorism in historical context encourage us to think more cautiously about the uniqueness of this particular security paradigm. In fact, there are a number of more concrete precedents for it. For example, many of the war on terrorism's dominant narratives and counter-insurgency practices have their roots in colonial pacification campaigns against Native Americans and the colonial occupation of the Philippines and elsewhere (Rose 2004). More directly, they are firmly rooted in the first 'war on terrorism' launched by President Reagan in the 1980s (Wills 2003; Jackson 2006), as well as in President Clinton's second 'war on terrorism' in the 1990s. In these earlier responses to terrorism, many of the same narratives and discursive constructions were also present, as well as the primary reliance on military force. As such, the existence of these earlier narratives increased their persuasiveness for Americans and others when they were rearticulated after 9/11 (see pp. 62–7). At the same time, many of the war on terrorism's material manifestations can also be traced to long-standing practices and technologies of governance within American politics and beyond, including the 'red scares' and the so-called 'war on drugs' (Campbell 1998; Stokes 2005). Contemporary surveillance techniques or the techniques of immigration control, policing and public health, for example, draw on earlier efforts to identify and manage 'risky' behaviours (Feldman 2005). Similarly, the housing of terrorist suspects at Guantánamo Bay follows earlier programmes of housing Haitian illegal immigrations in camps there in the 1990s (Rose 2004).

Finally, to understand the pervasiveness of the war on terrorism, it is necessary to highlight the extent to which it has taken root within American politics. The central assumptions and ideas underpinning this war have been institutionalized in the structures of American government, with the creation of new departments such as the DHS, legislation such as the USA PATRIOT Act and strategic plans all serving to embed this discourse of threat within concrete political practices and procedures. Hundreds of thousands of employees in the DHS and private contractor companies, for example, now have careers in counter-terrorism that depend upon the continued widespread acceptance of the terrorist threat narrative and the ongoing commitment of resources to its control. Agencies like the military, the DHS and the CIA, moreover, depend upon the war on terrorism for large parts of their annual budgets, as well as the increased prestige and recognition that goes with it. Beyond this, other actors – like military contractors who supply the Pentagon, private security companies who supply airports and other actors with screening services and protection, and pharmaceutical firms who supply the government with vaccines in preparation for bioterrorism for example – also now have material interests in maintaining the war on terrorism. And, as we saw in Chapter 3, this war has also been reproduced across popular culture in mediums such as film, art, novels, computer games and television programmes. In these ways, the war on terrorism has taken on a concrete reality, becoming a durable part of modern society.

None of the above explanations is completely satisfactory by itself, and a comprehensive explanation would also need to look at other global and domestic trends outside of the USA and how these interacted with US dynamics. Nonetheless, the combination of all these factors at the particular historical moment following 9/11 – the psychological effects of the terrorist attacks, the rise of the Bush Doctrine, the influence of neoconservatism, the pre-eminence of US global power and its imperial interests, previously established approaches for dealing with issues like terrorism – help us to understand how the war on terrorism became the dominant paradigm and extensive global conflict it is today.

> ## Key Points
>
> - The roots and evolution of the war on terrorism lie in a series of psychological, political, economic and cultural factors.
> - The psychological trauma of 9/11 for the American public and political elites demanded an extensive and powerful response.
> - The war on terrorism was shaped by the Bush Doctrine's willingness to engage in preventive war, act unilaterally, spread American values and maintain American hegemony. The Bush Doctrine and the war on terrorism were also shaped by the presence and ideas of the neoconservatives.
> - Some critics view the war on terrorism as an exercise in American imperialism designed to promote more parochial national interests.
> - It is also possible to view the war on terrorism as a manifestation of more established traditions, myths and practices within American politics.
> - The war on terrorism has been embedded in American politics and culture, and is now a durable concrete reality that will not be easily changed.

## Conclusion

It is difficult to escape the conclusion that the war on terrorism has been highly problematic on almost every level, even if the security sector has made enormous profits (Pilkington 2010). Not only has it failed to achieve any of its core security objectives, it has resulted in enormous and long-lasting human, material, political and social costs to individuals and societies around the world. Moreover, the negative consequences of this conflict will in all likelihood be felt for generations to come, in the same way that the cold war has had a lasting impact on almost every aspect of the international system. Perhaps most disturbingly, the war on terrorism has in recent years transformed into a self-perpetuating, self-sustaining conflict. This is because, first, the military-industrial complex is now heavily invested in maintaining the campaign to sustain its system of profits, and, second, because it acts as a self-fulfilling prophesy in which foreign military intervention and internal repression prompts the very behaviour it seeks to prevent – thereby justifying ever greater counter-terrorism efforts. In effect, counter-terrorism has become pivotal in promoting terrorism (Zulaika 2009).

Although it is sometimes argued that the war on terrorism ended with President Obama's election in 2008, in fact its material, legal, institutional, cultural and discursive aspects have now been embedded and normalized across many countries and the institutions of international politics. These durable structures suggest that the guiding paradigm and practices of the war on terrorism are likely to remain with us for many years still, even if the term 'war on terrorism' is no longer used by politicians (Jackson 2011b). President Obama's failure to close down the Camp X-ray facilities at Guantánamo Bay, the expansion of the terrorist targeted killing campaign in Afghanistan, and the intensification of counter-insurgency in Afghanistan and its spread to Pakistan, Yemen, Somalia and elsewhere, offer but a few prominent examples of the difficulties involved in escaping the legacies of the past. In fact, there is always the possibility that the war on terrorism could intensify further and become more embedded over the next few years, particularly if there were another terrorist attack in the USA or Europe which caused large-scale loss of life.

In this book, we have tried to demonstrate that this global outcome – seemingly endless war and the normalization of counter-terrorism in nearly every area of life – was neither natural nor inevitable. Rather, it was the result of the way in which terrorism has been understood, studied and socially constructed over the past few decades, and the kinds of responses that this construction made possible. The internal logic of the war on terrorism is rooted in the widely accepted view that terrorism is no more than an evil to be eradicated. The value of the critical approach we have outlined in this book lies in the theoretical tools and analytical perspectives it provides for interrogating and deconstructing the terrorism framework and practices which are taken for granted, as well as the normative framework for evaluating the consequences of counter-terrorism. Ultimately, a critical approach to terrorism suggests that more positive and progressive change is always possible and that we can break out of seemingly endless cycles of terrorist/counter-terrorist violence, if only we can begin to think, study, speak and act outside of the dominant terrorism paradigm.

## Discussion Questions

1. What are the most important dimensions of the war on terrorism?
2. In what ways did other states participate in this US-led conflict?
3. What, if any, were the successes of the war on terrorism?
4. How has the war on terrorism impacted on international politics?
5. What were the war on terrorism's major consequences for human rights and civil liberties?
6. How might critical notions of emancipation be used to critique the war on terrorism?
7. What was the Bush Doctrine and how significant was it in shaping the war on terrorism?
8. Is the war on terrorism usefully understood as an exercise in American imperialism?
9. Was the war on terrorism an entirely new development?
10. Did the war on terrorism end with the election of Barack Obama?

## Recommended Reading

Amoore, L. and De Goede, M., eds, 2008. *Risk and the War on Terror*, London: Routledge. A collection of essays exploring the value of risk management as a lens through which to explore contemporary counter-terrorism programmes.

Bellamy, A., Bleiker, R., Davies, S. and Devetak, R., eds, 2008. *Security and the War on Terror*, London: Routledge. A critical introduction to some of the main consequences of the war on terrorism for security today.

Buckley, M. and Singh, R., eds, 2006. *The Bush Doctrine and the War on Terrorism: Global Responses, Global Consequences*, London: Routledge. An overview of the impact of the war on terrorism on the world's regions and its consequences for international security, law, finances and beyond.

Cole, D., 2005. *Enemy Aliens: Double Standards and Constitutional Freedoms in the War on Terrorism*, New York and London: The New Press; Cole, D., 2007. *Less Safe, Less Free: Why We Are Losing the War on Terror*, New York and London: The New Press. Powerful critiques of the erosion of civil liberties within the US-led war on terrorism by a prominent lawyer.

Miller, M. and Stefanova, B., eds, 2007. *The War on Terror in Comparative Perspective: US Security and Foreign Policy after 9/11*, Basingstoke: Palgrave Macmillan. An edited volume exploring the roots and global impacts of the war on terrorism.

→

Woodward, B., 2003. *Bush at War*, London: Pocket Books. Investigative journalist's 'insider' account of the Bush administration's activities in the first 100 days after 9/11.

## Suggested Websites

Archive of the speeches of George W. Bush: *www.presidentialrhetoric.com/speeches/bushpresidency.html*
Includes speeches related to terrorism and the war on terrorism.

The Counterterrorism Blog: *http://counterterrorismblog.org/*
Run by the Counterterrorism Foundation (CTF), a not-for-profit organization that 'seeks to increase public awareness of the daily happenings in the Global War on Terror (GWOT)'.

Report of the Eminent Jurists Panel on Terrorism, Counter-terrorism and Human Rights: *www.icj.org/default.asp?nodeID=349&sessID=&langage=1&myPage=Legal_Documentation&id=22936*
One of the most comprehensive surveys on counter-terrorism and human rights to date, the Report addresses the consequences of pursuing counter-terrorism within a war paradigm, the increasing importance of intelligence, the use of preventative mechanisms and the role of the criminal justice system in counter-terrorism.

Amnesty International's Counter Terror With Justice Campaign homepage: *www.amnestyusa.org/counter-terror-with-justice/page.do?id=1011329*
A wealth of resources and publications detailing the violation of international human rights law within the war on terrorism.

Cageprisoners: *www.cageprisoners.com/*
A human rights organization which works on issues related directly to the abuses occurring in the war on terrorism. Its primary areas of research and advocacy include the Guantánamo Bay detention centre, rendition and secret detention, and extra-judicial killing.

Report on the FBI's Counterterrorism Program since September 2001: *http://www.fbi.gov/stats-services/publications/fbi_ct_911com_0404.pdf*
Details all the domestic measures taken in the USA as part of the war on terrorism.

Official website of the Not in Our Name project: *www.notinourname.net/*
One of the most visible groups protesting against the war on terrorism between March 2002 and March 2008.

# Glossary of Terms

**Abu Musab al-Zarqawi**   The former leader of al-Qaeda in Iraq responsible for numerous attacks on Coalition forces and civilian targets. A Jordanian, al-Zarqawi was killed in a US air strike in June 2006.

**Al-Qaeda**   A loose jihadist network with roots in the anti-Soviet struggle in Afghanistan. The network's fluidity makes al-Qaeda notoriously difficult to define, despite the vast international attention it received after 11 September 2001. There is disagreement among scholars over whether al-Qaeda exists as a coherent organization or is simply a label for a broader ideological movement. Al-Qaeda's stated ambitions include overthrowing apostate regimes within the Muslim world and removing the Western military presence therein. Its most prominent figures include Osama bin Laden and Ayman al-Zawahiri.

**American imperialism**   A term used to compare US foreign policy to that of previous empires. While American imperialism is not driven by the direct acquisition of territory that motivated many of the earlier European imperial projects, critics and some advocates of contemporary US foreign policy have found the comparison useful for understanding the recent extension of American power across the world.

**Army of God**   A right-wing, anti-abortionist, militant Christian organization operating in the USA.

**Aum Shinrikyo**   A Japanese millenarian group led by Shoko Asahara. Aum achieved notoriety in March 1995 when members of the group launched a sarin gas attack on the Tokyo underground system, killing 12 people and injuring thousands more. Following the attack, its leaders were imprisoned. However, the movement continued and was renamed Aleph in 2000.

**Black September**   A militant Palestinian group responsible for an audacious attack on Israeli athletes during the 1972 Munich Olympics.

**Bloody Sunday**   The term used to describe the events surrounding a civil rights march in 1972 in Londonderry, Northern Ireland, when British armed forces opened fire on marchers. The shootings resulted in the deaths of 14 unarmed civilian protestors and numerous injuries. An inquiry into the events was established in January 1998 under British Prime Minister Tony Blair. It reported its findings in June 2010. Some scholars view the events as an example of state terrorism.

**Bush Doctrine**   The set of core principles underpinning the George W. Bush administration's political decisions and actions. The Bush Doctrine combined a determination to maintain US global hegemony with an interest in the spread of political values such as democracy across the world. Its fullest incarnation can be found in the 2002 National Security Strategy of the United States of America.

**Coercive diplomacy**   A term coined by Thomas Schelling to describe the threatened use of economic or military power by a state to compel adversaries to alter their behaviour. More colloquially, it is sometimes called 'gunboat diplomacy'.

**Constructivism**    A broad social scientific approach in which social, political and even material realities are understood as being created through shared ideas, practices and discourses. Constructivists highlight the key roles played by language, ideas, norms and meaning in constructing reality. Analyses inspired by constructivism have become increasingly influential within International Relations, Security Studies and Political Science, and much critical scholarship on terrorism may be viewed as broadly constructivist.

**Counter-hegemonic**    Knowledge claims or other political activities that challenge the dominance of established ideas and practices. The term is most frequently used approvingly in relation to progressive forms of political struggle.

**Counter-radicalization programmes**    Initiatives aimed at encouraging 'extremist' individuals to adopt more moderate political views, reject violent activities and join the legitimate political process. Some programmes have been criticized for their similarity to re-education programmes in totalitarian regimes and for focusing on imprisoned militants.

**Critical Security Studies**    Capitalized, Critical Security Studies typically describes the Welsh School approach to the study of International Security which is rooted in Critical Theory. Associated with the work of Ken Booth and Richard Wyn Jones, this approach ties the study and practice of security to the concept of emancipation. Where not capitalized, critical security studies typically refers to a broader range of perspectives on security that depart from the narrow realist orthodoxy in this subdiscipline, including post-colonial, feminist and post-structuralist approaches.

**Critical Theory/Approaches**    When capitalized, Critical Theory typically refers to scholarship inspired by the ideas of the Frankfurt School whose key figures included Max Horkheimer, Theodor Adorno, Herbert Marcuse and Walter Benjamin. Although a diverse group of thinkers, the Frankfurt School shared a concern with the generation of knowledge as a practice of emancipatory social change. In the discipline of International Relations, the term entered widespread usage through the writings of Robert W. Cox, who identified it with efforts to question the origins of established institutions and social power relations. Critical Approaches is a broader term than Critical Theory, and refers to social and political frameworks that are sceptical of established orthodoxies. These may include feminist, Marxist, constructivist and postmodern perspectives.

**Cultural grammar**    A term used in sociology, especially in relation to the study of social movements. It describes the underlying narratives, myths and identity of a society which are expressed through language, culture, memory, ritual and symbolism.

**Cultural violence**    A term used by Johan Galtung to describe the aspects of culture which legitimize other forms of violence, either direct or structural. More specifically, it refers to the aspects of key social phenomena such as language, ideology, art, religion and science which help make possible and justify the harms suffered by people.

**Culture**    Approached narrowly, culture refers to the sites of entertainment, artistic and intellectual endeavour within society, from the 'popular culture' of computer games and television programmes to the 'high culture' of ballet and opera. In a broader understanding, culture relates to the shared and evolving web of ideas, practices and values that make up a collective's habitual or established 'way of life'.

**Culture of fear** A social condition characterized by grossly exaggerated fears over perceived risks to the continuation of our individual and collective existence. Recent mass panics surrounding avian flu, African killer bees, paedophiles, terrorists and crime more generally are all indicative of this contemporary condition, as are the disproportionate resources that are often afforded to these problems. Cultures of fear may be deliberately and instrumentally manufactured in the interests of elites or they may emerge more organically within the concerns of the general public.

**Department of Homeland Security (DHS)** A major new cabinet department of the US Federal Government that was established in January 2003. The department's primary responsibilities span counter-terrorism, border security, immigration control and disaster management. The DHS employs 180,000 people and has a budget that runs into tens of billions of dollars. It is now one of the most powerful actors in the US government.

**Discourse** Discourses are relatively coherent systems of words, statements, ideas and values that organize and constitute social and political reality. By establishing relationships between people, institutions and material phenomena, and legitimizing certain forms of knowledge and social practice, discourses attribute meaning to the world around us.

**Discourse analysis** A set of methodological approaches and techniques for studying the use of language and texts in written, spoken or symbolic form. Some forms of discourse analysis, such as critical discourse analysis (CDA), seek to understand the relationship between language and social action.

**Emancipation** The primary normative concern of Critical Theory, emancipation is a commitment to removing the sources of violence and oppression that confront people as individuals and communities. The sources of oppression are manifold and include direct violence, such as war, crime and terrorism, as well as indirect cultural or structural violence, such as poverty and disease. Advocates argue that emancipation should be thought of as a continuous process rather than an achievable condition or endpoint, while critics argue that it is a potentially dangerous notion which imposes values on the people it is seeking to liberate.

**Embedded experts** A critical term used to describe analysts, experts and scholars that have become heavily integrated within the state's apparatuses through institutional ties, research income or their sharing of a common worldview with policymaking elites. Critics argue that these relationships impede the objectivity of such experts who are unlikely to challenge state practices because of their interest in perpetuating the status quo.

**Empiricist epistemology** Empiricism is an epistemological position which holds that accurate knowledge of the world can only be based on one's direct experience of it, for example through scientific observation.

**Enemy combatants** A label used by the US government to identify, target and prosecute suspected terrorists within the war on terrorism. It was initially used to describe captured members of al-Qaeda and the Taliban in Afghanistan as a way of avoiding trying the detainees in criminal courts or treating them as prisoners of war. The term functions to suspend normal legal safeguards, affording the US government the latitude to detain captured foreign nationals indefinitely.

**Enforced disappearance**    A term used by human rights organizations to describe instances where individuals are imprisoned or killed by state agents or their proxies (such as death squads) who then deny all knowledge of the victim. Recently defined as a crime against humanity by the International Criminal Court (ICC), enforced disappearance typically involves kidnap, incarceration in a secret prison, murder and secret burial. Human rights organizations estimate that thousands of people are disappeared every year.

**Epistemic community**    A term used to describe a network of recognized experts that share a common view of the field in which they work, its core issues and ideas, and the nature of the problems that need to be solved. Because epistemic communities are organized around shared political ideas and values, members tend to advocate similar policy solutions to the issues with which they are engaged.

**Epistemology/epistemological**    Epistemology is the subfield of philosophy concerned with the study of knowledge or how we know what we know. In social science, epistemological positions refer to researchers' assumptions about the origins, formation and accuracy of particular knowledge claims.

**Ethnography**    A social scientific research methodology centred on immersion in one's field of study, often by interacting directly with the subjects of research. Ethnographic work seeks to provide 'thick', detailed descriptions of particular contexts or cultures to facilitate a deeper understanding of that which is being investigated.

**Eurocentrism**    A term used to describe knowledge claims and perspectives that privilege European or Western experiences and interests over others.

**Existential threat**    A term that describes extreme sources of danger that threaten the very existence of a particular referent object, for example an individual, state or collective identity. It is most often used to describe a physical danger that threatens the continued existence of a nation-state, such as nuclear war, invasion by a more powerful state or total social breakdown.

**Extra-judicial killing**    The murder or execution of perceived political opponents by state actors or their proxies (such as death squads) outside of the law or the legal parameters of armed conflict. Extra-judicial killings may take the form of enforced disappearance, deaths in custody, assassination and murder; they can be considered a form of terrorism in that they are directed towards intimidating political opposition. Controversially, some human rights organizations argue that the policy of targeted killings currently used in the war on terrorism amounts to the extra-judicial killing of terrorist suspects.

**FLN**    Acronym for Front de Libération Nationale (FLN) or the National Liberation Front, an organization established in 1954 to fight for Algeria's independence from French colonial rule. The FLN fought a bitter war of independence which ended in 1962, when it became the ruling part of Algeria.

**Frustration-aggression thesis**    A psychological model for explaining aggressive behaviour – such as violence – through the experience of frustration that occurs when an individual's efforts to achieve his or her goals are impeded. The thesis was made popular in terrorism studies through the work of Ted Robert Gurr and his relative-deprivation model of the causes of terrorism.

**Fundamental attribution error** A term from the study of psychology to describe people's willingness to explain the behaviour of others in terms of dispositional characteristics such as personality, attitude or character traits. The error of such explanations is their neglect of situational or environmental causes of behaviour – the contexts they are in when they act in particular ways.

**Gender hierarchies** The concept of gender hierarchy is based on the idea that sexism is a universal organizing principle in human society, whereby power and privilege is distributed in a manner that ensures that men in general are more powerful and privileged than women, and that men are therefore generally at the top of the hierarchy and women are at the bottom. The form that gender hierarchies take varies from society to society and from context to context.

**Genocide** The term used to describe a policy of a state or group which aims at the deliberate and systematic violent destruction, in whole or in part, of an ethnic, racial, religious or national group. The 1948 United Nations Convention on the Prevention and Punishment of the Crime of Genocide establishes an international obligation for states to try and prevent acts of genocide and punish individuals involved in it.

**Governmentality** A term derived from the writings of Michel Foucault to capture the changing character of the exercise of political power, in particular the practices and techniques liberal states have developed to construct self-regulating citizens suited to government priorities. Sometimes referred to as the art of government, it includes modern techniques of surveillance, control and regulation, such as identity cards, biometric testing, CCTV cameras, facial scanning, citizenship tests, financial tracking, immigration control and a multitude of other processes.

**Guantánamo Bay** Nicknamed 'Gitmo', Guantánamo Bay is the location of a series of US Detention Camps on land leased from Cuba. Previously used to hold illegal immigrants, the camp achieved notoriety after 9/11 as a holding and interrogation site for foreign nationals suspected of terrorism related activities. There have been numerous legal cases to determine whether or not the territory falls under the jurisdiction of the US Constitution and legal system.

**Guerrilla warfare** A form of military conflict in which a non-state group wages war against a stronger, usually state, adversary. Guerrilla warfare often involves the protracted conduct of surprise attacks against vulnerable or exposed targets and the avoidance of direct confrontation with a superior enemy.

**Hard man** A colloquial term used in working-class areas in Northern Ireland to refer to a tough, physically invulnerable, pugnacious, macho man. The term was taken up by anthropologist Allen Feldman in his analysis of male culture within paramilitary organizations, in which he argues, amongst other things, that the use of light weapons dispenses with the need for physical strength.

**Hearts and minds approaches** Programmes of counter-insurgency that target potential supporters or sympathizers of an enemy employing techniques of persuasion rather than armed force. Rooted in historical colonial pacification programmes, hearts and minds approaches entail efforts to win the loyalty of an occupied population to marginalize support for guerrillas or insurgents.

**Hegemony**  A Marxist term associated with Antonio Gramsci, it refers to a relation of dominance that operates as much through acquiring the consent of those subject to it as through direct coercion or force. Hegemonic ideas or practices appear detached from the particular interests behind their establishment, taking on the appearance of normality, even desirability within a broader population.

**Heteronormative/heteronormativity**  The term refers to norms and values that support the division of society into two distinct genders (male and female), associate 'natural' roles with each gender, and normalize heterosexual relations between males and females as the normal form of sexual relations. The term was first defined by Michael Warner in 1991 and forms the basis for queer theory.

**Historical materialism**  A Marxist-inspired framework for social analysis. Historical materialism ties social and political developments to the economic systems of production and distribution within a society.

**Human security**  An approach to security that places the individual, rather than the state, as the referent object to be secured and the main unit of analysis. The concept of human security came to prominence in the United Nations Development Project's (UNDP) 1994 Human Development Report, which defined it as safety from chronic threats such as hunger, disease and repression, as well as protection from sudden and hurtful disruptions to daily life.

**Ideograph**  Flexible and imprecise political labels that encapsulate a community's shared values or ideals. Freedom, democracy and justice are all examples of ideographs within Western political discourse. Negative ideographs, in contrast, are labels which help to define a community by condemning deplorable or anathematic behaviours. Tyranny and terrorism, for example, fulfil this role in much Western political discourse.

**Immanent critique**  A critical philosophical strategy which attempts to realize the potential for progress within society at a given historical moment, in part by locating and exposing the contradictions within social forms and systems and exposing their underlying ideological basis. It seeks to critique systems within historical reality, showing how these systems are the product of historical processes and forces.

**Inductive reasoning**  A methodological approach in which generalized theories build on the collection and aggregation of empirical evidence about the social and political world.

**Instrumentalism**  An approach to ideas or behaviour in which the ends are deemed more important than the means. Terrorism, for example, is often viewed as a form of instrumental violence because its victims are reduced to tools or instruments used towards the achievement of future goals.

**Invisible college**  A sociological term used to describe tight knit groups of scholars who maintain links and group cohesion through shared, yet often informal, research activities. It is related to, but not identical with, the idea of an epistemic community.

**Knowledge and power**   A perspective rooted in the ideas of Michel Foucault which recognizes that power is based upon, and makes use of, knowledge. At the same time, power reproduces and shapes knowledge for its own purposes. More simply, it is the recognition that knowledge always works for someone and for something. The fact that knowledge is viewed as neutral helps to disguise the ways in which it operates as a form of power.

**Manifest Destiny**   An American political myth encapsulating the idea that the USA is uniquely fated to spread its political ideals and systems around the world.

**Media frames**   A framework or schema of interpretation employed in the news media to help audiences make sense of events. Media frames package stories according to identifiable narrative structures or stereotypes, thereby simplifying and ordering complex events and processes for the audience. As such, media frames are an important meaning-making process.

**MI5**   The UK's national security intelligence agency. MI5's primary responsibilities include counter-espionage, counter-terrorism and counter-proliferation.

**Military-industrial complex**   A term first used by former US President, Dwight D. Eisenhower, to describe the overlapping interests of the military and the manufacturers who supply the military, and the way in which their interests became increasingly intertwined in the cold war. Critics of the military-industrial complex argue that the two sectors frequently work in concert to promote policies that satisfy their own narrow material interests above those of the broader society.

**Minimal foundationalism**   A philosophical position which argues that there are some basic truths or insights which are relatively secure. These truths can be used as anchors to build further knowledge upon.

**Moral panics**   Exaggerated, frequently short-lived, widespread and intense social fears around things that are seen to be radical threats to society and its core values. Often hyped by the popular media and vastly out of proportion to the actual risk, examples of moral panics include periods of intense social fear of knife crime, paedophiles, illegal drugs, immigrants, hooded teenagers, disease and terrorism.

**Narrative**   A socially constructed, coherent story in which events are linked to one another to form a meaningful plot. Essential for making sense of the world, collectives employ public narratives to maintain group identity and values, while personal narratives enable individuals to find a meaningful place in society.

**National security**   A term that emerges from the realist approach to international relations, 'national security' refers to the aggregate of issues deemed vital to the survival and core interests of a particular state.

**Neoconservatives**   A US-based intellectual movement with a shared belief in US power as a force for moral and political progress. Critics argue that the neoconservatives, or 'neocons', had their most powerful moment when they exerted an undue influence over the early part of George W. Bush administration's war on terrorism.

**Normative**   Knowledge claims, arguments or positions based on values and ethics. Normative claims which suggest how things ought to be are often contrasted with objective descriptions of how things are.

**Northern Alliance**   A loose coalition of groups which had been fighting a civil war against the ruling Taliban regime in Afghanistan since the mid-1990s. The Northern Alliance came to international prominence following the invasion of Afghanistan after the 9/11 attacks when they allied with US forces to defeat the Taliban.

**Objectivity**   A term used to describe the scientific search for accurate knowledge which is impartial and testable because it does not depend on the observer's values or perspectives.

**Ontology/ontological**   Ontology is the philosophical study of the nature of being, existence or reality more generally. It asks questions about how things exist in the world, the nature of their existence and how they exist in relation to other things.

**Operation Enduring Freedom**   The official public codename of the US-led military operation to topple the Taliban regime in Afghanistan launched in October 2001 in response to 9/11. Every military chooses codenames for its operations, but the names chosen for operations in the war on terrorism have become part of the US military's public diplomacy and are therefore seen to be important in their choice of words.

**Operation Iraqi Freedom**   The official public codename of the US-led military operation to overthrow Iraq's Saddam Hussein regime in March 2003. Operation Iraqi Freedom was argued to be the second front in the war on terrorism by the Bush administration.

**Organic intellectuals**   A term from the work of Antonio Gramsci to describe scholars and other intellectuals who are embedded in particular social structures and institutions such as the state, and who therefore form part of the hegemonic structure of dominance. Through a series of institutional, financial, political and ideological relationships, organic intellectuals function to reproduce the consciousness or worldview that is dominant within, and which helps to sustain, existing power structures.

**Orientalism**   Originally a term used to describe the study of any aspect related to 'Eastern' cultures, through the work of Edward Said it has come to describe a broad system of knowledge – or a system of representations – through which Western scholars and writers have constructed 'the Orient' as a simultaneously exotic, dangerous and inferior place. Said's analysis demonstrates the interlinking of academic, political and cultural enterprises in this formulation of knowledge and the link between power and knowledge in the way in which Orientalism helped to justify the colonial project of subjugating these regions.

**Osama bin Laden**   Figurehead and founder of the al-Qaeda movement. The son of a wealthy construction magnate, bin Laden's first experience of political violence came with the Afghan resistance to the Soviet invasion of 1979. Prior to the 9/11 attacks, bin Laden lived in exile from Saudi Arabia in Afghanistan. He remains at large despite the war on terrorism's efforts to apprehend or kill him.

**Paradigm**   A coherent, often taken-for-granted, framework of thought and knowledge that determines the concepts, methodologies and appropriate objects of study in a particular field of inquiry. Paradigms function to exclude ideas, subjects and approaches which are not seen to fit within the existing framework.

**Patriarchal**   A term from feminist theory which broadly describes male domination and the subjugated position of women in society. More specifically, it refers to social and cultural processes, practices, structures and forms of knowledge that privilege masculine experiences or interests.

**PLO**   The Palestine Liberation Organization (PLO) was an umbrella liberation movement established in 1964 to coordinate the fight for Palestinian independence from Israel. Recognized as the official voice of the Palestinian people and led by Yasser Arafat, the PLO fought a long campaign of guerrilla warfare and terrorism attacks against Israel which ended following the Oslo Peace Accords in 1993.

**Pogroms**   Originally used to describe periods of extensive violence directed at Jews in the Russian empire, the term describes violent mob attacks, whether approved by the authorities or not, aimed at a particular ethnic, religious or other group. Typically, the attacks are characterized by widespread killing and the destruction of homes, businesses and places of worship.

**Politicide**   Similar to genocide, politicide refers to systematic attempts to destroy physically a group of people who are viewed as belonging to the same political movement. The murder of 500,000 suspected communists by the Indonesian government in 1965 is seen as an example of a politicide, as is the murder of a million opponents of the Khmer Rouge in Kampuchea after 1975.

**Positivism**   An epistemological perspective which holds that the best approach to social or political analysis is the scientific method involving the collection of observable, measurable evidence and the formulation and testing of hypotheses.

**Post-positivism**   In IR, this term refers collectively to a number of contemporary approaches to social or political analysis that share a scepticism towards positivist assumptions, such as the analyst's claim to objectivity or impartiality. Constructivism, post-structuralism and some forms of feminist theorizing are examples of post-positivist approaches.

**Post-structuralism**   A loose and sometimes controversial term commonly associated with continental theorists such as Michel Foucault and Jacques Derrida. It describes a number of approaches to social analysis which aim at revealing and deconstructing the contingent and incomplete character of social or political reality and its component parts. Post-structuralism is based on a rejection of positivism, the fixity of meaning and Enlightenment ideas of progress and the superiority of reason.

**Praxis**   A Marxist term which describes purposive practical action in the world, usually aimed at normative transformation. It is illustrated by Marx's famous dictum: 'Philosophers have hitherto only interpreted the world in various ways; the point is to change it'.

**Precautionary principle**   An approach to risk management which has its origins in debates over climate change. It suggests that even in a condition of scientific uncertainty or low probability of occurrence, if the potential consequences of an event would have devastating consequences for human life, the authorities have a responsibility to take the necessary preventive action. The precautionary principle has also long been at the heart of counter-proliferation and anti-nuclear activities. The sociologist, Ulrich Beck, argues that modern society is now a 'risk society' which embodies this principle.

**Preventive war** A term used to describe wars launched in the belief that future conflict or serious security threat will occur, even if it is not imminent. Pre-emptive war, by contrast, is war launched as a first strike when war is otherwise imminent. Arguably illegal under current international law, preventive war is often launched to forestall a shift in the balance of power or, as was argued by the Bush administration in the lead-up to the attack on Iraq in 2003, to prevent the emergence of future catastrophic threats.

**Problem of definition** A shorthand label for the difficulties associated with accurately or objectively capturing the meaning of a concept. These difficulties vary depending upon the theoretical standpoint of the analyst, but they also include some permanent challenges, including: the problem that any concept will be defined by, and in relation to, other concepts; the changes in meaning that occur over time; the problem of subjective interpretation; and the values of the analyst.

**Problem-solving theory** A term popularized in IR by Robert W. Cox but originally drawn from the critical theory of Max Horkheimer, it describes those theories and approaches which do not question the world's organization and structures of power, but instead seek to understand and address any actors or processes which challenge or destabilize the status quo. Cox contrasted problem-solving theory with critical theory which seeks to interrogate the ways in which the status quo is implicated in problems and challenges to the dominant world order.

**Profiling** Related to criminal profiling within policing, in current debates about counter-terrorism 'profiling' refers to the practice of narrowing down the pool of potential terrorist suspects for closer scrutiny based on a set of demographic, racial, religious or appearance-based characteristics thought to be associated with terrorism.

**Pro-insurgency** The term used to describe a state's policy of encouraging and supporting an insurgent movement, usually with arms, advisers and political support, in contrast to counter-insurgency strategies aimed at defeating an insurgency. During the cold war, the USA adopted pro-insurgency in countries like Nicaragua, Angola and Afghanistan, and counter-insurgency in places like Vietnam and El Salvador.

**Project for the New American Century (PNAC)** The PNAC was an influential neoconservative think tank and lobby group based in Washington from 1997 to 2006. It aimed 'to promote American global leadership' in the belief that American leadership was both good for America and good for the world, and it promoted the Reaganite ideas of military strength and moral clarity. The PNAC was arguably quite influential on the direction and policies of the early Bush administration.

**Psychological operations (psych-ops)** Planned information-based operations aimed at influencing the emotions, beliefs, reasoning and ultimately behaviour of a targeted group. Typically, psychological operations attempt to persuade, cajole, intimidate, confuse and demoralize the enemy without recourse to direct physical violence through techniques such as the dropping of propaganda leaflets, radio broadcasts, disinformation campaigns in the media, the use of agents provocateurs and the spread of rumours.

**Public diplomacy** A campaign of targeted communications aimed at projecting a positive image of a state or society or explaining the basis for particular policies to foreign audiences. Public diplomacy campaigns often try to make use of the elements of a state's soft power, including film, television, radio, sport, cultural exchange and education.

**Rational choice**   An influential positivist approach to the study of social and political dynamics. Rational choice theory argues that social processes and events are best explained by the decisions and actions of individuals who are presumed to be self-interested and instrumental. Criticisms of the approach include its neglect of the structural contexts that shape individual interests and behaviours and its inability to account for actions not motivated by self-interest.

**Rationalism**   An epistemological position which views reason as the primary and most important route to gaining knowledge, in large part because it provides a strong basis for judging between rival truth claims.

**Red Army Faction (RAF)**  Also called the Baader–Meinhof group by the media, the RAF was a radical left-wing German organization which conducted a campaign of urban terrorism for more than 30 years. It reached its zenith in the 1970s before its original founders were imprisoned. The history of the group was represented in a popular film of 2008 entitled *The Baader–Meinhof Complex.*

**Red Brigades**   Formed in 1970, the Red Brigades (Brigate Rosse in Italian) were an extreme left-wing organization who sought to bring about revolution in Italy. They launched a campaign of terrorism and urban warfare which involved kidnappings and attacks on factories. Most famously, they kidnapped and murdered the former Italian prime minister, Aldo Moro, in 1978. The group disintegrated in the mid-1980s due to internal division and police pressure.

**Reflectivist approaches**   A term used in IR to describe those approaches which oppose realism and, more generally, positivism. Constructivism, post-structuralism, feminist theory and critical theory are examples of reflectivist approaches.

**Reflexivity**   A term referring broadly to an attitude of critical self-awareness about one's own political and normative commitments and values in the research process. More specifically, it refers to a methodological process in which a field's main theories are applied equally to the object of research and the field itself.

**Regime of truth**   A term taken from the writings of Michel Foucault to refer to the set of discourses, institutions, social roles and procedures that determine whether a statement should be viewed as true or false. Regimes of truth emerge within and perpetuate specific forms of social organization and are therefore best viewed as historical rather than objective or inevitable structures.

**Rendition**   Also referred to as 'extraordinary rendition', rendition is a CIA-directed programme involving the forcible abduction (kidnapping) and transfer of terrorist suspects across national borders to specialist facilities for questioning and interrogation. It is undertaken by US security agents, usually in cooperation with the security services of other states. Some rendered individuals have been tortured, while others have been forcibly disappeared.

**Rhetorical theory**   A broad term referring to the study of language and discourse and its variety of forms and effects.

**Risk**    A calculated projection of future danger which combines the likelihood and potential impact of a specific harm befalling an individual or community. In a universe of infinite possibilities and dangers, and because they cannot be objectively calculated, risks are always socially constructed and contingent to history and place.

**Rogue states**    A pejorative term employed in international politics and the media to describe states who are perceived to pose a serious threat to regional or international security because of their unpredictable behaviour. The term is most frequently used in relation to certain states seen to be sponsoring international terrorism, pursuing WMD or acting in defiance of international law. Some states avoid being labelled with the term due to their relations with powerful Western states.

**Saddam Hussein**    The former President of Iraq and leader of the Ba'ath Party. The Saddam regime was overthrown by the US-led invasion in 2003. He was later captured by Coalition forces and executed for crimes against humanity in 2006.

**Securitization**    A term developed within the field of Critical Security Studies, 'securitization' refers to the process by which an issue is constructed by powerful elites as an existential threat, thereby justifying removing it from the political process and applying extraordinary measures. Securitization is achieved through a speech act by authoritative actors and is successful when the audience accepts the construction of the threat.

**Security certificate**    A legal mechanism used by the Canadian government to detain and deport foreign nationals and non-citizens on the grounds that they pose a threat to national security or have been accused of human rights violations. Used primarily against individuals suspected of involvement in terrorism, they have been heavily criticized for their violation of civil rights and have been challenged in the courts.

**Social facts**    A term used in sociology to describe the values, norms and social structures external to individuals and sufficiently durable to shape human thought and behaviour. Phenomena like sovereignty, law and sport are social facts created through collectively held beliefs, institutions and practices. Social facts can be understood in relation to brute facts, which are material or physical in nature: money, for example, is a social fact, while the paper it is printed on is a brute fact.

**Social movement theory**    A broad area of interdisciplinary study that seeks to explain the conditions under which social mobilization occurs, its different forms and manifestations, and its social, political and cultural consequences.

**Social performance**    Known also as 'performativity', this is a term used in a range of disciplines to refer to the way in which speech or other forms of behaviour such as dress, gestures or other actions, shape social interactions, identity and the course of human events. The notion has been addressed by a range of philosophers such as Derrida, Sedgewick Austin and particularly in the work of queer theorists like Judith Butler.

**Societal security**    A term used within Critical Security Studies which defines security as it relates to societies or social groups, rather than the nation-state. Taking society as the referent object of security takes the notion of threat beyond narrow military issues to factors like crime, poverty, migration and any other factor which threatens a society's values and institutions.

**Soft power**   A term coined by Joseph Nye and widely used in IR to describe how power operates through persuasion and cooption, rather than through coercion. Soft power relates to a state's values, culture, policies and institutions, and the extent to which it can attract other actors to follow its point of view. Soft power operates through processes such as diplomacy, strategic communication, development assistance and cultural products like cinema, music and fashion.

**State of exception**   A term used in legal theory to describe a situation in which the state can transcend the rule of law in the name of the public good. Through the work of the philosopher, Giorgio Agamben, it has more recently been used to describe a paradigm of governance where extraordinary security measures, such as the suspension of legal safeguards, have become normalized.

**State-centric**   The term describes approaches in IR that privilege the state as the most important actor in world politics and that make state perspectives and priorities the primary focus of analysis.

**State-sponsored terrorism**   The sponsorship of, or support for, terrorist groups acting as proxies for a state or its ruling regime. State-sponsored terrorism can be direct or indirect, active or passive, and can include financial, military, political or ideological assistance. Some examples of state sponsorship of terrorism include US support for the Contras, Taliban-ruled Afghan support for al-Qaeda, and Iranian and Syrian support for Palestinian terrorist groups.

**Structural violence**   A term used by Johan Galtung to describe the systematic ways in which social structures and social institutions harm people by preventing them from meeting their basic needs and reaching their full potential. Examples of structural violence include racism, sexism, nationalism, economic exploitation and political oppression, and it often produces social conflict characterized by physical violence.

**Subjective/Subjectivity**   Subjective beliefs, ideas or experiences are those derived from a person's individual position as a researcher or social actor. Subjectivity refers to the inability of individuals to escape these ideas or experiences in their work.

**Subject/object distinction**   An approach to social analysis that maintains an ontological separation between the world (the object) and its observers or analysts (the subjects). Scholars of terrorism that draw upon Frankfurt School approaches to Critical Theory seek to maintain this distinction, while arguing that the two shape each other in a continuous, dialectical dynamic.

**Subject positions**   A term used to describe the places within social frameworks or discourses that people inhabit and negotiate in their everyday lives. Student, wife, footballer, extremist or terrorist are all examples of subject positions within broader social discourses.

**Surrogate state terrorism**   A form of indirect state terrorism whereby one or more states provide support for, assistance to, or act as role models for other states more able or willing to employ their own forms of state terrorism.

**Suspect communities**   A term first introduced by Paddy Hillyard in his analysis of the Irish community's experiences under UK anti-terrorism legislation. It describes the differential treatment that is meted out to communities that have come to be viewed with widespread suspicion by virtue of their ethnic or cultural background.

**Taboo**   An anthropological term which describes a particular kind of prohibition or ban which a society puts on activities declared as sacred, forbidden, dangerous or unclean, either physically or spiritually. Breaking taboos is usually considered objectionable or abhorrent to society, and may have serious consequences, such as imprisonment or social ostracism.

**Taliban**   Also called the Taleban, they are a Sunni Islamist movement that arose during the period of civil war following the withdrawal of the Soviets from Afghanistan. After taking control of Kabul and most of the country, they ruled from 1996 until they were overthrown in the US-led invasion in 2001. During their rule, the Taliban practised one of the strictest forms of sharia law seen in the Muslim world and were internationally isolated. Since 2004, they have regrouped to lead a serious insurgency against Coalition forces in the country.

**Tamil Tigers**   The popular name for the Liberation Tigers of Tamil Eelam (LTTE), a separatist Tamil movement that waged a violent struggle for self-determination in Sri Lanka. The LTTE were militarily defeated by Sri Lankan forces in 2009 following nearly 30 years of civil war. The LTTE were at one time the primary practitioners of suicide terrorist attacks.

**Targeted killing**   A force-based counter-terrorism tactic involving the assassination of individuals suspected of involvement in terrorism. They are most often carried out by unmanned drones or other kinds of air attack. Targeted killings have been criticized for being extra-judicial and causing collateral damage, and may be considered a form of state terrorism when they are part of a campaign of intimidation against political opposition.

**Terrorism experts**   The term used to describe a high-profile group of terrorism scholars that gained increasing public and academic recognition from the 1970s onwards. Viewed as 'experts', they continue to make regular appearances in the media and provide advice to policymakers. Advocates of critical terrorism studies are sceptical about claims to expertise in the field of terrorism because of the term's association with objective and neutral knowledge, and because knowledge cannot be separated from power and interests.

**Terrorism industry**   A term used to describe the range of actors involved in producing and disseminating information on terrorism and the threat that it poses. These actors include political elites such as government officials, the opinion formers associated with think tanks, private security firms responsible for assessing and managing the risk posed by terrorism, and academic experts that publish on the topic of terrorism. The term captures the connections between, and shared interests of, these different agencies.

**Terrorology**   A term used by some critical scholars to describe the orthodox study of terrorism, especially in terms of its problem-solving orientation, the close links between its scholars and the state, and its role in counter-terrorism.

**Traditional theory/approaches**   A term originally employed by Max Horkheimer, traditional theory refers to the efforts of scholars employing positivist and scientific approaches who attempt to explain the world and derive parsimonious generalizations or laws about it. Contrasting traditional theory with critical theory, Horkheimer argued that social scientific generalizations cannot be made because the researchers themselves are located within a particular historical and cultural context which ideologically shapes their thinking. Problem-solving theory is a kind of traditional theory.

*Ummah*   The Arabic term for the worldwide community of Muslim believers.

**Unilateralism**   The actions of a state that are conducted independently from multilateral frameworks or engagements.

**UNSC Resolution 1371**   A Resolution adopted by the UN Security Council on 28 September 2001 in response to the 9/11 attacks. The Resolution aims to improve international efforts to fight terrorism and calls on all states to adjust their national laws to conform to international conventions on terrorism and to reflect the seriousness of terrorist crimes with harsher penalties. It also calls on states to cooperate with each other in counter-terrorism matters and establishes the UNSC Counter Terrorism Committee (CTC) to monitor states' compliance with the Resolution. The Resolution is binding on all member states of the United Nations.

**USA PATRIOT Act**   The acronym for the Uniting and Strengthening America by Providing Appropriate Tools Required to Intercept and Obstruct Terrorism Act of 2001. The USA Patriot Act constituted a dramatic strengthening of US counter-terrorism powers and was criticized by civil liberties advocates for its draconian measures and suspension of many established legal protections.

**Water-boarding**   A painful and distressing form of torture in which water is used repeatedly to take a prisoner to the point of drowning without killing him or her. Banned by all international and domestic law, water-boarding gained notoriety when the Bush administration attempted to redefine it as a harsh but legitimate interrogation technique, and admitted using it extensively on terrorist suspects after 9/11. President Barack Obama banned US agencies from engaging in the practice in 2009.

**Weapons of Mass Destruction (WMD)**   A generic label used to describe chemical, biological, radiological and nuclear weapons, and to distinguish them from conventional weapons. There are a number of international conventions which regulate the use and development of these kinds of weapons, and there appears to be a widespread taboo over their use, especially by states.

**Weathermen**   Also known as the Weather Underground Organization, the Weathermen were a small radical leftist group formed in 1969 out of the Students for a Democratic Society organization in the USA. The Weathermen bombed a number of public buildings as part of a broader campaign aimed at the overthrow of US imperialism and the establishment of world communism. The group disintegrated and became inactive after 1973 when the USA withdrew from Vietnam.

**WMD terrorism**   Terrorist activities involving the threat or use of chemical, biological, radiological or nuclear weapons. The most serious successful WMD terrorist attack was the 1995 sarin gas attack by the Japanese Aum Shinrikyo cult. Many terrorism experts see it as a significant threat and argue that it is only a matter of time before a major WMD attack occurs.

# References

Abdallah, S., 2003. 'Interview with Leila Khaled – 2003', United Press International, July 21, 2003. Available online at http://www.pflp.ps/english/?q=interview-leila-khaled-2003, accessed 10 October, 2010.

Abu-Nimer, M., 2003. *Nonviolence and Peace Building in Islam: Theory and Practice*, Gainesville, FL: University Press of Florida.

ACTA (American Council of Trustees and Alumni), 2001. 'Blame America First: College Campuses Respond to The War on Terror'. *Defending Civilization: How Our Universities Are Failing America and What Can Be Done about It.* Available online at: http://www.goacta.org/publications/Reports/defciv.pdf, accessed May 24 2008.

Adele, A., 1993. *Women Fighters of the Liberation Tigers*, Jaffna: Thasan Printers.

Agger, I. and Jensen, S., 2006. *Trauma and Healing Under State Terrorism*, London: Zed.

Al-Sumait, F., Lingle, C. and Domke, D., 2009. 'Terrorism's Cause and Cure: The Rhetorical Regime of Democracy in the US and UK', *Critical Studies on Terrorism*, 2(1): 7–25.

Aldrich, R., 2004. 'Transatlantic Intelligence and Security Cooperation', *International Affairs*, 80(4): 731–53.

Alexander, Y. and Swetnam, M., eds, 1999. *Cyber Terrorism and Information Warfare: Threats and Responses*, Oxford: Oxford University Press.

Alison, M., 2004. 'Women as Agents of Political Violence: Gendering Security', *Security Dialogue*, 35(4): 447–63.

Alison, M., 2009. *Women and Political Violence: Female Combatants in Ethno-national Conflict*, London: Routledge.

Alker, H., 2004. 'Emancipation in the Critical Security Studies Project', in Booth, K., ed., *Critical Security Studies and World Politics*, Boulder, CO: Lynne Rienner.

Allan, S., 2002. 'Reweaving the Internet: Online News of September 11', in Zelizer B. and Allan, S., eds, *Journalism After September 11*, London: Routledge, pp. 119–40.

Allen, J., 2005. 'Warrant to Torture? A Critique of Dershowitz and Levinson', ACDIS Occasional Paper. Available online at: https://www.ideals.illinois.edu/bitstream/handle/2142/40/AllenOP.pdf;jsessionid=0C3EFE8C79C93C629B625E56E2299EA7?sequence=1, accessed 29 September 2010.

Allison, G., 2004. *Nuclear Terrorism: The Ultimate Preventable Catastrophe*, New York, NY: Times Books.

Allison, G., 2008. 'I am more worried about a Nuclear Attack Today than I was on 9/11', available online at: http://www.aapss.org/news/2008/09/11/graham-allison-i-am-more-worried-about-a-nuclear-attack-today-than-i-was-on-9-11, accessed 29 September 2010.

Altheide, D., 2002. *Creating Fear: News and the Construction of Crisis*, Hawthorne, NY: Walter de Gruyter.

290

Altheide, D., 2006. *Terrorism and the Politics of Fear*, Lanham, MD: Alta Mira Press.

Altheide, D., 2009. 'Terrorism Programming', *Critical Studies on Terrorism*, 2(1): 68–80.

America.gov, 2003. 'Bush, Indonesia's Megawati Denounce Linking of Terrorism and Religion: Joint US-Indonesian Statement After Presidential Talks in Bali', 22 October 2003. Available online at: http://www.america. gov/st/washfile-english/2003/October/20031022085833esrom0.6787989.html, accessed 11 March 2010.

Amnesty International, 2002. *Israel/Occupied Territories: Palestinians Suffer New Collective Punishments*. Available online at: http://web.amnesty. org/library/Index/ENGMDE151002002?open&of=ENG-398, accessed 5 December 2007.

Amoore, L. and de Goede, M., 2005. 'Governance, Risk and Dataveillance in the War on Terror', *Crime, Law and Social Change*, 43: 149–73.

Amoore, L. and de Goede, M., 2008. *Risk and the War on Terror*, London: Routledge.

Anderson, B., 1983. *Imagined Communities: Reflections on and Spread of Nationalism*, London: Verso.

Anker, E., 2005. 'Villains, Victims and Heroes: Melodrama, Media and September 11', *Journal of Communication*, 55(1): 22–37.

Anti-Defamation League, 2010. 'Press Release: Statement on Islamic Community Center Near Ground Zero', Anti-Defamation League, July 28, 2010. Available online at: http://www.adl.org/PresRele/CvlRt_32/5820_32. htm, accessed 10 October 2010.

Antiwar.com, 2006. 'The Abu Ghraib Prison Photos', February 16, 2006. Available online at: http://www.antiwar.com/news/?articleid=2444, accessed 4 September 2010.

Applebaum, A., 2005. 'The Torture Myth', *Washington Post*, January 12, 2005, available online at: http://www.washingtonpost.com/wp-dyn/articles/ A2302–2005Jan11.html, accessed 29 September 2010.

Araj, B., 2008. 'Harsh State Repression as a Cause of Suicide Bombing: The Case of the Palestinian-Israeli Conflict', *Studies in Conflict & Terrorism*, 31(4): 284–303.

Aretxaga, B., 2001. 'Terror as Thrill: First Thoughts on the "War on Terrorism"', *Anthropological Quarterly*, 75(1): 139–50.

Arkin, W., 2002. 'The Secret War', *Los Angeles Times*, 27 October 2002. Available online at: http://ics.leeds.ac.uk/papers/pmt/exhibits/821/arkin.pdf, accessed 20 July 2010.

Arquilla, J. and Ronfeldt, D., 2001. *Networks and Netwars: The Future of Terror, Crime, and Militancy*, Santa Monica, CA: RAND.

Asad, T., 2007. *On Suicide Bombing*, New York, NY: Columbia University Press.

Ashcroft, J., Mueller, R., Giuliani, R. and Pataki, G., 2001. 'Remarks from Press Conference at WTC, New York', 21 September 2001. Available online at: http://www.usdoj.gov/archive/ag/speeches/2001/agcrisisremarks9_20.htm, accessed 17 April 2003.

Ashley, R., 1981. 'Political Realism and Human Interests', *International Studies Quarterly*, 25(2): 204–36.

Ayoob, M., 2005. 'The Future of Political Islam: The Importance of External Variables', *International Affairs*, 81(5): 951–61.

Aysha, 2005. 'September 11 and the Middle East Failure of US "Soft Power": Globalisation contra Americanisation in the "New" US Century', *International Relations* 19(2): 193–210.

Badey, T., 1998. 'Defining International Terrorism: A Pragmatic Approach', *Terrorism and Political Violence*, 10(1): 90–107.

Bahdi, R., 2003. 'No Exit: Racial Profiling and Canada's War Against Terrorism', *Osgoode Hall Law Journal,* 41(2–3): 293–316.

Bakunin, M., 1870. 'Letters to a Frenchman on the Present Crisis'. Available online at: http://marxists.org/reference/archive/bakunin/works/1870/letter-frenchman.htm, accessed 27 June 2009.

Barber, B., 2002. 'Democracy and Terror in the Era of Jihad vs. McWorld', in Booth K. and Dunne, T., eds, *Worlds in Collision: Terror and the Future of Global Order*, New York, NY: Palgrave Macmillan.

Barker, J., 2002. *The No-Nonsense Guide to Terrorism*, London: Verso.

Bartolucci, V., 2010. 'Terrorism as Discourse: The Elite Political Discourse on Terrorism and its Implications 2001–2008', PhD Dissertation, University of Bradford.

Bay, M., 2001. *Pearl Harbor*, Touchstone Pictures.

BBC, n.d. 'Editorial Guidelines in Full: War, Terror & Emergencies'. Available online at: http://www.bbc.co.uk/guidelines/editorialguidelines/edguide/war/mandatoryreferr.shtml, accessed 26 March 2010.

BBC News Online, 1999. 'America's Bush No Whizz on Foreign Quiz'. Available online at: http://news.bbc.co.uk/1/hi/506298.stm, accessed 20 July 2010.

BBC News Online, 2001a. 'Whalers Battle Protestors'. Available online at: http://news.bbc.co.uk/1/hi/world/asia-pacific/1715174.stm, accessed 12 June 2009.

BBC News Online, 2001b. 'Transcript: Bin Laden video excerpts', 27 December 2001. Available online at: http://news.bbc.co.uk/1/hi/world/middle_east/1729882.stm, accessed 9 September 2010.

BBC News Online, 2007. 'Anti-terror Spending to Rise £1 Billion'. Available online at: http://news.bbc.co.uk/1/hi/uk/7036121.stm, accessed 1 October 2010.

BBC News Online, 2008. 'IRA Bomber Event Held at Stormont', 7 March 2008. Available online at: http://news.bbc.co.uk/1/hi/northern_ireland/7283227.stm, accessed 5 September 2010.

Becker, T., 2006. *Terrorism and the State: Rethinking the Rules of State Responsibility*, Oxford: Hart Publishing.

*Behavioural Sciences of Terrorism and Political Aggression*, 2011. Special Issue: The Definition of Terrorism, January.

Bell, J., 2008. *The Secret Army: The IRA*, revised 3rd edn, Basingstoke: Palgrave Macmillan.

Bellamy, A., 2006. 'No Pain, No Gain? Torture and Ethics in the War on Terror', *International Affairs*, 82(1): 121–48.

Bellamy, A., Bleiker, R., Davies, S. and Devetak, R., eds, 2008. *Security and the War on Terror*, London: Routledge.

Bergen, P., 2001. *Holy War Inc: Inside the Secret World of Osama bin Laden*, London: Weidenfeld & Nicolson.

Biernatzki, W., 2002. 'Terrorism and Mass Media', *Communication Research Trends*, 21(1–3): 1–27.

Bird, B., 2004. *The Incredibles*, Walt Disney Pictures.

Bjørgo, T., 2005a. 'Conflict Processes Between Youth Groups in a Norwegian City: Polarisation and Revenge', *European Journal of Crime, Criminal Law and Criminal Justice*, 13(1): 44–74.

Bjørgo, T., ed., 2005b. *Root Causes of Terrorism: Myths, Reality and Ways Forward*, London: Routledge.

Bjørgo, T., 2009. 'Processes of Disengagement from Violent Groups of the Extreme Right', in Horgan, J. and Bjørgo, T., eds, *Leaving Terrorism Behind: Individual and Collective Disengagement*, London: Routledge.

Black, C., 2003. 'Press Conference for 2002 Annual Report "Patterns of Global Terrorism"', Washington, DC, April 30, 2003. Available online at: http://usinfo.org/wf-archive/2003/030430/epf309.htm, accessed 29 September 2010.

Blair, A., 2001. 'Speech by Prime Minister Tony Blair at the Labour Party Conference', 2 October 2001. Available online at: http://www.guardian.co.uk/politics/2001/oct/02/labourconference.labour6, accessed 9 May 2004.

Blair, T., 2003. 'Speech to the House of Commons in Favour of War with Iraq', 18 March 2003. Available online at: http://www.guardian.co.uk/politics/2003/mar/18/foreignpolicy.iraq1, accessed 15 August 2009.

Blakeley, R., 2007. 'Bringing the State Back into Terrorism Studies', *European Political Science*, 6(3): 228–53.

Blakeley, R., 2009. *State Terrorism and Neoliberalism: The North in the South*, Abingdon: Routledge.

Blee, K., 1991. *Women of the Klan: Racism and Gender in the 1920s*, Berkeley and Los Angeles, CA: University of California Press.

Blomberg, S. and Hess, G., 2008. 'The Lexus and the Olive Branch', in Keefer, P. and Loayza, N., eds, *Terrorism, Economic Development and Political Openness*, Cambridge: Cambridge University Press.

Bloom, M., 2005. *Dying to Kill: The Allure of Suicide Terror*, New York, NY: Columbia University Press.

Bloom, M., 2007. 'Female Suicide Bombers: A Global Trend', *Daedalus*, Winter: 94–102.

Booth, K., 1991. 'Security and Emancipation', *Review of International Studies*, 17(4): 313–26.

Booth, K., 2005. *Critical Security Studies and World Politics*, London: Lynne Rienner.

Booth, K., 2007. *Theory of World Security*, Cambridge: Cambridge University Press.

Booth, K., 2008. 'The Human Faces of Terror: Reflections in a Cracked Looking Glass', *Critical Studies on Terrorism*, 1(1): 65–79.

Brass, P., 1997. *Theft of an Idol: Text and Context in the Representation of Collective Violence*, Princeton, NJ: Princeton University Press.

Braudy, L., 2003. *From Chivalry to Terrorism: War and the Changing Nature of Masculinity*, New York, NY: Vintage Books.

Brecher, R., 2007. *Torture and the Ticking Bomb*, London: Wiley-Blackwell.

Breen Smyth, M., 2009. 'Subjectivities, "Suspect Communities", Governments, and the Ethics of Research on Terrorism', in Jackson, R., Breen Smyth, M. and Gunning, J., eds, *Critical Terrorism Studies: A New Research Agenda*, London: Routledge, pp. 194–215.

Brown, C., 2007. 'Global Terror and the International Community', in Ankersen, C. with O'Leary M., eds, *Understanding Global Terror*, Cambridge: Polity, pp. 17–36.

Brown, W., 2006. 'American Nightmare: Neoliberalism, Neoconservatism and De-Democratization', *Political Theory*, 34(6): 690–714.

Bryan, B. and Conybeare, J., 1994. 'Retaliating Against Terrorism', *American Journal of Political Science*, 38(1): 196–210.

Bryan, D., Kelly, L. and Templer, S., forthcoming. 'The Failed Paradigm of "Terrorism"', *Behavioral Sciences of Terrorism and Political Aggression*, 2 (1).

Brzezinski, Z., 2007 'Terrorized by War on Terror', *Washington Post*, 25 March 2007. Available online at: http://www.washingtonpost.com/wp-dyn/content/article/2007/03/23/AR2007032301613.html, accessed 20 July 2010.

Buckley, M., 2006. 'Reactions in the Russian Federation and Security in Central Asia', in Buckley, M. and Singh, R., eds, *The Bush Doctrine and the War on Terrorism: Global Responses, Global Consequences*, London: Routledge, pp. 57–74.

Buckley, M. and Singh, R., 2006. 'Introduction', in Buckley, M. and Singh, R., eds, *The Bush Doctrine and the War on Terrorism: Global Responses, Global Consequences*, London: Routledge, pp. 1–11.

Bunn, M. and Wier, A., 2005. 'The Seven Myths of Nuclear Terrorism', *Current History*, 106: 153–61.

Burke, A., 2008. 'The End of Terrorism Studies', *Critical Studies on Terrorism*, 1(1): 37–49.

Burke, J., 2004. *Al-Qaeda: The True Story of Radical Islam*, Harmondsworth: Penguin.

Burnett, J. and Whyte, D., 2005. 'Embedded Expertise and the New Terrorism', *Journal for Crime, Conflict and the Media*, 1(4): 1–18.

Burnham, G., Lafta, R., Doocy, S. and Roberts, L., 2006. 'Mortality after the 2003 Invasion of Iraq: A Cross-sectional Cluster Sample Survey', *The Lancet*, 368 (9545): 1421–28.

Bushnell, P., Schlapentokh, V., Vanderpool, C. and Jeyaratnam, S., eds, 1991. *State Terror: The Case of Violent Internal Repression*, Boulder, CO: Westview.

Butler, J., 1990. *Gender Trouble: Feminism and the Subversion of Identity*, London: Routledge.

Butler, J., 2006. *Precarious Life: The Powers of Mourning and Violence*, London: Verso.

Byman, D., 2003. 'Al-Qaeda as an Adversary: Do We Understand Our Enemy?', *World Politics*, 56(1): 139–63.

Byman, D., 2005. *Confronting Passive Sponsors of Terrorism*, Analysis Paper No. 4, The Saban Center for Middle East Policy, The Brookings Institution, pp. 21–7.

Campbell, B., 2000. 'Death Squads: Definition, Problems, and Historical Context', in Campbell, B. and Brenner, A., eds, *Death Squads in Global Perspective: Murder with Deniability*, New York, NY: St Martin's Press.

Campbell, B. and Brenner, A., eds, 2000. *Death Squads in Global Perspective: Murder with Deniability*, New York, NY: St Martin's Press.

Campbell, D., 1998. *Writing Security: United States Foreign Policy and the Politics of Identity*, revised edn, Manchester: Manchester University Press.

Campbell, D., 2002. 'Times is Broken: The Return of the Past in the Response to September 11', *Theory and Event*, 5(4).

Carlson, E., 2006. 'The Hidden Prevalence of Male Sexual Assault During War: Observations on Blunt Trauma to the Male Genitals', *British Journal of Criminology*, 46(1): 16–25.

Cavanaugh, W., 2004. 'The Violence of "Religion": Examining a Prevalent Myth', Kellogg Institute for International Studies, Working Paper 310, Notre Dame, IN: KI. Available online at: http://www.nd.edu/~kellogg/publications/workingpapers/WPS/310.pdf, accessed 18 January 2008.

CDC (Centre for Disease Control), n.d. Available online at: http://www.cdc.gov/malaria/facts.htm, accessed 15 August 2009.

Chandler, D., 2000. *Voices from S-21: Terror and History in Pol Pot's Secret Prison*, Berkeley and Los Angeles, CA: University of California Press.

Cheney, R., 2009. 'Full Text of Cheney's Speech at American Enterprise Institute'. Available online at: http://www.azstarnet.com/sn/hourlyupdate/293873.php, accessed 2 September 2009.

Chermak, S., 2003. 'Marketing Fear: Representing Terrorism After September 11', *Journal for Crime, Conflict and the Media*, 1(1): 5–22.

Chomsky, N., 1979. *The Washington Connection and Third World Fascism*, Cambridge, MA: South End Press.

Chomsky, N., 1991. 'International Terrorism: Image and Reality', in George, A., ed., *Western State Terrorism*, Cambridge: Polity Press.

Chomsky, N., 2002. *Pirates and Emperors Old and New: International Terrorism in the Real World*, London: Pluto.

Chomsky, N. and Herman, E., 1979. *The Political Economy of Human Rights, Volume I: The Washington Connection and Third World Fascism*, Nottingham: Spokesman.

Clarke, R., 2004. *Against All Enemies: Inside America's War on Terror*, London: Simon & Schuster.

CNN, 2010. 'Intelligence Chiefs Say Another Terror Attempt in U.S. is "Certain"', 3 February 2010. Available online at: http://edition.cnn.com/2010/POLITICS/02/02/us.terror.attacks/, accessed 4 February 2010.

Coady, C.A.J., 2004. 'Defining Terrorism', in Primoratz, I., ed., *Terrorism: The Philosophical Issues*, Basingstoke: Palgrave Macmillan, pp. 3–14.

Coaffee, J., O'Hare, P. and Hawkesworth, M., 2009. 'The Visibility of (In)security: The Aesthetics of Planning Urban Defences Against Terrorism', *Security Dialogue*, 40(4–5): 489–511.

Colarik, A., 2006. *Cyber Terrorism: Political and Economic Implications*, Hershey, PA: Idea Group Publishing.

Colás, A. and Saull, R., 2006. 'Introduction: The War on Terror and the American Empire After the Cold War', in Colás, A. and Saull, R., eds, *The War on Terrorism and the American Empire after the Cold War*, London: Routledge, pp. 1–23.

Cole, D., 2003/2005. *Enemy Aliens: Double Standards and Constitutional Freedoms in the War on Terrorism*, New York, NY: The New Press.

Cole, D., 2007. *Less Safe, Less Free: Why We Are Losing the War on Terror*, New York, NY: The New Press.

Cole, D., 2010. 'No: Respecting Civil Liberties and Preventing Executive Overreach are Critical to Preserving America's Security and its Ideals', in

Gottlieb, S., ed., *Debating Terrorism and Counterterrorism: Conflicting Perspectives on Causes, Contexts and Responses*, Washington, DC: CQ Press.

Commission on the Prevention of Weapons of Mass Destruction Proliferation and Terrorism, 2008. *World At Risk: The Report of the Commission on the Prevention of Weapons of Mass Destruction Proliferation and Terrorism*, New York, NY: Vintage Books.

Connell, R., 2009. *Gender*, Polity Short Introductions, Cambridge: Polity.

Coogan, T., 2002a. *The IRA*, Basingstoke: Palgrave Macmillan.

Coogan, T., 2002b. *The Troubles: Ireland's Ordeal and the Search for Peace*, Basingstoke: Palgrave Macmillan.

Cooper, A., 2002. 'Terrorism: The Problem of Definition Revisited', in Kushner, H., ed., *Essential Readings on Political Terrorism: Analyses of Problems and Prospects for the 21st Century*, Lincoln, NE: Gordian Knot Books.

Copeland, T., 2001. 'Is the New Terrorism Really New? An Analysis of the New Paradigm for Terrorism', *Journal of Conflict Studies*, XXI(2): 91–105.

Corradi, J., Fagen, W. and Garretón, M., eds, 1992. *Fear at the Edge: State Terror and Resistance in Latin America*, Berkeley and Los Angeles, CA: University of California Press.

Cox, M., 2002. 'American Power Before and After 11 September: Dizzy with Success?', *International Affairs*, 78(2): 261–76.

Cox, M., 2004. 'Empire, Imperialism and the Bush Doctrine', *Review of International Studies*, 30(4): 585–608.

Cox, M., 2005. 'Empire by Denial: The Strange Case of the United States', *International Affairs*, 81(1): 15–30.

Cox, R., 1981. 'Social Forces, States and World Orders: Beyond International Relations Theory', *Millennium: Journal of International Studies*, 10(2): 126–55.

Cox, R., 1986. 'Social Forces, States and World Orders: Beyond International Relations Theory', in Keohane, R., ed., *Neorealism and Its Critics*, New York, NY: Columbia University Press.

Cox, R., 1996. 'Social Forces, States and World Orders: Beyond International Relations Theory', in Cox, R. with Sinclair, T., eds, *Approaches to World Order*, Cambridge: Cambridge University Press.

Cragin, K. and Daly, S., 2009. *Women as Terrorists: Mothers, Recruiters, Martyrs*, Westport, CT: Praeger.

Crelinsten, R., 2003. 'The World of Torture: A Constructed Reality', *Theoretical Criminology*, 7(3): 293–318.

Crelinsten, R., 2009. *Counterterrorism*, Cambridge: Polity.

Crelinsten, R. and Schmid, A., 1993. 'Western Responses to Terrorism: A Twenty-Five Year Balance Sheet', in Schmid, A. and Crelinsten, R., eds, *Western Responses to Terrorism*, London: Frank Cass.

Crenshaw, M., 1981. 'The Causes of Terrorism', *Comparative Politics*, 13(4), July: 379–99.

Crenshaw, M., 1995. *Terrorism in Context*, University Park, PA: Pennsylvania State University Press.

Crenshaw, M., 2008. '"New" vs "Old" Terrorism: A Critical Appraisal', in Coolsaet, R., ed., *Jihadi Terrorism and the Radicalisation Challenge in Europe*, Aldershot: Ashgate.

Crenshaw, M. and Pimlott, J., eds, 1996. *Encyclopedia of World Terrorism*, Armonk, NY: M.E. Sharpe.

*Critical Studies on Terrorism*, 2008. Symposium: Critical Terrorism Studies: Foundations, Issues, Challenges, 1(1–2).

*Critical Studies on Terrorism*, 2010. Special Issue: Views from the 'Others' of the War on Terror, 3(1).

Croft, S., 2006. *Culture, Crisis and America's War on Terror*, Cambridge: Cambridge University Press.

Croft, S., 2010. 'New Security Challenges in an Interdependent World', in Hay, C., ed., *New Directions in Political Science: Responding to the Challenges of an Interdependent World*, Basingstoke: Palgrave Macmillan, pp. 189–210.

Cronin, A., 2009. *How Terrorism Ends: Understanding the Decline and Demise of Terrorist Campaigns*, Princeton, NJ: Princeton University Press.

Cunningham, K., 2003. 'Cross-Regional Trends in Female Terrorism', *Studies in Conflict and Terrorism*, 26: 171–95.

Danner, M., 2004. *Torture and Truth: America, Abu Ghraib, and the War on Terror*, New York, NY: New York Review of Books.

Dannreuther, R., 2007. *International Security: The Contemporary Agenda*, Cambridge: Polity.

David, S., 2002. *Fatal Choices: Israel's Policy of Targeted Killing*, The Begin-Sadat Center for Strategic Studies, Bar-Ilan University. Available online at: http://www.biu.ac.il/Besa/david.pdf, accessed 19 June 2010.

Davies, N., 2010. 'Afghanistan War Logs: Task Force 373 – Special Forces Hunting Top Taliban', *The Guardian*, 25 July 2010. Available online at: http://www.guardian.co.uk/world/2010/jul/25/task-force-373–secret-afghanistan-taliban, accessed 13 August 2010.

Davis, D. and Silver, B., 2004. 'Public Opinion in the Context of the Terrorist Attacks on America', *American Journal of Political Science*, 48(1): 28–46.

Denton, R., 2004. 'The Language, Symbols, and Media of 9/11: An Introduction', in Denton, R., ed., *Language, Symbols, and the Media: Communication in the Aftermath of the World Trade Center Attack*, London: Transaction.

Department of Homeland Security (DHS), n.d. *What We Do and How We're Doing It*. Available online at: http://www.dhs.gov/xabout/responsibilities.shtm, accessed 15 July 2010.

Der Derian, J., 2009. *Virtuous War: Mapping the Military-Industrial-Media-Entertainment Network*, 2nd edn, London: Routledge.

Derrida, J., 1981. *Positions*, trans. Alan Bass. London: Athlone.

Dershowitz, A., 2002. *Why Terrorism Works*, New Haven, CT: Yale University Press.

Dershowitz, A., 2007. 'Rape as Terrorism', *The Huffington Post*, 28 February 2007. Available online at: http://www.huffingtonpost.com/alan-dershowitz/rape-as-terrorism_b_42309.html, accessed 5 September 2010.

Dershowitz, A., 2010. 'No: There is a Need to Bring an Unfortunate Practice within the Bounds of Law', in Gottlieb, S., ed., *Debating Terrorism and Counterterrorism: Conflicting Perspectives on Causes, Contexts and Responses*, Washington, DC: CQ Press.

Devetak, R., 2005. 'The Gothic Scene of International Relations: Ghosts,

Monsters, Terror and the Sublime after September 11', *Review of International Studies*, 31(4): 621–43.

DFID, 2005. *Fighting Poverty to Build a Safer World: A Strategy for Security and Development*, London: DFID.

DFID, 2010. 'Alexander and Miliband on Yemen Conference', DFID Media Room, News Stories, 27 January. Available online at: http://webarchive. nationalarchives.gov.uk/, accessed 29 August 2010.

Dodds, K., 2007. 'Steve Bell's Eye: Cartoons, Geopolitics and the Visualization of the "War on Terror"', *Security Dialogue*, 38(2): 157–77.

Doty, R., 1993. 'Foreign Policy as Social Construction: A Post-Positivist Analysis of U.S. Counter-Insurgency Policy in the Philippines', *International Studies Quarterly*, 37(3): 297–320.

Dugdale-Pointon, T., 2007. *Gudrun Ensslin (1940–1977)*, 29 August. Available online at: http://www.historyofwar.org/articles/people_ensslin. html, accessed 10 October 2010.

Dunn, D., 2003. 'Myths, Motivations and "Misunderestimations": The Bush Administration and Iraq', *International Affairs*, 79(2): 279–97.

Dunne, M., 2003. 'The United States, the United Nations and Iraq: "Multilateralism of a Kind"', *International Affairs*, 79(2): 257–77.

Duvall, R. and Stohl, M., 1988. 'Governance by Terror', in Stohl, M., ed., *The Politics of Terrorism*. 3rd edn, New York, NY: Marce Dekker, Inc.

Duyvesteyn, I., 2004. 'How New is the New Terrorism?', *Studies in Conflict & Terrorism*, 27(5): 439–54.

Eager, P., 2008. *From Freedom Fighters to Terrorists: Women and Political Violence*, Aldershot: Ashgate.

Eckstein, H. and Gurr, T., 1975. *Patterns of Authority: A Structural Basis for Political Inquiry*, New York: John Wiley & Sons.

Edel, U., 2008. *The Baader-Meinhof Complex*, Constantin Film Produktion.

Egerton, D., 2009. *Death or Liberty: African Americans and Revolutionary America*. Oxford: Oxford University Press.

Ellis, S., 2001. *The Mask of Anarchy: The Destruction of Liberia and the Religious Dimension of an African Civil War*, New York, NY: New York University Press.

Enders, W. and Sandler, T., 1993. 'The Effectiveness of Anti-Terrorism Policies: A Vector-Autoregression-Intervention Analysis', *American Political Science Review*, 87(4): 829–44.

English, R., 2003. *Armed Struggle: The History of the IRA*. Oxford: Oxford University Press.

English, R., 2006. *Irish Freedom: The History of Nationalism in Ireland*, London: Pan Macmillan.

English, R., 2009. *Terrorism: How to Respond*, Oxford: Oxford University Press.

Enloe, C., 2000. *Bananas, Beaches and Bases: Making Feminist Sense of International Politics*, Berkeley, CA: University of California Press.

Entman, R., 1991. 'Framing US Coverage of International News: Contrasts in Narratives of the KAL and Iran Air Incidents', *Journal of Communication*, 41(4): 6–27.

Erickson, C., 2007. 'Counter-Terror Culture: Ambiguity, Subversion, or Legitimization?', *Security Dialogue*, 38(2): 197–214.

Esparza, M., Huttenbach, H. and Feierstein, eds, 2009. *State Violence and Genocide in Latin America: The Cold War Years*, Abingdon: Routledge.

Eurobarometer 66 (2007) *Public Opinion in the European Union*. Available at: http://ec.europa.eu/public_opinion/archives/eb/eb66/eb66_en.pdf, accessed 20 October 2010.

Evans, M., 2006. 'International Law and Human Rights in a Pre-Emptive Era', in Buckley, M. and Singh, R., eds, *The Bush Doctrine and the War on Terrorism: Global Responses, Global Consequences*, London: Routledge, pp. 189–99.

Falk, O. and Morgenstern, H., 2009. *Suicide Terror: Understanding and Confronting the Threat*, Hoboken, NJ: Wiley.

Falkenrath, R., Newman, R. and Thayer, B., 1998. *America's Achilles' Heel: Nuclear, Biological and Chemical Terrorism and Covert Attack*, Cambridge, MA: MIT Press.

Fangen, K., 1997. 'Separate or Equal? The Emergence of an All-Female Group in Norway's Rightist Underground', *Terrorism and Political Violence*, 9(3): 122–64.

Farnen, R., 1990. 'Terrorism and the Mass Media: A Systematic Analysis of a Symbiotic Process', *Terrorism*, 13(2): 99–143.

FBI (Federal Bureau of Investigation), 2007. 'Crime in the United States 2007', available online at: http://www.fbi.gov/ucr/cius2007/data/table_20.html, accessed 22 August 2009.

Feith, D., 2003. 'Council on Foreign Relations: Progress in the Global War on Terrorism, Washington, DC', 13 November 2003. Available online at: http://www.defenselink.mil/policy/sections/public_statements/speeches/archi ve/former_usdp/feith/2002/april_21_02.html, accessed 3 October 2006.

Fekete, L., 2004. 'Anti-Muslim Racism and the European Security State', *Race and Class*, 46(1): 3–29.

Feldman, A., 1994. *Formations of Violence: The Narrative of the Body and Political Terror in Northern Ireland*, revised edn, Chicago, IL: The University of Chicago Press.

Feldman, A., 2005. 'On the Actuarial Gaze', *Cultural Studies*, 19(2): 203–26.

Ferguson, Y., 2008. 'Approaches to Defining Empire and Characterizing United States Influence in the Contemporary World', *International Studies Perspectives*, 9(3): 272–80.

Ferree, M. and Miller, F., 1985. 'Mobilization and Meaning: Toward an Integration of Social Psychological and Resource Mobilization Perspectives on Social Movements', *Sociological Inquiry*, 55(1): 38–51.

Finn, P., 2005. 'One Year Later, Beslan's School Tragedy Still Haunts : Siege that Ended with 331 Dead Leaves Sorrow, Ire', in *Washington Post*, 2 September 2005. Available online at: http://www.boston.com/news/world/ europe/articles/2005/09/02/one_year_later_beslans_school_tragedy_still_ haunts/, accessed 5 February 2010.

Foot, R., 2005. 'Collateral Damage: Human Rights Consequences of Counter-Terrorist Action in the Asia-Pacific', *International Affairs*, 81(2): 411–25.

Foster, R., 2005. 'Cynical Nationalism', in Heller, D., ed., *The Selling of 9/11: How a National Tragedy Became a Commodity*, Basingstoke: Palgrave Macmillan.

Foucault, M., 1970. *The Order of Things: An Archaeology of the Human Sciences*, London: Tavistock Publications.

Foucault, M., 1984. 'The Order of Discourse', in Shapiro, M., ed., *Language and Politics: Readings in Social and Political Theory*, Oxford: Basil Blackwell, pp. 108–38.

Foucault, M., 1988. 'Practicing Criticism', in Kritzman, L., ed., *Michel Foucault: Politics, Philosophy, Culture: Interviews and Other Writings 1977–1984*, London: Routledge.

Foucault, M., 1991. *Discipline and Punish: The Birth of the Prison*, Harmondsworth: Penguin.

Frascina, F., 2005. 'Advertisements For Itself: *The New York Times*, Norman Rockwell, and the New Patriotism', in Heller, D., ed., *The Selling of 9/11: How a National Tragedy Became a Commodity*, Basingstoke: Palgrave Macmillan.

Freedman, B., 2010. 'Officially Blacklisted Extremist/Terrorist (Support) Organizations: A Comparison of Lists from Six Countries and Two International Organizations', *Perspectives on Terrorism*, IV(2): 46–52. Available online at: http://www.terrorismanalysts.com/pt/index.php?option=com_rokzine&view=article&id=112&Itemid=54, accessed 20 June 2010.

Fukuyama, F., 2006. *After the Neocons: America at the Crossroads*, London: Profile Books.

Furedi, F., 2002. *Culture of Fear: Risk-Taking and the Morality of Low Expectation*, revised edn, London: Continuum.

Gaddis, J., 2004. *Surprise, Security, and the American Experience*, Cambridge, MA: Harvard University Press.

Gallie, W.B., 1955–6. 'Essentially Contested Concepts', *Proceedings of the Aristotelian Society*, 56: 167–98.

Gambetta, D., ed., 2005. *Making Sense of Suicide Missions*, Oxford: Oxford University Press.

Ganor, B., 2005. *The Counter-Terrorism Puzzle: A Guide for Decision-Makers*, New Brunswick, NJ: Transaction.

Ganser, D., 2005. *NATO's Secret Armies: Operation GLADIO and Terrorism in Western Europe*, London: Routledge.

Garden, T., 2003. 'Iraq: The Military Campaign', *International Affairs*, 79(4): 701–18.

Gareau, F., 2004. *State Terrorism and the United States: From Counterinsurgency to the War on Terrorism*, London: Zed Books.

Garrett, S., 2004. 'Terror Bombing of German Cities in World War II', in Primoratz, I., ed., *Terrorism: The Philosophical Issues*, Basingstoke: Palgrave Macmillan.

Garrison, A., 2004. 'Defining Terrorism: Philosophy of the Bomb, Propaganda by Deed, and Change Through Fear and Violence', *Criminal Justice Studies*, 17(3): 259–79.

George, A., ed., 1991a. *Western State Terrorism*, Cambridge: Polity Press.

George, A., 1991b. 'The Discipline of Terrorology', in George, A., ed., *Western State Terrorism*, Cambridge: Polity Press.

Gerrits, R., 1991. 'Terrorists Perspectives: Memoirs', in Paletz, D. and Schmid, A., eds, *Terrorism and the Media*, London: Sage, pp. 29–61.

Gissinger, R. and Gleditsch, N., 1999. 'Globalization and Conflict: Welfare, Distribution, and Political Unrest', *Journal of World-Systems Research*, 5(2): 274–300.

Glassner, B., 1999. *The Culture of Fear: Why Americans are Afraid of the Wrong Things*, New York, NY: Basic Books.

Glassner, B., 2003. 'Narrative Techniques of Fear Mongering', *Social Research*, 71(4): 819–26.

Global Terrorism Database, n.d. Available online at: http://www.start.umd.edu/gtd/search/Results.aspx?charttype=pie&chart=regions&casualties_type=b&casualties_max=&dtp2=all&weapon=1,2,6,7,5,8,9,4,12,3,11,13,10&target=14, accessed 15 August 2009.

Glynos, J. and Howarth, D., 2007. *Logics of Critical Explanation in Social and Political Theory*, London: Routledge.

Gold-Biss, M., 1994. *The Discourse on Terrorism: Political Violence and Subcommittee on Security and Terrorism 1981–1986*, New York, NY: Peter Lang.

Gonzalez-Perez, M., 2008. *Women and Terrorism: Female Activity in Domestic and International Terror Groups*, London: Routledge.

Goodin, R. 2006. *What's Wrong with Terrorism?*, Cambridge: Polity Press.

Gow, J., 2006. 'Team America – World Police: Down-Home Theories of Power and Peace', *Millennium: Journal of International Studies*, 34(2): 563–68.

Graebner, W., 2008. *Patty's got a Gun: Patricia Hearst in 1970s America*, Chicago, IL: University of Chicago Press.

Greenberg, K., ed., 2006. *The Torture Debate in America*, Cambridge: Cambridge University Press.

Greenberg, K. and Dratel, J., eds, 2005. *The Torture Papers: The Road to Abu Ghraib*, Cambridge: Cambridge University Press.

Grey, R., 2006. 'Africa', in Buckley, M. and Singh, R., eds, *The Bush Doctrine and the War on Terrorism: Global Responses, Global Consequences*, London: Routledge, pp. 121–35.

Grey, S., 2006. *Ghost Plane: The Inside Story of the CIA's Secret Rendition Programme*, London: Hurst/ St Martin's Press.

Griset, P. and Mahan, S., 2003. *Terrorism in Perspective*, Thousand Oaks, CA: Sage.

Grosscup, B., 2006. *Strategic Terror: The Politics and Ethics of Aerial Bombardment*, London: Zed Books.

Guelke, A., 2008. 'Great Whites, Pedophiles and Terrorists: The Need For Critical Thinking in a New Age of Fear', *Critical Studies on Terrorism*, 1(1): 17–25.

Gunning, J., 2007a. 'A Case for Critical Terrorism Studies?', *Government and Opposition*, 42(3): 363–93.

Gunning, J., 2007b. *Hamas in Politics: Democracy, Religion, Violence*, London: Hurst.

Gunning, J., 2007c. 'Terrorism, Charities and Diasporas: Contrasting the Fundraising Practices of Hamas and al Qaeda Among Muslims in Europe', in Biersteker T. and Eckert, S., eds, *Countering the Financing of Terrorism*, London: Routledge, pp. 93–125.

Gunning, J., 2009. 'Social Movement Theory and the Study of Terrorism', in Jackson, R., Breen Smyth, M. and Gunning, J., eds, *Critical Terrorism Studies: A New Research Agenda*, London: Routledge.

Gunning, J., forthcoming. 'It's the Context, Stupid', in Deol, J. and Kazmi, Z., eds, *Contextualizing Jihadi Ideologies*, London: Hurst.

Gunning, J. and Jackson, R., forthcoming. 'What's so Religious about Religious Terrorism?', Scholl of Government and International Affairs Research Working Papers Series, University of Durham. Available online at: http://www.dur.ac.uk/sgia/working/.

Gurr, N. and Cole. B., 2000. *The New Faces of Terrorism: Threats from Weapons of Mass Destruction*, London: I.B. Tauris.

Gurr, T., 1970. *Why Men Rebel?*, Princeton, NJ: Princeton University Press.

Gurr, T., 1986. 'The Political Origins of State Violence and Terror: A Theoretical Analysis', in Stohl, M. and Lopez, G., eds, *Government Violence and Repression: An Agenda for Research*, Westport, CT: Greenwood Press, pp. 45–71.

Gurr, T., and Goldstone, J., 1986. 'Persisting Patterns of Repression and Rebellion', in Karns, M., ed., *Persistent Patterns and Emergent Structures in a Waning Century*, New York, NY: Praeger, pp. 324–52.

Haass, R., 2002. 'Defining U.S. Foreign Policy in a Post-Post-Cold War World: The 2002 Arthur Ross Lecture, Remarks to the Foreign Policy Association', 22 April 2002. Available online at: http://www.state.gov/s/p/rem/9632.htm, accessed 1 February 2007.

Hafez, K., ed., 2000. *Islam and the West in the Mass Media: Fragmented Images in a Globalizing World*, Cresskill, NJ: Hampton Press.

Hafez, M., 2003. *Why Muslims Rebel? Repression and Resistance in the Islamic World*, Boulder, CO: Lynne Rienner.

Hafez, M., 2006. *Manufacturing Human Bombs: The Making of Palestinian Suicide Bombers*, Washington, DC: United States Institute of Peace Press.

Halliday, F., 2002. *Two Hours that Shook the World: September 11, 2001: Causes & Consequences*, London: Saqi Books.

Ham, P. van, 2003. 'War, Lies and Videotape: Public Diplomacy and the USA's War on Terrorism', *Security Dialogue*, 34(4): 427–44.

Hamilton, K., 2009. 'The Deterrence Logic of State Warfare: Israel and the Second Lebanon War, 2006', in Jackson, R., Murphy, E. and Poynting, S., eds, 2009. *Contemporary State Terrorism: Theory and Cases*, Abingdon: Routledge.

Hancock, M. and Valeriano, B., 2006. 'Western Europe', in Buckley, M. and Singh, R., eds, *The Bush Doctrine and the War on Terrorism: Global Responses, Global Consequences*, London: Routledge, pp. 32–43.

Harmon, C., 2008. *Terrorism Today*, 2nd edn, London: Routledge.

Hart, W., 2005. 'The Country Connection: Country Music, 9/11 and the War on Terrorism' in D. Heller, ed., *The Selling of 9/11: How a National Tragedy Became a Commodity*, Basingstoke: Palgrave Macmillan, pp. 155–73.

Harvey, D., 2005. *The New Imperialism*, Oxford: Oxford University Press.

Harvey, O., 2009. 'Tiaras to Balaclavas', *The Sun*, 10 January 2009. Available online at: http://www.thesun.co.uk/sol/homepage/woman/real_life/article 2116482.ece#ixzz11rmWriKz, accessed 10 October 2010.

Hasenclever, A. and Rittberger, V., 2000. 'Does Religion Make a Difference? Theoretical Approaches to the Impact of Faith on Political Conflict,' *Millennium: Journal of International Studies*, 29(3): 641–74.

Hawthorne, S. and Winter, B., eds, 2002. *September 11, 2001: Feminist Perspectives*, North Melbourne, Victoria: Spinifex.

Hayner, P., 2002. *Unspeakable Truths: Confronting State Terror and Atrocity*, London: Routledge.

Hehir, A., 2007. 'The Myth of the Failed State and the War on Terror', *Journal of Intervention and Statebuilding*, 1(3): 307–26.

Heiberg, M., O'Leary B. and Tirman, J., eds, 2007. *Terror, Insurgency and the State: Ending Protracted Conflicts*, Philadelphia, PA: University of Pennsylvania Press.

Held, D., 1990. *Introduction to Critical Theory: Horkheimer to Habermas*, Cambridge: Polity.

Held, V., 2008. *How Terrorism Is Wrong: Morality and Political Violence*, Oxford: Oxford University Press.

Heller, D., 2005. 'Introduction: Consuming 9/11', in Heller, D., ed., *The Selling of 9/11: How a National Tragedy Became a Commodity*, Basingstoke: Palgrave, pp. 1–26.

Herman, E., 1982. *The Real Terror Network: Terrorism in Fact and Propaganda*, Cambridge, MA: South End Press.

Herman, E. and O'Sullivan, G., 1989. *The 'Terrorism' Industry: The Experts and Institutions that Shape our View of Terror*, New York, NY: Pantheon Books.

Herman, E., and O'Sullivan, G., 1991. '"Terrorism" as Ideology and Cultural Industry', in George, A., ed., *Western State Terrorism*, Cambridge: Polity Press.

Herring, E., 2008. 'Critical Terrorism Studies: An Activist Scholar Perspective', *Critical Studies on Terrorism*, 1(2): 197–212.

Hersh, S., 2004. *Chain of Command: The Road from 9/11 to Abu Ghraib*, Harmondsworth: Penguin.

Hewitt, C., 1984. *The Effectiveness of Anti-Terrorist Policies*, New York, NY: University Press of America.

Hill, A., 2009. *Re-Imagining the War on Terror: Seeing, Waiting, Travelling*, Basingstoke: Palgrave Macmillan.

Hillyard, P., 1993. *Suspect Community: People's Experience of the Prevention of Terrorism Acts in Britain*, London: Pluto.

Hirsh, M., 2002. 'Bush and the World', *Foreign Affairs*, 81(5): 18–43.

HM Government, 2008. *The Prevent Strategy: A Guide for Local Partners in England*, London: HM Government.

Hodgson, D., 2000. *Discourse, Discipline and the Subject: A Foucauldian Analysis of the UK Financial Services Industry*, Aldershot: Ashgate.

Hoffman, B., 2004. 'The Changing Face of Al Qaeda and the Global War on Terrorism', *Studies in Conflict & Terrorism*, 27(6): 549–60.

Hoffman, B., 2006. *Inside Terrorism*, revised edn, New York, NY: Columbia University Press.

Hoffman, B., 2007. 'Remember Al Qaeda? They're Baaack', *Los Angeles Times*, February 20 2007. Available online at: http://www.latimes.com/news/printedition/asection/la-oe-hoffman20feb20,1,1766338.story, accessed 27 September 2010.

Hollis, M., 1994. *The Philosophy of Social Science: An Introduction*, Cambridge: Cambridge University Press.

Hollis, M. and Smith, S., 1991. *Explaining and Understanding International Relations*, Oxford: Oxford University Press.

Holloway, D., 2008. *Cultures of the War on Terror: Empires, Ideology and the Remaking of 9/11*, Montreal: McGill/Queen's University Press

Holmes, S., 2005. 'Al Qaeda, September 11, 2001', in Gambetta, D., ed., *Making Sense of Suicide Missions*, Oxford: Oxford University Press.

Horgan, J., 2003. 'The Search for the Terrorist Personality', in Silke, A., ed., *Terrorists, Victims and Society: Psychological Perspectives on Terrorism and Its Consequences*, Chichester: Wiley.

Horgan, J., 2005. *The Psychology of Terrorism*, London: Frank Cass.

Horgan, J. and Boyle, M., 2008. 'A Case Against "Critical Terrorism Studies"', *Critical Studies on Terrorism*, 1(1): 51–64.

Horkheimer, M., 1972. *Critical Theory: Selected Essays*, New York: The Seabury Press.

Hoskins, A., 2006. 'Temporality, Proximity and Security: Terror in a Media-Drenched Age', *International Relations*, 20(4): 453–66.

Hough, P., 2004. *Understanding Global Security*, London: Routledge.

Hughes, R., 2003. *Myths America Lives By*, Urbana and Chicago, IL: University of Illinois Press.

Hulsse, R. and Spencer, A., 2008. 'The Metaphor of Terror: Terrorism Studies and the Constructivist Turn', *Security Dialogue*, 39(6): 571–92.

Human Rights Watch, 2006. 'Iraq: End Interior Ministry Death Squads', *News*, October 28 2006. Available online at: http://www.hrw.org/en/news/2006/10/28/iraq-end-interior-ministry-death-squads, accessed 13 August 2010.

Hunt, K. and Rygiel, K., eds, 2006. *(En)Gendering the War on Terror*, Surrey: Ashgate.

Ignatieff, M., 2003. 'The American Empire: The Burden', *New York Times Magazine*, 5 January.

Ikenberry, G., 2004. 'The End of the Neoconservative Moment', *Survival*, 46(1): 7–22.

Ilardi, G., 2004. 'Redefining the Issues: The Future of Terrorism Research and the Search for Empathy' in Silke, A., ed., *Research on Terrorism: Trends, Achievements and Failures*, London: Frank Cass.

*Independent, The*, 2002 'Bush Accepts Link Between Poverty and Terrorism', 23 March. Available online at: http://www.independent.co.uk/news/world/americas/bush-accepts-link-between-poverty-and-terrorism-655054.html accessed 29 September 2010.

International Committee of the Red Cross, 2007. *International Humanitarian Law and Gender: Report on International Expert Meeting: 'Gender Perspectives on International Humanitarian Law'*, Stockholm, Sweden, 4–5 October 2007. Available online at: http://www.icrc.org/web/eng/siteeng0.nsf/html/ihl-women-report-051008, accessed 10 October 2010.

*International Relations*, 2009. Forum: Bridge-Building and Terrorism, 23(1).

Iraq Body Count, 2010. Available online at: http://www.iraqbodycount.org/, accessed 10 January 2010.

Israeli, R., 1997. 'Islamikaze and Their Significance', *Terrorism and Political Violence*, 9(3): 96–121.

Jabri, V., 1996. *Discourses on Violence: Conflict Analysis Reconsidered*, Manchester: Manchester University Press.

Jackson, R., 2005. *Writing the War on Terrorism: Language, Politics and Counterterrorism*, Manchester: Manchester University Press.

Jackson, R., 2006. 'Genealogy, Ideology, and Counter-Terrorism: Writing Wars on Terrorism from Ronald Reagan to George W. Bush Jr', *Studies in Language and Capitalism*, 1: 163–93.

Jackson, R., 2007a. 'Playing the Politics of Fear: Writing the Terrorist Threat in the War on Terrorism' in Kassimeris, G., ed., *Playing Politics with Terrorism: A User's Guide*, New York, NY: Columbia University Press.

Jackson, R., 2007b. 'The Core Commitments of Critical Terrorism Studies', *European Political Science*, 6(3): 244–51.

Jackson, R., 2007c. 'Language, Policy and the Construction of a Torture Culture in the War on Terrorism', *Review of International Studies*, 33: 353–71.

Jackson, R., 2007d. 'Constructing Enemies: "Islamic Terrorism" in Political and Academic Discourse', *Government & Opposition*, 42(3): 394–426.

Jackson, R., 2007e. 'Critical Reflection on Counter-sanctuary Discourse', in M. Innes, ed., *Denial of Sanctuary: Understanding Terrorist Safe Havens*, Westport, CT: Praeger Security International, pp. 21–33.

Jackson, R., 2008. 'The Ghosts of State Terror: Knowledge, Politics and Terrorism Studies', *Critical Studies on Terrorism*, 1(3): 377–92.

Jackson, R., 2009a. 'Knowledge, Power and Politics in the Study of Political Terrorism', in Jackson, R., Breen Smyth, M. and Gunning, J., eds, *Critical Terrorism Studies: A New Research Agenda*, London: Routledge, pp. 66–83.

Jackson, R., 2009b. 'Critical Terrorism Studies: An Explanation, a Defence and a Way Forward', paper presented at the 3rd Annual CICA-STR International Conference, University of Ulster, Northern Ireland, 2–5 September.

Jackson, R., 2009c. 'The 9/11 Attacks and the Social Construction of a National Narrative', in Morgan, M., ed., *The Impact of 9/11 on the Media, Arts, and Entertainment: The Day That Changed Everything?* Basingstoke: Palgrave Macmillan, pp. 25–35.

Jackson, R., 2009d. 'Conclusion: Contemporary State Terrorism: Towards a New Research Agenda', in Jackson, R., Poynting, S. and Murphy, E., eds, *Contemporary State Terrorism: Theory and Cases*, Abingdon: Routledge, pp. 228–39.

Jackson, R., forthcoming a. 'In Defence of "Terrorism": Finding a Way Through a Forest of Misconceptions', *Behavioral Sciences of Terrorism and Political Aggression*.

Jackson, R., forthcoming b. 'Culture, Identity and Hegemony: Continuity and (the Lack of) Change in US Counter-Terrorism Policy from Bush to Obama', *International Politics*.

Jackson, R., Breen Smyth, M. and Gunning, J., eds, 2009a. *Critical Terrorism Studies: A New Research Agenda*, Abingdon: Routledge.

Jackson, R., Breen Smyth, M. and Gunning, J., 2009b. 'Critical Terrorism Studies: Framing a New Research Agenda', in Jackson, R., Breen Smyth, M. and Gunning, J., eds, *Critical Terrorism Studies: A New Research Agenda*, London: Routledge, pp. 216–36.

Jackson, R., Murphy, E. and Poynting, S., eds, 2009. *Contemporary State Terrorism: Theory and Cases*, Abingdon: Routledge.

Jarvis, L. 2008. 'Times of Terror: Writing Temporality into the War on Terror', *Critical Studies on Terrorism*: 1(2): 245–62.

Jarvis, L., 2009a. 'The Spaces and Faces of Critical Terrorism Studies', *Security Dialogue*, 40(1): 5–27.

Jarvis, L., 2009b. *Times of Terror: Discourse, Temporality and the War on Terror*, Basingstoke: Palgrave Macmillan.

Jarvis, L., 2010. 'Remember, Remember, 11 September: Memorialising 9/11 on the Internet', *Journal of War and Culture Studies*, 3(1): 69–82.

Jarvis, L. and Lister, M., 2010. 'Stakeholder Security: The New Western Way of Counter-Terrorism?', *Contemporary Politics*, 16(2): 173–88.

Jeffords, S., 1989. *The Remasculinization of America: Gender and the Vietnam War*, Bloomington, IN: Indiana University Press.

Jenkins, B., 1975. 'International Terrorism: A Balance Sheet', *Survival*, 17(4): 158–64.

Jenkins, B., 1986. 'Defense against Terrorism', *Political Science Quarterly*, 101(5): 773–86.

Jenkins, B., 1998. 'Will Terrorists Go Nuclear? A Reappraisal', in Kushner, H., ed., *The Future of Terrorism: Violence in the New Millennium*, London: Sage.

Jenkins, P., 2003. *Images of Terror: What We Can and Can't Know About Terrorism*, New York, NY: Aldine de Gruyter.

Jervis, R., 2003. 'Understanding the Bush Doctrine', *Political Science Quarterly*, 118(3): 365–88.

Johnson, C., 2004. *Blowback: The Costs and Consequences of the American Empire*, 2nd edn, New York, NY: Holt.

Johnson, E., 2000. *Nazi Terror: Gestapo, Jews and Ordinary Germans*, New York, NY: Basic Books.

Johnston, H., 2008. 'Ritual, Strategy and Deep Culture in the Chechen National Movement', *Critical Studies on Terrorism*, 1(3), 321–42.

Jones, D., 1997. *Women Warriors: A History*, Washington, DC: Brassey's.

Jones, D. and Smith, M.L.R., 2009. 'We Are All Terrorists Now: Critical – Or Hypocritical – Studies on Terrorism?', *Studies in Conflict and Terrorism*, 32(4): 292–302.

Jones, E., Woolven, R., Durodie, B. and Wessely, S., 2006. 'Public Panic and Morale: Second World War Civilian Responses Re-Examined in the Light of the Current Anti-Terrorist Campaign', *Journal of Risk Research*, 9(1): 57–73.

Jones, S. and Libicki, M., 2008. *How Terrorist Groups End: Lessons for Countering al Qa'ida*, Santa Monica, CA: RAND Corporation.

Joseph, J., 2009. 'Critical of What? Terrorism and its Study', *International Relations*, 23(1): 93–8.

Josselin, D., 2006. 'The Global Economy', in Buckley, M. and Singh, R., eds, *The Bush Doctrine and the War on Terrorism: Global Responses, Global Consequences*, London: Routledge, pp. 164–72.

Juergensmeyer, M., 2000. *Terror in the Mind of God: The Global Rise of Religious Violence*, Berkeley, CA: University of California Press.

Kampfner, J., 2003. 'The Truth about Jessica', *The Guardian*, Thursday 15 May.

Kapitan, T., 2004. 'Terrorism in the Arab-Israeli Conflict', in Primoratz, I., ed., *Terrorism: The Philosophical Issues*, Basingstoke: Palgrave Macmillan.

Kaplan, A., 2004. 'Violent Belongings and the Question of Empire Today: Presidential Address to the American Studies Association, Hartford, CT, October 17, 2003', *American Quarterly*, 56(1): 1–18.

Kaplan, D. and Marshall, A., 1996. *The Cult at the End of the World: The Terrifying Story of the Aum Doomsday Cult, from the Subways of Tokyo to the Nuclear Arsenals of Russia*, New York, NY: Random House.

Kassimeris, G., ed., 2007. *Playing Politics With Terrorism: A User's Guide*, New York, NY: Columbia University Press.

Kaufman, C., 1996. 'Intervention in Ethnic and Ideological Civil Wars: Why One Can Be Done and the Other Can't', *Security Studies*, 6(1): 62–100.

Kaufman, C., 1998. 'When All Else Fails: Ethnic Population Transfers and Partitions in the Twentieth Century', *International Security*, 23(2): 120–56.

Kaufman, S., 2001. *Modern Hatreds: The Symbolic Politics of Ethnic War*, London: Cornell University Press.

Kearney, R., 1981. 'Women in Politics in Sri Lanka', *Asian Survey*, 21 (7): 729–46.

Kellner, D., 2002. 'September 11, the Media, and War Fever', *Television & New Media*, 3(2): 143–51.

Kelly, O., 2008. 'Women: The Secret Weapon of Modern Warfare?', *Hypatia*, 23(2): 1–16.

Kennedy, L., 2003. 'Remembering September 11: Photography as Cultural Diplomacy', *International Affairs*, 79(2): 315–26.

Kennedy, L. and Lucas, S., 2005. 'Enduring Freedom: Public Diplomacy and US Foreign Policy', *American Quarterly*, 57(2): 309–33.

Khaled, L., 1973. *My People Shall Live: The Autobiography of a Revolutionary*, London: Hodder & Stoughton.

Kibbe, J., 2004. 'The Rise of the Shadow Warriors', *Foreign Affairs*, 83(2): 102–15.

Klare, M., 1989. 'Subterranean Alliances: America's Global Proxy Network', *Journal of International Affairs*, 43(1): 97–118.

Klare, M. and P. Kornbluh, 1989. 'The New Interventionism: Low-Intensity Warfare in the 1980s and Beyond', in Klare, M. and Kornbluh, P., eds, *Low-Intensity Warfare: How the USA Fights Wars Without Declaring Them*, London: Methuen.

Kornbluh, P., 2003. *The Pinochet File: A Declassified Dossier on Atrocity and Accountability*, New York, NY: The New Press.

Krueger, A., 2007. *What Makes a Terrorist: Economics and the Roots of Terrorism*, Princeton, NJ: Princeton University Press.

Krueger, A. and Malečková, J., 2003. 'Education, Poverty and Terrorism: Is There a Causal Connection?', *Journal of Economic Perspectives*, 17(4): 119–44.

Kuhn, T., 1996. *The Structure of Scientific Revolutions*, 3rd edn, Chicago, IL: University of Chicago Press.

Kurki, M., 2008. *Causation in International Relations: Reclaiming Causal Analysis*, Cambridge: Cambridge University Press.

Kurrild-Klitgaard, P., Justesen, M. and Klemensen, R., 2006. 'The Political Economy of Freedom, Democracy and Transnational Terrorism', *Public Choice*, 128(1–2): 289–315.

Kurzman, C., 1996. 'Structural Opportunity and Perceived Opportunity in Social-Movement-Theory: The Iranian Revolution of 1979', *American Sociological Review*, 61(1): 153–70.

Lake, D., 2008. 'The New American Empire?', *International Studies Perspectives*, 9(3): 281–9.

Lakoff, G., 1987. *Women, Fire, and Dangerous Things: What Categories Reveal about the Mind*, Chicago, IL: University of Chicago Press.

Laqueur, W., 1987. *The Age of Terrorism*, London: Weidenfeld & Nicolson.

Laqueur, W., 1999. *The New Terrorism, Fanaticism and the Arms of Mass Destruction*, New York, NY: Oxford University Press.

Laqueur, W., 2001. *A History of Terrorism*, New Brunswick, NJ: Transaction Publishers.

Laqueur, W., 2003. *No End to War: Terrorism in the Twenty-First Century*, New York, NY: Continuum.

Laqueur, W. and Alexander, Y., 1987. *The Terrorism Reader: A Historical Anthology*, 2nd edn, New York, NY: Meridian.

Lasslett, K., 2009. 'Winning Hearts and Mines: The Bougainville Crisis, 1988–90', in Jackson, R., Murphy, E. and Poynting, S., eds, *Contemporary State Terrorism: Theory and Cases*, Abingdon: Routledge.

Lawrence, B., ed., 2005. *Messages to the World: The Statements of Osama Bin Laden*, translated by James Howarth, London: Verso.

Leffler, M., 2003. '9/11 and the Past and Future of American Foreign Policy', *International Affairs*, 79(5): 1045–63.

Lesser, I., Hoffman, B., Arquilla, J., Ronfeldt, D. and Zanini, M., 1999. *Countering the New Terrorism*, Santa Monica, CA: Rand.

Leung, R., 2004. 'His Year in Hell', *CBS News*, January 21. Available online at: http://www.cbsnews.com/stories/2004/01/21/48hours/main594974.shtml, accessed 9 February 2010.

Levitt, M., 2006. *Hamas: Politics, Charity, and Terrorism in the Service of Jihad*, New Haven, CT: Yale University Press and the Washington Institute for Near East Policy.

Li, Q. and Schaub, D., 2004. 'Economic Globalization and Transnational Terrorism: A Pooled Time-Series Analysis', *Journal of Conflict Resolution*, 48(2): 203–58.

Lia, B. and Skjolberg, K., 2005. 'Causes of Terrorism: An Expanded and Updated Review of the Literature', FFI-report 2004/04307. Kjeller, Norway: Norwegian Defence Research Establishment (FFI).

Lichbach, M. and Gurr, T., 1981. 'The Conflict Process: A Formal Model', *Journal of Conflict Resolution*, 25(1), 3–29.

Light, M., 2007. 'Russia and the War on Terrorism', in Ankersen, C. with O'Leary, M., eds, *Understanding Global Terror*, Cambridge: Polity, pp. 95–110.

Lisle, D., 2007. 'Benevolent Patriotism: Art, Dissent and the American Effect', *Security Dialogue*, 38(2): 233–50.

Litwak, R., 2002. 'The New Calculus of Pre-Emption', *Survival*, 44(4): 53–80.

Live Science, n.d. 'The Odds of Dying', available online at: http://www.livescience.com/environment/050106_odds_of_dying.html, accessed 22 September 2009.

Lombrozo, T., 2009. 'Explanation and Categorization: How "Why?" Informs "What?"', *Cognition*, 110: 248–53.

Lorber, J., 2002. 'Heroes, Warriors, and Burqas', *Sociological Forum*, 17(3): 377–96.

Luban, D., 2002. 'The War on Terrorism and the End of Human Rights', in Gehring, V., ed., *War After September 11*, Oxford: Rowman and Littlefield.

Luban, D., 2005. 'Liberalism, Torture and the Ticking Bomb', *Virginia Law Review*, 91: 1425–61.

Lustick, I., 2006. *Trapped in the War on Terror*, Philadelphia, PA: University of Pennsylvania Press.

Mac Ginty, R., 2010. 'Social network analysis and counterinsurgency: a counterproductive strategy?', *Critical Studies on Terrorism*, 3(2), 209–26.

MacDonald, E., 2001. *Shoot the Women First*, New York, NY: Random House.

MacDonald, P., 2009. 'Those Who Forget Historiography are Doomed to Republish It: Empire, Imperialism and Contemporary Debates About American Power', *Review of International Studies*, 35(1): 45–67.

Mahmood, C., 1996. *Fighting for Faith and Nation: Dialogues with Sikh Militants*, Philadelphia, PA: University of Pennsylvania Press.

Malik, O., 2000. *Enough of the Definition of Terrorism*, London: The Royal Institute of International Affairs.

Malji, A., 2008. 'Female Suicide Bombers', Adani. Available online at: http://adani.by/en/news-and-events/in-the-news/female-suicide-bombers.html, accessed 10 October 2010.

Mann, B., 2006. 'How America Justifies Its War: A Modern/Postmodern Aesthetics of Masculinity and Sovereignty', *Hypatia*, 21(4): 147–63.

Margon, R., 2003. 'Token Terrorist: The Demon Lover's Woman,' in Grisset, P. and Mahon, S., eds, *Terrorism in Perspective*, Thousand Oaks, CA: Sage.

Marsden, P., 2003. 'Afghanistan: The Reconstruction Process', *International Affairs*, 79(1): 91–105.

Martin, G., 2003. *Understanding Terrorism: Challenges, Perspectives, and Issues*, Thousand Oaks, CA: Sage.

Marvel Comics, 2001. *Heroes: The World's Greatest Superhero Creators Honor the World's Greatest Heroes*, New York, NY: Marvel.

Masters, C., 2009. 'Femina Sacra: The "War on/of Terror", Women and the Feminine', *Security Dialogue*, 40(1) 29–49.

Masters, D., 2008. 'The Origin of Terrorist Threats: Religious, Separatist, or Something Else?', *Terrorism and Political Violence*, 20(3): 396–414.

Mayer, J., 2005. 'Outsourcing Torture: The Secret History of America's "Extraordinary Rendition" Program', *The New Yorker*, 14 February. Available online at: http://www.newyorker.com/archive/2005/02/14/050214 fa_fact6, accessed 4 May 2010.

McAdam, D., 1982. *Political Process and the Development of Black Insurgency, 1930–1970*, Chicago, IL: University of Chicago Press.

McCafferty, N., 1981. *The Armagh Women*, Dublin: Co-op Books.

McCauley, C., ed., 1991. *Terrorism and Public Policy*, London: Frank Cass.

McDonald, E., 1992. *Shoot the Women First*, London: Random House.

McDonald, M., 2009. 'Emancipation and Critical Terrorism Studies', in Jackson, R., Breen Smyth, M. and Gunning, J., eds, *Critical Terrorism Studies: A New Research Agenda*, London: Routledge, pp. 109–23.

McGee, M., 1999. 'The "Ideograph": A Link Between Rhetoric and Ideology', in Lucaites, J., Condit, C. and Caudill, S., eds, *Contemporary Rhetorical Theory: A Reader*, London: The Guilford Press, pp. 425–40.

McGreal, C., 2010. 'US Supreme Court: Nonviolent Aid to Banned Groups Tantamount to "Terrorism"', *The Guardian*, 21 June. Available online at:

http://www.guardian.co.uk/law/2010/jun/21/nonviolent-aid-banned-groups-terrorism, accessed 13 August 2010.

McInnes, C., 2003. 'A Different Kind of War? September 11 and the United States' Afghan War', *Review of International Studies*, 29(2): 165–84.

McLean Hilker, L., Khan, S., Ladbury, S. and Gunning, J., 2009. *A Scoping Study for Developing a Research Agenda on the Drivers of Radicalisation and Violent Extremism*, Report for DFID Research. Available online at: http://research4development.info, accessed 29 September 2010.

McLoughlin, B. and McDermott, K., eds, 2002. *Stalin's Terror: High Politics and Mass Repression in the Soviet Union*, Basingstoke: Palgrave Macmillan.

McSherry, J., 2002. 'Tracking the Origins of a State Terror Network: Operation Condor', *Latin American Perspectives*, 29(1): 38–60.

McTiernan, 1998. *Die Hard* (film), Twentieth-Century Fox.

Meisels, T., 2005. 'How Terrorism Upsets Liberty', *Political Studies*, 53(1), 162–81.

Meisels, T., 2006. 'The Trouble With Terror: The Apologetics of Terrorism – A Refutation', *Terrorism and Political Violence*, 18(3): 465–83.

Menjívar, C. and Rodríguez, N., eds, 2005. *When States Kill: Latin America, the US, and Technologies of Terror*, Austin, TX: Texas University Press.

Menkhaus, K., 2007. 'Constraints and Opportunities in Ungoverned Spaces: The Horn of Africa', in M. Innes, ed., *Denial of Sanctuary: Understanding Terrorist Safe Havens*, Westport, CT: Praeger Security International

Merari, A., 1993. 'Terrorism as a Strategy of Insurgency', *Terrorism and Political Violence*, 5(4): 213–51.

Mertus, J., 2001 'Judgment of Trial Chamber II in the Kunarac, Kovac and Vukovic Case', *American Society of International Law*. Available online at: http://www.asil.org/insigh65.cfm, accessed 10 October 2010.

Mervis, C. and Rosch, E., 1981. 'Categorization of Natural Objects', *Annual Review of Psychology*, 32: 89–115.

Mickler, D., 2009. 'Darfur's Dread: Contemporary State Terrorism in the Sudan', in Jackson, R., Poynting, S. and Murphy, E., eds, *Contemporary State Terrorism: Theory and Cases*, Abingdon: Routledge

Miller, D. and Mills, T., 2009. 'The Terror Experts and the Mainstream Media: The Expert Nexus and its Dominance in the News Media', *Critical Studies on Terrorism*, 2(3): 414–37.

Miller, M., 2007. 'Disquiet on the Western Front: Sleeper Cells, Transatlantic Rift and the War in Iraq', in Miller, M. and Stefanova, B., eds, *The War on Terror in Comparative Perspective: US Security and Foreign Policy after 9/11*, Basingstoke: Palgrave Macmillan, pp. 111–20.

Miller, M. and Stephanova, B., eds, 2007. *The War on Terror in Comparative Perspective: US Security and Foreign Policy After 9/11*, Basingstoke: Palgrave Macmillan.

Mishal, S. and Rosenthal, M., 2005. 'Al Qaeda as a Dune Organization: Towards a Typology of Islamic Terrorist Organizations', *Studies in Conflict & Terrorism*, 28(4): 275–93.

Modood, T., Hansen, R., Bleich, E., O'Leary, B. and Carens, J., 2006. 'The Danish Cartoon Affair: Free Speech, Racism, Islamism, and Integration', *International Migration*, 44(5): 3–62.

Mogensen, K., 2008. 'Terrorism Journalism During Terror Attacks', *Media, War & Conflict*, 1(1): 31–49.

Moore, C., 2010. 'You Cannot Stop the Terrorist Threat if You are Unable to Profile It', *The Daily Telegraph*, 29 January. Available online at: http://www.telegraph.co.uk/comment/columnists/charlesmoore/7104133/You-cannot-stop-the-terrorist-threat-if-you-are-unable-to-profile-it.html, accessed 1 February 2010.

Morgan, M., 2004. 'The Origins of the New Terrorism', *Parameters*, XXXIV(1): 29–43.

Morgan, M., 2009. 'Introduction', in Morgan, M., ed., *The Impact of 9/11 on the Media, Arts, and Entertainment: The Day That Changed Everything?* Basingstoke: Palgrave Macmillan, pp. 1–5.

Morgan, R., 1980. 'Theory and Practice: Pornography and Rape', in Lederer, L. ed., *Take Back the Night: Women on Pornography*. New York, NY: William Morrow.

Muller, E., 1985. 'Income Inequality, Regime Repressiveness, and Political Violence', *American Sociological Review*, 50(1): 47–61.

Muller, E. and Weede, E., 1990. 'Cross-National Variation in Political Violence: A Rational Actor Approach', *Journal of Conflict Resolution*, 34(4): 624–51.

Mueller, J., 2005. 'Six Rather Unusual Propositions about "Terrorism" and "Response"', *Terrorism and Political Violence*, 17: 487–505, 523–28.

Mueller, J., 2006. *Overblown: How Politicians and the Terrorism Industry Inflate National Security Threats and Why We Believe Them*, New York, NY: The Free Press.

Mueller, J., 2009. *Atomic Obsession: Nuclear Alarmism From Hiroshima to Al-Qaeda*, Oxford: Oxford University Press.

Mutimer, D., 2007. 'Sovereign Contradictions: Maher Arar and the Indefinite Future', in Masters, C., ed., *The Logics of Biopower and the War on Terror: Living, Dying, Surviving*, Basingstoke: Palgrave Macmillan, pp. 159–79.

Nacos, B., 1994. *Terrorism and the Media*, New York, NY: Columbia University Press.

Nacos, B., 2002. *Mass-Mediated Terrorism: The Central Role of the Media in Terrorism and Counterterrorism*, Lanham, MD: Rowman & Littlefield.

Nacos, B., 2008. 'The Portrayal of Female Terrorists in the Media: Similar Framing Patterns in the News Coverage of Women in Politics and in Terrorism', in Ness, C., ed., *Female Terrorism and Militancy: Agency, Utility and Organisation*, London: Routledge.

Nacos, B., 2010. 'No: There is a Need to Focus More on Building Bridges', in Gottlieb, S., ed., *Debating Terrorism and Counterterrorism: Conflicting Perspectives on Causes, Contexts and Responses*, Washington, DC: CQ Press.

Nagengast, C., 1994. 'Violence, Terror and the Crisis of the State', *Annual Review of Anthropology*, 23: 109–36.

Nankivell, K. and Boutilier, J., 2007. 'Southeast Asia and Global Terror', in Ankersen, C. with O'Leary, M., eds, *Understanding Global Terror*, Cambridge: Polity, pp. 111–29.

Nasr, S., 2009. 'Israel's Other Terrorism Challenge', in Jackson, R., Poynting, S. and Murphy, E., eds, *Contemporary State Terrorism: Theory and Cases*, Abingdon: Routledge.

Ness, C., ed., 2008. *Female Terrorism and Militancy: Agency, Utility and Organisation*, London: Routledge.

Neumann, P., 2009. *Old and New Terrorism: Late Modernity, Globalization and the Transformation of Political Violence*, Cambridge: Polity.

*New Internationalist*, 2009. 'Terror Takeover', Issue 427, 2009. Available online at: http://www.newint.org/issues/2009/11/01/, accessed 19 June 2010.

Nexon, D., 2008. 'What's This, Then? "Romanes Eunt Domus"?', *International Studies Perspectives*, 9(3): 300–8.

Norris, P., Kern, M. and Just, M., 2003. 'Framing Terrorism', in Norris, P., Kern, M. and Just, M., eds, *Framing Terrorism: The News Media, the Government and the Public*, London: Routledge, pp. 3–23.

Nye, J., 2004. 'The Decline of America's Soft Power: Why Washington Should Worry', *Foreign Affairs*, 83(3): 16–20.

Obama, President Barack, 2009. 'Remarks by the President on a New Strategy for Afghanistan and Pakistan', Room 450, Dwight D. Eisenhower Executive Office Building, the White House Office of the Press Secretary, 27 March. Available online at: http://www.whitehouse.gov/the_press_office/Remarks-by-the-President-on-a-New-Strategy-for-Afghanistan-and-Pakistan/, accessed 14 July 2009.

Office of Public Affairs, 2002. *International Contributions to the War Against Terrorism: Fact Sheet June 7, 2002 (Revised June 14, 2002)*. Available online at: http://www.defense.gov/news/Jun2002/d20020607contributions.pdf, accessed 8 May 2010.

Óghra Shinn Féin, 2010. '"Women in Struggle" Honouree – Rose Dugdale', May 17. Available online at: http://ograshinnfein.blogspot.com/2010/05/women-in-struggle-honouree-rose-dugdale.html, accessed 5 September 2010.

O'Kane, R., 1996. *Terror, Force and States: The Path From Modernity*, Cheltenham: Edward Elgar.

O'Leary, B. and Silke, A., 2007. 'Understanding and Ending Persistent Conflicts: Bridging Research and Policy', in Heiberg, M., Tirman, J. and O'Leary, B., eds, *Terror, Insurgency, and the State: Ending Protracted Conflicts*, Philadelphia, PA: University of Pennsylvania Press, pp. 387–426.

Oliver, J., 2007. 'US Foreign Policy After 9/11: Content and Prospect', in Miller, M. and Stefanova, B., eds, *The War on Terror in Comparative Perspective: US Security and Foreign Policy After 9/11*, Basingstoke: Palgrave Macmillan, pp. 19–45.

Oliverio, A., 1998. *The State of Terror*, New York, NY: State University of New York Press.

O'Neil, A., 2003. 'Terrorist Use of Weapons of Mass Destruction: How Serious is the Threat?', *Australian Journal of International Affairs*, 57(1): 99–112.

Pape, R., 2005. *Dying to Win: The Strategic Logic of Suicide Terrorism*, New York, NY: Random House.

Pappe, I., 2009. 'De-Terrorising the Palestinian National Struggle: The Roadmap to Peace', *Critical Studies on Terrorism*, 2(2): 127–46.

Parker, T., 2004. *Team America: World Police*, Paramount Pictures.

Parker, T., 2007. 'Fighting the Antaean Enemy: How Democratic States Unintentionally Sustain the Terrorist Movements They Oppose', *Terrorism and Political Violence*, 19(2): 155–79.

Patai, R., 1973. *The Arab Mind*, New York, NY: Simon & Schuster.

Patman, R., 2007. 'Uneasy Coexistence: Globalization and the US National

Security State', in Miller, M. and Stefanova, B., eds, *The War on Terror in Comparative Perspective: US Security and Foreign Policy After 9/11*, Basingstoke: Palgrave Macmillan, pp. 46–68.

Pearlstein, R., 1991. *The Mind of the Political Terrorist*, Wilmington, DE: SR Books.

Pedahzur, A., 2005. *Suicide Terrorism*, Cambridge: Polity.

Pedahzur, A., ed., 2006. *Root Causes of Suicide Terrorism: The Globalization of Martyrdom*, London: Routledge.

Perdue, W., 1989. *Terrorism and the State: A Critique of Domination Through Fear*, London: Praeger.

Peterson, P., 2002. 'Public Diplomacy and the War on Terrorism', *Foreign Affairs*, 81(5): 74–94.

Piazza, J., 2006. 'Rooted in Poverty? Terrorism, Poor Economic Development, and Social Cleavages', *Terrorism and Political Violence*, 18(1), 159–77.

Piazza, J., 2009. 'Is Islamist Terrorism More Dangerous? An Empirical Study of Group Ideology, Organization, and Goal Structure', *Terrorism and Political Violence*, 21(1): 62–88.

Picard, R., 1991. 'News Coverage as the Contagion of Terrorism: Dangerous Charges Backed by Dubious Science', in O. Alali, ed., *Media Coverage Of Terrorism*, London: Sage.

Pilkington, E., 2010. 'America's Secret Army: How the "War on Terror" Created a New Industry', *The Guardian*, July 20. Available online at: http://www.guardian.co.uk/world/2010/jul/19/us-spies-triple-since-2001, accessed 20 July 2010.

Plumer, B., 2005. 'Death Squads in Iraq', *MotherJones*, November 29. Available online at: http://motherjones.com/mojo/2005/11/death-squads-iraq, accessed 13 August 2010.

PoKempner, D., 2007. 'Terrorism and International Law', in Ankersen, C. with O'Leary, M., eds, *Understanding Global Terror*, Cambridge: Polity, pp. 151–70.

Poole, E. and Richardson, J., 2006. *Muslims and the News Media*, London: I. B. Tauris.

Porta, D. della, 1992. 'Introduction: On Individual Motivations in Underground Political Organizations', in della Porta, D., ed., *Social Movements and Violence: Participation in Underground Organizations*, London: JAI Press, pp. 3–28.

Porta, D. della, 1995a. 'Left-Wing Terrorism in Italy', in Crenshaw, M., ed., *Terrorism in Context*, University Park, PA: Pennsylvania State University Press, pp. 105–59.

Porta, D. della, 1995b. *Social Movements, Political Violence, and the State: A Comparative Analysis of Italy and Germany*, Cambridge: Cambridge University Press.

Post, J., 1990. 'Terrorist Psycho-Logic: Terrorist Behavior as a Product of Psychological Forces', in Reich, W., ed., *Origins of Terrorism: Psychologies, Ideologies, Theologies, States of Mind*, Cambridge: Cambridge University Press, pp. 25–40.

Post, J., 2005. 'The Socio-Cultural Underpinnings of Terrorist Psychology: "When Hatred is Bred in the Bone"', in Bjørgo, T., ed., *Root Causes of Terrorism*, London: Routledge.

Power, M., 2007. 'Digitized Virtuosity: Video War Games and Post-9/11 Cyber-Deterrence', *Security Dialogue*, 38(2): 271–88.

Pratt, M. and Werchick, L., 2004. *Sexual Terrorism: Rape as a Weapon of War in Eastern Democratic Republic of Congo*, PeaceWomen Portal. Available online at: http://www.peacewomen.org/resources/DRC/USAIDD-CHADRC.pdf, accessed 10 October 2010.

Price, E., 2010. 'Dissertations and Theses on (Counter-)Terrorism and Political Violence (1980–2010)', *Perspectives on Terrorism*, 4(3): 58–63. Available online at: http://www.terrorismanalysts.com/pt/, accessed 8 August 2010.

Primoratz, I., 2004a. 'Introduction', in Primoratz, I., ed., *Terrorism: The Philosophical Issues*, Basingstoke: Palgrave Macmillan, pp. x–xxiv.

Primoratz, I., 2004b. 'State Terrorism and Counter-terrorism', in Primoratz, I., ed., *Terrorism: The Philosophical Issues*, Basingstoke: Palgrave Macmillan.

Prince, S., 2009. *Firestorm: American Film in the Age of Terrorism*, New York, NY: Columbia University Press.

Puar, J., 2007. *Terrorist Assemblages: Homonationalism in Queer Times*, Durham, NC: Duke University Press.

Puar, J., and Rai, A., 2002. 'Monster, Terrorist, Fag: The War on Terrorism and the Production of Docile Patriots', *Social Text*, 20(3): 117–48.

Puchala, D., 1971. 'Of Blind Men, Elephants, and International Integration', *Journal of Common Market Studies*, 10(3): 267–84.

Pullella, P., 2007. 'Vatican Says Gay Marriage Evil and Abortion Terrorism', Reuters, UK. Available online at: http://uk.reuters.com/article/idUKL 2336409320070423?pageNumber=1&virtualBrandChannel=0, Accessed 15 June 2009.

Rai, A., 2004. 'Of Monsters: Biopower, Terrorism and Excess in Genealogies of Monstrosity', *Cultural Studies*, 18(4): 538–70.

Rajaee, B., 2007a. 'US Foreign Policy and Radical Islam', in Miller, M. and Stefanova, B., eds, *The War on Terror in Comparative Perspective: US Security and Foreign Policy after 9/11*, Basingstoke: Palgrave Macmillan, pp. 69–95.

Rajaee , B., 2007b. 'The United States and Southwest Asia After 9/11: Trends and Flashpoints', in Miller, M. and Stefanova, B., eds, *The War on Terror in Comparative Perspective: US Security and Foreign Policy after 9/11*, Basingstoke: Palgrave Macmillan, pp. 151–68.

Rajan, V., forthcoming. *Female Suicide Bombers: Narratives of Violence*, Abingdon: Routledge.

Ramsay, M., 2006. 'Can the Torture of Terrorist Suspects be Justified', *The International Journal of Human Rights*, 10(2): 103–19.

Ranstorp, M., 1996. 'Terrorism in the Name of Religion', *Journal of International Affairs*, 50(1): 41–62.

Ranstorp, M., ed., 2006. *Mapping Terrorism Research: State of the Art, Gaps and Future Direction*, London: Routledge.

Ranstorp, M., 2009. 'Mapping Terrorism Studies After 9/11: An Academic Field of Old Problems and New Prospects', in Jackson, R., Breen Smyth, M. and Gunning, J., eds, *Critical Terrorism Studies: A New Research Agenda*, Abingdon: Routledge.

Raphael, S., 2009. 'In the Service of Power: Terrorism Studies and US Intervention in the Global South', in Jackson, R., Breen Smyth, M. and Gunning, J., eds, *Critical Terrorism Studies: A New Research Agenda*, Abingdon: Routledge.

Raphael, S., 2010. 'Terrorism Studies, the United States and Terrorist Violence in the Global South', PhD Thesis, King's College, University of London.

Rapin, A., 2009. 'Does Terrorism Create Terror?', *Critical Studies on Terrorism*, 2(2): 165–79.

Rapoport, D., 1984. 'Fear and Trembling: Terrorism in Three Religious Traditions', *American Political Science Review*, 78(3): 658–77.

Rapoport, D., 2004. 'The Four Waves of Modern Terrorism', in Cronin A. and Ludes, J., eds, *Attacking Terrorism: Elements of a Grand Strategy*, Washington, DC: Georgetown University Press, pp. 46–73.

Rathmell, A., 2005. 'Planning Post-Conflict Reconstruction in Iraq: What Can we Learn?', *International Affairs*, 81(5): 1013–38.

Rees, W. and Aldrich, R., 2005. 'Contending Cultures of Counterterrorism: Transatlantic Divergence or Convergence?', *International Affairs*, 81(5): 905–23.

Reid, E., 1993. 'Terrorism Research and the Diffusion of Ideas', *Knowledge and Policy*, 6(1): 17–37.

Reid, E., 1997. 'Evolution of a Body of Knowledge: An Analysis of Terrorism Research', *Information Processing and Management*, 33(1): 91–106.

Reif, L., 1986. 'Women in Latin American Guerrilla Movements: A Comparative Perspective', *Comparative Politics*, 18(2): 147–69.

Rejali, D., 2007 *Torture and Democracy*, Princeton, NJ: Princeton University Press.

Relatives for Justice, n.d. 'Mairéad Farrell'. Available online at: http://www. relativesforjustice.com/mairead-farrell.htm, accessed 10 October 2010.

Reuter, C., 2004. *My Life Is a Weapon*, Princeton, NJ: Princeton University Press.

Richards, A., 2010. 'Countering the Psychological Impact of Terrorism: Challenges for Homeland Security', in Silke, A., ed., *The Psychology of Counter-Terrorism*, Abingdon: Routledge.

Richardson, J., 2004. *(Mis)Representing Islam: The Racism and Rhetoric of British Broadsheet Newspapers*, Amsterdam: John Benjamins.

Richardson, L., 2006. *What Terrorists Want: Understanding the Terrorist Threat*, London: John Murray.

Riegler, T., 2010. 'Through the Lenses of Hollywood: Depictions of Terrorism in American Movies', *Perspectives on Terrorism*, IV(2): 35–45. Available online at: http://www.terrorismanalysts.com/pt/index.php?option=com_rokzine&view=article&id=112&Itemid=54, accessed 20 June 2010.

Robin, C., 2004. *Fear: The History of a Political Idea*, Oxford: Oxford University Press.

Rogers, P., 2009. *Global Security After the War on Terror*, Oxford Research Group Briefing Paper.

Rogers, P., 2010. *Losing Control: Global Security in the 21st Century*, London: Pluto.

Rose, D., 2004. *Guantánamo: America's War on Human Rights*, London: Faber & Faber.

Ross, J., 2007. 'Deconstructing the Terrorism News Media Relationship', *Crime Media Culture*, 3(2): 215–25.

Rotberg, R., ed., 2005. *Battling Terrorism in the Horn of Africa*, Baltimore, MD: Brookings Institution Press.

Roy, S., 2007. *Failing Peace: Gaza and the Palestinian-Israeli Conflict*, London: Pluto.

Rummel, R., 1994. *Death by Government*, Somerset, NJ: Transaction Books.

Rummel, R., 1995, 'Democracy, Power, Genocide and Mass Murder', *Journal of Conflict Resolution*, 39(1): 3–26.

Ryan, S., 2006. 'The United Nations', in Buckley, M. and Singh, R., eds, *The Bush Doctrine and the War on Terrorism: Global Responses, Global Consequences*, London: Routledge, pp. 173–88.

Sageman, M., 2004. *Understanding Terror Networks*, Philadelphia, PA: University of Pennsylvania Press.

Sageman, M., 2008. *Leaderless Jihad: Terror Networks in the Twenty-First Century*, Philadelphia, PA: University of Pennsylvania Press.

Said, E., 1978. *Orientalism*, London: Routledge.

Said, E., 2003. *Culture and Resistance: Conversations with Edward W. Said: Interviews by David Barsamian*, Cambridge, MA: South End Press.

Sapolsky, H., Gholz, E. and Talmadge, C., 2009. *US Defense Politics: The Origins of Security Policy*, London: Routledge.

Saull, R., 2008. 'Empire, Imperialism and Contemporary American Global Power', *International Studies Perspectives*, 9(3): 309–18.

Scarry, E., 1985. *The Body in Pain*, New York, NY: Oxford University Press.

Scarry, E., 2004. 'Five Errors in the Reasoning of Alan Dershowitz', in Levinson, S., ed., *Torture: A Collection*, Oxford: Oxford University Press.

Scham, P. and O. Abu-Irshaid, 2009. 'Hamas: Ideological Rigidity and Political Flexibility', US Institute of Peace Special Report 224, Washington, DC: USIP. Available online at: http://www.usip.org/resources/hamas, accessed 29 September 2010.

Scheff, T., 2006. 'Hypermasculinity and Violence as a Social System', *Universitas*, 2(2): 1–10. Available online at: http://www.uni.edu/universitas/fall06/pdf/art_scheff.pdf, accessed 10 October, 2010.

Schlesinger, P., 1991. '"Terrorism", the Media and the Liberal-Democratic State: A Critique of the Orthodoxy', in P. Schlesinger, ed., *Media, State, and Nation: Political Violence and Collective Identities*, London: Sage.

Schmid, A., 2004. 'Frameworks for Conceptualising Terrorism', *Terrorism and Political Violence*, 16(2): 197–221.

Schmid, A. and Jongman, A., 1988/2005. *Political Terrorism: A New Guide to Actors, Authors, Concepts, Databases, Theories and Literature*, Oxford and New York, NY: North-Holland/Transaction.

Schmitt, E., 2004. 'Military Women Reporting Rapes By U.S. Soldiers', *New York Times*, February 26, p. A1.

Schneier, B., 2007. 'Security Matters: Portrait of the Modern Terrorist as an Idiot', *Wired*. Available online at: http://www.wired.com/politics/security/commentary/securitymatters/2007/06/securitymatters_0614, accessed 9 August 2010.

Schweitzer, Y., ed., 2006. *Female Suicide Bombers: Dying for Equality?*, Tel Aviv: Jaffee Center for Strategic Studies.

Sedgwick, M., 2004. 'Al-Qaeda and the Nature of Religious Terrorism', *Terrorism and Political Violence*, 16(4): 795–814.

Shah, A., 2010. 'Poverty Around the World', *Global Issues*. Available online at: http://www.globalissues.org/article/4/poverty-around-the-world, accessed 10 March 2010.

Shaheen, J., 2001. *Reel Bad Arabs: How Hollywood Vilifies a People*, Northampton, MA: Interlink Publishing Group.

Shanahan, T., 2010. 'Betraying a Certain Corruption of Mind: How (and How not) to Define "Terrorism"', *Critical Studies in Terrorism*, 3(2): 173–90.

Sharlach, L., 2008. 'Four Walls and a Veil: A State of Terror in Pakistan', *Critical Studies on Terrorism*, 1(1): 95–110.

Sharp, T., 2009. 'Growth in U.S. Defense Spending Over the Last Decade', The Centre for Arms Control and Non-proliferation, available online at: http://www.armscontrolcenter.org/policy/securityspending/articles/022609_fy10_topline_growth_decade/, accessed 22 August 2009.

Shue, H., 1978. 'Torture', *Philosophy and Public Affairs*, 7(2): 124–43.

Shultz, R. and Vogt, V., 2003. 'It's War! Fighting Post-11 September Global Terrorism Through a Doctrine of Preemption', *Terrorism and Political Violence*, 15(1): 1–30.

Silberstein, S., 2002. *War of Words: Language, Politics and 9/11*, London: Routledge.

Silke, A., 1998. 'Cheshire-Cat Logic: The Recurring Theme of Terrorist Abnormality in Psychological Research', *Psychology, Crime and Law*, 4: 51–69.

Silke, A., 2004a. 'An Introduction to Terrorism Research', in Silke, A., ed., *Research on Terrorism: Trends, Achievements and Failures*, London: Frank Cass, pp. 1–29.

Silke, A., ed., 2004b. *Research on Terrorism: Trends, Achievements and Failures*, London: Frank Cass.

Silke, A., 2004c. 'The Road Less Travelled: Recent Trends in Terrorism Research', in Silke, A., ed., *Research on Terrorism: Trends, Achievements and Failures*, London: Frank Cass, pp. 186–213.

Silke, A., 2009. 'Contemporary Terrorism Studies: Issues in Research', in Jackson, R., Breen Smyth M. and Gunning, J., eds, *Critical Terrorism Studies: A New Research Agenda*, London: Routledge, 34–48.

Simon, R., 1989. *The Middle East in Crime Fiction: Mysteries, Spy Novels, and Thrillers From 1916 to the 1980s*, New York, NY: Lilian Barber Press.

Simon, S. and Benjamin, D., 2000. 'America and the New Terrorism', *Survival*, 42(1): 59–75.

Simpson, D., 2006. *9/11: The Culture of Commemoration*, Chicago, IL: Chicago University Press.

Singh, R., 2006. 'The Bush Doctrine', in Buckley, M. and Singh, R., eds, *The Bush Doctrine and the War on Terrorism: Global Responses, Global Consequences*, London: Routledge, pp. 12–31.

Sisler, V. 2008. 'Digital Arabs: Representation in Video Games', in *European Journal of Cultural Studies*, 11(2): 203–19.

Sjoberg, L. and Gentry, C., 2007. *Mothers, Monsters, Whores: Women's Violence in Global Politics*, London: Zed.

Skaine, R., 2006. *Female Suicide Bombers*, Jefferson, NC: McFarland.
Slack, J., 2008. 'Government Renames Islamic Terrorism as "Anti-Islamic Activity" to Woo Muslims', 17 January. Available online at: http://www.dailymail.co.uk/news/article-508901/government-renames-islamic-terrorism-anti-islamic-activity-woo-muslims.html, accessed 2 February 2010.
Sluka, J., 1989. *Hearts and Minds, Water and Fish: Support for the IRA and INLA in a Northern Irish Ghetto*, Greenwich, CT: JAI Press.
Sluka, J., ed., 2000. *Death Squad: The Anthropology of State Terror*, Philadelphia, PA: University of Pennsylvania Press.
Sluka, J., 2009. 'The Contribution of Anthropology to Critical Terrorism Studies', in Jackson, R., Breen Smyth, M. and Gunning, J., eds, *Critical Terrorism Studies: A New Research Agenda*, London: Routledge.
Smith, S., 2004. 'Singing Our World into Existence: International Relations Theory and September 11', *International Studies Quarterly*, 48: 499–515.
Smith, N., 2006. 'The Endgame of Globalization', *Political Geography*, 25(1): 1–14.
Soberg, L. and Gentry, C., 2007. *Mothers, Monsters, Whores: Women's Violence in Global Politics*, London: Zed.
*Social Research*, 2004. Special Issue on 'Fear: Its Political Uses and Abuses', 71(4).
Sorel, J., 2003. 'Some Questions about the Definition of Terrorism and the Fight against Its Financing', *European Journal of International Law*, 14(2): 365–78.
Sorenson, J., 2009. 'Constructing Terrorists: Propaganda About Animal Rights', *Critical Studies on Terrorism*, 2(2): 237–56.
Spencer, A., 2006. 'Questioning the Concept of "New Terrorism"', *Peace, Conflict & Development*, 8: 1–33.
Spivak, G., 1999. *A Critique of Postcolonial Reason: Toward a History of the Vanishing Present*. Cambridge, MA: Harvard University Press.
Sprinzak, E., 1998. 'The Great Superterrorism Scare', *Foreign Policy*, 112: 110–24.
Spruyt, H., 2008. '"American Empire" as an Analytical Question or a Rhetorical Move?', *International Studies Perspectives*, 9(3): 290–9.
Stern, J., 2003. *Terror in the Name of God: Why Religious Militants Kill*, New York, NY: HarperCollins.
Stern, J., 2010. *Denial: A Memoir of Terror*, New York, NY: Ecco.
Steuter, E. and Wills, D., 2010. '"The Vermin Have Struck Again": Dehumanizing the Enemy in Post 9/11 Media Representations', *Media, War & Conflict*, 3(2): 152–67.
Stewart, F., 2008. *Horizontal Inequalities and Conflict: Understanding Group Violence in Multiethnic Societies*, London: Palgrave Macmillan.
Stewart, M., and Mueller, J., 2008. 'Assessing the Costs and Benefits of United States Homeland Security Spending', Centre for Infrastructure Performance and Reliability, University of Newcastle (Australia), Research Report 265.04.08. Available online at: http://polisci.osu.edu/faculty/jmueller/stewarr1.pdf, accessed 14 September 2009.
Stohl, M., 1979. 'Myths and Realities of Political Terrorism', in Stohl, M., ed., *The Politics of Terrorism*, New York, NY: Marcel Dekker, pp. 1–19.
Stohl, M., 1986. 'The Superpowers and International Terrorism', in Stohl, M.

and Lopez, G., eds, *Government Violence and Repression: An Agenda for Research,* Westport, CT: Greenwood Press.

Stohl, M., ed., 1988. *The Politics of Terrorism,* 3rd edn, New York, NY: Marce Dekker, Inc.

Stohl, M., 2005. 'Expected Utility and State Terrorism', in Bjorgo, T., ed., *Root Causes of Terrorism: Myths, Reality and Ways Forward,* Abingdon: Routledge.

Stohl, M., 2006. 'The State as Terrorist: Insights and Implications', *Democracy and Security,* 2(1): 1–25.

Stohl, M., 2008. 'Old Myths, New Fantasies and the Enduring Realities of Terrorism', *Critical Studies on Terrorism,* 1(1): 5–16.

Stohl, M. and Lopez, G., eds, 1984. *The State as Terrorist: The Dynamics of Governmental Violence and Repression,* Westport, CT: Greenwood Press.

Stohl, M. and Lopez, eds, 1986. *Government Violence and Repression: An Agenda for Research,* Westport, CT: Greenwood Press.

Stokes, D., 2005. *America's Other War: Terrorising Colombia,* London: Zed Books.

Stokes, D., 2006. '"Iron Fists in Iron Gloves": The Political Economy of US Terrorocracy Promotion in Colombia', *The British Journal of Politics & International Relations,* 8(3): 368–87.

Stokes, D., 2009. 'Ideas and Avocados: Ontologising Critical Terrorism Studies', *International Relations,* 23(1): 85–92.

Stone, D., 1996. *Capturing the Political Imagination: Think Tanks and the Policy Process,* London: Frank Cass.

Suarez-Orozco, M., 1987. 'The Treatment of Children in the "Dirty War": Ideology, State Terrorism, and the Abuse of Children in Argentina', in Scheper-Hughes, N., ed., *Child Survival: Anthropological Perspectives on the Treatment and Maltreatment of Children,* Dordrecht: Reidel, pp. 219–59.

Suganami, H., 2002. 'Explaining War: Some Critical Observations', *International Relations,* 16(3): 307–26.

Sussman, D., 2005. 'What's Wrong with Torture?', *Philosophy and Public Affairs,* 33(1): 1–33

Sylvester, C., and Parashar, S., 2009. 'The Contemporary "Mahabharata" and the many "'Draupadis": Bringing Gender to Critical Terrorism Studies', in Jackson, R., Breen Smyth, M. and Gunning, J., eds, *Critical Terrorism Studies: A New Research Agenda,* London: Routledge, pp. 178–93.

'Symposium: The Case for Critical Terrorism Studies', *European Political Science,* 6(3): 225–59.

'Symposium: Critical Terrorism Studies: Foundations, Issues, Challenges', 2007, *Critical Studies on Terrorism,* 1(1–2).

Taylor, C., 2000. 'And Don't Forget to Clean the Fridge: Women in the Secret Sphere of Terrorism,' in DeGroot, G. and Peniston-Bird, C., eds, *A Soldier and a Woman: Sexual Integration in the Military,* New York, NY: Longman.

Terry, J., 1980. 'State Terrorism: A Juridical Examination in Terms of Existing International Law', *Journal of Palestine Studies,* 10(1): 94–117.

Thakrah, J., 2004. *Dictionary of Terrorism,* 2nd edn, London: Routledge.

Thatcher, M., 1985. 'Speech to American Bar Association'. Available online

at: http://www.margaretthatcher.org/speeches/displaydocument.asp?docid=
106096, accessed 27 June 2009.

The 9/11 Commission Report, 2004. *Final Report of the National Commission on Terrorist Attacks Upon the United States (Authorized Edition)*, London: W.W. Norton & Company.

The Center on Law and Security, 2008. 'Terrorist Trial Report Card: September 11 2008', New York University, The Centre for Law and Security. Available online at: http://www.lawandsecurity.org/publications/Sept08TTRCFinal.pdf, accessed 22 September 2009.

Thomas, E., 2004. 'Explaining Lynndie England', *Newsweek*, May 15. Available online at: http://www.newsweek.com/2004/05/14/explaining-lynndie-england.html, accessed 10 October, 2010.

Thomas, S., 2005. *The Global Resurgence of Religion and the Transformation of International Relations*, New York, NY: Palgrave Macmillan.

Thorup, M., 2010. *An Intellectual History of Terror: War, Violence and the State*, Abingdon: Routledge.

Thyne, C., 2006. 'ABC's, 123's and the Golden Rule: The Pacifying Effect of Education on Civil Conflict, 1980–1999', *International Studies Quarterly*, 50: 733–54.

Tilly, C., 2004. 'Terror, Terrorism, Terrorists', *Sociological Theory*, 22(1): 5–13.

*Time*, 1974. 'Renegade Debutante', Time.com, 20 May. Available online at: http://www.time.com/time/magazine/article/0,9171,944833–1,00.html, accessed 10 October 2010.

Toros, H., 2008. 'Terrorists, Scholars and Ordinary People: Confronting Terrorism Studies with Field Experiences', *Critical Studies on Terrorism*, 1(2): 297–92.

Toros, H. and Gunning, J., 2009. 'Exploring a Critical Theory Approach to Terrorism Studies', in Jackson, R., Breen Smyth, M. and Gunning, J., eds, *Critical Terrorism Studies: A New Research Agenda*, London: Routledge, pp. 87–108.

Townshend, C., 1983. *Political Violence in Ireland: Government and Resistance Since 1848*, Oxford: Oxford University Press.

Townshend, C., 2002. *Terrorism: A Short Introduction*, Oxford: Oxford University Press.

Townshend, C., 2007. 'Terrorism: In Search of the Definite Article', *Open Democracy*. Available online at: http://www.opendemocracy.net/conflicts/democracy_terror/what_is_terrorism, accessed 27 March 2010.

Tripp, C., 2004. 'The United States and State-Building in Iraq', *Review of International Studies*, 30(4): 545–58.

Tucker, D., 2001. 'What is New About the New Terrorism and How Dangerous is It?', *Terrorism and Political Violence*, 13(3): 1–14.

Tuman, J., 2003. *Communicating Terror: The Rhetorical Dimensions of Terrorism*, London: Sage.

United Kingdom Home Office, 2009. 'Statistics on Terrorism Arrests and Outcomes Great Britain: 11 September 2001 to 31 March 2008', *Home Office Statistical Bulletin*, 13 May. Available online at: http://www.state-watch.org/news/2009/may/uk-ho-terrorism-arrests.pdf, accessed 12 September 2009.

United States Department of State, 2009. *Country Reports on Terrorism 2008.* Available online at: http://www.state.gov/documents/organization/122599.pdf, accessed 14 February 2010.

US Department of Justice 2009. *The Department of Justice's Internal Controls Over Terrorism Reporting,* U.S. Department of Justice Office of the Inspector General, Audit Division, Audit Report 07–20, February 2007. Available online at: http://trac.syr.edu/tracreports/terrorism/177/include/DOJ_IG_terrorism_070220.pdf, accessed 21 September 2009.

USA Today, 2005. 'Russia Mourns for Beslan School Siege 1 Year Later', 1 September. Available online at: http://www.usatoday.com/news/world/2005–09–01–beslan-anniversary_x.htm, accessed 2 February 2010.

Valls, A., 2000. 'Can Terrorism be Justified?', in A. Valls, ed., *Ethics in International Affairs: Theories and Cases,* Lanham, MD: Rowman & Littlefield.

Van Bruinessen, M., 1996. 'Turkey's Death Squads', *Middle East Report,* 26(2): 20–3.

Versluys, K. 2009. '9/11 in the Novel', in Morgan, M., ed., *The Impact of 9/11 on the Media, Arts, and Entertainment: The Day That Changed Everything?,* Basingstoke: Palgrave Macmillan, pp. 141–50.

Victor, B., 2003. *Army of Roses: Inside the World of Palestinian Women Suicide Bombers,* New York, NY: Rodale.

Waldron, J., 2003. 'Security and Liberty: The Image of Balance', *The Journal of Political Philosophy,* 11(2): 191–210.

Walter, E., 1969. *Terror and Resistance,* New York, NY: Oxford University Press.

Weber, C., 2007. 'Securitizing the Unconscious: The Bush Doctrine of Pre-emption and *Minority Report*', in E. Dauphinee and Masters, C., eds, *The Logics of Biopower and the War on Terror: Living, Dying, Surviving,* Basingstoke: Palgrave Macmillan, pp. 109–27.

Weinberg, L. and P. Davies, 1989. *Introduction to Political Terrorism,* New York, NY: McGraw-Hill.

Weinberg, L. and Eubank, W., 1987. 'Italian Women Terrorists', *Terrorism: An International Journal,* 9(3): 241–62.

Weinberg, L. and Eubank, W., 2008. 'Problems with the Critical Studies Approach to the Study of Terrorism', *Critical Studies on Terrorism,* 1(2): 185–95.

Weinstein, L., 2007. 'The Significance of the Armagh Dirty Protest', *Eire-Ireland,* 41(3–4): 11–41.

Wellman, C., 1979. 'On Terrorism Itself', *The Journal of Value Inquiry,* 13(4): 250–8.

Wendt, A. 1987. 'The Agent-Structure Problem in International Relations Theory', *International Organization,* 41(3): 335–50.

Wendt, A., 2001. 'On Constitution and Causation in International Relations', *Review of International Studies,* 24(5): 101–18.

Whaley Eager, P., 2008. *From Freedom Fighters to Terrorists: Women and Political Violence,* Aldershot: Ashgate.

White House, 2003. 'Operation Iraqi Freedom Coalition Members', 27 March. Available online at: http://georgewbush-whitehouse.archives.gov/news/releases/2003/03/20030327–10.html, accessed 9 July 2010.

WHO (World Health Organization), n.d. 'Causes of Death 2001', available online at: http://www.who.int/mip/2003/other_documents/en/causesofdeath. pdf, accessed 22 August 2009.

WHO (World Health Organization), 2008. World Health Statistics, available online at: http://www.who.int/whosis/whostat/EN_WHS08_Full.pdf, accessed 12 September 2009.

Wickham, C., 2004. 'Interests, Ideas, and Islamist Outreach in Egypt', in Wiktorowicz, Q., ed., *Islamic Activism: A Social Movement Theory Approach*, Bloomington, ID: Indiana University Press.

Wikipedia Talk: Definition of Terrorism, n.d. Available online at: http://en. wikipedia.org/wiki/talk:definition_of_terrorism, accessed, 27 March 2010.

Wiktorowicz, Q., 2005. 'A Genealogy of Radical Islam', *Studies in Conflict & Terrorism*, 28(2): 75–97.

Wiktorowicz, Q. and Kaltner, J., 2003. 'Killing in the Name of Islam: Al-Qaeda's Justification for September 11', *Middle East Policy*, X(2): 76–92.

Wilkins, K. and Downing, J., 2002. 'Mediating Terrorism: Text and Protest in Interpretations of *The Siege*', *Critical Studies in Media Communication*, 19(4): 419–37.

Wilkinson, P., 1986. *Terrorism and the Liberal State,* Basingstoke: Macmillan.

Wilkinson, P., 2006. *Terrorism Versus Democracy: The Liberal State Response*, 2nd edn, London: Routledge.

Williams, M., 2005. 'What is the National Interest? The Neoconservative Challenge in IR Theory', *European Journal of International Relations*, 11(3): 3037–337.

Williams, P., 2008. 'Security Studies, 9/11 and the Long War', in Bellamy, A., Bleiker, R., Davies, S. and Devetak, R., eds, *Security and the War on Terror*, London: Routledge, pp. 9–24.

Wills, D., 2003. *The First War on Terrorism: Counter-Terrorism Policy During the Reagan Administration*, Lanham, MD: Rowman & Littlefield.

Winkler, C., 2006. *In the Name of Terrorism: Presidents on Political Violence in the Post-World War II Era*, Albany, NY: State University of New York Press.

Wolfendale, J., 2006. 'Training Torturers', *Social Theory and Practice*, 322(2): 269–87.

Wolfendale, J., 2007. 'Terrorism, Security and the Threat of Counterterrorism', *Studies in Conflict & Terrorism*, 30(1): 75–92.

Wolff, K., 1998. 'New New Orientalism: Political Islam and Social Movement Theory', in A.S. Moussalli, ed., *Islamic Fundamentalism: Myths and Realities*, Reading: Ithaca, pp. 41–73.

Wood, M., 1998. *In Search of the Trojan War*, Berkeley and Los Angeles: University of California Press.

Woods, N., 2005. 'The Shifting Politics of Foreign Aid', *International Affairs*, 81(2): 393–409.

Woodward, B., 2003. *Bush at War*, New York, NY: Simon & Schuster.

Wright, T., 2007. *State Terrorism in Latin America: Chile, Argentina, and International Human Rights*, Lanham, MD: Rowman & Littlefield.

Wyk, J van., 2007. 'Africa and the War on Terror: From Kalashnokovs to Quarans to Cooperation', in Miller, M. and Stefanova, B., eds, *The War on*

*Terror in Comparative Perspective: US Security and Foreign Policy after 9/11*, Basingstoke: Palgrave Macmillan, pp. 121–38.

Wyn Jones, R., 2005. 'On Emancipation: Necessity, Capacity, and Concrete Utopias', in Booth, K., ed., *Critical Security Studies and World Politics*, Boulder, CO: Lynne Rienner.

Yin, T., 2008. 'Jack Bauer Syndrome: Hollywood's Depiction of National Security Law', *Southern California Interdisciplinary Law Journal*, 17: 279–300.

Yoo, J., 2010. 'Yes: The United States Needs to Reasonably Limit Civil Liberties and Bolster Executive Powers', in Gottlieb, S., ed., *Debating Terrorism and Counterterrorism: Conflicting Perspectives on Causes, Contexts and Responses*, Washington, DC: CQ Press.

Yunus, M., 2006. *Nobel Lecture*, Oslo, December 10. Available online at: http://nobelprize.org/nobel_prizes/peace/laureates/2006/yunus-lecture-en. html, accessed 10 March 2010.

Zedalis, D., 2004. *Female Suicide Bombers*, Honolulu: University Press of the Pacific.

Zulaika, J., 1988. *Basque Violence: Metaphor and Sacrament*, Reno, NA: University of Nevada Press.

Zulaika, J., 1995. 'The Anthropologist as Terrorist', in Nordstrum C., and Robben, A., eds, *Fieldwork Under Fire: Contemporary Studies of Violence and Survival*, Berkeley, CA: University of California Press, pp. 203–22.

Zulaika, J., 2003. 'The Self-Fulfilling Prophecies of Counterterrorism', *Radical History Review*, 85: 191–99.

Zulaika, J., 2009. *Terrorism: The Self-Fulfilling Prophesy*, Chicago, IL: University of Chicago Press.

Zulaika, J. and Douglass, W., 1996. *Terror and Taboo: The Follies, Fables, and Faces of Terrorism*, London: Routledge.

Zwick, E., 1998. *The Siege* (film), Bedford Falls Productions.

# Index